Essentials

W9-DAY-417

of PSYCHOLOGICAL ASSESSMENT *Series*

Everything you need to know to administer, interpret, and score the major psychological tests.

I'd like to order the following
ESSENTIALS OF PSYCHOLOGICAL ASSESSMENT:

- ❏ **WAIS-III Assessment / 28295-2 / $34.95**
- ❏ **CAS Assessment / 29015-7 / $34.95**
- ❏ **Millon Inventories Assessment / 29798-4 / $34.95**
- ❏ **Forensic Psychological Assessment / 33186-4 / $34.95**
- ❏ **Bayley Scales of Infant Development-II Assessment / 32651-8 / $34.95**
- ❏ **Myers-Briggs Type Indicator® Assessment / 33239-9 / $34.95**
- ❏ **WISC-III and WPPSI-R Assessment / 34501-6 / $34.95**
- ❏ **Career Interest Assessment / 35365-5 / $34.95**
- ❏ **Rorschach Assessment / 33146-5 / $34.95**
- ❏ **Cognitive Assessment with KAIT and Other Kaufman Measures 38317-1 / $34.95**
- ❏ **MMPI-2 Assessment / 34533-4 / $34.95**
- ❏ **Nonverbal Assessment / 38318-X / $34.95**
- ❏ **Cross-Battery Assessment / 38264-7 / $34.95**

Please send this order form with your payment (credit card or check) to:
JOHN WILEY & SONS, INC., Attn: J. Knott, 10th Floor
605 Third Avenue, New York, N.Y. 10158-0012

Name _____

Affiliation _____

Address _____

City/State/Zip _____

Phone _____ E-mail _____

❏ **Would you like to be added to our e-mailing list?**

Credit Card: ❏ MasterCard ❏ Visa ❏ American Express
(All orders subject to credit approval)

Card Number _____

Exp. Date _____ Signature _____

TO ORDER BY PHONE, CALL 1-800-225-5945
Refer to promo code #1-4081

To order online: www.wiley.com/essentials

Essentials of Psychological Assessment Series

Series Editors, Alan S. Kaufman and Nadeen L. Kaufman

Essentials

of Cross-Battery Assessment

Dawn P. Flanagan

Samuel O. Ortiz

 John Wiley & Sons, Inc.

NEW YORK · CHICHESTER · WEINHEIM · BRISBANE · SINGAPORE · TORONTO

Library of Congress Cataloging-in-Publication Data:

Flanagan, Dawn P.

    Essentials of cross-battery assessment / Dawn P. Flanagan, Samuel O. Ortiz.

       p. cm. — (Essentials of psychological assessment series)

    Includes index.

    ISBN 0-471-38264-7 (pbk. : alk. paper)

    1. Intelligence tests. 2. Intellect. I. Ortiz, Samuel O., 1958– II. Title. III. Series.

BF431 .F437 2000

153.9′3—dc21

00-038211

Printed in the United States of America.

10 9 8 7 6 5 4 3 2 1

To our families for their constant love and support

My mother, Maryann; sister, Gale; brother, Frank

And in loving memory of my father
—DPF

My wife, Denise; and children, Katie, Sammy, Bella, Alisa, and Carlos

And in honor of my mother and father
—SOO

CONTENTS

SERIES PREFACE

In *Essentials of Cross-Battery Assessment,* the authors demonstrate an efficient means of conducting comprehensive assessments of cognitive abilities and processes in a psychometrically and theoretically defensible manner that advances current practice. By recognizing both the strengths and limitations of single battery assessments, these authors show practitioners how to systematically augment individual intelligence batteries with tests from another battery (or batteries) to ensure that a wider range of cognitive functions is measured and in a manner consistent with modern intelligence theory.

Two cross-battery methods are offered: *Comprehensive Cross-Battery assessment,* which ensures that the widest range of broad cognitive abilities and processes is represented in assessments in accordance with contemporary psychometric theory and research; and *Selective Cross-Battery assessment,* which ensures that the abilities and processes that are most closely related (either empirically or logically) to well-defined referral issues are assessed thoroughly. In this book, the authors also extend their cross-battery procedures further in order to address issues of interpretive bias and nondiscriminatory assessment that often arise when assessing individuals with cultural and linguistic backgrounds that differ from those of the U.S. mainstream. The step-by-step cross-battery assessment procedures presented in this book are firmly grounded in decades of research on (a) the structure of human cognitive abilities; (b) construct validation; and (c) the relations between cognitive abilities and processes and specific academic skills. Through their provision of easy-to-follow steps, data summary sheets, and worksheets, these authors demonstrate how practitioners can improve upon reliability and validity in assessment and use current theory and research to enrich and inform interpretations of cognitive function and dysfunction.

One

OVERVIEW

For the past six decades, cognitive ability tests have made significant contributions to psychology research and practice. Although individually administered intelligence batteries continue to be used widely by clinicians, they do not adequately measure many of the cognitive abilities that contemporary psychometric theory and research specify as important in understanding learning and problem solving. The lack of representation of important cognitive abilities on most current intelligence batteries creates a gap between theories of the structure of intelligence and the traditional practice of measuring these abilities (Flanagan & McGrew, 1997). In order to narrow the theory-practice gap, commonly used intelligence tests need to be modernized so that a broader range of cognitive abilities can be both measured and interpreted in a more valid and defensible manner. The CHC (Cattell-Horn-Carroll) Cross-Battery approach described in this volume was developed specifically by McGrew and Flanagan (1998) as a method to update assessment practice by grounding it solidly within contemporary psychometric theory.

HISTORY AND DEVELOPMENT OF CHC CROSS-BATTERY ASSESSMENT

The process of analyzing and classifying human cognitive abilities "has intrigued scientists for centuries" (Kamphaus, Petoskey, & Morgan, 1997, p. 33). Attempts to define the construct of intelligence and to explain and classify individual differences in cognitive functions have been characterized by significant variability for decades. The differences among theories of intelligence are exemplified by the numerous multiple-intelligences models that have been offered over the years to explain the structure of intelligence. Some of the most popular models include Carroll's Three-Stratum Theory of Cognitive Abilities, Gardner's Theory of Multiple Intelligences, the Cattell-Horn Fluid-Crystallized (*Gf-Gc*) theory, Feuerstein's Theory of Structural Cognitive Modifiability (SCM), the Luria-Das Model of Information Processing, and Sternberg's Triarchic Theory of Intelligence (see Flanagan, Genshaft, & Harrison, 1997, for a comprehensive description of these theories). Each of these theories represents an attempt to comprehend a class of phenomena and, ultimately, to fulfill the chief goal of science: "to minimize the mental effort needed to understand complex phenomena through classification" (Thurstone, 1935, p. 45; cited in Flanagan, McGrew, & Ortiz, 2000). To achieve this goal each theory of intelligence provides a taxonomic framework for classifying and analyzing the nature of the cognitive characteristics that account for the variability in observed intellectual performance among and between individuals (Flanagan, McGrew, et al., 2000).

Among the popular theoretical frameworks, psychometric theories are the oldest and most well established. Furthermore, the psychometric approach is the most research-based and has produced the most economically efficient and practical instruments for measuring cognitive abilities in applied settings (Neisser et al., 1996; Taylor, 1994). The reader is referred to Carroll (1993), Gustafsson and Undheim (1996), Ittenbach, Esters, and Wainer (1997), Kamphaus (1993), Sattler (1988), and Thorndike and Lohman (1990) for historical information on the development of psychometric theories of intelligence.

Recently, psychometric theories of intelligence have converged on a more complete multiple–cognitive abilities taxonomy ("complete" in a relative sense, because theories are never truly complete), which reflects a review of the extant factor-analytic research conducted over the past 60 years. This taxonomy serves as the organizational framework for both the Carroll and Cattell-Horn models (Carroll, 1983, 1989, 1993, 1997; Gustafsson, 1984, 1988; Horn, 1988, 1991, 1994; Horn & Noll, 1997; Lohman, 1989; Snow, 1986), the two most prominent psychometric theories of intelligence proposed to date (Flanagan, McGrew, et al., 2000; McGrew & Flanagan, 1998; Sternberg & Kaufman, 1998; Woodcock, McGrew, & Mather, 2001).

Recent theory-driven, joint, or "cross-battery" factor analyses of the major intelligence batteries (e.g., Flanagan & McGrew, 1998; Keith, Kranzler, & Flanagan, 2000; McGhee, 1993; McGrew, 1997; Woodcock, 1990; Woodcock, et al., 2001) indicated that the majority of current intelligence tests do not adequately assess the complete range of *broad* cognitive abilities included in either Horn's (1991, 1994) or Carroll's (1993, 1997) model of the structure of intelligence. Of course, this is not surprising because the vast majority of extant intelligence tests were never specifically designed or developed to operationalize CHC theory. Therefore, use of the CHC Cross-Battery approach provides practitioners with two unique advantages: (a) It allows data gathered both within and across test batteries to be organized and interpreted in a theoretically and empirically meaningful way; and (b) it specifies and allows examination of the empirically validated links between specific cognitive abilities and specific areas of academic functioning. These advantages have profound implications for examiners and examinees, given the emergence of research that indicates that many of the cognitive abilities that contribute significantly to the explanation of academic skills are either not measured or not measured well by existing intelligence tests (Keith, 1999; McGrew, Flanagan, Keith, & Vanderwood, 1997; Vanderwood, McGrew, Flanagan, & Keith, 2000). The need to have readily available tests with which to clearly specify and validly measure cognitive abilities, along with the need to examine the known links between specific cognitive abilities and specific academic skills, helped to spark the development of the CHC Cross-Battery approach and provide compelling reasons for its adoption and use (Flanagan & McGrew, 1997; Flanagan, McGrew, & Ortiz, 2000; McGrew & Flanagan, 1998).

RATIONALE FOR THE CHC CROSS-BATTERY APPROACH

In the intellectual assessment literature, Woodcock (1990) was first to advance the notion of crossing intelligence batteries to measure a more complete range of broad abilities included in contemporary psychometric theory, following his compilation of a series of cross-battery factor analyses of several intelligence batteries. Similarly, although Kaufman did not use the term *cross-battery,* he has long advocated the practice of *supplementing* intelligence batteries (particularly the Wechsler Scales) to gain a more complete understanding of cognitive functioning (e.g., Kaufman, 1994). Because it is clear that most single intelligence batteries provide limited information when considered within the context of contemporary theory and research, CHC Cross-Battery assessment emerged in response to this need and as a way of advancing the science of assessment (Flanagan & McGrew, 1997).

Briefly, the CHC Cross-Battery approach was developed to (a) provide practitioners with a way to conduct more valid and comprehensive assessments of cognitive abilities and processes; (b) circumvent the significant weaknesses in intracognitive discrepancy models for the diagnosis of learning disability; (c) provide researchers with a multiplicity of theory-driven and empirically supported classifications of intelligence tests that can be used to design and improve research studies on human cognitive abilities (Flanagan & McGrew, 1997; McGrew & Flanagan, 1998); and (d) provide test developers with a classification system, a blueprint that can be used to conceptualize new tests and evaluate and modify existing ones. The reader is referred to Flanagan, McGrew, and colleague (2000) for a detailed discussion of the more specific and fundamental reasons for the development of the cross-battery method.

Definition

The CHC Cross-Battery approach is designed to spell out how practitioners can conduct assessments that approximate the total range of broad cognitive abilities more adequately than most single intelligence batteries can (Carroll, 1997, p. 129). According to Carroll (1998), this approach "can be used to develop the most appropriate information about an individual in a given testing situation" (p. xi). Likewise, Kaufman (2000) stated that the approach can serve to "elevate [test] interpretation to a higher level, to add theory to psychometrics and thereby to improve the quality of the psychometric assessment of intelligence" (p. xv).

According to McGrew and Flanagan (1998) the CHC *Cross-Battery approach* is a time-efficient method of cognitive assessment that is grounded in contemporary psychometric theory and research on the structure of intelligence. More specifically, it allows practitioners to measure validly a wider range (or a more selective but in-depth range) of abilities than can be represented by a single intelligence battery. The approach is based on three foundational sources or pillars of information (Flanagan & McGrew, 1997; McGrew & Flanagan, 1998). Together, the three pillars (summarized in Rapid Reference 1.1) provide the knowledge base necessary to organize theory-based, comprehensive, reliable, and valid assessments of cognitive abilities.

≡Rapid Reference 1.1

Three Pillars of the CHC Cross-Battery Approach

• The first pillar of the approach is a relatively complete taxonomic framework for describing the structure and nature of intelligence. This taxonomy is reflected by the Cattell-Horn-Carroll theory of cognitive abilities (CHC theory).

• The second pillar of the CHC Cross-Battery approach is the CHC *broad (stratum II) classifications* of cognitive ability tests (as measures of *Gf, Gc, Gv, Ga, Gsm, Glr, Gs,* and *Gq*).

• The third pillar of the cross-battery approach is the CHC *narrow (stratum I) classifications* of cognitive ability tests (e.g., Block Design is classified as a measure of Spatial Relations [SR], a narrow ability subsumed by *Gv*).

Pillar #1: A Well-Validated Theoretical Foundation

The first pillar of the approach is a relatively complete taxonomic framework for describing the structure and nature of intelligence. This taxonomy is reflected by the Cattell-Horn-Carroll theory of cognitive abilities (CHC theory). Hence, CHC theory represents an integration of Carroll's (1993) three-stratum theory and the Cattell-Horn *Gf-Gc* theory (Horn, 1994; see also Flan–agan, McGrew, et al., 2000; McGrew, 1997; McGrew & Flanagan, 1998; Woodcock et al., 2001; Woodcock, personal communication, July 16, 1999).[1] The reader is referred to Carroll (1993, 1997) and Horn and Noll (1997) for comprehensive descriptions of their respective theories.

Although there are several important differences between the Carroll (1993) and Horn (1991, 1994) models (see McGrew & Flanagan, 1998), in order to realize the practical benefits of the calls for more theory-based inter-

---

[1] Recently, it has come to our attention that Drs. John Horn and John Carroll would prefer that "modern *Gf-Gc* theory" (Horn, 1994) and the *Gf-Gc* based three-stratum theory (Carroll, 1993) be called the "Cattell-Horn-Carroll Theory of Cognitive Abilities," or simply, "CHC theory" (Woodcock, personal communication, July 16, 1999). In this book, we have adopted this new terminology and have replaced "*Gf-Gc*" with "CHC" in reference to modern *Gf-Gc* theory, *Gf-Gc* abilities, *Gf-Gc* cross-battery assessment, and the like, to be consistent with the request of these theorists.

pretation (Kaufman, 1979, 1994; Kamphaus, 1998; Kamphaus et al., 1997), it was considered necessary to settle upon a single, integrated cognitive abilities taxonomy (McGrew, 1997). A first effort to create a single CHC taxonomy for use in the evaluation and interpretation of intelligence batteries was proposed by McGrew (1997). McGrew and Flanagan (1998) and Flanagan, McGrew, and colleague (2000) subsequently presented slightly revised integrated models based on additional research. The integrated CHC model presented in Flanagan and McGrew (2000) is used in the current work and is the validated framework upon which cross-battery assessments are based. The CHC model is presented in Figure 1.1.

In the CHC model, cognitive abilities are classified at three strata that differ in degree of generality (Carroll, 1993). The broadest or most general level of ability in the CHC model is represented by stratum III, located at the apex of the hierarchy. This single cognitive ability, which subsumes both broad (stratum II) and narrow (stratum I) abilities, is interpreted by Carroll as representing a general factor (i.e., g) that is involved in complex higher-order cognitive processes (Gustafsson & Undheim, 1996).

The exclusion of g in Figure 1.1 does not mean that the CHC model used in this book does not subscribe to a separate general human ability or that g does not exist. Rather, it was omitted by McGrew (1997), McGrew and Flanagan (1998), and Flanagan, McGrew, and colleague (2000) because it was judged to have little practical relevance to this method of assessment and interpretation. That is, the CHC Cross-Battery approach was designed to improve psychological and psycho-educational assessment practice by describing the unique pattern of specific (stratum II) cognitive abilities of individuals (McGrew & Flanagan, 1998).

The most prominent and recognized abilities in the model are located at stratum II. These *broad* abilities include Fluid Intelligence (*Gf*), Crystallized Intelligence (*Gc*), Visual Processing (*Gv*), and so forth (see Figure 1.1) and represent "basic constitutional and longstanding characteristics of individuals that can govern or influence a great variety of behaviors in a given domain" (Carroll, 1993, p. 634). The broad CHC abilities vary in their emphasis on process, content, and manner of response. Approximately 70 narrow (stratum I) abilities are subsumed by the broad CHC abilities (see Figure 1.1). *Narrow* abilities "represent greater specializations of abilities, often in quite specific ways

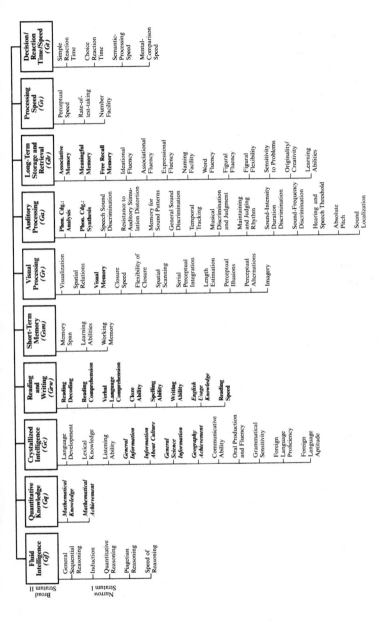

Figure 1.1 The Cattell-Horn Theory of Cognitive Abilities (CHC Theory)

Italic font indicates abilities that were not included in Carroll's three-stratum model but were included by Carroll in the domains of knowledge and achievement. **Bold font** indicates abilities that are placed under different CHC broad abilities than in Carroll's model. These changes are based on the Cattell-Horn model and/or recent research (see Flanagan, McGrew, et al., 2000; McGrew, 1997, and McGrew & Flanagan, 1998).

See Rapid References 1.2–1.9 for definitions of narrow abilities.

that reflect the effects of experience and learning, or the adoption of particular strategies of performance" (Carroll, 1993, p. 634).

It is important to recognize that the abilities within each level of the hierarchical CHC model typically display positive intercorrelations (Carroll, 1993; Gustafsson & Undheim, 1996). For example, the different stratum I (narrow) abilities that define the various CHC domains are correlated positively to varying degrees. These intercorrelations give rise to and allow for the estimation of the stratum II (broad) ability factors. Likewise, the positive correlations among the stratum II (broad) CHC abilities are sometimes used as justification for the estimation of a stratum III (general) *g* factor (e.g., Carroll, 1993). The positive factor intercorrelations within each level of the CHC hierarchy indicate that the different CHC abilities do not reflect independent—that is, uncorrelated—traits (Flanagan & McGrew, 2000).

Overall, the CHC conception of intelligence is supported extensively by factor-analytic (i.e., structural) evidence as well as by developmental, neurocognitive, and heritability evidence (see Horn & Noll, 1997, and Messick, 1992, for a summary). In addition, a mounting body of research is available on the relations between the broad CHC abilities and many academic and occupational achievements (see McGrew & Flanagan, 1998, for a review of this literature). Furthermore, studies have shown that the CHC structure of intelligence is invariant across the lifespan (e.g., Bickley, Keith, & Wolfe, 1995), and across ethnic groups and gender (e.g., Carroll, 1993; Gustafsson & Balke, 1993; Keith, 1997, 1999). In general, the CHC theory is based on a more thorough network of validity evidence than are other contemporary multidimensional ability models of intelligence (see Kranzler & Keith, 1999; McGrew & Flanagan, 1998; Messick, 1992; Sternberg & Kaufman, 1998). According to Daniel (1997), the strength of the multiple (CHC) cognitive abilities model is that it was arrived at "by synthesizing hundreds of factor analyses conducted over decades by independent researchers using many different collections of tests. Never before has a psychometric ability model been so firmly grounded in data" (p. 1042–1043). The broad and narrow abilities of the CHC model are defined briefly as follows.

Broad and Narrow CHC Ability Definitions

The definitions provided here are consistent with those presented in McGrew and Flanagan (1998) and Flanagan, McGrew, and colleague (2000). They were derived from an integration of the writings of Carroll (1993), Gustafsson and Undheim (1996), Horn (1991), McGrew (1997), McGrew, Werder, and Woodcock (1991), and Woodcock (1994).

Fluid Intelligence (Gf)   *Fluid Intelligence* encompasses mental operations that an individual uses when faced with a novel task that cannot be performed automatically. These mental operations include forming and recognizing concepts, perceiving relationships among patterns, drawing inferences, comprehending implications, problem solving, extrapolating, and reorganizing or transforming information. Inductive and deductive reasoning are considered to be the hallmark narrow ability indicators of *Gf* (Carroll, 1993; McGrew & Flanagan, 1998). Definitions as well as corresponding task demands and select subtests of the *Gf* narrow abilities are presented in Rapid Reference 1.2.

Crystallized Intelligence (Gc)   *Crystallized Intelligence* refers to the breadth and depth of a person's accumulated knowledge of a culture and the effective use of that knowledge. This store of predominately verbal or language-based knowledge represents those abilities that have been developed largely through the investment of other abilities during educational and general life experiences (Horn & Noll, 1997). *Gc* abilities are those mentioned most often by lay persons who are asked to describe an "intelligent" person (Horn, 1988). The image of a sage captures to a large extent the essence of *Gc* (McGrew & Flanagan, 1998). Definitions as well as corresponding task demands and select subtests of the *Gc* narrow abilities are presented in Rapid Reference 1.3.

Quantitative Knowledge (Gq)   *Quantitative Knowledge* encompasses an individual's store of accumulated quantitative, declarative, and procedural knowledge. The *Gq* knowledge base is necessary to use quantitative information and manipulate numeric symbols.

The difference between *Gq* and Quantitative Reasoning (RQ; subsumed by *Gf*) is noteworthy. While *Gq* represents an individual's store of accumulated mathematical knowledge, RQ represents the ability to reason inductively and deductively when solving quantitative problems. For example, when a task requires math skills and general math knowledge (e.g., knowing what the multiplication symbol means), *Gq* would be evident. When a task involves solving for a missing number in a number sequence task (e.g., 1,2,4,8,16, ____), RQ would be required. The narrow *Gq* abilities are described in Rapid Reference 1.4.

Reading / Writing Ability (Grw)   *Reading / Writing Ability*, like *Gc* and *Gq*, is an accumulated store of knowledge. The *Grw* knowledge base includes basic reading

Rapid Reference 1.2

Description of Select *Gf* Narrow Ability Definitions and Task Examples

Narrow Stratum I Name (Code)	Definition	Task Example	Subtest Examples
General Sequential Reasoning (RG)	Ability to start with stated rules, premises, or conditions, and to engage in one or more steps to reach a solution to a novel problem.	An examinee is presented with an incomplete logic puzzle and must deduce the missing components following careful analysis of the presented stimuli.	WJ-R/III Analysis Synthesis KAIT Logical Steps UNIT Cube Design
Induction (I)	Ability to discover the underlying characteristic (e.g., rule, concept, process, trend, class membership) that governs a problem or a set of materials.	An examinee is presented with a certain pattern of related stimuli and must select one of several stimuli that would complete or continue the pattern.	WAIS-III Matrix Reasoning WJ-R/III Concept Formation DAS Matrices KSNAP Four-Letter Word
Quantitative Reasoning (RQ)	Ability to inductively and deductively reason with concepts involving mathematical relations and properties.	An examinee is presented with an incomplete series of related numbers and must select the number(s) that best complete(s) the series.	SB:IV Equation Building DAS Sequential and Quantitative Reasoning SB:IV Number Series

Note. Narrow ability definitions are from "Analysis of the Major Intelligence Batteries According to a Proposed Comprehensive *Gf-Gc* Framework," by K. S. McGrew, in *Contemporary Intellectual Assessment: Theories, Tests, and Issues* (pp. 151–180), edited by D. P. Flanagan, J. L. Genshaft, and P. L. Harrison, 1997, New York: Guilford. Copyright 1997 by Guilford. Adapted with permission. All rights reserved. Two-letter factor codes (e.g., "RG") are from *Human Cognitive Abilities: A Survey of Factor-Analytic Studies*, by J. B. Carroll, 1993, Cambridge, UK: Cambridge University Press. Task examples are from *The Wechsler Intelligence Scales and CHC Theory: A Contemporary Approach to Interpretation* (pp. 32–41), by D. P. Flanagan, K. S. McGrew, and S. O. Ortiz, 2000, Boston: Allyn & Bacon. Copyright 2000 by the publisher. Adapted with permission of Allyn & Bacon. All rights reserved.

Rapid Reference 1.3

Description of Select *Gc* Narrow Ability Definitions and Task Examples

Narrow Stratum I Name (Code)	Definition	Task Example	Subtest Examples
Language Development (LD)	General development, or the understanding of words, sentences, and paragraphs (*not requiring reading*), in spoken native language skills.	An examinee is presented with everyday problems and must offer solutions that demonstrate an understanding of social rules and concepts.	WECH Comprehension SB:IV Absurdities
Lexical Knowledge (VL)	Extent of vocabulary that can be understood in terms of correct word meanings.	An examinee must provide oral definitions for words of increasing difficulty.	WECH Vocabulary DAS Word Definitions WJ-R Oral Vocabulary
Listening Ability (LS)	Ability to listen to and comprehend oral communications.	An examinee is presented with an incomplete verbal passage and must provide a word that completes the passage.	WJ-R Listening Comprehension WJ III Oral Comprehension NEPSY Comprehension of Instructions

(continued)

Narrow Stratum I Name (Code)	Definition	Task Example	Subtest Examples
General (Verbal) Information (KO)	Range of general knowledge.	An examinee must provide specific responses to questions of general factual information.	WECH Information WJ III General Information DTLA-3/4 Basic Information
Information About Culture (K2)	Range of cultural knowledge (e.g., music, art).	An examinee is presented with pictures of historical figures and must identify the individual in the picture.	KAIT Famous Faces

Note. Narrow ability definitions are from "Analysis of the Major Intelligence Batteries According to a Proposed Comprehensive Gf-Gc Framework," by K. S. McGrew, in *Contemporary Intellectual Assessment: Theories, Tests, and Issues* (pp. 151–180), edited by D. P. Flanagan, J. L. Genshaft, and P. L. Harrison, 1997, New York: Guilford. Copyright 1997 by Guilford. Adapted with permission. All rights reserved. Two-letter factor codes (e.g., "LD") are from *Human Cognitive Abilities: A Survey of Factor-Analytic Studies*, by J. B. Carroll, 1993, Cambridge, UK: Cambridge University Press. Task examples are from *The Wechsler Intelligence Scales and CHC Theory: A Contemporary Approach to Interpretation* (pp. 32–41), by D. P. Flanagan, K. S. McGrew, and S. O. Ortiz, 2000, Boston: Allyn & Bacon. Copyright 2000 by the publisher. Adapted with permission of Allyn & Bacon. All rights reserved.

≡Rapid Reference 1.4

Description of Select *Gq* Narrow Ability Definitions and Task Examples

Narrow Stratum I Name (Code)	Definition	Task Example	Subtest Examples
Mathematical Achievement (A3)	Measured mathematics achievement.	An examinee is required to perform simple mathematical calculations using pencil and paper.	WJ-R Calculation WISC-III Arithmetic
Mathematical Knowledge (KM')	Range of general knowledge about mathematics.	An examinee is asked to demonstrate knowledge of basic mathematical facts and operations.	WJ-R Applied Problems

Note. Narrow ability definitions are from "Analysis of the Major Intelligence Batteries According to a Proposed Comprehensive *Gf-Gc* Framework," by K. S. McGrew, in *Contemporary Intellectual Assessment: Theories, Tests, and Issues* (pp. 151–180), edited by D. P. Flanagan, J. L. Genshaft, and P. L. Harrison, 1997, New York: Guilford. Copyright 1997 by Guilford. Adapted with permission. All rights reserved. Two-letter factor codes (e.g., "KM'") are from *Human Cognitive Abilities: A Survey of Factor-Analytic Studies*, by J. B. Carroll, 1993, Cambridge, UK: Cambridge University Press. Task examples are from *The Wechsler Intelligence Scales and CHC Theory: A Contemporary Approach to Interpretation* (pp. 32–41), by D. P. Flanagan, K. S. McGrew, and S. O. Ortiz, 2000, Boston: Allyn & Bacon. Copyright 2000 by the publisher. Adapted with permission of Allyn & Bacon. All rights reserved.

and writing skills necessary for comprehending written language and expressing thoughts and ideas through writing. It includes both basic abilities (e.g., reading decoding, spelling) and complex abilities (e.g., reading comprehension and writing composition). Currently, *Grw* is not well defined or researched within the CHC framework. In applied settings, *Grw* (and *Gq*) are conceived of as achievement domains and are therefore measured by achievement tests, not by intelligence tests. In Carroll's (1993) three-stratum model, eight narrow reading and writing abilities are subsumed by *Gc* in addition to other abilities. In the CHC models presented by McGrew (1997), McGrew and Flanagan (1998), and Flanagan, McGrew, and colleague (2000), these eight narrow abilities define the broad *Grw* ability (see Figure 1.1). Because *Grw* abilities are measured predominantly by achievement tests, they will not be discussed in detail here.

Short-Term Memory (Gsm)   *Short-Term Memory* refers to the apprehension and holding of information in immediate awareness as well as the ability to use the information within a few seconds. *Gsm* is described as a limited-capacity system because most individuals can retain only seven "chunks" of information (plus or minus two) in this system at one time. Examples of *Gsm* include the ability to remember a telephone number long enough to dial it, and the ability to retain a sequence of spoken directions long enough to complete the task. Because there is a limit to the amount of information that can be held in short-term memory, information is typically lost after only a few seconds. When a new task requires an individual to use his or her *Gsm* to store new information, the previous information held in short-term memory is either lost or stored in the acquired knowledge bases of the individual (i.e., *Gc, Gq, Grw*) through the use of long-term storage and retrieval abilities. The *Gsm* narrow abilities are described in Rapid Reference 1.5.

Visual Processing (Gv)   *Visual Processing* refers to the generation, perception, analysis, synthesis, storage, retrieval, manipulation, and transformation of visual patterns and stimuli (Lohman, 1994). An individual who can effectively reverse and rotate objects mentally, interpret how objects change as they move through space, perceive and manipulate spatial configurations, and maintain spatial orientation would be regarded as having a strength in *Gv* abilities (McGrew & Flanagan, 1998). Various narrow abilities subsumed by *Gv* are described in Rapid Reference 1.6.

Auditory Processing (Ga)   At the broadest level, auditory abilities "are cognitive abilities that depend on sound as input and on the functioning of our hearing

Description of Select *Gsm* Narrow Ability Definitions and Task Examples

Narrow Stratum I Name (Code)	Definition	Task Example	Subtest Examples
Memory Span (MS)	Ability to attend to and immediately recall temporally ordered elements in the correct order after a single presentation.	An examinee is presented with a series of numbers or words and must repeat them orally in the same sequence as presented.	WAIS-III Digit Span SB:IV Memory for Digits WJ-R/III Memory for Words
Working Memory (MW)	Ability to temporarily store and perform a set of cognitive operations on information that requires divided attention and the management of the limited capacity of short-term memory.	An examinee is presented a series of numbers and letters in a mixed-up order; then is required to reorder and say the complete list, numbers first, in order, followed by the letters in alphabetical order.	WAIS-III Letter-Number Sequencing WJ-R/III Numbers Reversed NEPSY Knock and Tap

Note. Narrow ability definitions are from "'Analysis of the Major Intelligence Batteries According to a Proposed Comprehensive Gf-Gc Framework," by K. S. McGrew, in *Contemporary Intellectual Assessment: Theories, Tests, and Issues* (pp. 151–180), edited by D. P. Flanagan, J. L. Genshaft, and P. L. Harrison, 1997, New York: Guilford. Copyright 1997 by Guilford. Adapted with permission. All rights reserved. Two-letter factor codes (e.g., "MS") are from *Human Cognitive Abilities: A Survey of Factor-Analytic Studies,* by J. B. Carroll, 1993, Cambridge, UK: Cambridge University Press. Task examples are from *The Wechsler Intelligence Scales and CHC Theory: A Contemporary Approach to Interpretation* (pp. 32–41), by D. P. Flanagan, K. S. McGrew, and S. O. Ortiz, 2000, Boston: Allyn & Bacon. Copyright 2000 by the publisher. Adapted with permission of Allyn & Bacon. All rights reserved.

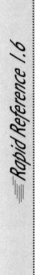

Rapid Reference 1.6

Description of Select *Gv* Narrow Ability Definitions and Task Examples

Narrow Stratum I Name (Code)	Definition	Task Example	Subtest Examples
Spatial Relations (SR)	Ability to perceive and manipulate relatively simple visual patterns rapidly, or to maintain orientation with respect to objects in space.	An examinee is required to view a stimulus pattern or design and reproduce the design using blocks or cubes.	WECH Block Design K-ABC Triangles SB:IV Pattern Analysis
Visual Memory (MV)	Ability to form and store a mental representation or image of a visual stimulus and then recognize or recall it later.	An examinee is required to reproduce or recognize a previously presented visual stimulus that has been removed.	WJ-R Picture Recognition DAS Recall of Designs SB:IV Bead Memory
Closure Speed (CS)	Ability to combine disconnected, vague, or partially obscured visual stimuli or patterns quickly into a meaningful whole, *without knowing in advance* what the pattern is.	An examinee is required to identify an object from a line drawing that has portions of the lines missing.	WECH Object Assembly K-ABC Gestalt Closure WJ-R/III Visual Closure
Visualization (Vz)	Ability to manipulate objects or visual patterns mentally and to "see" how they would appear under altered conditions.	An examinee is required to view a series of designs and identify a matching design.	WJ-R Spatial Relations DAS Block Building WPPSI-R Geometric Designs

Narrow Stratum I Name (Code)	Definition	Task Example	Subtest Examples
Flexibility of Closure (CF)	Ability to find, apprehend, and identify a visual figure or pattern embedded in a complex visual array, *when knowing in advance what the pattern is.*	An examinee must identify 10 animals that are embedded in a complex visual scene.	CAS Figure Memory Leiter-R Figure Ground
Spatial Scanning (SS)	Ability to survey a spatial field or pattern accurately and quickly and to identify a path through the visual field or pattern.	An examinee is required to complete a series of increasingly difficult mazes within a specified time period.	WISC-III Mazes UNIT Mazes NEPSY Route Finding
Serial Perceptual Integration (PI)	Ability to apprehend and identify a pictorial or visual pattern when parts of the pattern are presented rapidly in serial or successive order.	An examinee is required to correctly identify or name a stimulus when portions of the stimulus are presented serially (e.g., portions of a line drawing of a cat are passed through a small window).	K-ABC Magic Window

Note. Narrow ability definitions are from "Analysis of the Major Intelligence Batteries According to a Proposed Comprehensive Gf-Gc Framework," by K. S. McGrew, in *Contemporary Intellectual Assessment: Theories, Tests, and Issues* (pp. 151–180), edited by D. P. Flanagan, J. L. Genshaft, and P. L. Harrison, 1997, New York: Guilford. Copyright 1997 by Guilford. Adapted with permission. All rights reserved. Two-letter factor codes (e.g., "SR") are from *Human Cognitive Abilities: A Survey of Factor-Analytic Studies,* by J. B. Carroll, 1993, Cambridge, UK: Cambridge University Press. Task examples are from *The Wechsler Intelligence Scales and CHC Theory: A Contemporary Approach to Interpretation* (pp. 32–41), by D. P. Flanagan, K. S. McGrew, and S. O. Ortiz, 2000, Boston: Allyn & Bacon. Copyright 2000 by the publisher. Adapted with permission of Allyn & Bacon. All rights reserved.

apparatus" (Stankov, 1994, p. 157) and reflect "the degree to which the individual can cognitively control the perception of auditory stimulus inputs" (Gustafsson & Undheim, 1996, p. 192). *Auditory Processing (Ga)* requires the perception, analysis, and synthesis of patterns among auditory stimuli as well as the discrimination of subtle differences in patterns of sound (e.g., complex musical structure) and speech when presented under distorted conditions. Although *Ga* abilities do not require language comprehension (*Gc*), they appear to be important in the development of language skills (e.g., Morris et al., 1998). *Ga* subsumes most of those abilities referred to as "phonological awareness/processing" (e.g., Phonetic Coding). However, the *Ga* domain is very broad and encompasses many specific abilities beyond phonological awareness and processing abilities. Select *Ga* abilities are described in Rapid Reference 1.7.

Long-Term Storage and Retrieval (Glr)   *Long-Term Storage and Retrieval* is the ability to store new or previously acquired information (e.g., concepts, ideas, items, names) in long-term memory and to retrieve it fluently later through association (Horn, 1991). *Glr* abilities have been prominent in creativity research, where they have been referred to as idea production, ideational fluency, and associational fluency (Carroll, 1993; McGrew & Flanagan, 1998). *Glr* has been confused often with a person's stores of acquired knowledge (i.e., *Gc, Gq,* and *Grw*). It is important to realize, however, that *Gc, Gq,* and *Grw* represent *what* is stored in long-term memory, while *Glr* is the *efficiency* by which this information is stored in and later retrieved from long-term memory (Flanagan, McGrew, et al., 2000).

It is also important to distinguish between the different processes involved in *Glr* and *Gsm*. Although the expression *long-term* carries with it the connotation of days, weeks, months, and years, long-term storage processes can begin within a couple of minutes or hours of performing a task. Therefore, the time between initial task performance and recall of information related to that task is not of critical importance in defining *Glr*. Rather, the occurrence of an intervening task that engages short-term memory during the interim before the attempted recall of the stored information (e.g., *Gc*) is the critical or defining characteristic of *Glr* (Woodcock, 1994). Rapid Reference 1.8 describes several narrow *Glr* memory and fluency abilities.

Processing Speed (Gs)   *Processing Speed* is akin to mental quickness and is frequently associated with intelligent behavior (Nettelbeck, 1994). Processing speed involves performing cognitive tasks fluently and automatically, par-

≡ Rapid Reference 1.7

Description of Select *Ga* Narrow Ability Definitions and Task Examples

Narrow Stratum I Name (Code)	Definition	Task Example	Subtest Examples
Phonetic Coding: Analysis (PC:A)	Ability to segment larger units of speech sounds into smaller units of speech sounds.	An examinee is presented with the pronunciation of a word and must identify the beginning and ending sounds.	WJ III Incomplete Words NEPSY Phonological Processing Test of Phonological Awareness
Phonetic Coding: Synthesis (PC:S)	Ability to blend smaller units of speech together into larger units of speech.	An examinee is presented with the isolated sounds for a word and must blend the sounds together and identify the word.	WJ-R/III Sound Blending
Speech/General Sound Discrimination (US/U3)	Ability to detect differences in speech sounds under conditions of little distraction or distortion.	An examinee is presented with a series of tape-recorded, nonmeaningful sounds and must identify whether the sounds are the same or different.	WJ III Auditory Attention WJ-R Sound Patterns

(continued)

Narrow Stratum I Name (Code)	Definition	Task Example	Subtest Examples
Resistance to Auditory Stimulus Distortion (UR)	Ability to understand speech and language that has been distorted or masked in one or more ways.	An examinee must identify mono- and multisyllabic words while listening to an increasing level of noise pre- sented through earphones.	WJ III Auditory Attention
Memory for Sound Patterns (UM)	Ability to retain, on a short- term basis, auditory events such as tones, tonal patterns, and voices.	An examinee is presented with a se- ries of tone patterns and later must identify whether subsequently pre- sented patterns were among those originally heard.	Not measured by the major intelligence batteries

Note. Narrow ability definitions are from "Analysis of the Major Intelligence Batteries According to a Proposed Comprehensive Gf-Gc Framework," by K. S. McGrew, in *Contemporary Intellectual Assessment: Theories, Tests, and Issues* (pp. 151–180), edited by D. P. Flanagan, J. L. Genshaft, and P. L. Harrison, 1997, New York: Guilford. Copy- right 1997 by Guilford. Adapted with permission. All rights reserved. Two-letter factor codes (e.g., "PCA") are from *Human Cognitive Abilities: A Survey of Factor-Analytic Studies*, by J. B. Carroll, 1993, Cambridge, UK: Cambridge University Press. Task examples are from *The Wechsler Intelligence Scales and CHC Theory: A Contemporary Ap- proach to Interpretation* (pp. 32–41), by D. P. Flanagan, K. S. McGrew, and S. O. Ortiz, 2000, Boston: Allyn & Bacon. Copyright 2000 by the publisher. Adapted with permis- sion of Allyn & Bacon. All rights reserved.

Rapid Reference 1.8

Description of Select *Glr* Narrow Ability Definitions and Task Examples

Narrow Stratum I Name (Code)	Definition	Task Example	Subtest Examples
Associative Memory (MA)	Ability to recall one part of a previously learned but unrelated pair of items when the other part is presented (i.e., paired-associative learning).	An examinee is presented with a set of visual stimuli paired with nonsense words and must correctly identify the nonsense word that had been presented with a certain visual stimulus.	WJ-R Memory for Names CMS Word Pairs KAIT Rebus Learning
Meaningful Memory (MM)	Ability to recall a set of items where there is a meaningful relation between items or the items comprise a meaningful story or connected discourse.	An examinee is presented with a short story and must retell the story as accurately as possible immediately following a single presentation.	WMS-III Logical Memory II CMS Stories 2
Free-recall Memory (M6)	Ability to recall as many unrelated items as possible, in any order, after a large collection of items is presented.	An examinee is presented with a series of objects and, after they are removed, must recall the objects in any order.	WMS-III Word Lists I DAS Recall of Objects NEPSY List Learning
Ideational Fluency (FI)	Ability to produce rapidly a series of ideas, words, or phrases related to a specific condition or object. Quantity, not quality, is emphasized.	An examinee is asked to name quickly what he or she would do in preparation for a week-long trip.	WJ III Retrieval Fluency
Associational Fluency (FA)	Ability to produce rapidly words or phrases associated in meaning (semantically associated) with a given word or concept.	An examinee must name as many examples of objects that fit into a specified category (e.g., name as many fruits as you can think of) within a specified time limit.	WJ III Retrieval Fluency

(continued)

Narrow Stratum I Name (Code)	Definition	Task Example	Subtest Examples
Expressional Fluency (FE)	Ability to think of and organize words or phrases rapidly into meaningful complex ideas under high general or more specific cueing conditions.	An examinee must rapidly name a category that best represents a series of presented words (e.g., pattern, material, thread . . . things to make clothing).	Not measured by the major intelligence batteries
Naming Facility (NA)	Ability to produce names for concepts rapidly when presented with a pictorial or verbal cue.	An examinee must rapidly provide the general name of a category when shown specific pictorial stimuli (e.g., a picture of an apple, shirt, and bus, would require the reply: fruit, clothing, transportation).	WJ III Rapid Picture Naming CAS Expressive Attention NEPSY Speeded Naming
Word Fluency (FW)	Ability to produce words rapidly that have specific phonemic, structural, or orthographic characteristics (independent of word meanings).	An examinee must name as many words as he or she can think of that start with the sh sound within a specified time limit.	Not measured by the major intelligence batteries
Figural Fluency (FF)	Ability to draw or sketch several examples or elaborations rapidly when given a starting visual or descriptive stimulus.	An examinee must draw as many things as he or she can when presented with a nonmeaningful starting visual stimulus.	NEPSY Design Fluency

Note. Narrow ability definitions are from "Analysis of the Major Intelligence Batteries According to a Proposed Comprehensive *Gf-Gc* Framework," by K. S. McGrew, in *Contemporary Intellectual Assessment: Theories, Tests, and Issues* (pp. 151–180), edited by D. P. Flanagan, J. L. Genshaft, and P. L. Harrison, 1997, New York: Guilford. Copyright 1997 by Guilford. Adapted with permission. All rights reserved. Two-letter factor codes (e.g., "MA") are from *Human Cognitive Abilities: A Survey of Factor-Analytic Studies*, by J. B. Carroll, 1993, Cambridge, UK: Cambridge University Press. Task examples are from *The Wechsler Intelligence Scales and CHC Theory: A Contemporary Approach to Interpretation* (pp. 32–41), by D. P. Flanagan, K. S. McGrew, and S. O. Ortiz, 2000, Boston: Allyn & Bacon. Copyright 2000 by the publisher. Adapted with permission of Allyn & Bacon. All rights reserved.

ticularly when under pressure to maintain focused attention and concentration. The expression *attentive speediness* appears to capture the essence of *Gs*. *Gs* abilities require little complex thinking or mental processing and are usually measured by fixed-interval timed tasks. Three different narrow speed-of-processing abilities are subsumed by *Gs* in the present CHC model. These narrow abilities are described in Rapid Reference 1.9.

Decision/Reaction Time or Speed (Gt)   Both Carroll and Horn in their respective cognitive ability models include a broad speed ability that differs from *Gs*. The ability proposed by Carroll, Processing Speed (Decision/Reaction Time or Speed; *Gt*), subsumes narrow abilities that reflect an individual's quickness in reacting (reaction time) and making decisions (decision speed). The ability proposed by Horn, Correct Decision Speed (CDS), is quite similar to Carroll's *Gt* ability and is typically measured by recording the time an individual needs to provide an answer to a problem on a variety of tests (e.g., letter series, classifications, vocabulary; Horn, 1988, 1991). After a review of the descriptions of *Gt* and CDS offered by Carroll and Horn, respectively, it appeared that CDS is a much narrower ability than *Gt*. Therefore, CDS is subsumed by *Gt* in the CHC model used in this book (for details, see Figure 1.1; Flanagan et al., 2000; McGrew, 1997; and McGrew & Flanagan, 1998).

It is important to understand the difference between *Gt* and *Gs*. According to Flanagan and McGrew (2000),

> *Gt* abilities reflect the immediacy with which an individual can react (typically measured in seconds or parts of seconds) to stimuli or a task, while *Gs* abilities reflect the ability to work quickly over a longer period of time (typically measured in intervals of 2–3 minutes). Being asked to read a passage (on a self-paced scrolling video screen) as quickly as possible and, in the process, touch the word "the" with a stylus pen each time it appears on the screen, is an example of *Gs*. The individual's *Gs* score would reflect the number of correct responses (taking into account errors of omission and commission). In contrast, *Gt* may be measured by requiring a person to read the same text at their normal rate of reading and press the space bar as quickly as possible whenever a light is flashed on the screen. In this latter paradigm, the individual's score is based on the average response latency or the time interval between the onset of the stimulus and the individual's response. (pp. 44–45)

☰ Rapid Reference 1.9

Description of Select Gs Narrow Ability Definitions and Task Examples

Narrow Stratum I Name (Code)	Definition	Task Example	Subtest Examples
Perceptual Speed (P)	Ability to search for rapidly and compare known visual symbols or patterns presented side-by-side or separated in a visual field.	An examinee must rapidly view rows of stimuli and cross out those stimuli that are similar within the presented row within a specified time limit.	WAIS-III Symbol Search WJ-R/III Visual Matching CAS Receptive Attention
Rate-of-Test-Taking (R9)	Ability to perform rapidly tests that are relatively easy or that require very simple decisions.	An examinee is required to pair numbers with symbols according to a presented key as rapidly as possible.	WISC-III Coding WPPSI-R Animal Pegs CAS Planned Codes
Number Facility (N)	Ability to manipulate and deal with numbers rapidly and accurately, from elementary skills of counting and recognizing numbers to advanced skills of adding, subtracting, multiplying, and dividing numbers.	An examinee is required to complete a series of arithmetic problems using paper and pencil in a specified time limit.	WJ III Decision Speed CAS Number Detection DAS Speed of Information Processing

Because *Gt* is not measured by any of the major intelligence batteries, it will not be discussed further in this book.

The reader is referred to Carroll (1993, 1997), Flanagan, McGrew, and colleague (2000), Horn (1991, 1994), Horn and Noll (1997), and McGrew and Flanagan (1998) for a comprehensive description of CHC theory and the abilities it encompasses, as well as for supporting evidence for and limitations of the theory. For a discussion of additional developments and potential future refinements and extensions of the CHC model, see Flanagan, McGrew, and colleague (2000) and Woodcock et al. (2001).

We realize that other structural models and theories of cognitive abilities have made significant contributions to the intelligence knowledge base and have unique features that may lead to modifications in and perhaps illuminate possible shortcomings of CHC theory. Notwithstanding, contemporary CHC theory is presented here because it is currently the most researched, empirically supported, and comprehensive descriptive hierarchical psychometric framework from which to organize thinking about intelligence-test interpretation. According to Gustafsson and Undheim (1996), "the empirical evidence in favor of [this] hierarchical arrangement of abilities is overwhelming" (p. 204). As such, the CHC theory is the taxonomic framework around which cross-battery assessment and interpretation are organized (see also Carroll, 1997, 1998; Flanagan et al., 1997; Genshaft & Gerner, 1998; McGrew, 1997; McGrew & Flanagan, 1998; Woodcock, 1990; Ysseldyke, 1990).

Pillar #2: Broad Cognitive Ability Classifications

The second pillar of the CHC Cross-Battery approach is the CHC *broad (stratum II) classifications* of cognitive ability tests. Specifically, based on the results of a series of cross-battery confirmatory factor-analysis studies of the major intelligence batteries, McGrew and Flanagan (1998) and Flanagan, McGrew, and colleague (2000) classified all the subtests of these batteries according to the particular CHC broad cognitive abilities they measure. Their CHC classifications based on these analyses are presented in Table 1.1.

The gaps or holes in Table 1.1 exemplify the theory-practice gap that exists in the field of intellectual assessment. The data in the table show that the WPPSI-R, K-ABC, KAIT, and CAS batteries measure only two to three broad CHC abilities adequately. The WPPSI-R measures primarily *Gv* and *Gc*. The K-ABC measures primarily *Gv* and *Gsm,* and to a much lesser extent, *Gf;* while the KAIT measures

Table 1.1 CHC Broad (Stratum II) Empirical Classifications of Intelligence Batteries (based on cross-battery studies published since 1990)

CHC Factor	WJ-R/III	Wechslers	SB:IV	DAS*	K-ABC*/KAIT	CAS
Long-term Storage and Retrieval (*Glr*)	Memory for Names Visual-Auditory Learning Delayed Recall-MN Delayed Recall-VAL Retrieval Fluency (*Gr*) Rapid Picture Naming (*Gs*)		—	*	Rebus Learning Delayed Recall-Rebus Learning Delayed Recall-Auditory Comprehension (*Gc*)*	Expressive Attention
Short-Term Memory (*Gsm*)	Memory for Words Numbers Reversed Auditory Working Memory (*Gf/Gs*) Memory for Sentences (*Gc*)	Digit Span Letter-Number Sequencing	Memory for Digits Memory for Objects Memory for Sentences (*Gc*)	Recall of Designs	Number Recall Word Order Hand Movements or Move (*Gf*)	Word Series Sentence Repetition Sentence Questions
Processing Speed (*Gs*)	Visual Matching Cross Out (*Gp*) Decision Speed (*Gp*) Pair Cancellation	Coding/Digit Symbol Symbol Search		*	—	Matching Numbers Receptive Attention Planned Codes Number Detection Planned Connections
Auditory Processing (*Ga*)	Incomplete Words Sound Blending Auditory Attention Sound Patterns	—	—	—	—	—

CHC Factor	WJ-R/III	Wechslers	SB:IV	DAS[a]	K-ABC/KAIT	CAS
Visual Processing (Gv)	**Spatial Relations** Picture Recognition Visual Closure	**Block Design** **Object Assembly** Mazes Picture Completion (Gv) Picture Arrangement (Gv)	**Pattern Analysis** Copying Paper Folding (Gq)	Pattern Construction	**Triangles** Gestalt Closure Spatial Memory Matrix Analogies (Gf) Photo Series (Gf) **Memory for Block Designs**	**Figure Memory** **Verbal Spatial Relations**
Crystallized Intelligence (Gc)	**Picture Vocabulary** **Oral Vocabulary** **Verbal Comprehension** **General Information** **Listening Comprehension**	**Information** **Similarities** **Vocabulary** **Comprehension**	**Vocabulary** **Verbal Relations** Comprehension Absurdities	**Word Definitions** **Similarities**	Faces & Places Riddles Expressive Vocabulary **Famous Faces** Definitions (Grw) Double Meanings (Grw) Auditory Comprehension (Gsm)	—
Fluid Reasoning (Gf)	**Analysis-Synthesis** **Concept Formation**	Matrix Reasoning	Matrices	Matrices Sequential-Quantitative Reasoning (Gq)	**Logical Steps** **Mystery Codes**	Nonverbal Matrices
Quantitative Ability (Gq)	**Calculation** **Applied Problems** Math Concepts	**Arithmetic**	**Quantitative** **Number Series**	*	Arithmetic	—

Note. Strong measures of CHC factors are reported in bold type; measures not in bold type are moderate or mixed indicators of CHC abilities. Primary measures of CHC factors for the WJ-R/III are based on the empirical analyses of Woodcock (1990) and Woodcock, McGrew, and Mather (2001); CHC factor classifications of the SB:IV, Wechslers, and K-ABC are reported in Woodcock (1990); classifications for the DAS and KAIT are reported in McGhee (1993) and Flanagan and McGhee (1998), respectively. Classifications for the CAS are reported in Keith, Flanagan, and Kranzler (2000). For additional information on CHC factor classifications of major intelligence test batteries see Flanagan and colleagues (2000). CHC codes, reported in parentheses next to subtest names, identify the factor(s) upon which the subtest had a second factor loading. These subtests are *mixed* measures of abilities. Adapted from "A Cross-Battery Approach to Assessing and Interpreting Cognitive Abilities: Narrowing the Gap between Practice and Cognitive Science," in *Contemporary Intellectual Assessment: Theories, Tests, and Issues* (pp. 314–325), edited by D. P. Flanagan, J. L. Genshaft, and P. L. Harrison, 1997, New York: Guilford. Copyright 1997 by Guilford. Adapted with permission. All rights reserved.

[a]Only a subset of DAS and K-ABC tests were joint factor analyzed by McGhee (1993) and Woodcock (1990), respectively. Therefore, only the tests that were included in these analyses are reported in this table. The CHC factor classifications of *all* DAS and K-ABC tests following a logical task analysis and expert consensus are reported in McGrew and Flanagan (1998) and Flanagan and colleagues (2000).

*Tests measuring these abilities (i.e., Glr, Gs, Gq) are included on the DAS battery but have yet to be included in CHC organized confirmatory cross-battery factor analyses.

primarily *Gf, Gc,* and *Glr,* and to a much lesser extent, *Gv* and *Gsm.* The CAS measures primarily *Gs, Gsm,* and *Gv.* Finally, while the DAS, SB:IV, WISC-III, and WAIS-III do not provide sufficient coverage to narrow the theory-practice gap, their comprehensive measurement of approximately four CHC abilities, as depicted in Table 1.1, is nonetheless an improvement over the previously mentioned batteries (Flanagan, McGrew, et al., 2000; McGrew & Flanagan, 1998).

The results of the cross-battery factor analyses presented in Table 1.1 demonstrate that the amount of information yielded by most single intelligence batteries is limited; thus, it may be necessary to supplement any one the of the major batteries with tests from other batteries to ensure that certain abilities are well represented in an assessment as dictated by referral concerns. In order to supplement an intelligence test in a defensible and valid manner, however, it is necessary to understand what abilities underlie the major cognitive batteries.

Classification of all tests at the broad ability level is necessary to improve upon the validity of cognitive assessment and interpretation (McGrew & Flanagan, 1998). Specifically, broad ability classifications are necessary because they ensure that the CHC constructs that underlie such assessments are minimally affected by construct-irrelevant variance (Messick, 1989, 1995). In other words, knowing what tests measure what abilities enables clinicians to organize tests into clusters that contain only measures that are *relevant* to the construct or ability of interest.

To clarify, *construct-irrelevant variance* is present when an "assessment is too broad, containing excess reliable variance associated with other distinct constructs . . . that affects responses in a manner irrelevant to the interpreted constructs" (Messick, 1995, p. 742). For example, the WISC-III Verbal IQ (VIQ) has construct-irrelevant variance because, in addition to its four indicators of *Gc* (i.e., Information, Similarities, Vocabulary, Comprehension), it has one indicator of *Gq* (i.e., Arithmetic). Therefore, the VIQ is a *mixed* measure of two distinct, broad CHC abilities (*Gc* and *Gq*); it contains reliable variance (associated with *Gq*) that is irrelevant to the interpreted construct of *Gc* (McGrew & Flanagan, 1998). This represents a grouping together of subtests on the basis of face validity (e.g., grouping tests together that appear to measure the same common concept), an inappropriate aggregation of subtests that can actually decrease reliability and validity (Epstein, 1983). The purest *Gc* composite on the WISC-III is the Verbal Comprehension Index, because it contains only construct-*relevant* variance.

Construct-irrelevant variance can also operate at the subtest (as opposed to composite) level. For example, the Verbal Analogies test on the WJ-R measures both *Gc* and *Gf*. That is, in factor-analytic studies, the Verbal Analogies test had significant loadings on both the *Gc* and *Gf* factors. Therefore, this test is considered factorially complex—a situation that complicates interpretation of this measure (e.g.: Is poor performance due to low vocabulary knowledge [*Gc*] or to poor reasoning ability [*Gf*], or both?).

In short, interpretation is far less complicated when composites are derived from relatively pure measures of the underlying construct (e.g., tests printed in bold type in Table 1.1). "[A]ny test that measures more than one common factor to a substantial degree yields scores that are psychologically ambiguous and very difficult to interpret" (Guilford, 1954, p. 356; cited in Briggs & Cheek, 1986). Therefore, CHC Cross-Battery assessments are designed using only empirically strong or moderate (but not factorially complex or mixed) measures of CHC abilities, following the information presented in Table 1.1[2] (i.e., tests printed in bold).

To date, more than 250 CHC broad ability classifications have been made based on the results of cross-battery factor-analytic studies (such as those presented in Table 1.1) and the logical task analyses of intelligence-test experts (see Flanagan, McGrew, et al., 2000, for a discussion). These classifications of cognitive ability tests guide practitioners in identifying measures that assess various aspects of the broad cognitive abilities (such as *Gf* and *Gc*) represented in CHC theory. These classifications have been integrated into the CHC Cross-Battery Worksheets provided in Appendix A.

If constructs are broad and multifaceted, like those represented at stratum

---

[2] Classifications of cognitive ability tests as strong, moderate, or mixed measures of CHC abilities were based on the following criteria: A classification of *strong* was given to a test that had a substantial factor loading (> .50) on a primary factor and a secondary factor loading (if present) that was equal to or less than ½ of its loading on the primary factor. A classification of *moderate* was given to a test that had a primary factor loading of < .50 and a secondary factor loading (if present) that was less than ½ of the primary loading, or any primary factor loading with a secondary loading between ½ and 7⁄10 of the primary loading. A classification of *mixed* was given to a test that had a factor loading on a secondary factor that was greater than 7⁄10 of its loading on the primary factor. These criteria were derived from Woodcock (1990).

DON'T FORGET

Invalidity in Assessment

- *Construct-irrelevant variance*— excess reliable variance associated with other distinct constructs that affects responses in a manner irrelevant to the interpreted constructs

The cross-battery approach guards against this major source of invalidity in assessment by ensuring that only validated measures of a cognitive ability (e.g., Visual Processing) are included in a cross-battery composite designed to measure that ability.

The cross-battery worksheets assist practitioners in designing valid composites of important cognitive abilities.

II in the CHC model, then each component (i.e., CHC broad ability) "should be specified and measured as *cleanly* as possible" (Briggs & Cheek, 1986, p. 130, emphasis added). Because the approach is designed to include only em-pirically strong or moderate (but not mixed) measures of CHC abilities into appropriate (i.e., construct-relevant) composites, CHC Cross-Battery assessment offers a more valid means of measuring the CHC constructs than that offered by most single intelligence batteries (see Flanagan, in press).

Pillar #3: Narrow Cognitive Ability Classifications

The third pillar of the cross-battery approach is the CHC *narrow (stratum I) classifications* of cognitive ability tests. These classifications were originally reported in McGrew (1997), then later reported in McGrew and Flanagan (1998) and Flanagan, McGrew, and colleague (2000) following minor modifications. Classifications of cognitive ability tests according to content, format, and task demand at the narrow (stratum I) ability level were necessary to improve further upon the validity of intellectual assessment and interpretation (see Messick, 1989). Specifically, these narrow ability classifications were necessary to ensure that the CHC constructs that underlie assessments are well represented. According to Messick (1995), *construct underrepresentation* is present when an "assessment is too narrow and fails to include important dimensions or facets of the construct" (p. 742).

Interpreting the Wechsler Block Design (BD) test as a measure of Visual Processing (i.e., the broad *Gv* ability) is an example of construct underrepresentation. This is because the BD test measures only *one* narrow aspect of *Gv* (i.e., Spatial Relations). At least one other *Gv* measure (i.e., subtest) that is qualitatively different from Spatial Relations (measured by BD) is necessary to include in an assessment to ensure adequate representation of the *Gv* construct. That is, two or more qualitatively different indicators (i.e., measures of two or more narrow abilities subsumed by the broad ability) are needed for appropriate construct representation (see Comrey, 1988; Messick, 1989, 1995). The aggregate of BD (a measure of Spatial Relations at the narrow ability level) and Object Assembly (a measure of Closure Speed at the narrow ability level), for example, would provide a good estimate of the broad *Gv* ability because these tests are strong measures of *Gv* (see Table 1.1) and represent qualitatively different aspects of this broad ability.

The Verbal Comprehension Index (VCI) of the WAIS-III is an example of good construct representation. This is because the VCI includes Vocabulary (VL), Similarities (LD/VL), Comprehension (LD), and Information (K0), which represent qualitatively different aspects of *Gc*. Despite the fact that the construct of *Gc* is well represented on the Wechsler Intelligence Scales, there are few composites among the major intelligence batteries that are both relatively pure (i.e., containing only construct-relevant tests) and well represented (i.e., containing qualitatively different measures of the broad ability represented by the composite; see Flanagan, McGrew, et al., 2000, for a review). In fact, most major intelligence batteries yield composites characterized by construct-irrelevant variance and have two or more constructs that are underrepresented (McGrew & Flanagan, 1998).

In addition to interpreting a single subtest as a measure of a *broad* ability, construct underrepresentation occurs when the aggregate of two or more measures of the *same narrow (stratum I) ability* is interpreted as measuring a broad (stratum II) CHC ability. For example, the Memory for Names and Visual-Auditory Learning tests of the WJ-R are interpreted as measuring the broad ability of *Glr* (Woodcock & Mather, 1989), even though they are primarily measures of Associative Memory (MA), a narrow ability subsumed by *Glr*. Thus, the *Glr* cluster of the WJ-R is most appropriately interpreted as an estimate of Associative Memory (a narrow ability) rather than an estimate of Long-Term Storage and Retrieval (a broad ability).

"A scale [or broad CHC ability cluster] will yield far more information—and, hence, be a more valid measure of a construct—if it contains more differentiated items [or tests]" (Clarke & Watson, 1995). CHC Cross-Battery assessment circumvents the misinterpretations that can result from underrepresented constructs by specifying the use of two or more qualitatively different indicators to represent

DON'T FORGET

....

Invalidity in Assessment

- *Construct underrepresentation*—present when an assessment is too narrow and fails to include important dimensions or facets of a construct

The cross-battery approach guards against this major source of invalidity in assessment by ensuring that at least two different components of a broad ability (e.g., Fluid Intelligence) are included in a cross-battery composite designed to measure that ability.

The cross-battery worksheets organize the subtests of the major intelligence batteries according to the narrow abilities they measure to assist practitioners in designing assessments that measure important cognitive abilities well.

each broad CHC ability. In order to ensure that qualitatively different aspects of broad abilities are represented in assessment, classification of cognitive ability tests at the narrow (stratum I) ability level was necessary. This process involved the use of a systematic expert consensus process to classify the more than 250 cognitive ability tests previously mentioned according to the narrow (stratum I) abilities they measure (see Flanagan, McGrew, et al., 2000). These classifications aid in the selection of qualitatively different test indicators for each of the broad abilities represented in CHC Cross-Battery assessments. Thus, construct va-lidity is maximized rather than compromised (McGrew & Flanagan, 1998; Mes-sick, 1995). The tests of the major intelligence batteries are classified at both the broad and narrow ability levels on the CHC Cross-Battery Worksheets available in Appendix A.

In sum, the latter two cross-battery pillars guard against two ubiquitous sources of invalidity in assessment: construct-irrelevant variance and construct underrepresentation. Taken together, the three pillars underlying the cross-battery approach provide the necessary foundation from which to organize assessments of cognitive abilities that are more theoretically driven, comprehensive, and valid. The subsequent chapters in this book will describe how to organize and interpret CHC Cross-Battery assessments as well as instruct practitioners in the appropriate use of the related worksheets and summary sheets.

Cross-Battery Assessment in Perspective

It is important to realize that the crossing of batteries described in this book is not an entirely new method of intellectual assessment per se, as it is a common practice in neuropsychological assessment (e.g., Lezak, 1976, 1995; Wilson, 1992) and is carried out routinely by astute practitioners (Brackett & McPherson, 1996). In fact, Kaufman continues to advocate for and instruct practitioners in supplemental testing methods (see Kaufman, 2000). Kaufman, Lichtenberger, and Naglieri's (1999) suggestion for "test integration" is one such example (p. 332). Notwithstanding, a time-efficient method for crossing intelligence batteries was not formally operationalized until recently (Flanagan, McGrew, et al., 2000; McGrew & Flanagan, 1998). The CHC Cross-Battery approach defined here provides a systematic means for clinicians to make valid, *up-to-date* interpretations of current intelligence batteries, in particular, and to augment them in a way that is consistent with the empirically supported CHC theory of cognitive abilities.

Through an understanding of the breadth and depth of broad and narrow CHC cognitive abilities and their relations to outcome criteria (e.g., specific academic skills), it will become clear that the measurement of these abilities, via cross-battery assessment, supercedes global IQ in the evaluation of learning and problem-solving capabilities (Flanagan, 2000; Flanagan, McGrew, et al., 2000). Moving beyond the boundaries of a single test kit by adopting the psychometrically and theoretically defensible cross-battery principles represents a significantly improved method of measuring cognitive abilities (Carroll, 1998; Kaufman, 2000). Furthermore, because the cross-battery approach is theory-focused (rather than test kit–focused), its principles and procedures can be used with any intelligence battery.

THE NEED FOR A CROSS-BATTERY ASSESSMENT APPROACH

The need to have cross-battery assessment techniques to broaden the assessment of cognitive functioning beyond the confines of a single battery not only is apparent in school and clinical psychology (e.g., Brackett & McPherson, 1996; Flanagan & McGrew, 2000; Kaufman, 1994; Kaufman et al., 1999; Woodcock, 1990), it is also apparent in neuropsychology (e.g., Lezak, 1976, 1995; Wilson, 1992). In fact, as previously stated, neuropsychological assessment has been characterized for years by the crossing of various standardized tests in an attempt to measure a broader range of brain functions than that offered by a single instrument (Lezak, 1976, 1995). Unlike Flanagan and McGrew's approach, however, the omnipresent techniques of crossing batteries within the field of neuropsychological assessment do not appear to

<table>
<tr><td>

DON'T FORGET
....

**Broad Use of
Cross-Battery Approach**

Because the cross-battery approach is theory-focused (rather than test kit–focused), its principles and procedures can be used with any intelligence battery and in any assessment-related discipline.

</td></tr>
</table>

be grounded in a systematic process that is both psychometrically and theoretically defensible. Thus, as Wilson (1992) cogently pointed out, the field of neuropsychological assessment is in need of an eclectic approach that can guide practitioners through the selection of measures that would result in more specific and delineated patterns of function and dysfunction—an approach that provides more clinically useful information than one that is "wedded to the utilization of subscale scores and IQs" (p. 382).

Indeed, all fields involved in the assessment of cognitive functioning have a need for an approach that can aid practitioners in their attempts to "touch all of the major cognitive areas, with emphasis on those most suspect on the basis of history, observation, and on-going test findings" (Wilson, 1992, p. 382; see also Brackett & McPherson, 1996). Although the theories and conceptual models that underlie neuropsychological assessment may differ from those underlying other types of assessment (e.g., psychoeducational), the principles and procedures that define the CHC Cross-Battery approach to assessment can be adopted for use within any field.

APPLICATION OF THE CHC CROSS-BATTERY APPROACH

In order to ensure that CHC Cross-Battery assessment procedures are psychometrically and theoretically defensible, it is recommended that practitioners adhere to three guiding principles. These principles are presented in Rapid Reference 1.10 and are described briefly in the following pages. (It is important to note that the CHC Cross-Battery Worksheets that comprise Appendix A incorporate these principles in order to facilitate the application of this method of assessment.)

Guiding Principle I

When constructing broad (stratum II) ability composites or clusters, one should include only *relatively pure CHC indicators* (i.e., those tests that had either *strong* or *moderate* [but not mixed] loadings on their respective CHC factors in cross-battery factor

≡Rapid Reference 1.10

Guiding Principles of CHC Cross-Battery Assessment

Guiding Principle 1: When constructing broad (stratum II) ability composites or clusters, include only relatively pure CHC indicators (i.e., those tests that had either strong or moderate [but not mixed] loadings on their respective CHC factors in cross-battery factor analyses).

Guiding Principle 2: When constructing broad (stratum II) ability composites, include two or more qualitatively different narrow (stratum I) ability indicators for each CHC domain.

Guiding Principle 3: When conducting CHC Cross-Battery assessments, select tests from the smallest number of batteries to minimize the effect of spurious differences between test scores that may be attributable to differences in the characteristics of independent norm samples.

Following the worksheets in Appendix A will ensure adherence to Guiding Principles 1 and 2. The information presented in Chapter 3 of this book will assist practitioners with Guiding Principle 3.

analyses). There is one exception to this principle: A test that was classified *logically* at the broad (stratum II) level may be used in cross-battery assessments if there is a clear, established relation between it and the format of a test that was classified *empirically*. For example, although the WMS-III Digit Span test has not been included in adequately designed CHC cross-battery factor analyses to date, it is most likely a good indicator of Memory Span (MS), a narrow ability of *Gsm*. This is because it is very similar in testing format (e.g., administration procedure, task demand, nature of stimuli) to the Wechsler Intelligence Scales' Digit Span tests, which have had consistently strong loadings on *Gsm* factors in CHC theory–driven cross-battery factor analyses (e.g., Woodcock, 1990; Woodcock et al., 2001). As a general rule of thumb, empirically classified tests should be selected over logically classified tests whenever feasible. This will ensure that only *construct-relevant* tests are included in cross-battery assessments. (Empirically and logically classified tests are clearly marked on the CHC Cross-Battery Worksheets presented in Appendix A.)

DON'T FORGET

Empirical vs. Logical Classification

Empirically classified tests should be selected over logically classified tests whenever it is feasible to do so.

Guiding Principle 2

When constructing broad (stratum II) ability composites, include *two or more qualitatively different* narrow (stratum I) ability indicators for each CHC domain to ensure appropriate construct representation. Without sufficient empirically or logically classified tests available to represent constructs adequately, inferences about an individual's broad (stratum II) ability cannot be made. For example, when a composite is derived from two measures of Vocabulary (VL; for example, WJ-R Oral Vocabulary and Picture Vocabulary), it is inappropriate to generalize about an individual's *broad Gc* ability because the *Gc* construct is underrepresented. In this case the composite (i.e., WJ-R Comprehension-Knowledge [or *Gc*] Cluster) is best interpreted as a measure of Lexical Knowledge (a narrow stratum I ability) rather than as *Gc* (a broad stratum II ability). Alternatively, inferences can be made about an individual's broad *Gc* ability based on a composite that is derived from one measure of Lexical Knowledge and one measure of General Information (i.e., two qualitatively different indicators of *Gc;* see *Gc* worksheet in Appendix A). Of course, as stated earlier, the more broadly an ability is represented (i.e., through the derivation of composites based on multiple qualitatively different narrow ability indicators), the more confidence one has in drawing inferences about that broad ability based on the composite score. A minimum of two qualitatively different indicators per CHC composite is recommended for practical reasons (viz., time-efficient assessment; McGrew & Flanagan, 1998; Woodcock et al., 2001).

CAUTION

Minimum Number of Indicators

A minimum of two qualitatively different indicators per CHC composite is recommended for practical reasons (viz., time-efficient assessment).

Guiding Principle 3

When conducting CHC Cross-Battery assessments, it is important to select tests from the *smallest number* of batteries to minimize the effect of spurious differences among test scores that may be attributable to differences in the characteristics of independent norm samples (Mc-

Grew, 1994). For example, the *Flynn effect* (Flynn, 1984) indicates that there is, on average, a difference of three standard-score points between the test scores of any two tests that were standardized 10 years apart. Using the WJ-R to augment the WISC-III and DAS, or the WJ III to augment the CAS or WAIS-III, following the steps that follow will ensure a valid and comprehensive assessment of most CHC broad abilities (see Keith, Flanagan, et al., 2000). Because the WISC-III and WJ-R, for example, were normed within 2 years of one another and both were found to have exemplary standardization sample characteristics (Kamphaus, 1993; Kaufman, 1990; Salvia & Ysseldyke, 1991), this combination of batteries would be appropriate for CHC Cross-Battery assessments (see Hanel, 2001; Mascolo, 2001).

There are times, however, when crossing more than two batteries is necessary to gain enough information to test hypotheses about cognitive strengths or weaknesses or to answer specific referral questions. For example, since *Glr* is not measured (or at least, not adequately) by most intelligence batteries, it is often necessary to supplement tests, such as the Wechslers, SB:IV, KAIT, K-ABC, and CAS, with tests from more than one additional battery to gain enough qualitatively different measures of *Glr* to constitute broad representation of this ability in assessment. Although crossing more than two batteries may not seem desirable from a psychometric standpoint, it is important to realize that "when cross-battery assessments are implemented *systematically* and adhere to the recommendations for development, use, and interpretation, the potential error introduced due to crossing norm groups is likely negligible and has far *fewer* implications than the error associated with the improper use and interpretation of cognitive ability performance associated with the traditional assessment approach (e.g., subtest analysis)" (Flanagan, McGrew, et al., 2000, p. 223, emphasis in original).

In summary, the pillars and guiding principles underlying the CHC Cross-Battery approach provide the necessary foundation from which to conduct comprehensive assessments of the broad CHC abilities that define the structure of intelligence in current psychometric theory and research. Preliminary studies have shown that assessments organized around CHC theory, following cross-battery principles and procedures (see Chapter 2), are valid and explain certain academic skills (e.g., reading decoding, reading comprehension) better than do assessments organized around traditional models (e.g., Wechsler models). These studies are summarized in the next section.

RESEARCH FOUNDATION OF CHC CROSS-BATTERY ASSESSMENT

The entire CHC Cross-Battery approach was built on research. Kaufman (2000) commented that this new approach to assessment and interpretation "is based on an impressive compilation and integration of research investigations" (p. xv). Specifically, the approach ensures that assessments are organized and interpreted according to the well-researched CHC theory of cognitive abilities. In addition, the classifications necessary to organize assessments according to CHC theory are either empirically based or the result of an expert consensus process. Thus, the CHC Cross-Battery approach rests on a solid research foundation. Notwithstanding, the validity of the assessment *method* was not fully evaluated until very recently.

Because the CHC Cross-Battery approach was formally introduced to the field only 2 years ago, little research on its utility is available. The few investigations that have been conducted using cross-battery data sets, however, are promising. Summaries of these investigations are organized around two important questions about the approach.

Does use of the CHC classifications and procedures of the CHC Cross-Battery approach result in valid measurement of CHC constructs?   Preliminary studies suggest that the CHC clusters that are derived following cross-battery classifications and procedures are valid. For example, confirmatory factor analysis with WISC-R/WJ-R cross-battery data demonstrated that they fit a seven-factor CHC model well and significantly better than a traditional three-factor WISC-R model. In a similar investigation of the cross-battery principles and procedures for organizing tests in assessment, Mascolo (2001) demonstrated the configural invariance of Flanagan's seven-factor structural model in an independent cross-battery dataset. Likewise, Keith, Kranzler, and Flanagan (in press) showed the configural invariance of the same CHC seven-factor model in an independent evaluation of CAS/WJ III data. Thus, when the WISC-R, WISC-III, and CAS were supplemented with select tests from the WJ-R/WJ III in a systematic manner, following the steps of the CHC Cross-Battery approach, the resultant CHC structural model underlying these data sets was supported by and indeed consistent with the extant factor-analytic cognitive abilities research. In addition, these cross-battery data fit a contemporary CHC seven-factor model better than competing traditional models of the structure of intelligence. To demonstrate fully the utility of the CHC Cross-Battery approach, it is necessary to cross-validate the previous findings and conduct similar research with intelligence batteries other than the WJ-R/WJ III following cross-battery principles and procedures.

Do CHC cross-battery assessments provide a better understanding of academic skills than traditional (Wechsler Scale) assessments? Preliminary research suggests that assessments organized around cross-battery principles and procedures lead to better prediction of academic skills as well as to a more accurate description of the specific cognitive abilities that contribute to the explanation of specific academic achievements. For example, Flanagan (in press) found that the general ability (or g) factor underlying a WISC-R–based cross-battery CHC model accounted for substantially more variance in reading achievement (approximately 25%) than did the g factor underlying a more traditional three-factor Wechsler model (Verbal Comprehension [VC]–Perceptual Organization [PO]–Freedom From Distractibility [FFD]). Similarly, Hanel (2001) found that the g factor underlying a WISC-III–based cross-battery model accounted for substantially more variance in reading achievement than did the more frequently interpreted four-factor WISC-III model (i.e., VC-PO-FFD-Processing Speed). In addition, both Flanagan and Hanel found that when assessments are organized around the strong CHC model, specific cognitive abilities, such as *Gc, Ga,* and *Gs,* explained a significant portion of the variance in reading achievement beyond that accounted for by g. Their findings were consistent with the g/specific abilities literature (e.g., Keith, 1999; McGrew et al., 1997; Vanderwood et al., 2000) and suggest that these abilities may be particularly important to assess in addition to general ability in young children referred for reading problems. Following the cross-battery principles and procedures will ensure that these abilities are represented adequately in assessment.

These initial validity studies demonstrated that the application of the CHC Cross-Battery approach to the WISC-R, WISC-III, and CAS resulted in structurally valid CHC measures. Additional validity support for the resultant cross-battery CHC constructs was demonstrated through their significant (and expected) relations to external measures (viz., general and specific reading abilities; see Flanagan, in press, for details). Although it is recognized that these studies so far offer only limited evidence regarding the validity of the CHC

Cross-Battery approach, they are nonetheless quite promising in their findings. Clearly, much more validity evidence will be necessary in order to substantiate fully the benefits and utility of the CHC Cross-Battery approach. Considering the strong research and theoretical foundations of the CHC Cross-Battery approach and given the results of these current studies, there appears to be every reason to believe that the direction of such future research is likely to be positive and consistent with what has already been found. As supporting validity evidence continues to emerge, the unique benefits and advantages provided by the approach (i.e., valid measurement of constructs using data from crossed batteries and better prediction of academic skills through accurate measurement of related cognitive abilities) are likely to become valuable, if not indispensable, tools in cognitive assessment.

COMPREHENSIVE REFERENCES ON THE CHC CROSS-BATTERY APPROACH

The Intelligence Test Desk Reference (ITDR): Gf-Gc *Cross-Battery Assessment* (Mc-Grew & Flanagan) and *The Wechsler Scales and* Gf-Gc *Theory: A Contemporary Approach to Interpretation* (Flanagan, McGrew, et al., 2000) currently provide the most detailed information on the development and implementation of the CHC Cross-Battery approach. In addition, these books provide a detailed description of the specific steps necessary to organize a cognitive ability evaluation according to current theory and research. While the former book provides the most comprehensive description of the psychometric, theoretical, content, and interpretive features of all current intelligence tests as well as numerous special-purpose tests (information necessary to make informed decisions about supplementing a given intelligence battery), the latter book provides a comprehensive and defensible organizational framework for interpreting cross-battery data using the Wechsler Intelligence Scales.

REFERENCES

Bickley, P. G., Keith, T. Z., & Wolfe, L. M. (1995). The three-stratum theory of cognitive abilities: Test of the structure of intelligence across the life span. *Intelligence, 20,* 309–328.

Brackett, J., & McPherson, A. (1996). Learning disabilities diagnosis in postsecondary students: A comparison of discrepancy-based diagnostic models. In N. Gregg, C. Hoy, & A. F. Gay (Eds.), *Adults with learning disabilities: Theoretical and practical perspectives* (pp. 68–84). New York: Guilford.

Briggs, S. R., & Cheek, J. M. (1986). The role of factor analysis in the development and evaluation of personality scales. [Special Issue: Methodological developments in personality research]. *Journal of Personality, 54*(1), 106–148.

Carroll, J. B. (1983). Studying individual differences in cognitive abilities: Through and beyond factor analysis. In R. F. Dillon (Ed.), *Individual differences in cognition* (Vol. 1, pp. 1–33). New York: Academic.

Carroll, J. B. (1989). Factor analysis since Spearman: Where do we stand? What do we know? In R. Kanfer, P. L. Ackerman, & R. Cudeck (Eds.), *Abilities, motivation, and methodology* (pp. 43–67). Hillsdale, NJ: Erlbaum.

Carroll, J. B. (1993). *Human cognitive abilities: A survey of factor-analytic studies.* Cambridge, UK: Cambridge University Press.

Carroll, J. B. (1997). The three-stratum theory of cognitive abilities. In D. P. Flanagan, J. L. Genshaft, & P. L. Harrison (Eds.), *Contemporary intellectual assessment: Theories, tests, and issues* (pp. 122–130). New York: Guilford.

Carroll, J. B. (1998). Foreword. In K. S. McGrew & D. P. Flanagan, *The intelligence test desk reference (ITDR): Gf-Gc cross-battery assessment* (pp. xi–xii). Boston: Allyn & Bacon.

Clarke, L. A., & Watson, D. (1995). Constructing validity: Basic issues in objective scale development. *Psychological Assessment, 7,* 309–319.

Comrey, A. L. (1988). Factor-analytic methods of scale development in personality and clinical psychology. *Journal of Consulting and Clinical Psychology, 56*(5), 754–761.

Daniel, M. H. (1997). Intelligence testing: Status and trends. *American Psychologist, 52,* 1038–1045.

Epstein, S. (1983). Aggression and beyond: Some basic issues on the prediction of behavior. *Journal of Personality, 51,* 360–392.

Flanagan, D. P. (in press). Wechsler-based CHC cross-battery assessment and reading achievement: Strengthening the validity of interpretations drawn from Wechsler test scores. *School Psychology Quarterly.*

Flanagan, D. P., Genshaft, J. L., & Harrison, P. L. (Eds.). (1997). *Contemporary intellectual assessment: Theories, tests, and issues.* New York: Guilford.

Flanagan, D. P., & McGrew, K. S. (1997). A cross-battery approach to assessing and interpreting cognitive abilities: Narrowing the gap between practice and cognitive science. In D. P. Flanagan, J. L. Genshaft, & P. L. Harrison (Eds.), *Contemporary intellectual assessment: Theories, tests, and issues* (pp. 314–325). New York: Guilford.

Flanagan, D. P., & McGrew, K. S. (1998). Interpreting intelligence tests from contemporary Gf-Gc theory: Joint confirmatory factor analyses of the WJ-R and KAIT in a nonwhite sample. *Journal of School Psychology, 36,* 151–182.

Flanagan, D. P., McGrew, K. S., & Ortiz, S. O. (2000). *The Wechsler intelligence scales and CHC theory: A contemporary approach to interpretation.* Boston: Allyn & Bacon.

Flynn, J. R. (1984). The mean IQ of Americans: Massive gains 1932 to 1978. *Psychological Bulletin, 95,* 29–51.

Genshaft, J. L., & Gerner, M. E. (1998). Gf-Gc cross-battery assessment: Implications for school psychologists. *Communique, 26*(8), 24–27.

Guilford, J. P. (1954). *Psychometric methods* (2nd ed.). New York: McGraw-Hill.

Gustafsson, J. E. (1984). A unifying model for the structure of intellectual abilities. *Intelligence, 8,* 179–203.

Gustafsson, J. E. (1988). Hierarchical models of individual differences in cognitive abilities. In R. J. Sternberg (Ed.), *Advances in the psychology of human intelligence* (Vol. 4, pp. 35–71). Hillsdale, NJ: Erlbaum.

Gustafsson, J. E., & Balke, G. (1993). General and specific abilities as predictors of school achievement. *Multivariate behavioral research, 28*(4), 407–434.

Gustafsson, J. E., & Undheim, J. O. (1996). Individual differences in cognitive functions. In C. D. Berliner & R. C. Cabfee (Eds.), *Handbook of educational psychology* (pp. 186–242). New York: Macmillan.

Hanel, C. (2001). *CHC cross-battery assessment: Examining the relationship between specific cognitive abilities and reading, writing, and math achievement in a referred sample.* Unpublished doctoral dissertation, Saint John's University.

Horn, J. L. (1988). Thinking about human abilities. In J. R. Nesselroade & R. B. Cattell (Eds.), *Handbook of multivariate psychology* (Rev. ed., pp. 645–685). New York: Academic.

Horn, J. L. (1991). Measurement of intellectual capabilities: A review of theory. In K. S. McGrew, J. K. Werder, & R. W. Woodcock (Eds.), *Woodcock-Johnson technical manual* (pp. 197–232). Chicago: Riverside.

Horn, J. L. (1994). Theory of fluid and crystallized intelligence. In R. J. Sternberg (Ed.), *Encyclopedia of human intelligence* (pp. 443–451). New York: Macmillan.

Horn, J. L., & Noll, J. (1997). Human cognitive capabilities: *Gf-Gc* theory. In D. P. Flanagan, J. L. Genshaft, & P. L. Harrison (Eds.), *Contemporary intellectual assessment: Theories, tests, and issues* (pp. 53–91). New York: Guilford.

Ittenbach, R. F., Esters, I. G., & Wainer, H. (1997). The history of test development. In D. P. Flanagan, J. L. Genshaft, & P. L. Harrison (Eds.), *Contemporary intellectual assessment: Theories, tests, and issues* (pp. 17–31). New York: Guilford.

Kamphaus, R. W. (1993). *Clinical assessment of children's intelligence.* Boston: Allyn & Bacon.

Kamphaus, R. W. (1998). Intelligence test interpretation: Acting in the absence of evidence. In A. Prifitera & D. Saklofske (Eds.), *WISC-III clinical use and interpretation.* San Diego: Academic.

Kamphaus, R. W., Petoskey, M. D., & Morgan, A. W. (1997). A history of test intelligence interpretation. In D. P. Flanagan, J. L. Genshaft, & P. L. Harrison (Eds.), *Contemporary intellectual assessment: Theories, tests, and issues* (pp. 32–51). New York: Guilford.

Kaufman, A. S. (1979). *Intelligent testing with the WISC-R.* New York: Wiley.

Kaufman, A. S. (1990). *Assessing adolescent and adult intelligence.* Boston: Allyn & Bacon.

Kaufman, A. S. (1994). *Intelligent testing with the WISC-III.* New York: Wiley.

Kaufman, A. S. (2000). Foreword. In D. P. Flanagan, K. S. McGrew, & S. O. Ortiz, *The Wechsler intelligence scales and Gf-Gc theory: A contemporary approach to interpretation.* Boston: Allyn & Bacon.

Kaufman, A. S., Lichtenberger, E. O., & Naglieri, J. A. (1999). Intelligence testing in the schools. In C. R. Reynolds & T. B. Gutkin (Eds.), *The handbook of school psychology* (pp. 307–349). New York: Wiley.

Keith, T. Z. (1997). Using confirmatory factor analysis to aid in understanding the constructs measured by intelligence tests. In D. P. Flanagan, J. L. Genshaft, & P. L. Harrison, *Contemporary intellectual assessment: Theories, tests, and issues* (pp. 373–402). New York: Guilford.

Keith, T. Z. (1999). Effects of general and specific abilities on student achievement: Similarities and differences across ethnic groups. *School Psychology Quarterly, 14*(3), 239–262.

Keith, T. Z., Kranzler, J. H., & Flanagan, D. P. (in press). What does the Cognitive Assessment System (CAS) measure? Joint confirmatory factor analysis of the CAS and the Woodcock-Johnson Tests of Cognitive Ability–Third Edition (WJ III). *School Psychology Review.*

Kranzler, J. H., & Keith, T. Z. (1999). Independent confirmatory factor analysis of the Cognitive Assessment System (CAS): What does the CAS measure? *School Psychology Review, 28,* 117–144.

Lezak, M. D. (1976). *Neuropsychological assessment.* New York: Oxford University Press.

Lezak, M. D. (1995). *Neuropsychological assessment* (3rd ed.). New York: Oxford University Press.

Lohman, D. F. (1989). Human intelligence: An introduction to advances in theory and research. *Review of Educational Research, 59*(4), 333–373.

Lohman, D. F. (1994). Spatial ability. In R. J. Sternberg (Ed.), *Encyclopedia of human intelligence* (pp. 1000–1007). New York: Macmillan.

Mascolo, J. (2001). *Interpreting Cross-Battery data from contemporary theory: Cross-validation of the CHC model in a referred sample.* Unpublished doctoral dissertation, St. John's University.

McGhee, R. L. (1993). Fluid and crystallized intelligence: Confirmatory factor analysis of the Differential Abilities Scale, Detroit Tests of Learning Aptitude–3, and Woodcock-Johnson Psycho-Educational Assessment Battery–Revised. *Journal of Psychoeducational Assessment, Monograph Series: Woodcock-Johnson Psycho-Educational Battery–Revised,* 20–38.

McGrew, K. S. (1994). *Clinical interpretation of the Woodcock-Johnson Tests of Cognitive Ability–Revised.* Boston: Allyn & Bacon.

McGrew, K. S. (1997). Analysis of the major intelligence batteries according to a proposed comprehensive *Gf-Gc* framework. In D. P. Flanagan, J. L. Genshaft, & P. L. Harrison (Eds.), *Contemporary intellectual assessment: Theories, tests, and issues* (151–180). New York: Guilford.

McGrew, K. S., & Flanagan, D. P. (1998). *The intelligence test desk reference (ITDR):* Gf-Gc cross-battery assessment. Boston: Allyn & Bacon.

McGrew, K. S., Flanagan, D. P., Keith, T. Z., & Vanderwood, M. (1997). Beyond *g:* The impact of *Gf-Gc* specific cognitive abilities research on the future use and interpretation of intelligence tests in the schools. *School Psychology Review, 26*(2), 189–210.

McGrew, K. S., Werder, J. K., & Woodcock, R. W. (1991). *Woodcock-Johnson Psycho-Educational Battery–Revised technical manual.* Chicago: Riverside.

Messick, S. (1989). Validity. In R. Linn (Ed.), *Educational Measurement* (3rd ed., pp. 131–104). Washington, DC: American Council on Education.

Messick, S. (1992). Multiple intelligences or multilevel intelligence? Selective emphasis on distinctive properties of hierarchy: On Gardner's *Frames of Mind* and Sternberg's *Beyond IQ* in the context of theory and research on the structure of human abilities. *Psychological Inquiry, 3*(4), 365–384.

Messick, S. (1995). Validity of psychological assessment: Validation of inferences from persons' responses and performances as scientific inquiry into score meaning. *American Psychologist, 50,* 741–749.

Morris, R. D., Stuebing, K. K., Fletcher, J. M., Shaywitz, S. E., Lyon, G. R., Shankweiler, D. P., Katz, L., Francis, D. J., & Shaywitz, B. A. (1998). Subtypes of reading disability: Variability around a phonological core. *Journal of Educational Psychology, 90*(3), 347–373.

Neisser, U., Boodoo, G., Bouchard, T. J., Boykin, A. W., Brody, N., Ceci, S. J., Halpern, D. F., Loehlin, J. C., Perloff, R., Sternberg, R. J., & Urbina, S. (1996). Intelligence: Knowns and unknowns. *American Psychologist, 51,* 77–101.

Nettelbeck, T. (1994). Speediness. In R. J. Sternberg (Ed.), *Encyclopedia of human intelligence* (pp. 1014–1019). New York: Macmillan.

Salvia, J., & Ysseldyke, J. (1991). *Assessment in special and remedial education* (5th ed.). Boston: Houghton-Mifflin.

Sattler, J. M. (1988). *Assessment of children's intelligence and special abilities* (2nd ed.). San Diego: Sattler.

Snow, R. E. (1986). Individual differences and the design of educational programs. *American Psychologist, 41,* 1029–1039.

Stankov, L. (1994). Auditory abilities. In R. J. Sternberg (Ed.), *Encyclopedia of human intelligence* (pp. 157–162). New York: Macmillan.

Sternberg, R. J., & Kaufman, J. C. (1998). Human abilities. *Annual Review of Psychology, 49,* 479–502.

Taylor, T. R. (1994). A review of three approaches to cognitive assessment, and a proposed integrated approach based on a unifying theoretical framework. *South African Journal of Psychology, 24*(4), 183–193.

Thorndike, R. M., & Lohman, D. F. (1990). *A century of ability testing.* Chicago: Riverside.

Thurstone, L. L. (1935). *The vectors of mind.* Chicago: University of Chicago Press.

Vanderwood, M., McGrew, K. S., Flanagan, D. P., & Keith, T. Z. (2000). *Examination of the contribution of general and specific cognitive abilities to reading achievement.* Manuscript submitted for publication.

Wilson, B. C. (1992). The neuropsychological assessment of the preschool child: A branching model. In I. Rapm & S. I. Segalowitz (Eds.), *Handbook of neuropsychology: Child neuropsychology* (Vol. 6, pp. 377–394).

Woodcock, R. W. (1990). Theoretical foundations of the WJ-R measures of cognitive ability. *Journal of Psychoeducational Assessment, 8,* 231–258.

Woodcock, R. W. (1994). Measures of fluid and crystallized intelligence. In R. J. Sternberg (Ed.), *The encyclopedia of intelligence* (pp. 452–456). New York: Macmillan.

Woodcock, R. W., & Mather, N. (1989). WJ-R tests of cognitive ability—Standard and supplemental batteries: Examiner's manual. In R. W. Woodcock & M. B. Johnson (Eds.), *Woodcock-Johnson Psycho-Educational Battery* (Rev. ed.). Chicago: Riverside.

Woodcock, R. W., McGrew, K. S., & Mather, N. (2001). *Woodcock-Johnson Psycho-Educational Battery–Third Edition (WJ III).* Itasca, IL: Riverside.

Ysseldyke, J. (1990). Goodness of fit of the Woodcock-Johnson Psycho-Educational Battery—Revised to the Horn-Cattell *Gf-Gc* theory. *Journal of Psychoeducational Assessment, 8,* 268–275.

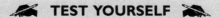

✎ TEST YOURSELF ✎

....

1. **The majority of current intelligence tests do not adequately assess the complete range of broad cognitive abilities included in either Horn's (1991, 1994) or Carroll's (1993, 1997) model of the structure of intelligence.** True or False?

2. **Fluid Intelligence (*Gf*), Crystallized Intelligence (*Gc*), and Visual Processing (*Gv*) are examples of**

   (a) general (stratum III) ability.

   (b) broad (stratum II) abilities.

   (c) narrow (stratum I) abilities.

3. **How can one best describe *Gq* and the Quantitative Reasoning (*RQ*) ability that is subsumed by *Gf*?**

   (a) *Gq* represents the ability to reason inductively and deductively when solving quantitative problems, whereas RQ represents an individual's store of acquired mathematical knowledge.

   (b) *Gq* represents an individual's store of acquired mathematical knowledge, whereas RQ represents the ability to reason inductively and deductively when solving quantitative problems.

   (c) Both *Gq* and RQ represent the same thing: an individual's store of acquired mathematical knowledge.

   (d) Both *Gq* and RQ represent the same thing: the ability to reason inductively and deductively when solving quantitative problems.

4. **When defining Long-Term Storage and Retrieval (*Glr*), the most important aspect of the word *long-term* is**

   (a) a significantly long period of time between the storage and retrieval of information (e.g., days, weeks, months, or years).

   (b) the occurrence of an intervening task that engages short-term memory during the interim before the attempted recall of the stored information.

(continued)

5. **How can one best describe Decision/Reaction Time or Speed (Gt) and Processing Speed (Gs)?**

   (a) Gt abilities reflect the immediacy with which an individual can react (typically measured in seconds or parts of seconds) to stimuli or a task, whereas Gs abilities reflect the ability to work quickly over a longer period of time (typically measured in intervals of 2–3 min).

   (b) Gt abilities reflect the ability to work quickly over a longer period of time (typically measured in intervals of 2–3 min) whereas Gs abilities reflect the immediacy with which an individual can react (typically measured in seconds or parts of seconds) to stimuli or a task.

   (c) Both Gt and Gs represent the same thing: the immediacy with which an individual can react (typically measured in seconds or parts of seconds) to stimuli or a task.

   (d) Both Gt and Gs represent the same thing: the ability to work quickly over a longer period of time (typically measured in intervals of 2–3 min).

6. **Which is the "purest" Gc composite on the WAIS-III?**

   (a) Verbal IQ

   (b) Perceptual Organization Index

   (c) Verbal Comprehension Index

   (d) Working Memory Index

7. **Most composites that are found in the major intelligence batteries are both relatively pure (i.e., containing only construct relevant tests) and well represented (i.e., containing qualitatively different measures of the broad ability represented by the composite).** True or False?

8. **Which of the following is *not* a good descriptor of the CHC Cross-Battery approach?**

   (a) time-efficient

   (b) theory-focused

   (c) test kit–focused

   (d) empirically supported

9. **When constructing broad (stratum II) ability composites or clusters in cross-battery assessment, one should *not* include**

   (a) relatively pure CHC indicators.

   (b) tests that are classified as mixed measures of CHC abilities.

   (c) two or more qualitatively different narrow (stratum I) ability indicators.

10. **When conducting cross-battery assessments, it is important to select tests from the smallest number of batteries possible.** True or False?

Answers: 1. True; 2. b; 3. b; 4. b; 5. a; 6. c; 7. False; 8. c; 9. b; 10. True

Two

HOW TO ORGANIZE AND ADMINISTER A CHC CROSS-BATTERY ASSESSMENT

This chapter describes the fundamental principles for organizing and administering CHC Cross-Battery assessments. Clear, step-by-step instructions of the approach will be presented that allow practitioners to select, organize, and administer subtests and batteries that are most appropriate to particular referral concerns and purposes of assessment. Specific issues related to the differences that arise when conducting comprehensive versus selective cross-battery assessments will be outlined in order to clarify the decision-making process. To assist practitioners in conducting CHC Cross-Battery assessments, specific materials and their applications in the process are introduced in the form of worksheets, reference tables, and summary sheets.

ORGANIZING CHC CROSS-BATTERY ASSESSMENT: BASIC PRINCIPLES AND METHODS

Overview

The discussion in Chapter 1 provided the rationale for using contemporary intelligence theory to drive assessment, as well as evidence that the most empirically supported model of intelligence is the Cattell-Horn-Carroll Theory of Cognitive Abilities (referred to simply as *CHC theory*). Chapter 1 also provided evidence to indicate that no single extant intelligence battery possesses the capacity to measure validly the wide range of human cognitive abilities specified by this CHC taxonomy. Therefore, Carroll (1997, 1998) and others have recommended that research be used to guide both the organization and the selection of tests that may be used to measure the abilities of interest accurately and reliably. The CHC Cross-Battery approach (Flanagan, McGrew, & Ortiz,

2000; McGrew & Flanagan, 1998) was specifically developed to assist practitioners in conducting assessments that approximate the total range of broad cognitive abilities more adequately than through the use of any single intelligence battery. In general, CHC Cross-Battery assessment is a time-efficient method of cognitive assessment that is grounded in contemporary psychometric theory and research on the structure of intelligence. Using the guidelines for Comprehensive CHC Cross-Battery (C-CB), assessment practitioners are able to measure in a valid manner a wider range of abilities than that represented by any single intelligence battery. Using the guidelines for Selective CHC Cross-Battery (S-CB) assessment, practitioners are also able to measure a selective range, or even a specific ability, validly and with more depth and adherence to empirical evidence than what can ordinarily be obtained using a single battery.

Utilization of Specific Referral Information

The ability to measure cognitive abilities broadly and selectively with increased empirical and theoretical confidence is not to be considered a haphazard exercise. Rather, CHC Cross-Battery assessment should be tailored to meet the unique demands of each situation in which it is determined that standardized data on cognitive abilities are to be collected. Therefore, decisions about test selection and organization must utilize the accompanying specific referral information that is a part of any need for engaging in such evaluations. There are three basic scenarios that best highlight how such information affects the decision-making process with respect to test selection and organization within the CHC Cross-Battery assessment framework.

The first scenario relates to the need to evaluate the relationship between an individual's manifest performance (e.g., academic skills) and cognitive abilities. This is often the situation in evaluations conducted in accordance with the Individuals with Disabilities Education Act (1997; often referred to as IDEA or PL 105-17), which seeks to deter-

> ### DON'T FORGET
>
> ### Tailoring to the Situation
>
> CHC Cross-Battery assessment should be tailored to meet the unique demands of each situation in which it is determined that standardized data on cognitive abilities are to be collected.

mine the presence of a disability that may be used to establish eligibility for special education programs and services. In such cases, practitioners should relate the current literature on the relationship of manifest skills to the examinees' respective underlying cognitive abilities in order to select tests that have been empirically demonstrated to have a significant relationship to such development. In other words, if there are concerns with reading skills, practitioners should review any research that provides evidence linking particular cognitive abilities with reading achievement. The practitioner should then ensure that measures of these specific cognitive abilities are included in the proposed assessment. McGrew and Flanagan (1998) reviewed the extant research on the relations between cognitive abilities and reading and math achievement. A summary of their findings of more than a decade of research in this area is presented in Table 2.1.

Another scenario that illustrates the effect of referral concerns on decision making occurs when attention must be paid to practical or legal considerations. With respect to practical limitations, it is unreasonable to expect that every practitioner possesses every published test or that every practitioner has expertise in administering any given test. Therefore, although the CHC Cross-Battery approach is not constrained by such issues, the practitioner is, and, thus, decisions regarding test selection and organization will be directly influenced by these issues. Similarly, there are times when legal prescriptions require the collection of certain types of data (e.g., IQ or global ability scores). This most often occurs in special education assessment but is not restricted solely to that domain. In this circumstance the practitioner may find it necessary to administer either an entire core battery to obtain the required score, or at the very least, to administer some additional tests that may not be directly relevant to CHC Cross-Battery purposes. The availability of brief measures for such things as IQ or global ability may attenuate this consideration to a certain degree (this issue is discussed in more detail in Chapter 4).

The third most common scenario in which decisions regarding test selection and organization are affected by specific referral concerns involves testing individuals who possess characteristics that set them apart from the mainstream. Practitioners are often called upon to assess the abilities of people who have sensory or perceptual impairments (deafness, blindness, etc.), who are motorically impaired (individuals with cerebral palsy, tremors, seizure activity, etc.), or people who are culturally and linguistically diverse. Obviously, if

Table 2.1 Summary of Significant Relations between CHC Abilities and Reading and Math Achievement

CHC Ability	Reading Achievement	Math Achievement
Gf	Inductive (I) and General Sequential Reasoning (RG) abilities play a moderate role in reading comprehension.	**Inductive (I) and General Sequential Reasoning (RG) abilities are consistently very important at all ages.**
Gc	**Language Development (LD), Lexical Knowledge (VL), and Listening Ability (LS) are important at all ages. These abilities become increasingly more important with age.**	**Language Development (LD), Lexical Knowledge (VL), and Listening Ability (LS) are important at all ages. These abilities become increasingly more important with age.**
Gsm	Memory Span (MS) is important especially when evaluated within the context of working memory.	Memory Span (MS) is important especially when evaluated within the context of working memory.
Gv		May be important primarily for higher-level or advanced mathematics (e.g., geometry, calculus).
Ga	**Phonetic Coding (PC) or "phonological awareness/ processing" is very important during the elementary school years.**	

Gf-Gc Ability	Reading Achievement	Math Achievement
Glr	**Naming Facility (NA) or "rapid automatic naming"** is **very important during the elementary school years.** Associative memory (MA) may be somewhat important at select ages (e.g., age 6).	
Gs	**Perceptual Speed (P) abilities are important during all school years, particularly the elementary school years.**	**Perceptual Speed (P) abilities are important during all school years, particularly the elementary school years.**

Note. The absence of comments for a particular CHC ability and achievement area (e.g., *Ga* and mathematics) indicates that the research reviewed either did not report any significant relations between the respective CHC ability and the achievement area, or if significant findings were reported, they were weak and were for only a limited number of studies. Comments in bold represent the CHC abilities that showed the strongest and most consistent relations with the respective achievement domains. From *The Wechsler Intelligence Scales and Gf-Gc theory: A Contemporary Approach to Interpretation* (p. 286), by D.P. Flanagan, K.S. McGrew, and S.O. Ortiz, 2000, Boston: Allyn & Bacon, copyright 2000 by Allyn & Bacon; and *The intelligence test desk reference (ITDR): Gf-Gc Cross-Battery Assessment* (p. 422), by K. S. McGrew and D. P. Flanagan, 1998, Boston: Allyn & Bacon, copyright 1998 by Allyn & Bacon. Reproduced with permission. The reader is referred to McGrew and Flanagan (1998) for a detailed discussion.

an individual is unable to manipulate objects because he or she cannot see them or cannot hold them, test selection and organization will be significantly affected. Such decisions are not, of course, necessarily specific to conducting CHC Cross-Battery assessments, but they must be appropriately considered nevertheless. The classification of the major intelligence batteries and nonverbal tests (e.g., UNIT, Leiter-R, CTONI, etc.) according to CHC theory can assist in this process (see McGrew & Flanagan, 1998; Flanagan, McGrew, et al. 2000).

In the case of individuals who are culturally and linguistically diverse, the cultural and linguistic extensions of the CHC Cross-Battery approach can be utilized in order to make decisions that respond directly to issues of dual-language development and proficiency as well as acculturation (Flanagan, McGrew, et al., 2000; Ortiz & Flanagan, 1998). These particular procedures, described in detail in Chapter 5 and in one of the case studies presented in Chapter 7, allow practitioners the opportunity to construct test batteries that not only provide a very sophisticated empirical and statistical basis, but that are also highly tailored to specific referral needs and factors related to individual culture and language variables.

Integrating Guiding Principles with Decision Making

In both Comprehensive Cross-Battery (C-CB) and Selective Cross-Battery (S-CB) assessments, organization and selection of tests is a process that is integrated within the context of the basic guiding principles. Practitioners must review information on several aspects of available tests in order to make appropriate decisions regarding final organization and selection. The information necessary to engage in this process is contained in Appendix B; by reviewing and referring to the information contained in this appendix, practitioners are able to arrive at decisions that meet the specific needs and purpose of the assessment to be conducted. The decision-making process varies slightly as a function of whether the practitioner seeks to engage in C-CB or S-CB. In very general terms, if one is interested in measuring comprehensive (or broad-based) intellectual functioning (e.g., Gf, Gc, Gv, Gsm, Gs, etc.) then a wide range of broad (stratum II) ability tests should be selected (i.e., do not use mostly or only tests of Gv). Similarly, if one is interested in measuring selective broad abilities (e.g., only Gc and Gs), then only tests of Gc and Gs should be used. This is, of course, only the initial step. The following text provides additional guidelines that must be considered in order to organize and assemble the most appropriate final battery. Although the amount of information included in Appendix B may appear daunting at first, practitioners must nevertheless become very familiar with its contents in order to make the most appropriate decisions possible. Appendix B is essentially the beginning point for organizing and selecting tests for CHC Cross-Battery assessment and is indispensable to establishing the validity of the process.

Beyond deciding simply whether the assessment is to be broad (C-CB) or narrow (S-CB) in focus, the practitioner must make decisions that are supported by theory and empirical data, and that are statistically defensible. Therefore, in order to ensure that CHC Cross-Battery assessment procedures are psychometrically and theoretically sound, practitioners must also adhere to the three guiding principles outlined in Chapter 1 when reviewing the information in Appendix B and making decisions regarding specific test selection. Although the information presented in Appendix B along with the guiding principles of CHC Cross-Battery assessment may appear overwhelming, at least initially, all of this information is integrated in an easy-to-follow format on the CHC Cross-Battery worksheets discussed in this chapter.

CHC Cross-Battery Worksheets

To facilitate the decision-making process and streamline the statistical calculations necessary in CHC Cross-Battery assessment, worksheets have been created for practitioner use. These worksheets can be found in Appendix A and are essentially a reorganization of the information contained in Appendix B in a manner consistent with the CHC Cross-Battery guiding principles. The worksheets are especially helpful when decisions regarding which constructs are of interest have already been made, because the practitioner is able to refer directly to a set of tests that have been classified jointly along this dimension. These worksheets, together with the step-by-step approach to cross-battery assessment that follows, provide a bridge between CHC theory and practice and are explained here in more detail. Although many of the calculations can be easily completed by hand, the use of a calculator or a computer automated worksheet (see Chapter 6) is recommended in order to ensure accuracy and expedite the process.

These worksheets were originally presented in McGrew and Flanagan

(1998), were modified and presented again in Flanagan, McGrew, and colleague (2000), and have been updated and reproduced here again for convenience. Practitioners are encouraged to photocopy these worksheets from any of these sources and use them to facilitate the cross-battery assessment method presented here. There are seven cross-battery worksheets in all, one for each of the broad CHC abilities considered most critical in comprehensive or selective evaluations of intellectual functioning. As in Appendix B, each worksheet follows the same convention: Tests that have strong or moderate loadings on their respective CHC factor are printed in bold/uppercase and bold/lowercase letters, respectively, and those in bold letters (upper- or lowercase) represent empirically based classifications. Tests that are classified logically as measures of the respective broad CHC abilities are printed in regular lowercase letters. Additionally, each worksheet groups the subtests according to the narrow abilities that they measure. For example, the *Gf* worksheet groups subtests according to those that measure either Induction (I), General Sequential Reasoning (RG), or Quantitative Reasoning (RQ)—three narrow abilities subsumed by *Gf*.

As described in Chapter 1, CHC Cross-Battery assessment relies on the use of relatively pure measures of the broad ability constructs, preferably those with empirically validated loadings. This principle ensures that classification of tests along the dimension of broad constructs is based on contemporary research and statistical evaluation of actual data. The requirement is relaxed somewhat in the case of narrow ability indicators that may measure two different narrow abilities as long as both indicators remain within the scope of the same broad construct. This allowance is made because there is virtually no research to guide the classification of these indicators at the narrow ability level—thus, classification is based primarily on expert consensus procedures. Although use of narrow ability indicators that may measure two different aspects of the same broad ability may at times complicate interpretation at the narrow ability level, they do not in any way affect or preclude interpretation at the broad ability level. When a test is classified as a measure of two different narrow abilities (subsumed by the same broad ability), it is grouped with other measures of one narrow ability with the other narrow ability reported in parentheses next to the subtest. For example, a review of the *Gc* worksheet (see Figure 2.1) shows that the Wechsler Comprehension subtest is a measure of Language Development (LD), since it is grouped with other measures of LD on the worksheet. However, because the

Battery or Test	Age	Gc Narrow Abilities Tests	SS*	SS (100 ± 15)
		Language Development (LD)		
WECH	3–74	**COMPREHENSION (K0)**		
WECH	3–74	**SIMILARITIES (VL)**		
DAS	6–17	**SIMILARITIES**		
DAS	2–5	Verbal Comprehension (LS)		
SB:IV	12–24	**VERBAL RELATIONS**		
SB:IV	2–24	Comprehension (K0)		
SB:IV	2–14	Absurdities		
DTLA-4	6–17	Word Opposites		
DTLA-4	6–17	Story Construction		
Other				
		1. Sum of column		
		2. Divide by number of tests		
		3. Language Development average		
		Lexical Knowledge (VL)		
WECH	3–74	**VOCABULARY (LD)**		
DAS	6–17	**WORD DEFINITIONS (LD)**		
DAS	2–5	Naming Vocbulary (LD)		
SB:IV	2–24	**VOCABULARY (LD)**		
WJ-R	2–85+	**ORAL VOCABULARY (LD)**		
WJ-R	2–85+	**PICTURE VOCABULARY (K0)**		
WJ III	2–85+	**VERBAL COMP (LD)**		
NEPSY	3–4	Body Part Naming (K0)		
EVT	2–85+	Expressive Vocabulary Test (LD)		
K-BIT	4–90	Expressive Vocabulary (K0, LD)		
PPVT-3	2–85	Peab. Pic. Voc. Test (3rd ed.) (K0, LD)		
Other				
		1. Sum of column		
		2. Divide by number of tests		
		3. Lexical Knowledge average		
		Listening Ability (LS)		
WJ-R	4–85+	**LISTENING COMP. (LD)**		
WJ III	4–85+	**ORAL COMP. (LD)** (in ach. battery)		
NEPSY	3–12	Comprehension of Instructions (LD)		
Other				
		1. Sum of column		
		2. Divide by number of tests		
		3. Listening Ability average		
		General Information (K0)		
WECH	3–74	**INFORMATION**		
DTLA-4	6–17	Basic Information		
WJ III	2–85+	**GENERAL INFORMATION**		
Other				
		1. Sum of column		
		2. Divide by number of tests		
		3. General Information average		
		Information about Culture (K2)		
KAIT	11–85+	**FAMOUS FACES**		
Other				
		1. Sum of column		
		2. Divide by number of tests		
		3. Information about Culture average		

Name: _____
Age: _____
Grade: _____
Examiner: _____
Date of Evaluation: _____

Crystallized Intelligence: The breadth and depth of a person's acquired knowledge of a culture and the effective application of this knowledge.

Language Development: General development, or the understanding of words, sentences and paragraphs (not requiring reading) in spoken native-language skills.

Lexical Knowledge: Extent of vocabulary that can be understood in terms of correct word meanings.

Listening Ability: Ability to listen and comprehend oral communications.

General Information: Range of general knowledge.

Information about Culture: Range of cultural knowledge (e.g., music, art).

Cluster Average **

Sum/Number of Narrow Ability Averages

___ Broad (___)
___ Narrow (___)

Figure 2.1 Comprehensive Crystallized Intelligence (Gc) CHC Cross-Battery Worksheet

Note. from The intelligence test desk reference (ITDR): Gf-Gc Cross-Battery Assessment (p. 422), by K. S. Mc-Grew and D. P. Flanagan, 1998, Boston: Allyn & Bacon. Copyright 1998 by the publisher. Adapted with permission of Allyn & Bacon.

Comprehension subtest was classified also as a measure of General Information (K0), the code "K0" is printed in parentheses next to this subtest. The definitions of the respective broad and narrow abilities appear on the right side of each worksheet. Although brief, these definitions provide a quick reference and may facilitate test selection, test interpretation, and report writing.

IMPLEMENTING CHC CROSS-BATTERY ASSESSMENT STEP-BY-STEP

Step 1: Comprehensive or Selective Assessment

If it is determined that an assessment is to be selective in nature (S-CB), practitioners are free to focus exclusively on the constructs of interest and need not concern themselves with irrelevant constructs or full test batteries. However, if the assessment is to be comprehensive in nature (C-CB), then a *core* battery must be chosen that is appropriate and responsive to several factors, including age and developmental level of the examinee; availability of test batteries; examiner's familiarity and expertise with certain batteries; need to reduce duplication of test administration; and so forth. Once a core battery is selected, it is necessary to consider whether a Full Scale score is needed. This is because many state and professional classification systems (e.g., state guidelines adopted in compliance with IDEA, *DSM-IV*, AAMR mental retardation guidelines, etc.; see Jacobson & Mulick, 1996) may require the use of a Full Scale IQ in formulas designed to aid decision making in the diagnosis or identification of learning disabilities and developmental delays. It should be noted, however, that many of these formulas (e.g., those used in the discrepancy model for identifying significant ability-achievement differences to assist in diagnosing learning disability [LD]) are not only technically invalid, but are invalid for the very purpose for which they are used (e.g., to aid in the diagnosis of LD; see Flanagan, McGrew, et al., 2000, and Chapter 4 of this book).

If a complete intelligence battery must be administered to obtain a Full Scale score or general ability score, for whatever the reason, then cross-battery assessment may increase testing time. This is only because individual tests that do not meet the cross-battery guiding principles will need to be administered, depending on the core battery preference of the practitioner. If it is not necessary to use a complete battery to obtain a Full Scale score because it is either not relevant to the referral question or not required by formal criteria and regulations, then C-CB testing time will most likely remain equivalent to single-battery testing time. Of course, because of the specific focus on one or a few constructs, S-CB assessments will take significantly less time than single-battery administration.

Step 2: Identify the CHC Abilities of Interest

In the case of S-CB assessment, the practitioner merely needs to refer to the specific cross-battery worksheet(s) that correspond(s) to the ability or abilities that will form the focus of the evaluation. Within this framework, practitioners can readily review the relevant information that is needed in order to begin assembling the most appropriate measures for the abilities of interest. When an in-depth evaluation of a particular ability is the focus of assessment, the practitioner should keep in mind that the more qualitatively different indicators that are included to represent a given ability, the better the estimate of that ability.

With respect to C-CB assessment, the practitioner will first need to review the information in Appendix A or Appendix B to determine which CHC abilities are adequately represented on the chosen core battery from Step 1, and which are not. Again, if it is necessary to administer the full core intelligence battery (to obtain a Full Scale score), then all the test indicators (i.e., subtests) on the battery (that comprise the global score) will need to be administered even though they may be redundant or may contain significant construct-irrelevant variance (i.e., they may be

---

CAUTION

Invalidity of Discrepancy Formulas

Even though many state and professional classification systems require the use of a Full Scale IQ in formulas designed to aid decision making in the diagnosis or identification of learning disabilities and developmental delays, many of these formulas are not only technically invalid, but are invalid for the very purpose for which they are used (e.g., to aid in the diagnosis of LD).

DON'T FORGET

Including Qualitatively Different Indicators

The more qualitatively different indicators that are included to represent a given ability, the better the estimate of that ability.

mixed measures of two different abilities). For example, there are five WISC-III tests that comprise the VIQ, the analogue for *Gc*, but only two of those tests are necessary for C-CB assessment (i.e., two qualitatively different tests per CHC domain). The need for a Full Scale score thus makes administration of all five tests necessary, including one test (Arithmetic) that is irrelevant to the construct intended to be measured (*Gc*). If a Full Scale score is not needed, the practitioner should begin by examining the worksheets and identifying which two tests will be administered within the CHC domains that are represented adequately on the battery, since in some cases there may be more than two qualitatively different indicators that represent a particular broad ability.

The decision as to which two subtests are to be selected for each broad ability in C-CB assessment is based on joint consideration of several factors (see Rapid Reference 2.1). First, the two tests must represent qualitatively different aspects of the same broad ability. For example, in deciding how to measure *Gv*, two tests whose narrow ability (stratum I) classifications are the same (e.g., Spatial Relations [SR]) are not qualitatively different. Therefore, only one of these tests should be used and it should be coupled with a test that measures a qualitatively different aspect of *Gv*, such as Object Assembly or Gestalt Closure. Second, tests should be selected so as to be as responsive to the referral

≡ *Rapid Reference 2.1*

Considerations in Representing Broad Ability Domains

When selecting subtests to represent a broad ability domain, the following should be considered:

- The selected tests must represent qualitatively different aspects of the same broad ability.
- Selected tests should be as responsive to the referral concerns as possible. Some narrow abilities are more directly related to certain aspects of manifest functioning (e.g., academic skills) than are others.
- Age, developmental level, and other individual characteristics (e.g., cultural and linguistic background) of the examinee should be considered when selecting any particular test or combination of tests.
- Test reliability should be evaluated, especially when more than one subtest is available for the purpose of deriving a CHC cognitive ability cluster.

concerns as possible. Some narrow abilities are more directly related to certain aspects of manifest functioning (e.g., academic skills) than are others. Although the literature on this issue is just beginning to emerge (see Table 2.1), consideration should be given to identifying and using tests that have empirical or logical links to the cognitive processes that underlie the functional skills of interest. Third, attention to the issues mentioned previously—in particular age and developmental level of the child—should play a part in making final decisions regarding the suitability of any particular test or combination of tests. Fourth, practitioners should consider the reliability of the tests included in cross-battery assessments, and select tests with the highest reliability in situations in which more than one test could be used to represent an ability. Appendix C includes reliability information for all subtests for most major intelligence batteries, as well as select special-purpose tests.

Step 3: Identify Absence or Underrepresentation of CHC Abilities on the Core Battery

Identification of the relevant CHC abilities that are either not represented or that are underrepresented on a given core battery can be achieved by reviewing either Appendix B or the CHC Cross-Battery worksheets found in Appendix A. There are no published tests that provide adequate representation for the wide range of broad and narrow CHC cognitive abilities that have been validated empirically. Therefore, the practitioner will need to identify those abilities that will require supplementation through the use of tests from other batteries—hence the need to cross batteries. Even were tests available that could provide adequate coverage and representation of all such abilities, crossing batteries may yet prove useful in light of other considerations, such as task requirements, developmental appropriateness, cultural and linguistic implications, and so forth. Once again, in selecting tests that will be used to supplement the core battery, the practitioner should make every effort to accommodate the unique and idiosyncratic factors that may be involved so that assessment is tailored in a highly individualized manner.

Table 2.2 provides a quick reference for identifying abilities that are either not represented (i.e., absent) or not represented adequately (i.e., underrepresented) on the major intelligence batteries. By using this table, practitioners can quickly identify the areas in which a core battery needs to be supplemented.

Table 2.2 Representation of Broad CHC Abilities on Nine Major Intelligence Batteries

Battery	Gf	Gc	Gv
WISC-III	Not measured	Adequate **VOCABULARY (VL, LD)** **INFORMATION (K0)** **SIMILARITIES (LD, VL)** **COMPREHENSION (LD, K0)**	Adequate **BLOCK DESIGN (SR, Vz)** **OBJECT ASSEMBLY (CS, SR)** **Mazes (SS)**
WAIS-III	Underrepresented **MATRIX REASONING (I)**	Adequate **VOCABULARY (VL, LD)** **INFORMATION (K0)** **SIMILARITIES (LD, VL)** **COMPREHENSION (LD, K0)**	Adequate **BLOCK DESIGN (SR, Vz)** **OBJECT ASSEMBLY (CS, SR)**
WPPSI-R	Not measured	Adequate **VOCABULARY (VL, LD)** **INFORMATION (K0)** **SIMILARITIES (LD, VL)** **COMPREHENSION (LD, K0)**	Adequate **BLOCK DESIGN (SR, Vz)** **OBJECT ASSEMBLY (CS, SR)** **Mazes (SS)** Geometric Designs (Vz, P2)
KAIT	Adequate **MYSTERY CODES (I)** **LOGICAL STEPS (RG)**	Underrepresented **FAMOUS FACES (K2)**	Underrepresented **MEMORY FOR BLOCK** **DESIGNS (MV)**
K-ABC	Not measured	Not measured[a]	Adequate **TRIANGLES (SR)** Face Recognition (MV) **Gestalt Closure (CS)** Magic Window (PI)
CAS	Underrepresented Nonverbal Matrices (I)	Not measured	Adequate **FIGURE MEMORY (CF, MV)** **VERBAL-SPATIAL** **RELATIONS (PI)**
DAS	Adequate **MATRICES (I)** Picture Similarities (I) **SEQUENTIAL AND** **QUANTITATIVE** **REASONING (RQ, I)**	Adequate **SIMILARITIES (LD)** Verbal Comprehension (LD, LS) **WORD DEFINITIONS (VL,** **LD)** Naming Vocabulary (VL, LD)	Adequate Pattern Construction (SR) Block Building (Vz) Matching Letter-Like Forms (Vz) **RECALL OF DESIGNS (MV)** Recognition of Pictures (MV)

Gsm	*Glr*	*Ga*	*Gs*
Underrepresented **DIGIT SPAN (MS, MW)**	Not measured	Not measured	Adequate **SYMBOL SEARCH (P, R9)** **CODING (R9)**
Adequate **DIGIT SPAN (MS, MW)** **LETTER-NUMBER SEQUENCING (MW)**	Not measured	Not measured	Adequate **SYMBOL SEARCH (P, R9)** **DIGIT-SYMBOL CODING (R9)**
Not measured	Not measured	Not measured	Not measured
Not measured	Underrepresented **REBUS LEARNING (MA)** **REBUS DELAYED RECALL (MA)**	Not measured	Not measured
Underrepresented **NUMBER RECALL (MS)** **WORD ORDER (MS)**	Not measured	Not measured	Not measured
Underrepresented **WORD SERIES (MS)** **SENTENCE REPETITION (MS)** **SENTENCE QUESTIONS (MS)**	Underrepresented Expressive Attention	Not measured	Adequate **MATCHING NUMBERS (N, R9)** **RECEPTIVE ATTENTION (P, R4)** **PLANNED CODES (R9)** **NUMBER DETECTION (N7, R9)**
Underrepresented Recall of Digits	Underrepresented Recall of Objects (M6)	Not measured	Underrepresented Speed of Information Processing (N7, R9)

(continued)

Table 2.2 (continued)

Battery	*Gf*	*Gc*	*Gv*
WJ-R	Adequate **CONCEPT FORMATION (I)** **ANALYSIS-SYNTHESIS (RG)**	Adequate **ORAL VOCABULARY (VL, LD)** **PICTURE VOCABULARY (VL, K0)** **LISTENING COMPREHENSION (LS, LD)**	Adequate **Picture Recognition (MV)** **Visual Closure (CS)**
SB:IV	Adequate **MATRICES (I)** **EQUATION BUILDING (RQ)** Number Series (RQ)	Adequate **VERBAL RELATIONS (LD)** Comprehension (LD, K0) Absurdities (LD) **VOCABULARY (VL, LD)**	Adequate **PATTERN ANALYSIS (SR)** Bead Memory (MV) Memory for Objects (MV)

Note. Tests in bold, uppercase letters are strong measures as defined empirically; tests in bold, lowercase are moderate measures as defined empirically; tests in regular type, lowercase are classified logically. This table does not include tests that were classified as mixed measures of ability because mixed measures are not recommended in the initial phase of CHC Cross-Battery assessment.

[a]The K-ABC Achievement Test provides qualitatively different indicators of *Gc*.

Step 4: Select Tests Needed to Supplement the Core Battery

In determining which subtests are necessary in order to approximate or ensure adequate representation of absent or underrepresented abilities, one of the most important factors is the need to keep the number of batteries that will be used to a minimum (preferably two). There are some potential obstacles to be considered, however. For example, the fact that some broad (stratum II) CHC abilities (e.g., *Ga, Gsm, Glr*) can be represented by *only a few* qualitatively different indicators (e.g., three), as opposed to *many* qualitatively different subtests, highlights the limitations of intelligence instrumentation with respect to diversity of abilities measured and adherence to contemporary theory (a review of the *Ga* and *Gsm* worksheets compared to the *Gc* and *Gv* worksheets, for example, will make this point clear). Ideally, the universe of cognitive ability tests should allow for the selective measurement of multiple narrow (stratum I) abilities that comprise the broad (stratum II) abilities in contemporary CHC

Gsm	*Glr*	*Ga*	*Gs*
Adequate **MEMORY FOR WORDS (MS)** **NUMBERS REVERSED (MW)**	Underrepresented **MEMORY FOR NAMES (MA)** **VISUAL-AUDITORY LEARNING (MA, MM)** **DR: MEMORY FOR NAMES (MA)** **DR: VISUAL-AUDITORY LEARNING (MA, MM)**	Adequate **INCOMPLETE WORDS (PC:A)** **SOUND BLENDING (PC:S)** **SOUND PATTERNS (US/U3, UR)**	Adequate **VISUAL MATCHING (P, R9)** **CROSS-OUT (P)**
Underrepresented **MEMORY FOR DIGITS (MS, MW)**	Not measured	Not measured	Not measured

theory. Thus, there are times when choices may be rather limited or non-existent (depending on the availability of tests) and practitioners are advised to use their best judgment in deciding whether the potentially negative aspect of using, say, three different batteries, outweighs the negative aspects of not assessing a particular ability at all, or of not assessing it well.

Other instances in which one's choice of tests may be significantly affected include the need to assess individuals from a particular age range (e.g., preschool), or individuals with special needs (e.g., the deaf or blind), or individuals from different cultural or linguistic backgrounds. In such cases, the additional considerations imposed by the unique aspects of each individual case must be evaluated carefully in order to provide the most appropriate balance between the need for valid and reliable information and the need for practicality and efficiency in assessment. Some guidelines and recommendations for applying CHC Cross-Battery assessment within the context of various clinical applications are presented in Chapters 4 and 5.

Table 2.3 is an extension of Table 2.2 and provides only one example of several possibilities for ensuring adequate representation of the broad CHC abilities, depending on the core battery used in assessment. As can be seen in Table 2.3, some batteries may need to be crossed with tests from two additional batteries to provide for adequate representation of the broad CHC abilities.

Table 2.3 Examples of CHC Cross-Batteries for Nine Major Intelligence Tests

Battery	*Gf*	*Gc*	*Gv*
WISC-III	*WJ-R/III CONCEPT FORMATION (I)* *WJ-R/III ANALYSIS-SYNTHESIS (RG)*	**VOCABULARY (VL, LD)** **INFORMATION (K0)**	**BLOCK DESIGN (SR, Vz)** **OBJECT ASSEMBLY (CS, SR)**
WAIS-III	**MATRIX REASONING (I)** *WJ-R/III CONCEPT FORMATION (I)*	**VOCABULARY (VL, LD)** **INFORMATION (K0)**	**BLOCK DESIGN (SR, Vz)** **OBJECT ASSEMBLY (CS, SR)**
WPPSI-R	*WJ-R/III CONCEPT FORMATION (I)* *WJ-R/III ANALYSIS-SYNTHESIS (RG)*	**VOCABULARY (VL, LD)** **INFORMATION (K0)**	**BLOCK DESIGN (SR, Vz)** **OBJECT ASSEMBLY (CS, SR)**
KAIT	**MYSTERY CODES (I)** **LOGICAL STEPS (RG)**	**FAMOUS FACES (K2)** *WJ III VERBAL COMPREHENSION (VL, LD)*	**MEMORY FOR BLOCK DESIGN (MV)** *WJ-R/III SPATIAL RELATIONS (Vz, SR)*
K-ABC[a]	*MATRIX ANALOGIES (I)* *WJ-R/III ANALYSIS-SYNTHESIS (RG)*	*WJ III VERBAL COMPREHENSION (VL, LD)* *WJ III LISTEN ING COMPREHENSION (LS, LD)*	**TRIANGLES (SR)** Gestalt Closure (CS)
CAS	Nonverbal Matrices (Gf-I) *WJ-R/III ANALYSIS-SYNTHESIS (RG)*	*WJ III VERBAL COMPREHENSION (VL, LD)* *WJ III LISTEN ING COMPREHENSION (LS, LD)*	**FIGURE MEMORY (CF, MV)** **VERBAL SPATIAL RELATIONS (Gv-PI)**
DAS	**MATRICES (I)** **SEQUENTIAL & QUANTITATIVE REASONING (RQ, I)**	**SIMILARITIES (LD)** **WORD DEFINITIONS (VL, LD)**	Pattern Construction (SR) **RECALL OF DESIGNS (MV)**
WJ-R	**CONCEPT FORMATION (I)** **ANALYSIS-SYNTHESIS (RG)**	**ORAL VOCABULARY (VL, LD)** **LISTENING COMPREHENSION (LS, LD)**	**SPATIAL RELATIONS (Vz, SR)** Picture Recognition (MV)

Gsm	*Glr*	*Ga*	*Gs*
DIGIT SPAN (MS, MW) *WJ III AUDITORY WORKING MEMORY (MW)*	*WJ-R/III VISUAL AUDITORY LEARNING (MA)* *WJ III RAPID PICTURE NAMING (NA)*	*WJ-R/III INCOMPLETE WORDS (PC:A)* *WJ III AUDITORY ATTENTION (US/U3)*	**SYM SEARCH (P, R9)** **CODING (R9)**
DIGIT SPAN (MS, MW) **LETTER-NUMBER SEQUENCING (MW)**	*WJ-R/III VISUAL AUDITORY LEARNING (MA)* *WJ III RAPID PICTURE NAMING (NA)*	*WJ-R/III INCOMPLETE WORDS (PC:A)* *WJ III AUDITORY ATTENTION (US/U3)*	**SYMBOL SEARCH (P, R9)** **DIGIT-SYMBOL CODING (R9)**
WJ-R/III MEMORY FOR WORDS (MS) *WJ III AUDITORY WORKING MEMORY (MW)*	*WJ-R/III VISUAL AUDITORY LEARNING (MA)* *WJ III RAPID PICTURE NAMING (NA)*	*WJ-R/III INCOMPLETE WORDS (PC:A)* *WJ III AUDITORY ATTENTION (US/U3)*	*WJ-R/III VISUAL MATCHING (P, R9)* *WJ III DECISION SPEED (R7)*
WJ-R/III MEMORY FOR WORDS (MS) *WJ III AUDITORY WORKING MEMORY (MW)*	**REBUS LEARNING (MA)** *WJ III RAPID PICTURE NAMING (NA)*	*WJ-R/III INCOMPLETE WORDS (PC:A)* *WJ III AUDITORY ATTENTION (US/U3)*	*WJ-R/III VISUAL MATCHING (P, R9)* *WJ III DECISION SPEED (R7)*
WORD ORDER (MS) *WJ III AUDITORY WORKING MEMORY (MW)*	*WJ-R/III VISUAL AUDITORY LEARNING (MA)* *WJ III RAPID PICTURE NAMING (NA)*	*WJ-R/III INCOMPLETE WORDS (PC:A)* *WJ III AUDITORY ATTENTION (US/U3)*	*WJ-R/III VISUAL MATCHING (P, R9)* *WJ III DECISION SPEED (R7)*
WORD SERIES (MS) *WJ III AUDITORY WORKING MEMORY (MW)*	Expressive Attention *WJ III MEMORY FOR NAMES (MA)*	*WJ-R/III INCOMPLETE WORDS (PC:A)* *WJ III AUDITORY ATTENTION (US/U3)*	**MATCHING NUMBERS (N,R9)** **PLANNED CODES (R9)**
Recall of Digits (MS) *WJ III AUDITORY WORKING MEMORY (MW)*	Recall of Objects (M6) *WJ III MEMORY FOR NAMES (MA)*	*WJ-R/III INCOMPLETE WORDS (PC:A)* *WJ III AUDITORY ATTENTION (US/U3)*	Speed of Information Processing (R7, R9) *WJ-R/III VISUAL MATCHING (P, R9)*
MEMORY FOR WORDS (MS) **NUMBERS REVERSED (MW)**	**VISUAL AUDITORY LEARNING (MA)** DAS Recall of Objects (M6)	**INCOMPLETE WORDS (PC:A)** **SOUND BLENDING (PC:S)**	**VISUAL MATCHING (P, R9)** DAS Speed of Information Processing (R7, R9)

(continued)

Table 2.3 (*continued*)

Battery	*Gf*	*Gc*	*Gv*
SB:IV	**MATRICES (I)** **EQUATION BUILDING** **(RQ)**	**VERBAL RELATIONS (LD)** **VOCABULARY (VL, LD)**	**PATTERN ANALYSIS (SR)** **Bead Memory (MV)**

Note. Tests in bold, uppercase letters are strong measures as defined empirically; tests in bold, lowercase are moderate measures as defined empirically; tests in regular type, lowercase are classified logically. Tests printed in italics are supplementary. This table does not include tests that were classified as mixed measures of ability because mixed measures are not recommended in the initial phase of CHC Cross-Battery assessment. As may be seen by the tests printed in regular type, logically classified tests were used in constructing some of the cross-battery assessments presented in this table. In order to include only empirically classified tests, a more psychometrically rigorous approach, it is typically necessary to cross more than two batteries. Logically classified tests may be included in cross-battery assessments to keep the number of batteries crossed to a minimum. In the event that a logically classified tests deviates significantly from other tests within that domain or most other tests in the cross-battery in an unexpected or unexplained manner it will be necessary to re-evaluate that particular ability with empirically classified tests, if available.

[a]The K-ABC Achievement Test provides qualitatively different indicators of *Gc*.

Step 5: Administer and Score Core Battery and Supplemental Tests

Because CHC Cross-Battery assessment is not an individual test in and of itself, but rather a battery of tests that are individualized, organized, and constructed according to particular referral concerns and based on a contemporary theoretical perspective, there are no unique administration instructions to be followed apart from those already specified by the test publishers. Nevertheless, the practitioner must incorporate both general testing considerations applicable to the use of standardized tests as well as the specific guidelines provided by test publishers in the manuals of any tests that may be used.

Initially, practitioners must attend to issues such as the creation of an appropriate testing environment, proper use of testing materials and equipment, establishing and maintaining rapport with the examinee, and so forth (see

Gsm	Glr	Ga	Gs
MEMORY FOR DIGITS (MS, MW) **WJ III AUDITORY WORKING MEMORY (MW)**	*WJ-R/III VISUAL AUDITORY LEARNING (MA)* *WJ III RAPID PICTURE NAMING (NA)*	*WJ-R/III INCOMPLETE WORDS (PC:A)* *WJ III AUDITORY ATTENTION (US/U3)*	*WJ-R/III VISUAL MATCHING (P, R9)* *WJ III DECISION SPEED (R7)*

Kaufman, Lichtenberger, & Naglieri, 1999, pp. 15–19). Because CHC Cross-Battery assessment is accomplished through the use of standardized tests, it is imperative that these guidelines be followed just as they would be with any other standardized test battery in order to ensure optimum performance by the examinee. Second, the particular instructions provided by the publishers of any tests that are being administered within the context of CHC Cross-Battery assessment should also be followed scrupulously. There is no reason for any variance from specified procedures, and modification of these principles may reduce the confidence that can be placed in the validity and reliability of obtained results every bit as much as when using a single battery. Likewise, the scoring specifications and calculation instructions provided by the publishers of tests must be followed rigorously. In order to complete CHC Cross-Battery assessment, standard scores (or scaled scores) must be calculated for each test that is administered, in a manner consistent with the requirements of the test publisher and author(s) of the respective tests.

One concern raised in CHC Cross-Battery assessment relates to the issue of giving tests outside the comprehensive framework of standardization. The concern is one of whether, in cases in which a test battery was standardized using a particular order of subtest administration, using only selected tests necessarily violates standardization. In other words, in the absence of explicit instructions from the publisher that allow for the administration of only specific subtests, are we legally required to administer the entire test, even if we may be interested in only a particular set of tests or composite score? We believe the answer is *no,* and it is our contention that in a wide variety of cases, individuals have routinely been given only a portion of certain batteries because other portions were deemed invalid or inappropriate for that individual. For example, giving only the Wechsler Performance subtests to culturally or linguistically diverse children has been a common practice for decades and remains so to the present day.

DON'T FORGET

Practitioner Tips

In CHC Cross-Battery assessment, practitioners should always:

- Attend to issues such as the creation of an appropriate testing environment, proper use of testing materials and equipment, and establishing and maintaining rapport with the examinee.
- Carefully follow the particular instructions provided by the publishers of any tests that are being administered.
- Rigorously follow the scoring specifications and calculation instructions provided by the publishers of tests.
- Calculate standard scores (or scaled scores) for each test that is administered.

Similar selective administrations are often done with children who are blind, deaf, motor impaired, and so on, and selective test administration has been the foundation of many past and current procedures used in the field of neuropsychology. Therefore, unless a test's manual specifically states that the validity and reliability of the test is maintained *only when every single subtest is given,* we see no reason that CHC Cross-Battery methods should violate standardization any more or less than do the other selective procedures previously described that are in common practice today. In fact, in their respective standardizations, the test of the Woodcock-Johnson-Psycho-Educational Battery, Revised (Woodcock & Mather, 1989) and the diagnostic subtests of the Differential Abilities Scale (Elliott, 1990) utilized varied administration sequences. Moreover, not only do test publishers routinely *omit* prescriptions against using selected subtests or portions of the test, they also do not state that the use of the battery and interpretation of resulting scores are valid only if all subtests are administered. Therefore, it would seem that any alternative use of a test (whether with particular populations or through different theoretical foundations) is left up to the professional judgment of the examiner and that the examiner, in such cases, is wholly liable for providing a suitable (i.e., defensible) rationale for whatever decisions were made and actions taken. Clearly, the emphasis on both systematic evaluation and empirically based decision making inherent in the CHC Cross-Battery approach make it a method that is significantly more defensible than most other accepted procedures.

Step 6: Complete the CHC Cross-Battery Worksheets

Once the selected tests have been administered and initial standard scores calculated, the data can be recorded on the appropriate CHC Cross-Battery Worksheets in the column marked "SS*" (see Figure 2.2). The adjacent column, marked "SS (100 ± 15)" is used for recording the *converted* standard score in cases where tests utilize a metric that does not have a mean of 100 and a standard deviation of 15 (e.g., Wechsler individual subtest scaled scores). In such cases, the score must be converted to one that is consistent with this particular metric. A *Percentile-Rank and Standard-Score Conversion Table* is included in Appendix D for just this purpose. Tests that use this metric (e.g., WJ-R/III), may be entered directly in this second column since no conversion is necessary. Note also that most intelligence batteries provide only age-based norms, whereas, some tests (e.g., WJ-R/III) have both age- and grade-based norms. Therefore, when such tests are utilized, standard scores from the age-based norms should be used in order to derive appropriate comparisons with other batteries. It is also important to note that some tests (e.g., the WJ-R/III) yield *extended standard scores* (i.e., < 40 and > 160; McGrew, Werder, & Woodcock, 1991; Woodcock, McGrew, & Mather, 2001). This can be problematic when it comes to combining or comparing such standard scores with standard scores from other tests used in the assessment.

The standard scores for most intelligence batteries and supplemental tests represent *normalized standard scores* that are based on an area transformation of the raw score distribution. Very low or high normalized standard scores are typically calculated via extrapolation. As a result, low and high extrapolated scores are not based on real subjects (Woodcock, 1989). This problem is addressed typically by specifying a cutoff score at both the top and bottom of the standard-score scale. For example, the WISC-III norm tables include standard scores that range from 40 to 160 (Wechsler, 1991). In contrast, the WJ-R standard scores are not ex-

---

DON'T FORGET

Age-Based vs. Grade-Based Norms

Most intelligence batteries provide only *age-based* norms, whereas some tests (e.g., WJ-R/III) have both age- and grade-based norms. Therefore, when such tests are *utilized*, standard scores from the age-based norms should be used in order to derive appropriate comparisons with other batteries.

trapolated. They are based on the *linear transformation of W (Rasch) scores* that utilize two unique standard deviations to produce the observed 10th and 90th percentiles in the distribution. As a result, the WJ-R/III standard scores can range from 1 to 200 (Woodcock & Mather, 1989; Woodcock & McGrew, in press). Thus, combining extreme WJ-R standard scores (i.e., < 40 and > 160) with standard scores from other tests (e.g., WISC-III) that are constrained within a certain range (e.g., 40–160, inclusive) could potentially result in misleading cluster averages. Therefore, it is necessary to employ a method for reporting WJ-R/III standard scores that emulate those computed via more traditional methods. Following the logic of Woodcock and Mather (1989), whenever a standard score from any test that produces extended standard scores falls below 40, a value of 40 should be recorded on the appropriate CHC worksheet. Likewise, whenever a standard score (or a score from any test) exceeds 160, a score of 160 should be recorded.

Within each section related to a specific narrow ability, there is a simple three-step set of directions represented on the worksheet for calculating the average standard score for that narrow ability (see Rapid Reference 2.2). Although derivation of averages is very simple, from this point on the use of an electronic calculator or a computer automated worksheet (see Chapter 6) is highly recommended in order to ensure accuracy and provide efficiency in double-checking calculations. When scoring by hand, Step 1 is simply to sum the scores in the *converted* SS column and place the total in the corresponding box. In Step 2, the number of tests that comprise the total sum is entered in the next box just underneath the box containing the total sum. Step 3 involves dividing the sum total of standard scores by the number of tests that comprise it and putting the result in the final box within that section. This final score represents the respective *narrow ability average*. This three-step process is repeated for all narrow ability sections in which data exist.

Once all of the narrow ability averages are calculated, the shaded lines leading from the rows in which the narrow ability averages are recorded can be followed down to a box labeled "Sum/Number of Narrow Ability Averages." This box is used to record the total *sum* of the narrow ability averages followed by the *number* of narrow ability averages reported on the worksheet. The resulting ratio is calculated (i.e., total sum/number of averages) and entered in the final box at the far bottom, right-hand side of the worksheet and denotes

≡ Rapid Reference 2.2

Steps for Calculating CHC Cross-Battery Narrow Ability Averages

Step 1: Sum the scores in the *converted* SS column and place the total in the corresponding box.

Step 2: Enter the number of tests that comprise the total sum underneath the box containing the total sum.

Step 3: Divide the total sum of standard scores by the number of tests that comprise it and put the result in the final box within that section (this final score represents the respective *narrow ability average*).

Repeat this three-step process for all narrow ability sections in which data exist.

---

the *cluster average*. Averages that result in fractions of one-half or more are rounded up to the nearest whole number.

The final step in completing the worksheets involves specifying whether the cluster average should be interpreted as a broad or narrow estimate of the ability. This determination is indicated by checking off the appropriate description, found immediately above the cluster-average box. A cluster score (or average) would be considered a *broad* estimate of ability if it was derived by summing the standard scores or standard score averages that include at least two test indicators of qualitatively different narrow abilities subsumed by the broad ability in accordance with Guiding Principle 2 (see Chapter 1). When this is the case, a checkmark is placed next to the word *Broad* on the worksheet and the respective broad (stratum II) code (e.g., *Gf, Gc, Gv,* etc.) is written in the parentheses adjacent to the word *Broad.* Stated more simply, if the total cluster average includes tests from more than one narrow ability box on the worksheet, then the average is a broad estimate of the ability. Conversely, if the cluster

DON'T FORGET

Rounding Fractional Scores

Cluster averages that result in fractions of one half or more are rounded up to the nearest whole number.

average was derived by summing the standard scores of two or more test indicators of the same narrow ability, then this average would be interpreted most appropriately as representing a narrow (stratum I) ability rather than a broad (stratum II) ability. In other words, if the total cluster average includes tests from a single narrow ability box on the worksheet, then the average is a narrow estimate of the ability. In this case, a checkmark should be placed next to the word *Narrow* and the narrow (stratum I) code (e.g., RG-*Gf;* General Reasoning) should be written in the parentheses adjacent to the word *Narrow.*

The process of entering standard scores, converting standard scores (if necessary), computing narrow ability averages, computing cluster averages, and specifying measurement of narrow or broad abilities is completed for each of the measured CHC constructs. In the case of S-CB, this may represent only one or two such constructs (requiring use of only one or two worksheets), whereas in the case of C-CB, it is possible that all seven worksheets will need to be completed. However, even when there is a need for such comprehensive assessment of cognitive abilities, the amount of time necessary to complete the worksheets is not inordinately increased, since the calculations are quite simple. Of course, use of a computer automated worksheet eliminates the need and time for hand scoring entirely. An example of a properly completed worksheet is shown in Figure 2.2.

Step 7: Transfer Scores and Averages to CHC Summary Sheet

A three-part summary sheet for plotting CHC narrow ability test indicator standard scores and cluster averages from the cross-battery worksheets can be found in Appendix E. Use of the form is extremely helpful in organizing CHC Cross-Battery data in a highly visual manner (which greatly facilitates interpretation), and its completion should be considered a standard part of the entire process. The CHC Summary Sheet includes three main components: Part 1 is used for data summary only and is strictly numerical; Part 2 is used to summarize and graph data for normative analysis; and Part 3 is used to summarize and graph data for intracognitive analysis. Instructions for completion of each part are presented in this section.

The process of completing Part 1 of the CHC Summary Sheet (see Figure 2.3) begins with the transfer of data from the CHC Cross-Battery Worksheets

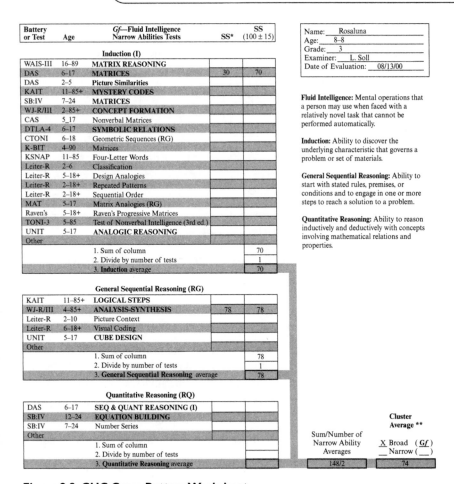

Figure 2.2 CHC Cross-Battery Worksheet

Battery or Test	Age	*Gf*—Fluid Intelligence Narrow Abilities Tests	SS*	SS (100 ± 15)
Induction (I)				
WAIS-III	16–89	**MATRIX REASONING**		
DAS	6–17	**MATRICES**	30	70
DAS	2–5	Picture Similarities		
KAIT	11–85+	**MYSTERY CODES**		
SB:IV	7–24	**MATRICES**		
WJ-R/III	2–85+	**CONCEPT FORMATION**		
CAS	5–17	Nonverbal Matrices		
DTLA-4	6–17	**SYMBOLIC RELATIONS**		
CTONI	6–18	Geometric Sequences (RG)		
K-BIT	4–90	Matrices		
KSNAP	11–85	Four-Letter Words		
Leiter-R	2–6	Classification		
Leiter-R	5–18+	Design Analogies		
Leiter-R	2–18+	Repeated Patterns		
Leiter-R	2–18+	Sequential Order		
MAT	5–17	Matrix Analogies (RG)		
Raven's	5–18+	Raven's Progressive Matrices		
TONI-3	5–85	Test of Nonverbal Intelligence (3rd ed.)		
UNIT	5–17	**ANALOGIC REASONING**		
Other				
		1. Sum of column		70
		2. Divide by number of tests		1
		3. Induction average		70
General Sequential Reasoning (RG)				
KAIT	11–85+	**LOGICAL STEPS**		
WJ-R/III	4–85+	**ANALYSIS-SYNTHESIS**	78	78
Leiter-R	2–10	Picture Context		
Leiter-R	6–18+	Visual Coding		
UNIT	5–17	**CUBE DESIGN**		
Other				
		1. Sum of column		78
		2. Divide by number of tests		1
		3. General Sequential Reasoning average		78
Quantitative Reasoning (RQ)				
DAS	6–17	**SEQ & QUANT REASONING (I)**		
SB:IV	12–24	**EQUATION BUILDING**		
SB:IV	7–24	Number Series		
Other				
		1. Sum of column		
		2. Divide by number of tests		
		3. Quantitative Reasoning average		

Name: Rosaluna
Age: 8–8
Grade: 3
Examiner: L. Soll
Date of Evaluation: 08/13/00

Fluid Intelligence: Mental operations that a person may use when faced with a relatively novel task that cannot be performed automatically.

Induction: Ability to discover the underlying characteristic that governs a problem or set of materials.

General Sequential Reasoning: Ability to start with stated rules, premises, or conditions and to engage in one or more steps to reach a solution to a problem.

Quantitative Reasoning: Ability to reason inductively and deductively with concepts involving mathematical relations and properties.

Sum/Number of Narrow Ability Averages: 148/2

Cluster Average **: 74

X Broad (**Gf**)   __ Narrow (__)

described in the previous section. By transferring the data collected and standard score ranges calculated and listed on the worksheets, data from the entire assessment can be condensed efficiently on a single summary sheet. Part 1 of the CHC Summary Sheet contains space for entering data on an ability cluster (as appropriate) as well as the standard score ranges for as many as six narrow ability indicators for each of the seven broad abilities that may have been measured. The names of tests used, and the name of the batteries from which they were drawn, as well as the CHC narrow ability code, are entered in the spaces

Name:	Rosaluna		

Name: Rosaluna
Age: 8-8 Grade: 3
Examiner: L. Soll Date: 08/13/00

CHC Cross-Battery Summary Sheet
Part 1: Normative Analysis Summary

Cluster	Test Battery	Subtest Name + (CHC ability code)	Standard Score	Standard Score Confidence Interval	Percentile Rank	Classification
Gf (Fluid Reasoning)		*Gf* Cluster Average =	74	69–79	4	Low
	DAS	Matrices—I	70	63–77	2	Low
	WJ III	Analysis-Synthesis —RG	78	71–85	8	Low
Gc (Crystallized Intelligence)		*Gc* Cluster Average =	105	100–110	65	Average
	DAS	Similarities—LD	100	93–107	50	Average
	WJ III	Verbal Comprehension—VL	109	102–116	75	Average

Figure 2.3 Sample Data Entry on Part 1, CHC Cross-Battery Summary Sheet

provided to the left. To the right of this information, the standard score, standard score confidence interval, percentile rank, and performance or normative classification for the narrow ability indicators and any broad or narrow ability clusters can be entered. Although this summary sheet is entirely numerical, it is an extremely efficient format for reporting the full breadth of the data that have been generated. One disadvantage, however, is that it does not easily facilitate the determination of convergent (overlapping or touching) standard score ranges. Nevertheless, this format may well meet the particular needs of practitioners; an example of how entered data would appear on the sheet is presented in Figure 2.3.

Part 2 of the CHC Cross-Battery Summary Sheet is used to display results from normative analysis and represents the visual counterpart to Part 1. It provides the means for graphing the broad (or narrow) cluster averages from each of seven CHC worksheets and for plotting the standard-score ranges (based on a mean of 100 and standard deviation of 15) for up to six narrow ability test indicators for each broad construct. The cluster averages are plotted on the *thick bars* and the standard scores for the narrow ability test indicators are plotted on the *thin bars*. The summary sheet contains a total of seven *sets of bars* (i.e., one thick and six thin in each set) for visually representing the scores derived from any one or all of the seven CHC Cross-Battery Worksheets.

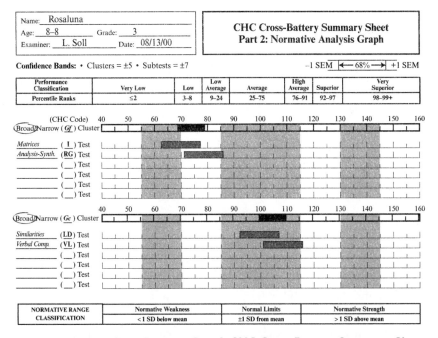

Figure 2.4 Sample Data Entry on Part 2, CHC Cross-Battery Summary Sheet

Note: Upon initial testing, in cases where the standard score bands for two qualitatively different narrow ability indicators fail to converge (do not touch or overlap), no circle is made to indicate a broad ability cluster and no band should be graphed. Similarly, in cases where the standard-score bands for two qualitatively similar narrow ability indicators fail to converge, no circle is made to indicate a Narrow cluster and no band should be graphed. Should assessment incorporate a second iteration in testing, then any new results related to the formation of convergent broad and narrow ability clusters may be marked and graphed as appropriate.

Data Transfer from Worksheets to Summary Sheet

The first step in completing Part 2 of the CHC Cross-Battery Summary Sheet is to transfer the appropriate data (cluster averages and individual-test standard scores) from any or all of the seven CHC Cross-Battery Worksheets completed according to specifications listed in the previous section. The data are transferred to the correct location on the summary sheet by placing a vertical hash mark on the thick bars corresponding to the standard score cluster averages, making sure to indicate by circling whether the average represents a broad or a narrow ability, as this is a critical component for test interpretation (see Chapter 3). This information is transferred from the bottom of the CHC Cross-Battery Worksheets, where a checkmark was placed next to *Broad* or *Narrow* and the CHC ability code appropriate to the descriptor was written in the adjacent parentheses. Next, the standard scores of the tests that comprise each cluster average should be recorded directly below their respective CHC cluster averages. The CHC codes corresponding to the narrow ability classifications of these tests should also be recorded in the parentheses located just to the right of the subtest names (a case example and corresponding worksheets and summary sheet will be presented in Chapter 3).

Specifying Confidence Bands on the Summary Sheet

The next step in completing Part 2 of the CHC Cross-Battery Summary Sheet is to specify and mark the appropriate *confidence band* for each CHC score that is recorded on the summary sheet. Confidence bands for cluster averages and narrow ability test indicator standard scores correspond to ± 1 standard error of measurement (SEM). Confidence bands represent the region in which an individual's true test score most likely will fall and extends from 1 SEM below the obtained score to 1 SEM above the obtained score. The SEM estimates for *all* cross-battery cluster averages is ± 5 and the SEM for individual test standard scores is ± 7. The confidence bands that were constructed for the CHC ability scores (based on ± 1 SEM) are also called *68% confidence bands* because they represent the standard score range in which an individual's true score falls two out of three times. Doubling the confidence bands or making them twice as wide (i.e., ± 2 SEM) would increase one's degree of confidence from 68% to 95%, representing the standard score range in which an individual's true score falls 19 out of 20 times. The purpose of reporting confidence bands is to demonstrate the degree of precision (or imprecision) that is present in the CHC scores. Examining a test score on a profile as a confidence band (rather than as a single or exact score) is usually preferred (Woodcock & Mather, 1989) and represents best practices. We recommend using 68% confidence bands because they are considered appropriate and sufficient for the type of clinical decision making that is characteristic of most comprehensive assessment approaches, including the CHC Cross-Battery approach.[1] Figure 2.4 provides an illustration regarding the manner in which data should be entered and depicted in Part 2.

The final component of the CHC Cross-Battery Summary Sheet is Part 3. This sheet is used to calculate, record, and display data generated for the purposes of intracognitive analysis. One of the major reasons for use of this form is that it allows for simultaneous evaluation and analysis of both intercognitive (normative based) and intracognitive (person relative) data. In addition, the space provided for making the calculations adds a great deal of efficiency to the process. Completing Part 3 is accomplished by simply following the numbers that appear in circles on the form in numerical order. Thus, the first step is to enter the cluster averages for each of the broad abilities that were measured. Practitioners should be careful to include only those broad clusters that were measured validly (i.e., two qualitatively different narrow ability indicators were used and the standard score bands converged [touched or overlapped]) in this form of analysis. Completion of Steps 2 through 4 includes calculating the sum of the cluster averages and dividing by the number of cluster averages (factors) used to derive the sum. This calculation yields the *Overall Average* for

---

[1] It should be noted that, given the large number of individual tests that can be used in CHC Cross-Battery assessment, it is not practical to calculate and report the composite reliability and SEM estimates for every possible combination of tests. Because the WJ-R *Gf-Gc* broad ability clusters are based on CHC theory (the foundation of CHC Cross-Battery assessment) and are derived from two-test combinations (like the clusters in CHC Cross-Battery assessment), the broad ability cluster SEMs reported in the *WJ-R Technical Manual* (McGrew et al., 1991) were used to estimate an SEM value for the broad CHC Cross-Battery clusters. For similar reasons it is impractical to report all published SEMs for all individual tests that might be interpreted in CHC Cross-Battery assessments. Therefore, the SEMs reported across the 21 WJ-R cognitive tests across all age ranges were reviewed to identify a reasonable SEM estimate that could be used as a general rule of thumb for all individual tests used in CHC Cross-Battery assessments. Furthermore, the respective subtest and composite SEMs reported for other intelligence batteries (e.g., WISC-III) were reviewed to ensure that these SEM rules-of-thumb values were reasonable approximate values across a variety of instruments. Thus, the values presented here (±5 and ±7) represent the average CHC cluster and subtest SEM (respectively) across all age ranges in the WJ-R norm sample.

the individual and is entered on the appropriate space denoted by the circled number *4*. The shading in this space is carried over to the spaces where the Overall Average is entered opposite the cluster averages (Step 5). Step 6 involves taking the difference between the cluster averages and the overall average and entering the result in the space provided, as well as indicating whether the result is positive or negative. These results are then transferred to the upper portion of the sheet also designated by a circled number *6* and entered accordingly in the spaces provided. Steps 7 and 8 involve indicating the manner in which the difference scores are to be interpreted. Rules for determining both relative and normative interpretation are provided on the form and are used to make decisions regarding classification of the obtained difference scores. The information from Step 7 is also recorded in the top portion of the sheet next to the difference score, primarily for reference. The graph is completed by placing a checkmark or *X* on the standard score line that corresponds to the cluster averages for each broad ability as originally entered in Step 1. The last step is to draw a vertical line down from the standard-score referent line at the top to the one on the bottom, which corresponds to the Overall Average calculated in Step 4. Completion of the graph in this manner provides a simple, visual display of the deviation between any single broad ability and the aggregate or composite average of all broad cognitive abilities. An example of what Part 3 looks like when completed is provided in Figure 2.5.

When completed properly, the CHC Cross-Battery Summary Sheet graphically displays the data obtained from the administration of the various tests chosen for the assessment in a clear and logical manner. As such, it provides a meaningful basis for making CHC-based cognitive ability comparisons that may be necessary in evaluating cognitive functioning (e.g., inter- and intracognitive strengths and weaknesses). Rapid Reference 2.3 provides a brief summary of the seven steps of CHC Cross-Battery assessment. Specific procedures for interpreting cross-battery results are presented in the next chapter.

SUMMARY

Through application and integration of the various guiding principles and methods described in this book, practitioners can effectively organize, select,

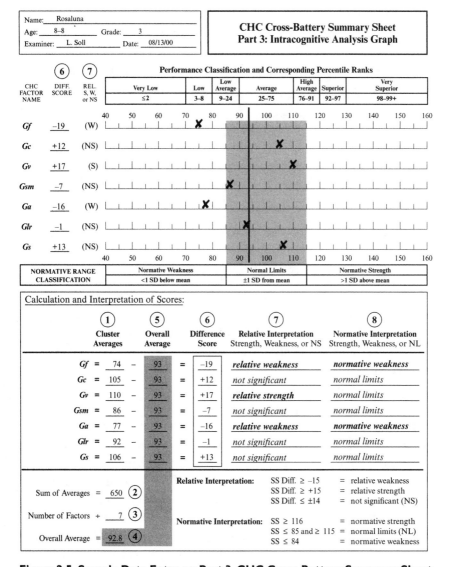

Figure 2.5 Sample Data Entry on Part 3, CHC Cross-Battery Summary Sheet

≡Rapid Reference 2.3

Steps for Implementing CHC Cross-Battery Assessment

1. Decide whether the assessment needs to be comprehensive or selective.
2. Identify the CHC abilities of interest.
3. Identify absence or underrepresentation of CHC abilities on the core battery.
4. Review and select tests needed to supplement the core battery.
5. Administer and score the core battery and supplemental tests.
6. Complete the CHC Cross-Battery Worksheets.
7. Transfer scores and averages to and complete the CHC Cross-Battery Summary Sheets.

administer, and evaluate the success of their CHC Cross-Battery assessment efforts. By careful augmentation of a preferred core battery, measurement of a wider range of broad and narrow cognitive abilities according to contemporary CHC theory and research can be accomplished—a result that cannot be achieved through the administration of any single intelligence battery in publication to date. The foundational sources of information upon which the CHC Cross-Battery approach was built (viz., the classification of the major intelligence batteries according to CHC theory discussed in Chapter 1) provide a means to systematically construct a theoretically driven, comprehensive, and valid measure of cognitive abilities. When the CHC Cross-Battery approach is applied, it is possible to measure important abilities that might otherwise go unassessed or that may be poorly assessed (e.g., *Gf, Ga, Glr*)—abilities that are important in understanding many educational, vocational, and occupational outcomes.

The CHC Cross-Battery approach allows for the effective measurement of the major cognitive areas specified in the CHC theoretical framework, with emphasis on those considered most critical on the basis of history, observation, and available test data. The CHC classifications of a multitude of cognitive ability tests (presented here and in Flanagan et al., 2000, and McGrew & Flanagan, 1998) bring strong content and construct validity evidence to the evaluation and interpretation process. With a strong research base and a multiplicity of CHC measures available, CHC Cross-Battery procedures can aid practitioners not only in the comprehensive measurement of cognitive abilities, but in the selective measurement of abilities that are deemed to be important with respect to the examinee's presenting problem(s). Adherence to the Guiding Principles, careful attention to key decision points, and integration of specific referral concerns can result in the creation of highly individualized and unique test batteries that are ideally suited for whatever the intended purpose of assessment may be.

REFERENCES

Carroll, J. B. (1997). The three-stratum theory of cognitive abilities. In D. P. Flanagan, J. L. Genshaft, & P. L. Harrison (Eds.), *Contemporary intellectual assessment: Theories, tests, and issues* (pp. 122–130). New York: Guilford.

Carroll, J. B. (1998). Foreword. In K. S. McGrew & D. P. Flanagan, *The intelligence test desk reference (ITDR): Gf-Gc cross-battery assessment* (pp. xi–xii). Boston: Allyn & Bacon.

Elliott, C. D. (1990). *Differential Ability Scales: Introductory and technical handbook.* San Antonio, TX: Psychological Corporation/Harcourt Brace Jovanovich.

Flanagan, D. P., & McGrew, K. S. (1998). Interpreting intelligence tests from contemporary *Gf-Gc* theory: Joint confirmatory factor analysis of the WJ-R and KAIT in a non-White sample. *Journal of School Psychology, 36,* 151–182.

Flanagan, D. P., McGrew, K. S., & Ortiz, S. O. (2000). *The Wechsler intelligence scales and Gf-Gc theory: A contemporary approach to interpretation.* Boston: Allyn & Bacon.

Individuals with Disabilities Education Act of 1997 (IDEA), 20 U.S.C. §§ 1400 *et seq.*

Jacobson, J. W., & Mulick, J. A. (Eds.). (1996). *Manual of diagnosis and professional practice in mental retardation.* Washington, DC: American Psychological Association.

Kaufman, A. S., Lichtenberger, E. O., & Naglieri, J. A. (1999). Intelligence testing in the schools. In C. R. Reynolds & T. B. Gutkin (Eds.), *The handbook of school psychology* (pp. 307–349). New York: Wiley.

McGrew, K. S., & Flanagan, D. P. (1998). *The intelligence test desk reference (ITDR):* Gf-Gc cross-battery assessment. Boston: Allyn & Bacon.

McGrew, K. S., Werder, J. K., & Woodcock, R. W. (1991). *Woodcock-Johnson Psycho-Educational Battery–Revised technical manual.* Chicago: Riverside.

Ortiz, S., & Flanagan, D. P. (1998). Enhancing cognitive assessment of culturally and linguistically diverse individuals: Selective *Gf-Gc* cross-battery assessment. *The School Psychologist, 52*(1), 6–9.

Wechsler, D. (1991). *Wechsler Intelligence Scale for Children* (3rd ed.). San Antonio, TX: Psychological Corporation.

Woodcock, R. (1989). *Emulation of the WISC-R type standard scores for users of the WJ-R.* Unpublished manuscript.

Woodcock, R. W., & Mather, N. (1989). WJ-R tests of cognitive ability—Standard and supplemental batteries: Examiner's manual. In R. W. Woodcock & M. B. Johnson (Eds.), *Woodcock-Johnson Psycho-Educational Battery* (Rev. ed.). Chicago: Riverside.

Woodcock, R. W., McGrew, K. S., & Mather, N. (2001). *Woodcock-Johnson—III tests of cognitive abilities.* Itasca, IL: Riverside.

🪶 TEST YOURSELF 🪶

1. **Crossing multiple (i.e., more than two) intelligence batteries during S-CB assessments (even those that are implemented systematically and that adhere to the recommendations for development, use, and interpretation) produces significantly less error than is obtained when improperly using and interpreting cognitive ability performance with the traditional methods (e.g., individual subtest analysis).** True or False?

2. **There currently are no published tests that provide adequate representation for the wide range of CHC cognitive abilities that have been empirically validated.** True or False?

3. **The CHC Cross-Battery approach is not a test in and of itself. It is a battery of cognitive ability tests individualized, organized, and constructed according to particular referral concerns and based on a valid theoretical perspective. Therefore, it is not necessary to follow general testing considerations applicable to the use of standardized tests or specific guidelines provided by test publishers in the manuals of the tests used in this approach.** True or False?

4. **Unless a test's manual specifically states that the validity and reliability of the test is maintained *only when every single subtest is given*, there does not appear to be a reason that CHC Cross-Battery methods should violate standardization any more or less than the other selective procedures that are in common practice today.** True or False?

5. **It is better to examine a test score on a profile as a single or exact score than as a confidence band.** True or False?

6. **Specific CHC Cross-Battery guidelines and procedures can be used to make decisions that respond directly to issues of dual-language development and proficiency as well as acculturation.** True or False?

7. **Which of the following situations would preclude a practitioner's using cross-battery procedures in the selection and organization of an assessment battery?**

   (a) the need to evaluate the relationship between an individual's manifest performance (e.g., academic skills) and his or her cognitive abilities

   (b) the need to pay attention to practical or legal considerations

   (c) the testing of individuals who possess characteristics that set them apart from the mainstream (e.g., perceptually impaired individuals)

   (d) none of the above

8. Which of the following is true of S-CB assessments?

(a) They take more time than single-battery assessments.

(b) They typically take less time than single-battery assessments.

(c) They do not require qualitatively different indicators of each broad ability represented in the assessment.

(d) They are useful when addressing specific referral concerns (e.g., reading difficulties).

(e) both (b) and (d)

9. If a cluster average on a *Gf* cross-battery worksheet was derived by summing the standard scores of two or more test indicators of Induction (I), then this average would be interpreted most appropriately as representing

(a) a narrow (stratum I) ability.

(b) a broad (stratum II) ability.

Answers: 1. True; 2. True; 3. False; 4. True; 5. False; 6. True; 7. d; 8. e; 9.

Three

HOW TO INTERPRET CHC CROSS-BATTERY DATA

Test data are relatively useless unless they can be reliably interpreted in a manner that is both theoretically and psychometrically defensible and that assists in deriving meaningful conclusions about performance. The application of modern theory that underlies the CHC Cross-Battery approach responds to this need because it provides an advancement over traditional practice in terms of both *measurement* and *meaning*. The ability to measure constructs with greater precision and accuracy, as described in the previous chapter, forms one of the two significant elements of the approach. The other—empirically based interpretation—is perhaps the most evident and practical benefit practitioners will derive from its use. The ability to derive meaning from data collected across batteries within the framework of an empirically validated theory of intelligence represents one of the cardinal features that distinguishes the CHC Cross-Battery approach. In this chapter, we provide guidelines for practitioners to follow that allow test data obtained from CHC Cross-Battery assessment (both comprehensive and selective) to be interpreted according to modern theory. The elements of interpretation for CHC Cross-Battery data are based primarily upon the CHC theoretical foundation presented in the previous chapters. Because of the close link between science and practice inherent in the CHC Cross-Battery approach, practitioners can have confidence that their collected data validly and reliably measure the cognitive abilities of interest, thereby making interpretation relatively clear and straightforward. In addition, interpretation adheres strictly to sound psychometric and statistical precepts that establish the basis for comparative evaluations of test performance, including inter- and intracognitive analysis of broad and narrow cognitive abilities. Interpretation must not, however, be thought of as an entirely separate or distinct endeavor from assessment. Rather, the two processes are highly interrelated, and each influences the other in many different ways.

In order to interpret CHC Cross-Battery data properly, the manner in which the assessment and interpretive processes are related must be specified. To this end, interpretation of CHC Cross-Battery data is embedded in a broader conceptual framework for assessment that relies on the generation and testing of functional assumptions or hypotheses regarding expected average performance. In general, both a priori and a posteriori assumptions are incorporated into the interpretive approach to control for confirmatory bias, which can arise when only assumptions regarding dysfunction accompany or guide the process of assessment. Therefore, discussion in this chapter will begin with an outline of an hypothesis-driven framework and its relationship to the iterative nature of CHC Cross-Battery assessment. The sections that follow will provide additional guidelines governing the direct interpretation of actual data patterns using psychometric and statistical principles. As will become evident, the process of assessment and interpretation is an exercise in integration and requires recursive, not linear, activities.

HYPOTHESIS-DRIVEN ASSESSMENT AND INTERPRETATION

Inherent in the CHC Cross-Battery approach is the value of conducting assessments from a broad, comprehensive framework, and the recognition that measurement methods, however precise, might form only a part of the entire scope of assessment-related activities. In general, CHC Cross-Battery assessment is used in cases for which standardized testing has been deemed necessary. In cases in which only standardized testing is accomplished, CHC Cross-Battery assessment may comprise the bulk of the assessment methods, whereas in other cases it might be only one aspect of a wide range of assessment practices. In either case, when standardized testing is to be carried out with the CHC Cross-Battery approach, practitioners should adhere to guidelines based on a philosophy of hypothesis generation and testing. Although psychometric data may seem to be rather objective, interpretation of such data is hardly an unambiguous exercise. Therefore, in order to reduce the chances of making incorrect inferences about data on the basis of preconceived ideas, hypothesis generation and testing is a necessary and crucial component in both selective and comprehensive CHC Cross-Battery assessment.

Confirmatory bias occurs when an examiner begins with preconceived notions regarding expected performance on a test. After the test is administered and the data are collected, the examiner reviews the data, looking specifically for patterns and results that support the preconception. In other words, the examiner becomes predisposed to seeing only those patterns in the data that support the prevailing assumptions, and tends to minimize or reject data that are counter to the assumption (Sandoval, Frisby, Geisinger, Scheuneman, & Grenier, 1998). In order to reduce the tendency to see patterns of disabilities or dysfunction in data where in fact none exist, diagnostic interpretation must not begin with the presumption of preexisting deficits. Rather, interpretation of test data must be guided by the assumption that the examinee is not impaired and that performance on tests (global functioning as well as functioning across individual subtests) will be within normal limits. This in essence forms the *null hypothesis,* which is evaluated statistically to determine whether it must be retained or rejected in favor of an alternative hypothesis (i.e., the hypothesis that performance is not average or not within normal limits). The *normal limit* is defined as ±1 SD inclusive (i.e., standard scores ranging from 85–115).

Adoption of the stance that expected performance will prove to be normal or within normal limits until convincingly contraindicated by the data reduces the chance that examiners will view standardized test data only in a manner that corroborates their beliefs going into the testing. All too often, the null hypothesis specifying average performance is ignored especially in cases in which testing is being accomplished on individuals whose functional deficits may be quite obvious. Moreover, even when it has been satisfactorily demonstrated that there are no external factors that might account for any observed manifest difficulties (e.g., with academic skills), this does not automatically imply that an internally based disability is present. In every

CAUTION

Confirmatory Bias

Confirmatory bias begins when an examiner begins with preconceived notions regarding expected performance on a test.

DON'T FORGET

Expect Normal Performance

Interpretation of test data must be guided by the assumption that the examinee is not impaired and that performance on tests (global functioning as well as functioning across individual subtests) will be within normal limits.

case the initial, fundamental hypothesis must remain in favor of the individual, recognizing that there is no reason to believe that performance will prove to be anything other than normal. This is not to say that practitioners cannot or must not entertain suspicions of dysfunction. After all, if standardized testing is being used then it is very likely that the examiner has already begun to suspect the possibility that a disability may exist. However, a clear distinction must be drawn between the specific hypotheses that are to be evaluated and the opinions, conjecture, or suppositions of the assessor. Only the hypotheses specified a priori or a posteriori are actually tested and evaluated directly in light of the data; opinion, conjecture, and suspicion are not. Therefore, only such hypotheses can be construed as either being supported or refuted by the data; opinion cannot. Consequently, unless and until the data strongly suggest otherwise, the null hypothesis that performance will be within normal limits must not be rejected, no matter how strong the examiner's belief to the contrary. Moreover, when the null hypothesis is rejected in favor of the alternative hypothesis, the examiner can be certain only that the data do not support the notion that performance is within normal limits and that performance is in all likelihood outside of normal limits. The alternative hypothesis does not provide de facto support for the presence of a disability, but rather only statistical evidence that suggests functioning cannot be considered normal. The reasons such performance has been found to be significantly deviant from the norm must be investigated further and corroborated by additional evidence and data (e.g., from review of school records, work samples, observations, diagnostic interviews, etc.).

CAUTION

Don't Diagnose by Default

Even when it has been satisfactorily demonstrated that there are no external factors that might account for any observed manifest difficulties (e.g., with academic skills), this does not automatically imply that an internally based disability is present.

CAUTION

Alternative Hypothesis and Evidence of Disability

The alternative hypothesis (performance is outside of normal limits) does not provide de facto support for the presence of a disability, but rather only statistical evidence that suggests functioning cannot be considered to be normal.

INTEGRATING HYPOTHESIS TESTING AND INTERPRETATION

Taking an hypothesis-driven approach to the interpretive process is the first step in a sequence of activities that form an iterative and recursive process. CHC Cross-Battery assessment has the potential to evaluate hypotheses in such a manner that it can guide the need for additional testing and the specification of additional (a posteriori) hypotheses. Thus, interpretation of CHC Cross-Battery data is an integrative process, as will become evident as each stage in this process is described (see Rapid Reference 3.1 for a summary of these stages).

The following guidelines are meant to assist practitioners in understanding and mastering the various stages of the CHC Cross-Battery assessment and interpretation process; they are essentially identical for the selective (S-CB) and comprehensive (C-CB) approaches. These stages are illustrated in Figure 3.1, and are based in part on Kamphaus's (1993) integrative method of test interpretation. It is assumed that the assessment and interpretation process described in this figure begins only when a focused evaluation of cognitive abilities through standardized testing is deemed necessary within the context of the broader, more comprehensive approach to assessment just described. The CHC Cross-Battery interpretive process continues to require careful evaluation of case history information (e.g., educational records; authentic measures of achievement; medical records); the inclusion of data from relevant sources (e.g., parents, siblings, teachers, friends, employers); and the framing of an individual's difficulties within the context of CHC theory and research. No matter how compelling, no single test

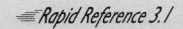

Rapid Reference 3.1

Stages of Interpretation for CHC Cross-Battery Assessment

Stage A: Knowledge Base of CHC Theory and Research

Stage B: Specification of A Priori Hypotheses

Stage C: Construction of Assessment Battery

Stage D: Administration and Scoring of Assessment Battery

Stage E: Interpretation and Evaluation of Hypotheses

Stage F: Specification of A Posteriori Hypotheses

Stage G: CHC Cross-Battery Psychological Report

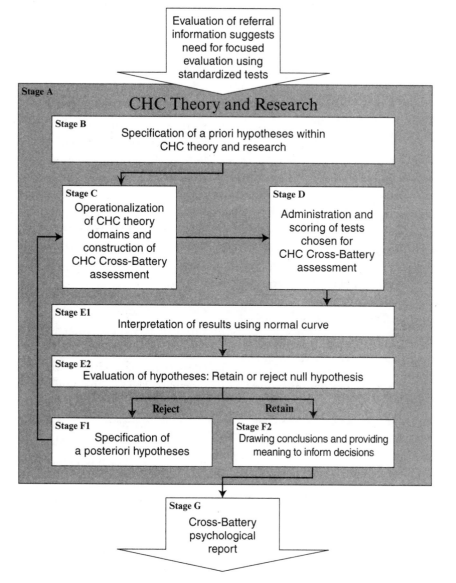

Figure 3.1 Stages of Interpretation for CHC Cross-Battery Assessment

DON'T FORGET

Corroborating Data

No matter how compelling, no single test or combination of tests should be used to make definitive interpretations or clinical decisions in the absence of other sources of corroborating data.

≡Rapid Reference 3.2

Items Included in Meaningful and Defensible Interpretation of CHC Cross-Battery Data

1. Literature on the relations between cognitive abilities specified by CHC theory and specific academic and occupational outcomes
2. Principles and philosophies that underlie the CHC Cross-Battery approach to assessing cognitive functioning
3. Network of validity evidence that exists in support of the structure and nature of abilities within CHC theory

or combination of tests should be used to make definitive interpretations or clinical decisions in the absence of other sources of corroborating data. The reader should refer often to Figure 3.1, as it will serve as the framework by which the various stages of CHC Cross-Battery assessment and interpretation will be discussed.

Stage A: Knowledge Base of CHC Theory and Research

In order to organize and then properly interpret a battery of tests assembled according to the CHC Cross-Battery approach, practitioners must possess or rely on a knowledge base of CHC theory and research. This is the initial step (Stage A) in CHC Cross-Battery interpretation, represented by the shaded area in Figure 3.1. Meaningful and defensible interpretation of CHC Cross-Battery data necessitates knowledge of contemporary theory and research (see Rapid Reference 3.2). A theory and research knowledge base is critical in the early stages of assessment because it serves to guide the reasoning related to the correspondence between deficits in academic skills or performance and suspected underlying cognitive impairments. On the basis of such logical deductions and presuppositions, the formation and subsequent testing of a priori hypotheses can occur.

Practitioners are encouraged to use reason and research to identify and select relationships between ability and manifest achievement that are relevant to the referral questions. It is the hypotheses regarding performance alone, however, that are formally tested irrespective of any suspicions on the part of the assessor regarding the potential existence of a disability. In addition, a priori hypotheses should be specified in the null manner, predicting average or normal functioning (the absence of any deficiency in performance) as was outlined previously.

Stage B: Specification of A Priori Hypotheses

Before a priori hypotheses can be generated, some type of logical or rational connection must be identified between the referral concerns and what the literature suggests. The precise definition of *a priori* as used for the purpose of CHC Cross-Battery assessment can be found in the *American Heritage Dictionary* (1994), which defines the term as: "From a known or assumed cause to a necessarily related effect; deductive . . . based on theory rather than on experiment." Use of an a priori approach "forces consideration of research and theory because the clinician is operating on the basis of research and theory when the hypothesis is drawn" (Kamphaus, 1993, p. 167). By coupling case history data and current information with knowledge of CHC theory and research (and perhaps with information from other fields [e.g., literature on learning disabilities]) defensible connections between academic achievement and cognitive functioning can be made. For example, when an individual presents with reading difficulties, the knowledge base assists the practitioner in identifying the most salient broad and narrow abilities related to reading achievement (e.g., *Ga*-PC:A, *Ga*-PC:S, *Gc*-VL, *Gc*-K0, *Gc*-LD, *Glr*-NA, etc.; see Chapter 2). On the basis of such research, the practitioner can logically assume that if there are indeed any cognitive impairments related to the individual's presenting reading difficulties, then those impairments are likely to be found through investigation of one or more of these abilities. The practitioner would of course be well advised to ensure that assessment of the individual provides adequate measures of these abilities in order to properly and reliably evaluate this relationship.

Although the practitioner has a suspicion that the individual's reading difficulties might be related to deficits in specific cognitive abilities (e.g., *Ga, Gc, Glr*), the a priori hypothesis remains null, specifying that expected performance on any ability test (measuring *Ga, Gc, Glr,* or any other ability for that matter) will be within normal limits. The practitioner must adhere to the stance that the data will show no evidence of anything other than normal functioning and must not abandon that position unless and until the data are convincing to the contrary.

Stage C: Construction of Assessment Battery

Once a connection has been identified between an individual's presenting difficulties and the cognitive abilities that may be related to those difficulties, and only after a priori hypotheses have been specified, does the practitioner begin to construct an appropriate collection of tests in accordance with the CHC Cross-Battery principles and procedures outlined in Chapters 1 and 2 of this book. Aside from all of the other issues that must be considered in organizing and selecting an appropriate set of tests, practitioners must ensure that they are providing adequate representation of the constructs that have been identified as relevant to the referral. As has been noted previously, this is an area in which CHC Cross-Battery methods prove superior to traditional approaches. Use of a single test battery will likely fail to measure certain constructs central to the need for assessment, whereas CHC Cross-Battery methods will ensure that they are measured. By ensuring that appropriate and sufficient data are collected with respect to the constructs of interest, interpretation of the data is greatly facilitated and meaningful conclusions are enhanced.

Stage D: Administration and Scoring of Assessment Battery

The detailed guidelines for administration and scoring within the context of CHC Cross-Battery assessment were presented in Chapter 2 and will not be reiterated here. Strictly speaking, this step is not actually a component of the *interpretive* process; however, it is a necessary component of the *overall* process. Because CHC Cross-Battery assessment is an integrative approach, inclusion of this step is required in order to delineate clearly that some assessment activities will stem from the need to test initial or a priori hypotheses and, as will be discussed shortly, that others may stem from evaluation of a posteriori hypotheses. Thus, the process of administration and scoring can be iterative in nature, and depending on interpretation of the initial collected data, it may well be a process that is accomplished more than once.

Stage E: Interpretation and Evaluation of Hypotheses

This step comprises the heart of the interpretive process. It is at this point that the examiner is able to accomplish several different levels of analysis with CHC Cross-Battery data. Such types of analyses include evaluation of inter-cognitive performance (normative comparison against same age- or grade-level peers); intracognitive discrepancies between broad (stratum II) ability clusters; and intracognitive discrepancies between narrow (stratum I) ability clusters. In general, CHC Cross-Battery assessment uses a hierarchical model of interpretation (presented in Figure 3.2) with preference given to analysis at the broadest level whenever possible (Level 1 in Figure 3.2). Figure 3.2 provides an illustration of the two basic layers involved in interpretation of CHC Cross-Battery data. The model depicts the emphasis that CHC Cross-Battery assessment places on the derivation and use of empirically based and statistically defensible factors or ability clusters. As explained in Chapter 1, such clusters are created through the careful selection and organization of test batteries that provide adequate construct representation. Although the interpretive levels themselves are rather straightforward, explanation of the decision-making steps that guide the interpretive process is more complex. Details regarding these methods for analysis of cross-battery data are discussed later in this chapter.

From a broad perspective, Stage E (Figure 3.1) comprises two major interpretive activities. In Stage E1, the practitioner must evaluate, in accordance with some normative standard, the numerical data collected within a CHC Cross-Battery assessment. CHC Cross-Battery assessment uses the properties of the normal probability curve for making such evaluative judgments and decisions. The normal probability curve was selected because it represents the most useful statistically-based comparative standard, and because it is able to accommodate the practice of crossing batteries (and, in effect, norm groups) in order to conduct more comprehensive and theoretically meaningful assessments. The utility of the normal probability curve is evident because it "has very practical applications for comparing and evaluating psychological data in that the position of any test score on a standard deviation unit scale, in itself, defines the proportion of people taking the test who will obtain scores above or below a given score" (Lezak, 1976, p. 123). In addition, with adherence to the practice of selecting tests that have been normed within a few years of one

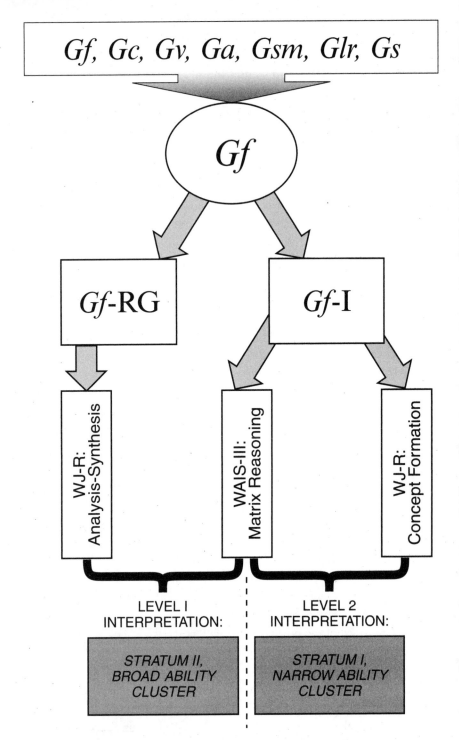

Figure 3.2 Interpretive Levels in CHC Cross-Battery Assessment

another (e.g., WAIS-III and WJ III), the potential for measurement error that may result from crossing batteries is significantly reduced.

Within Stage E1, two types of analyses will take place: intercognitive and intracognitive. *Intercognitive* analysis is accomplished through comparison of normative scores; it provides *population-relative* information and reveals *between*-individual differences. Thus, normative scores yield information concerning an individual's performance, functioning, or ability with respect to individuals of the same age or norm group (Anastasi & Urbina, 1997; Woodcock, 1994). Moreover, normative scores for one ability are not artificially altered by the individual's scores on other abilities as they are with intracognitive scores (discussed below).[1] Intercognitive analysis is used mainly to evaluate global and scale (or cluster) performance and to assist in formulating diagnostic impressions and classification.

Intracognitive analysis differs from intercognitive analysis in that the information is *person-relative* and reveals *within*-individual differences. This type of interpretation is broadly described as the generation of hypotheses about an individual's personal strengths or weaknesses and is based primarily on analysis of score deviation. In general, strengths are scores that deviate significantly above the aggregate average or mean calculated from the individual's

---

[1] Because cognitive ability tests show non-zero positive intercorrelations, the scores yielded by a given battery of tests will reflect these intercorrelations. That is, the higher the correlation between two cognitive ability measures the greater the likelihood that the traits underlying these measures will vary consistently. This is because "average intercorrelations of normative attributes is determined mainly by the relationships among the contents of attribute scales and the psychological characteristics of the respondent population: (McDermott et al., 1992, p. 509). Conversely, ipsative scores have near-zero (and often negative) intercorrelation. "The discovery of . . . near zero average relationships among ability attributes runs contrary to the theoretical expectation for constructs that might reflect some meaningful aspect of Spearman's *g*" (McDermott et al., 1992, p. 510). Thus, as opposed to normative scores, ipsative scores have "personological" ability dimensions (Brouerman, 1961). That is, through factor analysis of ipsative measures Brouerman observed that the "consequent dimensions retained a certain reciprocally exclusive character whereby, as an individual exhibited greater ability in one area, commensurate inability was apparent in another area" (cited in McDermott et al., 1992, p. 518).

other subtest scores. Likewise, weaknesses are scores that deviate significantly below the average or mean calculated from aggregation of the individual's other subtest scores. Consequently, unlike intercognitive analysis, the scaling of intracognitive scores is highly dependent upon the relative position of the obtained scores on every other ability attribute measured in that individual. Intracognitive analysis is used mainly to evaluate personal strengths and weaknesses in specific abilities and to assist in the development of appropriate interventions or treatment. They must, however, be evaluated within the context of normative differences since relative strengths and weaknesses can be easily misinterpreted in regard to actual functional impairment.

In summary, use of the normal probability curve in Stage E1 thus provides practitioners with a basis for accomplishing comparative evaluations of performance on any tests that may have been administered. Additional details and guidelines for making such judgments and decisions are contained in the sections that follow presentation of this overview.

Stage E2 is not actually a separate step from Stage E1. In Stage E1, practitioners must evaluate the viability of the a priori hypotheses that were generated prior to testing. Based on the evaluative judgments derived from normative comparisons of the data in Stage E1, practitioners must decide whether the data suggest that the null hypothesis is "correct," and should therefore be retained, or whether the data suggest that the null hypothesis is not supported and should be rejected in favor of an alternative hypothesis. This process is relatively straightforward in the sense that when the evaluative judgments in Stage E1 indicate that functioning or performance is outside of normal limits, then the null hypothesis is rejected in favor of the alternative that functioning is in fact, not within normal limits—that it is instead exceptional (high or low) in some way. Specifically, in intercognitive analysis, the null hypothesis specifies that the individual's measured performance on any test or tests of ability will fall within the normal limits of functioning as compared to measures of performance of other individuals of the same age. The null hypothesis in intracognitive analysis is virtually identical but slightly more complicated because of the potential shift in what constitutes the mean (or average) score for the individual. Thus, the null hypothesis in intracognitive analysis specifies that the individual's measured performance on any test or tests of ability will not deviate significantly from the average of all other measured abilities, *and* that it will fall within the normal limits of functioning as compared to other individuals of the same age. As will become evident, the fact that an individual's own mean or average score often deviates from the mean of a normative population (i.e., 100, or 50th percentile), means that distinctions must be drawn between relative and normative strengths and weaknesses. This will be discussed later in this chapter.

Stage F: Specification of A Posteriori Hypotheses

When CHC Cross-Battery assessment data are interpreted and evaluated according to the specified a priori hypotheses, there may be instances in which all functioning is

---

DON'T FORGET

Evaluating the Null Hypothesis

- In *intercognitive analysis*, the null hypothesis specifies that the individual's measured performance on any ability test or cluster will fall within the normal limits of functioning as compared to other individuals of the same age.

- In *intracognitive analysis*, the null hypothesis specifies that the individual's measured performance on any ability test or cluster will not deviate significantly from the average of all other measured abilities, *and* that it will fall within the normal limits of functioning compared to other individuals of the same age.

---

observed to fall within normal limits and thus all a priori hypotheses are retained (Stage F2). At this point, if the CHC Cross-Battery assessment was constructed in accordance with the principles and procedures set forth in Chapters 1 and 2, and if the assessment provides adequate representation of the constructs of interest (i.e., if cognitive abilities are not underrepresented), then practitioners can reasonably conclude that the individual demonstrates no measured impairments in functioning and thus, that no evidence is found within these data to support opinions or suspicions to the contrary. Standardized test data are not, however, the only or the most important source of information for making such determinations, and the lack of support from such procedures should not be construed as definitive evidence that no disability exists. Disability determinations must always remain based on multiple sources of information.

Because of the selective nature of referral and assessment, in the majority of cases, measurement of an individual's abilities is likely to produce one or more instances in which it cannot be maintained that performance is within normal limits and that functioning along some abilities will fall under the al-

CAUTION

Multiple Sources of Evidence of Disability

Standardized test data are not necessarily the only or most important source of information for making determinations about impairments in functioning. The lack of support from such procedures should not be construed as definitive evidence that no disability exists. Disability determination must always be based on multiple sources of information.

ternative hypothesis that such performance is not within normal limits. Disability determinations are concerned primarily with cases in which performance falls below the expected normal or average range, whereas identification of gifted and talented individuals focuses more on performance that is significantly above the average range. In those cases in which the data suggest that the null hypothesis should be rejected in favor of an alternative (Stage F1), or when the data provide contradictory, ambiguous, or insufficient evidence upon which to base such decisions, CHC Cross-Battery assessment becomes an iterative process.

When the initial CHC Cross-Battery data support the null hypotheses regarding expected normal functioning (Stage F2), further assessment via standardized testing is likely unwarranted; practitioners should draw appropriate conclusions and present those findings in a psychological report (Stage G). However, when one or more a priori hypotheses are not supported by the data, or when the data conflict (i.e., they do not provide convergence on broad or narrow ability factors), additional assessment may be warranted. When practitioners deem it necessary to investigate anomalous or ambiguous results, the process remains hypothesis-driven and is carried forth on the basis of a posteriori hypotheses. According to the *American Heritage Dictionary* (1994), *a posteriori* is defined as: "Reasoning from particular facts to general principles; empirical." The use of a posteriori hypotheses has a long history in clinical assessment and involves inferring causes from effects (Kamphaus, 1993).

The most common situation in which the use of a posteriori hypotheses and additional assessment will be pursued occurs when there is a significant difference between two measures of a particular cognitive ability that fail to converge as expected. For example, if the construct of interest revolves around *Gf*, then it would be expected that two independent measures of *Gf* (e.g., WJ III Analysis-Synthesis and WAIS-III Matrix Reasoning) would produce scores that are similar to each other, since each test measures the same broad construct. On occasion and for a wide variety of reasons (differences in narrow ability performance [e.g., general sequential reasoning vs. induction] or differences in task demands, administration influences, cultural or linguistic factors, chance, error, etc.), the scores may actually deviate significantly from each other, making interpretation of performance along that ability ambiguous at best. In this example, the broad ability (*Gf*) cannot be interpreted and no conclusions can be drawn about performance at this level (stratum II) within this domain (see Level 1 interpretation in Figure 3.2). Moreover, interpretations about the underlying narrow abilities (i.e., general sequential reasoning and induction) also cannot be made because there is only a single indicator (rather than two indicators) for each narrow ability; thus, it is insufficient to allow interpretation at the narrow ability (stratum I) level, either (see Level 2 interpretation in Figure 3.2). If *Gf* was not a construct central or relevant to the referral, and if performance on both tasks was within normal limits or above, practitioners may be able to live with the situation. However, if *Gf* was central to the referral, then the need to secure more definitive information about functioning along this or any other cognitive ability domain would necessitate the administration of additional tests in order to provide a defensible basis for interpretation.

Any such supplemental testing would be guided by the specification of a posteriori hypotheses. Such hypotheses are essentially identical to the a priori hypotheses specified previously, in that they also specify that performance on any additional tests that may be given will be within the normal limits of functioning. These hypotheses differ only with respect to the point in the assessment process at which they are generated: *A priori* hypotheses are generated prior to the administration of any CHC Cross-Battery assessment and prior to interpretation of any collected data; *a posteriori* hypotheses are generated following

---

DON'T FORGET

Use of A Posteriori Hypotheses and Additional Assessment

The most common situation in which the testing of a posteriori hypotheses and administration of additional tests occurs is when there is a significant difference between two measures of a particular cognitive ability that fail to converge as expected, particularly when the lower of the two scores falls greater than 1 SD below the normative mean.

such interpretation and continue the framework necessary for reducing or avoiding confirmatory bias. As can be seen in Figure 3.1, following specification of a posteriori hypotheses, practitioners return to Stage C in the process (operationalization of CHC theory domains and construction of CHC Cross-Battery assessment). Once again, knowledge of CHC theory and research is used to guide the selection of cognitive ability measures that will be used to gather additional information regarding functioning in a particular area, as well as to evaluate the a posteriori hypotheses. The recursive nature of the assessment process makes it clear that CHC Cross-Battery assessment and interpretation are iterative processes that may require the collection of additional data (via the administration of more cognitive tests) in order to properly evaluate individual performance or functioning. Going from Stage F1 back to Stage C represents another iteration in the assessment and interpretation process and is necessary in order to corroborate ambiguous, anomalous, or contradictory findings. Such iterations assist in "narrow[ing] down the possibilities" or reasons for the existence of a particular initial finding (Kamphaus, 1993, p. 166), and can be continued until all hypotheses are properly evaluated, allowing practitioners to draw valid conclusions.

Stage G: CHC Cross-Battery Psychological Report

Two examples of the way in which CHC Cross-Battery assessment data may be incorporated into psychological reports are presented in Chapter 7 of this book. Although there is no need to follow any strict format or template for the reporting of CHC Cross-Battery results, practitioners should be careful to include the major components shown in these samples. These components include primarily an analysis of intercognitive performance (or normative-based comparisons) and an analysis of intracognitive functioning (or person-relative comparisons). Within these analyses, specific strengths and weaknesses may be described at both the broad (stratum II) and narrow (stratum I) ability levels. Ability-achievement discrepancy analysis may also be part of data analysis within the context of CHC Cross-Battery assessment (see Chapter 4). In addition, practitioners should take care to provide clear explanations of the basis for assessment; the reasons that specific constructs may have been evaluated and others ignored; the relationship between substantiated deficits in cognitive ability and any presenting or referral concerns or manifest skill performance (e.g., academic functioning). Practitioners are also well-advised to remember that CHC Cross-Battery assessment, although systematic, defensible, and theory-driven, represents only one component of the broad framework of assessment. Therefore, any report that is built around CHC Cross-Battery assessment data should not be considered a complete report of psychological functioning. Psychological reports must also provide information and data that are consistent with and

CAUTION

Reporting CHC Cross-Battery Data

Any report that is built around CHC Cross-Battery assessment data should not be considered a complete report of psychological functioning. Standardized test data, even from CHC Cross-Battery assessment, represents only one component of a comprehensive report of psychological functioning.

support any conclusions drawn from the use of standardized tests. It is best practice to demonstrate that the evidence from multiple sources converged in order to form the basis for defensible conclusions about individual ability or functioning.

GUIDELINES FOR INTERCOGNITIVE ANALYSIS IN CHC CROSS-BATTERY ASSESSMENT

A general overview was presented in the previous section regarding intercognitive analysis and interpretation. The following discussion provides additional details and guidelines that are designed to assist practitioners in evaluating CHC Cross-Battery data in a manner that remains both theoretically and psychometrically defensible. Practitioners are urged to read the following sections carefully. The central issues related to CHC Cross-Battery assessment and interpretation are presented in detail and must be very well understood if valid and meaningful conclusions are to be drawn from the collected data.

When only a single battery is used in assessment, the data derived from the scoring process tend to remain on the same scale and are based on a norming sample that has the same mean and standard deviation. This, of course, provides for straightforward and direct comparison of scores and facilitates the interpretive process. In the case of CHC Cross-Battery assessment, the test scores come from at least two, and possibly more, different sources or tests.

Consequently, it is possible that each data source uses a different metric, making direct comparisons inappropriate (e.g., Wechsler subtests have a mean of 10 and SD of 3, whereas WJ III subtests have a mean of 100 and SD of 15). In addition, CHC Cross-Battery assessment may be carried out with a collection of tests that were developed at different times, in different places, on different samples, with different scoring procedures, and for different purposes (Lezak, 1976, 1995).

In CHC Cross-Battery assessment, these obstacles are overcome through the process of converting all test scores into a common metric and identifying a normative standard by which such scores may be appropriately compared. This process provides a basis for making inter- and intracognitive ability comparisons and interpretation of CHC Cross-Battery data psychometrically defensible. Step 5 of the guidelines for administering and scoring CHC Cross-Battery assessments (see Chapter 2) specified the need to convert all standard scores collected in cross-battery assessments to a common metric having a mean of 100 and standard deviation of 15. A "Percentile-Rank and Standard Score Conversion Table" is provided for just this purpose in Appendix D and contains conversion information for virtually every major intelligence battery and standard-score metric in use today. By converting all scores to this metric, concerns regarding the feasibility of drawing useful and valid conclusions from tests with different means and standard deviations are addressed directly. Practitioners can thus administer tests with different metrics and through the process of conversion are able to combine performance data from separate sources into reliable, construct-relevant clusters. Once this is accomplished, the practitioner then evaluates and compares these scores to a *normative standard*. Use of such a normative standard is necessary because cross-battery assessment has no internal norm group, and therefore some control must be made for potential differences across normative samples.

As discussed previously in Stage E, use of the normal probability curve provides the means for achieving normative-based comparisons of CHC Cross-Battery data. Table 3.1 provides practitioners with a description of the normal probability curve (i.e., percent of cases that fall under various portions of the normal curve) and a taxonomy of ability classifications or categories (e.g., low average, average, high average, etc.) that correspond to different stan-

Table 3.1   Descriptive and Evaluative Classifications of CHC Cross-Battery Data

Description of Performance			Evaluation of Performance	Standard Score & Percentile
Standard Score Range	Percentile Rank Range	Classification		
≥ 131	98–99+	Very Superior	Normative Strength (16% of the population) (> +1 standard deviation)	≥ 116 (85th percentile)
121–130	92–97	Superior		
116–120	85–91	High Average		
111–115	76–84	High Average	Normal Range (68% of the population)	115 (84th percentile) 85 (16 th percentile)
90–110	25–75	Average		
85–89	16–24	Low Average		
80–84	9–15	Low Average	(> –1 standard deviation) Normative Weakness (16% of the population)	≤ 84 (15 th percentile)
70–79	3–8	Low		
≤ 69	≤ 2	Very Low		

Note. These classifications correspond to those used in *The intelligence test desk reference (ITDR): Gf-Gc Cross-Battery Assessment,* by K. S. McGrew and D. P. Flanagan, 1998, Boston: Allyn & Bacon, and were adapted from "WJ-R Tests of Cognitive Ability—Standard and Supplemental Batteries: Examiner's Manual," by R. W. Woodcock and N. Mather, 1989, in *Woodcock-Johnson Psycho-Educational Battery* (Rev. ed., p. 403), edited by R. W. Woodcock and M. B. Johnson, 1989. Chicago: Riverside. Adapted with permission.

dard score and percentile rank ranges as well as qualitative and evaluative descriptions of performance. Note that there are actually two types of classification systems offered that follow the characteristics of the normal probability curve: a general, three-level normative classification (normative weakness, within normal limits, normative strength), and a multiple-category system for describing performance more specifically. These classification systems are often used interchangeably.

In general, the classifications provided in Table 3.1 closely approximate the classification schemata in common use (e.g., Wechsler intelligence tests) and are not significantly different from what practitioners are accustomed to using. The Evaluation of Performance column and its corresponding standard-score

DON'T FORGET

Criterion for Rejecting the Null Hypothesis

In order to reject the null hypothesis in favor of the alternative (viz., that an individual's performance is in fact significantly different than that of other individuals of the same age), the entire standard score range (including the uppermost and lowermost points of that range) must be greater than ±1 SD (15 points) from the normative mean (i.e., 100).

and percentile-rank cutoff points are provided as a means for establishing the criteria necessary to test the a priori and a posteriori hypotheses that guide the interpretive process. In CHC Cross-Battery assessment, the basic criterion for rejecting the null hypothesis is set at the level of > ±1 SD from the mean. Note that with the adoption of such a range, performance can be considered exceptional only when it falls either significantly above or below the mean, indicating both normative strengths and normative weaknesses in functioning, respectively.[2] As discussed previously, a great deal of assessment is conducted with respect to the investigation of potential or suspected deficits, and therefore, most attention will likely be paid to performance that is significantly *below* the mean.

The null hypothesis in intercognitive analysis with CHC Cross-Battery data was described earlier as the position that the measured performance on any test of cognitive ability would fall within the normal limits of functioning as compared to individuals of the same age. Therefore, in order to reject the null hypothesis in favor of the alternative (viz., that an individual's performance is in fact significantly different than that of other individuals of the same age), the entire standard score range (including the uppermost and lowermost points of that range) must be greater than ±1 SD (15 points) from the normative mean (i.e., 100). When this is the case, practitioners may confidently interpret such findings as indications that performance cannot be considered normal or average.

It is important to remember that CHC Cross-Battery interpretation and analysis (i.e., the testing of hypotheses) is carried out with two different types of data. Intercognitive (or normative) analysis is conducted with standard score ranges (i.e., confidence bands), whereas intracognitive (or relative) analysis by definition

---

[2] Typically, a sore that is > 1 SD above or below the mean is considered a normative strength or weakness, respectively (Lezak, 1976, 1995).

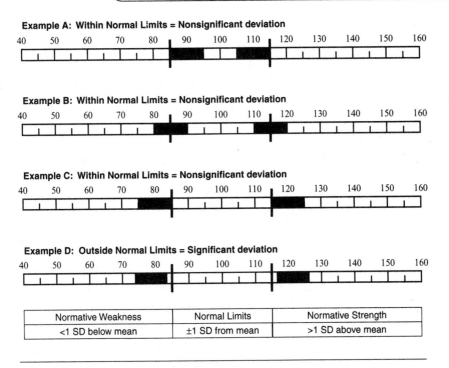

Figure 3.3 Interpretation of Significant Normative Deviation for Confidence Bands (> ±1 SD: < 85 or > 115)

is carried out with single, averaged scores. Thus, the decision process with respect to determining significant deviations and significant differences is not identical. Examples of how confidence bands are to be interpreted with respect to whether they are significantly deviant (both above and below the mean) are illustrated in Figure 3.3. Example A in this figure demonstrates a case in which the entire standard score range falls within normal limits. Two black bands are shown, each representing a typical standard score range and each illustrating that ranges can fall entirely above or below the cutoff points for significance (i.e., 85 and 115). Example B in Figure 3.3 also represents nonsignificant deviation, even though the midpoints of the standard score ranges fall right at the cutoff points. Note that constraining the deviation to the extreme points within the confidence bands, as opposed to the midpoint or average of the range, represents a conservative approach to defining significant deviation. Since the confidence bands represent the range in which practitioners can have 68% confidence that the individual's true score falls somewhere inside, use of the midpoint in this case would halve the confidence level as indicated in Example B. Likewise, Example C in Figure 3.3 is still nonsignificant because the possibility remains that the individual's true score (which can be anywhere within the range) might fall right on the cutoff point and therefore still be within normal limits. Example D in Figure 3.3 is the only illustration of a significant deviation, because the entire standard score range falls either below the lower cutoff point (normative weakness) or above the higher cutoff point (normative strength).

Application of this hypothesis-testing and -evaluation framework can be used whenever performance on any measure of cognitive ability is evaluated (including both narrow and broad ability clusters). Likewise, hypotheses related to functioning as measured by composite scores that are obtained within the scope of conducting CHC Cross-Battery assessment (e.g., WJ III General Intellectual Ability, Wechsler-based Verbal Comprehension Index, etc.) can also be evaluated through this method.

Additional Considerations in Intercognitive Analysis

From a normative standpoint, practitioners will find in some cases that the initial CHC Cross-Battery data fully support the null hypotheses regarding expected normal functioning as compared to peers in the general population. On the basis of such findings, it may well be appropriate to conclude that the individual's functioning is entirely within the normal range, and therefore, no further testing is necessary. Practitioners should recall, however, the Guiding Principles in CHC Cross-Battery assessment that specify the identification of convergence among indicators of ability (i.e., similar measures should produce similar results) and the need to interpret cluster scores only on the basis of two distinct, *nondiscrepant* measures. Therefore, additional interpretive guidelines are necessary when evaluating two or more confidence bands simultaneously. These guidelines are presented in the following section.

Before intercognitive analysis is carried out with cluster or composite scores, practitioners should examine the data in order to ensure that convergence among indicators is present. For the purposes of CHC Cross-Battery interpretation, convergence is defined as the touching or overlapping of two or more standard score ranges within broad ability domains, a condition predicted by CHC theory and the construct validation literature. Convergence is predicted by CHC theory to occur among the qualitatively different narrow abilities that subsume the same broad domain (e.g., WAIS-III Matrix Reasoning as a measure of Gf-Induction and WJ III Analysis-Synthesis as a measure of Gf-General Sequential Reasoning) as well as among qualitatively similar narrow abilities (e.g., WAIS-III Matrix Reasoning as a measure of Gf-I and WJ III Concept Formation as a measure of Gf-I). These measures are expected to correlate highly, and thus performance on one measure is expected to be consistent with performance on another related measure. Note that the ranges for broad abilities can overlap (e.g., the confidence band for Gf overlaps the band for Gv), indicating uniform ability across these domains. However, because CHC theory specifies that broad abilities are relatively distinct entities from one another and, therefore, only moderately intercorrelated, high performance on one broad ability does not necessarily suggest that performance should be high on any or all other broad abilities. When the standard score bands for measures that are expected to converge do, in fact, converge (i.e., the bands touch or overlap), the general rule for interpretation is accomplished via use of the relative position of the mean of the cluster's confidence band along the normal curve presented in Table 3.1. The manner in which a mean and confidence band for any given cluster is calculated was described in the previous chapter and it is important to remember that such means and bands are used only when an ability has been measured validly (i.e., two qualitatively different narrow ability indicators [for broad ability clusters] and two qualitatively similar narrow ability indicators [for narrow ability clusters]).

There is an exception, however, to the definition of convergence. On rare occasions, the standard score bands for two measures that are expected to converge may not actually touch or overlap as predicted, but may still fall completely within the same normative classification category. For example, the standard score bands for Gf-I and Gf-RG may be found to be discrepant (i.e., they do not touch or overlap) although the bands are both entirely within the classification range that represents a normative strength. In such cases, functioning in the broad domain (i.e., Gf) can be effectively interpreted as a normative strength since both narrow ability measures do in essence converge within the same normative range. Because it is extremely unlikely (statistically speaking) that true performance on this broad ability would fall outside this range, interpretation in this manner represents a rea-

Example 1: Non-convergent ability description as a normative weakness

NORMATIVE RANGE	Normative Weakness	Normal Limits	Normative Strength
CLASSIFICATION	<1 SD below mean	±1 SD from mean	> 1 SD above mean

40   50   60   70   80   90   100   110   120   130   140   150   160

Broad/Narrow (__) Cluster

Analysis-Synth. (**RG**) Test
Matrix Reas. (**I**) Test
_____ (__) Test
_____ (__) Test
_____ (__) Test
_____ (__) Test

Example 2: Non-convergent ability description within normal limits

NORMATIVE RANGE	Normative Weakness	Normal Limits	Normative Strength
CLASSIFICATION	< 1 SD below mean	±1 SD from mean	> 1 SD above mean

40   50   60   70   80   90   100   110   120   130   140   150   160

Broad/Narrow (__) Cluster

Analysis-Synth. (**RG**) Test
Matrix Reas. (**I**) Test
_____ (__) Test
_____ (__) Test
_____ (__) Test
_____ (__) Test

Example 3: Non-convergent ability description as a normative strength

NORMATIVE RANGE	Normative Weakness	Normal Limits	Normative Strength
CLASSIFICATION	< 1 SD below mean	±1 SD from mean	> 1 SD above mean

40   50   60   70   80   90   100   110   120   130   140   150   160

Broad/Narrow (__) Cluster

Analysis-Synth. (**RG**) Test
Matrix Reas. (**I**) Test
_____ (__) Test
_____ (__) Test
_____ (__) Test
_____ (__) Test

Figure 3.4 Examples of Interpretable Non-Convergent Ability Descriptions

sonable inference. This type of exception (i.e., interpreting broad ability performance using normative classification descriptions, such as *normative strength* or *normative weakness*) is referred to as a *non-convergent ability description* and can occur whenever two measures that are expected to converge do not (e. g., one measure of *Gf*-I and one measure of *Gf*-RG), although they still fall completely within the same normative range (strength, weakness, or within normal limits). This exception also applies to the interpretation of qualitatively similiar narrow abilities that do not converge as expected but still fall completely within the same normative range. In this case, normative classifications can be used to describe narrow ability performance. Note, however, that means and confidence bands for this type of cluster are not calculated, first because it remains statistically inappropriate, and second because there is no practical need to do so. Figure 3.4 provides a graphic illustration of the composition of the three possible non-convergent clusters that may result, albeit unexpectedly, in CHC Cross-Battery assessment.

An example was given previously in which the construct of interest centered on *Gf* and two measures of *Gf* were identified (WJ III Analysis-Synthesis and WAIS-III Matrix Reasoning). Both of these measures have been demonstrated to be strong, empirical measures of *Gf*, and therefore, administration of these two tests to the same individual should produce relatively similar results. Let us suppose for a moment, however, that the converted standard score range obtained on the WJ III Analysis-Synthesis was 103 to 117, and for the WAIS-III Matrix Reasoning, 63 to 77. The resulting average score calculated according to CHC Cross-Battery methods would be 90, with a range of 85 to 95, and gives an impression that this individual's functioning along the *Gf* ability domain is within the normal range. However, when these data are plotted on the CHC Cross-Battery Summary Sheet (see Appendix E), it will be readily apparent that the confidence bands for each measure do not overlap each other and they fall in different normative ranges. This situation is illustrated in Figure 3.5 using these scores as they might appear when graphed on the CHC Cross-Battery Summary Sheet.

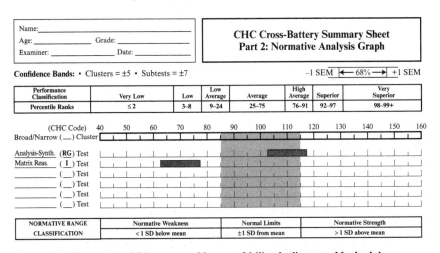

Figure 3.5 Example of Discrepant Narrow Ability Indicators Underlying Broad Ability

<table>
<tr><td>

DON'T FORGET

···

Guidelines for Interpreting Differences Between Standard Score Confidence Bands in CHC Cross-Battery Assessment

- If confidence bands touch or overlap, assume that the difference between them is not significant.
- If confidence bands *do not* touch or overlap, then assume that the difference between them is significant.

</td></tr>
</table>

There are two basic guidelines to follow in interpreting differences among standard score confidence bands as used in CHC Cross-Battery assessment. First, if the confidence bands for any two test scores or clusters touch or overlap, practitioners can assume that the difference between the ability scores being compared is not significant. Second, if the confidence bands for any two test scores or clusters do not touch or overlap, practitioners can assume that the difference between the ability scores being compared for any given individual is significant. These guidelines are consistent with research that demonstrates that when the non-overlapping guideline is used, practitioners can be 84% confident that there exists a true difference in scores (McGrew, Werder, & Woodcock, 1991). Given the clinical nature of the types of comparisons that are likely to be made in CHC Cross-Battery assessments, this level of confidence should prove adequate and acceptable in the vast majority of cases.

If we return for a moment to the example presented in Figure 3.5, it is clear that the confidence bands for the Matrix Reasoning and Analysis-Synthesis subtests do not overlap and that they fall in and span across different normative ranges. In accordance with the guidelines specified, the discrepancy between these two measures is significant and therefore precludes valid interpretation of the broad *Gf* ability cluster. The average of the two scores attenuates the fact that one narrow ability related to *Gf* (General Sequential Reasoning [RG], as measured by Analysis-Synthesis) crosses the normal limits and normative-strength ranges, whereas the other narrow ability related to *Gf* (Induction [I], as measured by Matrix Reasoning) is contained entirely within the normative weakness range. Thus, the true nature of the individual's functioning along the broad ability domain of *Gf* cannot be reliably determined on the basis of these data alone.

As stated previously, the relationships between and among narrow and broad ability indicators are empirically derived within CHC Cross-Battery assessment, and therefore it is expected that similar measures will converge. In other words, "persons high on the construct should score high on a variety of indicators of that construct" (Messick, 1989, p. 51). When scores on similar measures do not converge as expected in accordance with the theory underlying CHC Cross-Battery assessment, practitioners may not be able to determine exactly why one score is unusually different from the other. It was mentioned in the previous section that there are numerous reasons that this situation might occur, including inherent differences in an individual's narrow abilities; differences in the demands required by one task versus another; anomalous or extraneous influences that affect administration or performance; cultural or linguistic factors; chance; error; and so on. When the purpose of assessment is rather broad in nature, as in the use of the C-CB approach, practitioners may choose simply to leave broad ability clusters uninterpreted when the narrow ability indicators fail to converge as expected, especially if neither of the narrow ability scores falls *below* the normal range. When the approach is more focused, as with S-CB assessment, practitioners will often want to gain a better understanding of performance in a targeted area in which the results are ambiguous and potentially uninterpretable due to such lack of convergence among similar indicators. In either case, CHC Cross-Battery assessment allows practitioners the opportunity to investigate such discrepant findings in order to establish a stronger basis for defensible interpretation, as may be necessary or relevant to the purpose of assessment.

Irrespective of the logic and rationale behind the guidelines for interpretation presented here (particularly those that deal with significant differences), practitioners are reminded that such rules are not meant to replace clinical judgment but to augment it. There will be times when scores or score bands fall right at or close to the stated cutoff points, thereby complicating the interpretation and decision-making process. In such cases, strict adherence to the interpretive guidelines must never take precedence over professional or clinical judgment. Rather, test data and the accompanying rules for analysis are intended only to assist practitioners in evaluating performance and drawing inferences. In the final analysis, the meaning of the patterns seen in any and all data collected in the assessment process is determined in part by the professional opinion of the evaluator, rather than solely by the guidelines used by the evaluator.

In the example presented in Figure 3.5, it was noted that although the

Analysis-Synthesis and Matrix Reasoning subtests are measures of the same broad ability (*Gf*), convergence did not occur and a significant discrepancy was found between the two. When significantly disparate scores are found within broad ability domains, the meaning of the discrepancy is unlikely to be determined easily. Careful and selective additional assessment can, however, assist in clarifying the discrepancy and help determine whether this difference is simply an anomalous or irrelevant finding (Kamphaus, 1993). In CHC Cross-Battery assessment, interpretations and diagnostic conclusions should never be made on the basis of a single outlying test score, irrespective of the extent of deviation from the mean or from other scores (Atkinson, 1991; Lezak, 1995). Rather, CHC Cross-Battery assessment provides an iterative process that helps to shed additional light on any results that appear unusual or ambiguous.

To investigate functioning in areas that, for whatever reason, cannot be reliably interpreted after the initial round of testing, practitioners have the option of administering an additional measure. Although two additional measures could be given, one for each of the corresponding narrow abilities measured in the initial assessment (McGrew & Flanagan, 1998), in many cases this is not necessary or practical. This is because the focus of assessment is more often concerned with performance that is below the average range, not above it, as in the identification and diagnosis of disabilities or impairments (e.g., special education evaluation). Therefore, the focus on clarifying discrepant findings ordinarily will be on determining whether the lower standard score range, not the higher standard score range, is anomalous or not.

For practical reasons, most practitioners should thus select an additional narrow ability measure that corresponds to the narrow ability with the lowest standard score range. If we continue with the example already presented in Figure 3.5, Matrix Reasoning had the lower standard score range (63–77), compared to Analysis-Synthesis (103–117). A review of the CHC Cross-Battery Worksheets (see Appendix A) would provide practitioners with several options for supplementing investigation of the narrow ability reflected by Matrix Reasoning (i.e., *Gf*-Induction [I]). Because the example has so far supplemented only the core WAIS-III battery with the WJ III, it would make the most sense to select the Concept Formation subtest from the WJ III as the second measure of Induction since it would mean not having to cross a third battery. This is in accordance with the first guiding principle of CHC Cross-Battery assessment, which specifies the use of the least number of batteries possible. Much like before, an a posteriori hypothesis (i.e., that performance on this new test will be within normal limits as compared to same age peers in the general population) would be generated, and then the test would be administered and scored.

At this point in the assessment and interpretive process, there are five basic outcome scenarios. These outcomes are illustrated consecutively in Figures 3.6 through 3.10, using the CHC Cross-Battery Summary Sheet with the data from the initial assessment on *Gf* as presented previously. Outcome A, as depicted in Figure 3.6, shows the first possible scenario that could result whenever an additional test is given (in this case, Concept Formation). In this scenario, the resulting standard score range for Concept Formation (*Gf*-I) is lower than the standard score range originally obtained on the initial measure of Induction (i.e., Matrix Reasoning). The range for the additional *Gf*-I measure is indicated by the dark gray confidence band with the gray and white striped extension representing the area in which the band could fit and remain consistent with the interpretations offered for this scenario. Note that the bands for Matrix Reasoning and Concept Formation do not touch or overlap

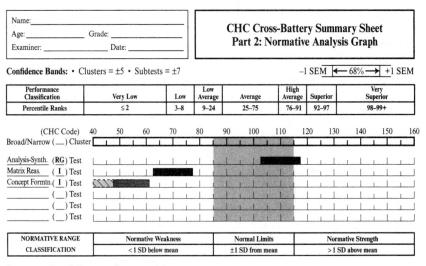

Interpretation of Outcome A:
 1. Broad ability *Gf* cannot be interpreted; and
 2. Narrow ability *Gf*-I can be interpreted as a Normative Weakness (non-convergent ability description).

Figure 3.6 Outcome A: Non-Convergent Narrow Ability Bands

as expected, indicating that there is a significant difference between the two Induction ability scores. However, although there is no convergence (as defined by overlap) among the two indicators, there is convergence with respect to normative classification since both are completely and entirely in the normative weakness range. This is an example in which a *non-convergent ability description* (i.e., normative weakness), as discussed previously, can be used to interpret performance in the area of Induction. However, an Induction cluster (i.e., the average of the two narrow ability Induction scores) is not represented on the graph, because calculation of a confidence band for this type of cluster is inappropriate. Note also that, as in the prior round of testing, the confidence band for the second measure of *Gf*-I does not overlap with the measure of *Gf*-RG. Thus, the lack of convergence and difference in normative ranges here precludes interpretation of a broad ability (*Gf*) cluster. Interpretation of Outcome A would be as follows: (a) Broad ability *Gf* cannot be interpreted because there is no convergence between any two qualitatively different narrow ability indicators (i.e., the standard score band for *Gf*-RG and any one of the bands for *Gf*-I do not touch or overlap, *and* no two different narrow ability bands are completely within the same normative range); (b) narrow ability *Gf*-I can be interpreted as a normative weakness because although the standard score ranges for both indicators do not touch or overlap each other, they both fall entirely and completely within the same range, allowing for a *non-convergent ability description*.

Outcome B, as depicted in Figure 3.7, shows the next possible scenario in this example. This illustration depicts a result in which the standard score range for the second measure of *Gf*-Induction is convergent with the standard score range originally obtained on the initial measure of *Gf*-Induction (i.e., Matrix Reasoning). In this figure, a dark gray confidence band for Concept Formation that corresponds closely to the existing band for Matrix Reasoning is shown. The new band is flanked by gray-and-white diagonal hash marks that, again, represent the potential degree to which the standard score range for Concept Formation could vary (depending on the obtained score) and still be considered convergent (nondiscrepant) with the results obtained previously with Matrix Reasoning, as well as consistent with the following interpretations. Because there is convergence among the two *Gf*-I narrow ability indicators, it is appropriate to calculate a confidence band for this cluster in order to guide interpretation. The dark gray band along the top of the graph represents the

Name:_____	
Age:_____ Grade:_____	**CHC Cross-Battery Summary Sheet**
Examiner:_____ Date:_____	**Part 2: Normative Analysis Graph**

Confidence Bands: • Clusters = ±5 • Subtests = ±7   –1 SEM |←— 68% —→| +1 SEM

Performance Classification	Very Low		Low	Low Average	Average	High Average	Superior	Very Superior
Percentile Ranks	≤2		3–8	9–24	25–75	76–91	92–97	98–99+

(CHC Code)	40	50	60	70	80	90	100	110	120	130	140	150	160

Broad(Narrow)(Gf-I) Cluster

Analysis-Synth. (RG) Test
Matrix Reas.   (I) Test
Concept Formtn.(I) Test
_____ (__) Test
_____ (__) Test
_____ (__) Test

NORMATIVE RANGE	Normative Weakness	Normal Limits	Normative Strength
CLASSIFICATION	<1 SD below mean	±1 SD from mean	>1 SD above mean

Interpretation of Outcome B:
1. Broad ability *Gf* cannot be interpreted; and
2. Narrow ability *Gf*-I can be interpreted as a normative weakness (convergent cluster).

Figure 3.7 Outcome B: Convergent Narrow Ability Bands

area in which this band could fall (again, depending on the obtained score on Concept Formation). Interpretation of Outcome B would be as follows: (a) Broad ability *Gf* cannot be interpreted because there is no convergence between any two qualitatively different narrow ability indicators (i.e., the standard score band for *Gf*-RG and any one of the bands for *Gf*-I do not touch or overlap, *and* no two different narrow ability bands are completely within the same normative range); (b) narrow ability *Gf*-I can be interpreted as a normative weakness because the standard score ranges for both indicators touch or overlap, forming a convergent cluster.

Outcome C is depicted in Figure 3.8 and shows the third variation of the possible scenarios for the current example. This case is similar to the initial one depicted in Figure 3.6, because the standard score range for Concept Formation (*Gf*-I) does not converge with the initial measure of Induction (i.e., Matrix Reasoning). However, in this example, the standard score range for Concept Formation is higher instead of lower. The dark gray confidence band and surrounding gray-and-white striped area show the range in which results would be subject to the interpretations that follow. Note that although the standard score range for Concept Formation is higher and discrepant from the standard score range for Matrix Reasoning, it still does not touch or overlap the confi-

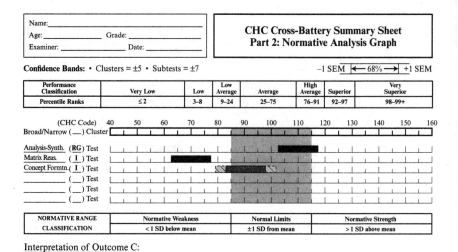

Figure 3.8 Outcome C: Non-Convergent Narrow Ability Bands

dence band for Analysis-Synthesis (*Gf*-RG). Therefore, no convergence is seen for the broad ability (*Gf*) and no cluster confidence bands are calculated or graphed. Accordingly, interpretation of Outcome C would be as follows: (a) Broad ability *Gf* cannot be interpreted because the standard score ranges for all of the narrow ability indicators (including *Gf*-I and *Gf*-RG) are all significantly discrepant from each other and no two indicators fall completely within the same normative range; and (b) narrow ability *Gf*-I cannot be interpreted because the standard score ranges for both *Gf*-I indicators do not converge (i.e., touch or overlap each other).

Outcome D is depicted in Figure 3.9 and illustrates the fourth variation of the possible scenarios in this example. This case is identical to the previous outcome depicted in Figure 3.8, with the exception that the standard score range for Concept Formation (*Gf*-I) now touches or overlaps the confidence band for General Sequential Reasoning (*Gf*-RG; Analysis-Synthesis). This overlap is indicated by the dark gray confidence band depicted directly under the black band originally obtained for *Gf*-RG. As before, the bands on either end of the new standard score range (shown by gray-and-white diagonal stripes) represent the area in which the standard score range for Concept Formation could vary and still maintain convergence, and thus remain subject to

Name:	CHC Cross-Battery Summary Sheet
Age: _____ Grade: _____	**Part 2: Normative Analysis Graph**
Examiner: _____ Date: _____	

Confidence Bands: • Clusters = ±5 • Subtests = ±7   –1 SEM ⟵ 68% ⟶ +1 SEM

Performance Classification	Very Low	Low	Low Average	Average	High Average	Superior	Very Superior
Percentile Ranks	≤2	3–8	9–24	25–75	76–91	92–97	98–99+

	(CHC Code)	40	50	60	70	80	90	100	110	120	130	140	150	160

Broad/Narrow (**Gf**) Cluster

Analysis-Synth. (**RG**) Test
Matrix Reas.   (**I**) Test
Concept Formtn.(**I**) Test
_____ (__) Test
_____ (__) Test
_____ (__) Test

NORMATIVE RANGE	Normative Weakness	Normal Limits	Normative Strength
CLASSIFICATION	< 1 SD below mean	±1 SD from mean	> 1 SD above mean

Interpretation of Outcome D:
1. Broad ability Gf can be interpreted as Within Normal Limits; and
2. Narrow ability Gf-I cannot be interpreted.

Figure 3.9 Outcome D: Non-Convergent Narrow Ability and Convergent Broad Ability Bands

the interpretations for this scenario. As in the previous case, the standard score range for Concept Formation is higher and discrepant from the standard score range for Matrix Reasoning, and they do not both fall within the same normative range. This lack of convergence precludes interpretation of Gf-Induction as a narrow ability cluster. However, the convergence between Concept Formation (Gf-I) and Analysis-Synthesis (Gf-RG) now represents a convergent broad ability cluster as a function of the overlap of two qualitatively different narrow ability indicators. Accordingly, the confidence band for this broad ability cluster is calculated and depicted at the top of the graph. Interpretation of Outcome D would be as follows: (a) Broad ability cluster Gf can be interpreted as being within normal limits because the average standard score ranges for two *different* narrow ability indicators (one Gf-I test and the Gf-RG test) converge; and (b) narrow ability Gf-I cannot be interpreted because the standard score ranges for both Gf-I indicators do not converge (i.e., touch or overlap each other).

The final scenario in this example is portrayed as Outcome E in Figure 3.10. This case is a variation on the previous outcome, with the exception that the standard score range for Concept Formation (Gf-I) no longer converges (does

Name:
Age: _____ Grade: _____
Examiner: _____ Date: _____

CHC Cross-Battery Summary Sheet
Part 2: Normative Analysis Graph

Confidence Bands: • Clusters = ±5 • Subtests = ±7

−1 SEM |←— 68% —→| +1 SEM

Performance Classification	Very Low	Low	Low Average	Average	High Average	Superior	Very Superior
Percentile Ranks	≤2	3–8	9–24	25–75	76–91	92–97	98–99+

(CHC Code) 40 50 60 70 80 90 100 110 120 130 140 150 160

Broad/Narrow (__) Cluster

Analysis-Synth. (**RG**) Test
Matrix Reas. (**I**) Test
Concept Formtn.(**I**) Test
_____ (__) Test
_____ (__) Test
_____ (__) Test

NORMATIVE RANGE CLASSIFICATION	Normative Weakness	Normal Limits	Normative Strength
	< 1 SD below mean	± 1 SD from mean	> 1 SD above mean

Interpretation of Outcome E:
1. Broad ability *Gf* cannot be interpreted; and
2. Narrow ability *Gf*-I cannot be interpreted.

Figure 3.10 Outcome E: Non-Convergent Narrow Ability and Non-Convergent Broad Ability Bands

not touch or overlap) with the standard score range for Matrix Reasoning (*Gf*-RG), but actually exceeds it. As can be seen in Figure 3.10, the standard score range for Concept Formation (represented by the dark gray confidence band) is completely above the standard score range for Matrix Reasoning. The gray-and-white diagonal stripes to the right of this band represent the area in which the standard score range for Concept Formation could fall, remain above and discrepant from the standard score range for Matrix Reasoning, and still be consistent with the following interpretations. The lack of actual statistical or normative range convergence precludes the formation of any valid ability cluster (convergent or nonconvergent), and therefore no cluster-level confidence bands are calculated or graphed. Interpretation of Outcome E is thus identical to that found in Outcome C and would be as follows: (a) Broad ability *Gf* cannot be interpreted because the standard score ranges for all of the narrow ability indicators (including *Gf*-I and *Gf*-RG) are all significantly discrepant from each other and no two indicators fall completely within the same normative range; and (b) narrow ability *Gf*-I cannot be interpreted because the standard score ranges for both *Gf*-I indicators do not converge (i.e., touch or overlap each other).

The examples illustrated (in Figures 3.6 through 3.10) relate primarily to cases in which two qualitatively different narrow abilities (from the same broad domain) are measured in the initial round of assessment, and the resulting discrepancy (lack of convergence) between the bands necessitates an additional iteration in the testing process. The same need for an additional iteration in testing can occur in some instances in which the initial measurement of abilities might deliberately include only two qualitatively similar narrow ability measures (from the same broad domain) such as in investigations of specific areas of functioning or ability. Such focus on narrow ability indicators, however, obviously precludes the measurement and interpretation of broad abilities (Level 1 interpretation). Nevertheless, if a practitioner is interested only in narrow abilities (Level 2 interpretation), there may well be occasions in which results from initial measurement of two similar narrow abilities are discrepant (do not converge), and thus, another iteration in testing is warranted. The second iteration of testing may well be accomplished with either a third qualitatively similar narrow ability indicator or with one that is qualitatively different depending on specific referral needs. Irrespective of the type of third narrow ability measure selected, the interpretive rules described previously are not altered in any way and should be followed as specified.

In summary, because the underlying CHC classification system of the CHC Cross-Battery approach allows for reasonably accurate selection of multiple

---

≡Rapid Reference 3.3

Situations in Which Additional Assessment within Broad Ability Domains is Generally Warranted

1. When a statistically significant difference is found between narrow abilities in a broad domain; *and*

2. When the lower of the two narrow abilities is suggestive of a significant normative weakness (i.e., more than 1 SD below the normative mean), or whenever both narrow abilities within the broad domain are more than 1 SD below the normative mean and significantly below that of most other CHC domains; *and*

3. When detailed analysis of the narrow ability (or abilities within the broad domain[s]) is deemed useful in understanding the individual's presenting difficulties (e.g., academic skill deficiencies)

CAUTION

....

Potentially Invalid Broad Ability Clusters

Whenever statistically significant differences exist between two qualitatively different narrow ability indicators, the broad ability cluster (i.e., the aggregate of the two narrow ability test scores) is likely to be a misleading estimate of the broad ability and should therefore not be calculated, graphed, or interpreted.

and varied indicators of constructs, it is expected that measured performance within broad ability domains will be relatively consistent. Therefore, in the majority of cases in which intercognitive analysis is applied, interpretation regarding performance will be made most appropriately at the broad ability level (e.g., *Gf, Gc, Gv,* etc.). However, in the event that measured performance within broad ability domains is not found to be consistent, it may be necessary to examine additional narrow ability indicators. Such examination takes the form of supplemental testing and represents the application of carefully constructed iterations in the testing and assessment process. Once completed, interpretation and inferences about measured performance will likely be made at the narrow ability level (e.g., inductive reasoning, general sequential reasoning, etc.). Irrespective of the level at which performance is examined (i.e., broad or narrow), proper interpretation requires that constructs be adequately represented. In the case of broad ability clusters, two qualitatively different indicators of the same broad ability (e.g., one *Gf*-I and one *Gf*-RG) are required. In the case of narrow ability clusters, two indicators of the same narrow ability (e.g., two measures of *Gf*-I) would be needed. The formation of interpretable but nonconvergent ability descriptions described previously represents the only exception to these rules. Adherence to these guidelines in constructing and interpreting clusters ensures an increase in reliability that is not attainable through the use of individual tests (i.e., subtests).

Cautions in the Interpretation of Cluster Scores

The main purpose of CHC Cross-Battery assessment is to identify both inter- and intracognitive strengths and weaknesses among the multiple broad (stratum II) abilities that essentially comprise the structure of intelligence as it is understood and explained by present-day theory. Because it is based on modern intelligence theory and because it incorporates many advances in cognitive psychology, CHC Cross-Battery assessment allows practitioners to measure a much broader range of skills and abilities specifically related to learning and other cognitive processes than that which can be measured through the use of a single battery (Flanagan, McGrew, & Ortiz, 2000; McGrew & Flanagan, 1998). The comprehensive method of CHC Cross-Battery assessment (C-CB) can generate up to seven broad ability cluster scores that can be reliably

> # DON'T FORGET
> ··
>
> ## Proper Interpretation Requires that Cognitive Ability Constructs be Represented Adequately
>
> - Proper interpretation at the broad ability level (i.e., *Gf, Gc, Gsm,* etc.) requires two qualitatively different indicators of the same broad ability (e.g., one *Gf*-I and one *Gf*-RG).
> - Proper interpretation at the narrow ability level requires at least two indicators of the same narrow ability (e.g., two measures of Induction).

and validly interpreted for the purpose of identifying cognitive processing strengths or weaknesses—an important consideration in documenting learning disabilities. However, because some of the scores that may be used for such purposes may represent the aggregate average of tests from two or more different test batteries, there are some cautions that should be noted.

Standard scores may be appropriately interpreted for individual tests and allow comparison of an individual's relative level of performance against a reference (norm) group. Because the underlying practice is to cross batteries in order to increase construct validity and measurement precision (i.e., reliability), the mean standard scores for broad clusters calculated and plotted in CHC Cross-Battery assessments must not be interpreted as if they represent actual cluster scores that were normed on a single norm group. These cluster scores are not exact or precise values and should not be substituted for other measures of aptitude or ability that may be necessary in order to make decisions regarding the significance of ability-achievement discrepancies. Although CHC Cross-Battery assessment is a psychometrically and theoretically defensible procedure for identifying intracognitive ability and processing strengths and weaknesses, broad clusters derived in the process are not recommended for use in discrepancy formulas (e.g., ability-achievement and aptitude-achievement). This is primarily because many of the assumptions carried by discrepancy models are not truly valid for the purpose of documenting learning disabilities. Nevertheless, CHC Cross-Battery assessment remains flexible enough to accommodate practitioners whose situations may require the identification of a cognitive processing deficit (or deficits) as well as an ability-achievement or aptitude-achievement discrepancy. Methods for accomplishing this type of assessment are discussed in detail in Chapter 4.

Another caution in the use of broad cluster scores derived from application of CHC Cross-Battery methods relates to the fact that actual normed cluster scores are not always equal to the average of the individual standard scores they comprise (McGrew, 1994). The basis for this statement is related to the magnitude of the intercorrelations and number of tests in the cluster (Paik & Nebenzahl, 1987). In general, the lower the intercorrelations between tests that contribute to a cluster score, the more extreme the difference will be between a cluster score that is normed and a cluster score that is based on the arithmetic average of tests. The only time a cluster standard score will equal the average of the individual tests that comprise it is when all the tests of the cluster are correlated perfectly, an obviously undesirable condition in test construction (Paik & Nebenzahl, 1987). As such, use of the simple averaging method for deriving cluster scores in CHC Cross-Battery assessment suggests that such scores will deviate *slightly* from what the normed cluster scores would have been. However, given the rigor with which the clusters have been constructed (e.g., based on the results of theory-driven, cross-battery factor analyses), it is highly probable that they would, in fact, not differ *significantly* from corresponding normed clusters based on a theoretical cross-battery norm group. Furthermore, when CHC Cross-Battery cluster scores are reported and interpreted with their corresponding confidence bands, deviation from normed averages is negligible and comparisons of performance relative to a normative standard (i.e., the normal probability curve), or relative to individual average performance, can be considered reliable. Practitioners are advised to view CHC Cross-Battery data as only one component in a multi-faceted assessment approach that seeks to find not only a convergence of indicators within cognitive ability testing, but convergence among various types and sources of data that support the overall conclusions and interpretations that may be offered.

GUIDELINES FOR INTRACOGNITIVE ANALYSIS IN CHC CROSS-BATTERY ASSESSMENT

Intracognitive (i.e., ipsative) analysis, or the *Kaufman Psychometric Approach* (Kamphaus, Petoskey, & Morgan, 1997), is a relatively popular method of test interpretation that seeks to explore an individual's own pattern of strengths and weaknesses in comparison to his or her performance across a variety of tests ostensibly measuring both similar and different cognitive abilities. Apart from gaining a better understanding of the individual's intellectual functioning, the major goal of this type of analysis involves the creation of a more defensible basis for the development of specific remedial strategies and interventions than that which typically emanate from global measures of ability. Unlike intercognitive analysis, emphasis is on *within*-individual differences rather than between-individual differences. Despite its popularity and clinical appeal, intracognitive analysis has been roundly criticized, primarily because few practitioners have stopped long enough to recognize and understand the significant limitations inherent in the process (Flanagan, Andrews, & Genshaft, 1997; McDermott & Glutting, 1997; McDermott, Fantuzzo, Glutting, Watkins, & Baggaley, 1992).

Limitations of Intracognitive Analysis

The major limitations of the intracognitive approach to interpretation are summarized in Rapid Reference 3.4. Given the breadth and depth of criticism leveled at this type of analysis, it would hardly seem prudent to recommend its use under most any circumstance, and in general, the practice of subtest-level interpretation can be a rather perilous endeavor with little potential benefit. Yet the use of intracognitive procedures seems to be a mainstay in clinical training and practice and shows little sign of slowing down. Although it has become a favorite tool in the repertoire of applied psychologists and practitioners, perhaps one of the reasons that intracognitive analysis has not fared nearly as well in the literature rests on the failure to ground such interpretive efforts in solid theory and research. Through the use and application of CHC Cross-Battery methods and procedures, some of the limitations of the intracognitive approach to interpretation can be addressed and effectively circumvented.

One reason that CHC Cross-Battery assessment may provide a more defen-

≡ *Rapid Reference 3.4*

Major Limitations of the Ipsative Approach to Interpretation

1. Ipsative scores have no construct validity
2. Ipsative scores have near zero (and typically negative) intercorrelations
3. Ipsative scores tend not to be stable over time
4. Ipsative scores have properties which make attempts at remediation a "no win" situation (e.g., their sum equals zero)
5. Ipsative scores have extremely poor predictive validity
6. Ipsative scores do not appear to provide any additional information beyond that generated by normative scores

Note. From McDermott, Fantuzzo, Glutting, Watkins, and Baggaley (1992).

sible framework for intracognitive analysis is that it is grounded in a well-validated structure of human cognitive abilities, unlike most previous attempts at interpretation that are not guided by either theory or research (McGrew, Flanagan, Keith, & Vanderwood, 1997; Vanderwood, McGrew, Flanagan, & Keith, 2000). The CHC Cross-Battery approach presented in this book is founded upon contemporary intelligence theory and extensive supporting research as well as sound measurement principles. These conditions greatly improve the ability of practitioners to draw clear and useful conclusions from the data (Daniel, 1997; Kamphaus, 1993, 1998; Kamphaus et al., 1997; Keith, 1988). Another reason that CHC Cross-Battery assessment is able to advance the practice of intracognitive analysis lies in the fact that when the broad clusters are ipsatized, the variance that is common to all clusters (i.e., *Gf, Gc, Gv, Ga,* etc.) is removed but the variance that is shared by the two tests that combine to yield the respective clusters remains. Consequently, when the broad (stratum II) clusters are ipsatized via CHC Cross-Battery methods (as opposed to ipsatization of individual tests as done in the traditional approach), proportionately more reliable variance remains. Clearly, interpretations of a specific cognitive ability (operationally defined by the reliable common variance shared by at least two empirically based and qualitatively different indicators) appears to represent a much more promising practice than has been found through misguided analysis of individual subtests. Finally, composition of the cognitive ability clusters in CHC Cross-Battery assessment is specifically designed to reduce construct-irrelevant variance and construct underrepresentation. This significantly enhances validity in the measurement and assessment of cognitive abilities far beyond the level that is typically associated with the use of individual tests in the context of test batteries that do not attend to these variables. The number of research investigations exploring the relationship between the broad clusters in CHC theory and numerous outcome criteria is beginning to

DON'T FORGET

Significance of Intracognitive Differences

Practitioners are well advised to remember that in the absence of additional convergent, and compelling evidence, intracognitive differences alone, despite being statistically significant, should not be construed as clinically meaningful.

provide significant validation evidence that enriches and informs the interpretive process. Considerably less corresponding validity evidence is available to support traditional ipsative-based, subtest-level interpretation.

A final note of caution regarding the limitations of the intracognitive approach involves recognition of the fact that a high degree of variation across tasks and item types is not uncommon in the normal population. Thus, it must be stressed that intracognitive differences alone are insufficient grounds upon which to base diagnostic, classification, or treatment decisions (Reschly & Grimes, 1995). Even when statistically significant intracognitive differences are found using CHC Cross-Battery data, the meaning of these differences must always be supported by a variety of other types and sources of data. Practitioners are well advised to remember that in the absence of additional convergent, and compelling evidence, intracognitive differences alone, despite being statistically significant, should not be construed as clinically meaningful.

Guidelines for Conducting an Intracognitive Analysis

The first step in conducting an intracognitive analysis is to sum the individual's CHC Cross-Battery cluster averages and divide by the total number of averages to obtain the individual's overall cluster mean or average of the averages (i.e., the average level of performance by the individual across all broad clusters that were measured). Next, *difference scores* are obtained by subtracting the overall cluster average from the individual cluster averages. The values should be preceded by either a "+" or a "−" sign to indicate positive or negative differences between the individual cluster scores and the overall cluster score.

Facilitation of the calculation and representation of intracognitive analysis is accomplished via Part 3 of the CHC Cross-Battery Summary Sheet (see Chapter 2 and Appendix E). This portion of the summary sheet not only provides a simple format and structure for generating the necessary data for intracognitive analysis, but also is designed to assist directly in the interpretive process. Finally, the practitioner must determine whether the absolute value of any of the difference scores is large enough for the corresponding broad (stratum II) ability to be considered a significant (relatively speaking) intracognitive strength or weakness for the examinee. It is extremely helpful to remember that intracognitive analysis is conducted with absolute (single) scores, in contrast to intercognitive analysis (discussed previously), which is conducted with score bands. The use of individual scores as opposed to a range of scores results in slight differences in the interpretive rules, particularly with respect to the definition of significant difference. In order to avoid confusion during analysis and interpretation of any test data, practitioners should remain aware of what type of data are being evaluated.

The number of human beings whose individual cognitive abilities are completely and uniformly developed is no doubt extremely small. Rather, some *variation in ability is normal,* and there is no reason to expect that patterns of cognitive abilities measured in individuals from the general population will demonstrate anything different. Some criterion must therefore be specified in order to establish some guidelines for practitioners to be able to ascertain whether one broad cluster varies *significantly* from the overall cluster. With respect to CHC Cross-Battery assessment, a criterion of ±15 standard score points was chosen to represent significant intracognitive (relative) strengths and weaknesses because it is most similar to the standards used in intracognitive analysis with other intelligence batteries (e.g., subtest analysis). A good example is the Wechsler Scales, in which subtests that differ by one or more standard deviations (i.e., ±3 points) from the average (mean) subtest scaled score have been suggested to represent possible strengths and weaknesses (Kaufman, 1979, 1990). Because all scores used in CHC Cross-Battery assessment are converted to the same metric having a mean of 100 and a SD of 15, use of a ±15 standard score point deviation ensures that differences in CHC Cross-Battery data are of equal magnitude to those specified by other rules. Generally speaking, a cluster standard score average that differs from the overall standard score average by ±15 points or more (i.e., ≥ 1 SD above or below the mean) can be considered as a possible intracognitive strength or weakness, respectively.

A common pitfall in intracognitive analysis is the failure to distinguish between relative and normative strengths and weaknesses. Frequently, practitioners who engage in intracognitive analysis will look only for discrepancies, and will attempt to interpret any such discrepancies as clinically meaningful without regard to where the scores fall compared to a normative standard. Figure 3.11 provides an illustration of this tendency to overlook the normative position of scores and blindly interpret significant differences that may in fact have little clinical relevance at all. Analysis of the seven broad cluster scores listed in the example reveals *Ga* as a relative weakness (falling 28 points below the overall cluster average of 120) and *Gsm* as a relative strength (16 points above the overall cluster average). All other comparisons were nonsignificant. In many cases, practitioners examine the extreme 28-point difference between *Ga* and the rest of the broad factors and assume that this discrepancy represents something of

Broad Cluster Average	Difference from Overall Average	Relative (Intracognitive) Interpretation	Normative (Intercognitive) Interpretation
Gf = 123	123 − 120 = +3	not significant	normative strength
Gc = 117	117 − 120 = −3	not significant	normative strength
Gv = 129	129 − 120 = +9	not significant	normative strength
Ga = 92	92 − 120 = −28	*relative weakness*	*not significant (within normal limits)*
Gsm = 136	136 − 120 = +16	*relative strength*	normative strength
Glr = 124	124 − 120 = +4	not significant	normative strength
Gs = 121	121 − 120 = +1	not significant	normative strength
Avg. = 120			

Figure 3.11 Distinguishing between Relative and Normative Strengths and Weaknesses in Interpretation

great clinical significance. Such large discrepancies often lead to the conclusion that the individual has deficits in this area. However, normative comparison of *Ga* ability shows that it is clearly within the normal limits of functioning (as indicated by the gray shaded area in Figure 3.11) as compared to other individuals of the same age. As such, proper interpretation of the clinical significance of this ability is not that it represents any deficit in functioning, but rather that it is merely within normal limits. The fact that all of the other broad abilities are well above the average range and represent normative strengths does not automatically make *Ga* deficient. Compared to the performance of other people of the same age in the general population, functional ability in *Ga* is quite normal. As such it can hardly be construed as evidence of any type of impairment, given that such functioning is falling at about the 29th percentile, and there is no expectation that an individual's abilities should all be uniformly well developed. Conversely, because measured performance in *Gsm* is significantly above the overall cluster average (+16) it represents a relative strength. In this case, however, the score of 136 is not merely within normal limits but is significantly above these limits and is thus also a normative strength. Again, the real clinical significance of this finding is rather limited (apart from the fact that it reflects exceptional performance) because it is relatively consistent with the majority of the other cluster scores. The fact that there is a significant discrepancy here provides no substantive basis whatsoever for any conclusions other than that the cluster average for *Gsm* reflects superior ability.

In order to clarify the distinctions that must be made between relative and normative strengths and weaknesses when making interpretations, the criteria and rules governing the decision process are outlined in Figure 3.12. There are two basic scenarios that can arise in intracognitive analysis. As illustrated in Figure 3.12, Case A represents the situation in which the average score for a broad cluster is found to be *discrepant* (≥ 15 points) from the overall cluster average score and the score for this broad cluster is *higher* than the overall cluster average score. When these are the findings, then one of the three listed interpretive rules must be followed:

1. The broad cluster score should be interpreted as a *normative weakness* when the score itself is still ≤ 84.
2. It should be interpreted as a *relative strength* when the score is between 85 and 115.

	Interpretation Rule #1	Interpretation Rule #2	Interpretation Rule #3
Case A: When the average score for a broad cluster is **discrepant** (≥ 15 points) from the overall cluster average score, **and** it is **higher** than the overall cluster average score, then interpret score as:	**NORMATIVE WEAKNESS** (If score is ≤ 84)	**RELATIVE STRENGTH** (If score is between 85 and 115)	**NORMATIVE STRENGTH** (If score is ≥ 116)
Case B: When the average score for a broad cluster is **discrepant** (≥ 15 points) from the overall cluster average score, **and** it is **lower** than the overall cluster average score, then interpret score as:	**NORMATIVE WEAKNESS** (If score is ≤ 84)	**RELATIVE WEAKNESS** (If score is between 85 and 115)	**RELATIVE WEAKNESS *BUT* NORMATIVE STRENGTH** (If score is > 116)

Figure 3.12 Criteria and Decision Rules for Interpretation of Relative and Normative Strengths and Weaknesses

  3. It should be interpreted as a *normative strength* when the score is ≥ 116.

These guidelines take into account the fact that relative strengths and weaknesses are dependent upon the position of the individual's overall mean and that when that mean falls at or near the upper end of the normal probability curve, significant discrepancies do not necessarily reflect normative-based weaknesses, even though there may be very large differences between scores. Figure 3.12 also depicts the second scenario that could occur, as illustrated by Case B. In this situation, when the average score for a broad cluster is *discrepant* (≥ 15 points) from the overall cluster average score and the score for this broad cluster is *lower* than the overall cluster average score, then interpretation should be as follows:

  1. If the score is ≤ 84, then it is a *normative weakness.*
  2. If the score is between 85 and 115, then it is a *relative weakness.*
  3. If the score is ≥ 116, then it is *both* a *relative weakness* and a *normative strength.*

After any significant intracognitive strengths and weaknesses have been identified and properly interpreted in accordance with the guidelines just spec-

DON'T FORGET

Relationship between Normative and Relative Functioning

Relative strengths and weaknesses are dependent upon the position of the individual's overall mean. When the individual's mean falls at or near the upper end of the normal probability curve, significant discrepancies do not necessarily reflect normative-based weaknesses even though there may be very large differences between scores.

ified, the findings need to be translated into meaningful descriptions of cognitive performance and functioning (Kamphaus, 1993; Kaufman, 1994; McGrew, 1994). One of the basic goals and perhaps the most utilitarian aspect of intracognitive analysis is to identify those tasks that the individual is most adept at handling and use them to aid in planning instructional or remedial programs that incorporate those strengths. Practically speaking, patterns of intracognitive strengths and weaknesses by themselves have very little *diagnostic* utility. There simply exists too little research evidence upon which to base appropriate diagnostic decisions derived from a profile of ipsatized scores (Glutting, McDermott, & Konold, 1997; Kamphaus, 1993; Kamphaus et al., 1997; McDermott et al., 1992; Watkins & Kush, 1994). Therefore, practitioners should be careful not to overestimate the significance of discrepancies that result from intracognitive analysis.

Nevertheless, when practitioners follow the guidelines and criteria specified in this chapter, intra- and intercognitive analyses can be effectively integrated in a manner that can assist in discovering clues about an individual's abilities that may help to clarify the functional nature of any observed or suspected learning problems. Couching intracognitive analysis within the context of CHC Cross-Battery methods creates a viable approach for the development of appropriate recommendations for clinical treatment, educational remediation, or vocational placement. Other times, however, intracognitive analysis may not uncover any pertinent or useful information that was not already available from intercognitive analysis. Practitioners will have to use good judgment to decide when and if engaging in intracognitive analysis will prove fruitful to the purpose of any given assessment.

The use of CHC Cross-Battery methods does not completely rectify many of the inherent problems found in the practice of intracognitive analysis. Practitioners should remain fully aware that despite some emerging research that may yet save this type of analysis, the process still lacks considerable empirical support and is almost completely indefensible when conducted outside the rigorous structure provided by assessment methods such as the CHC Cross-Battery approach. Therefore, such analysis should be de-emphasized in the interpretive process, and when it is used, it should be closely integrated with findings from intercognitive analysis in order to paint an accurate picture of the meaning and implications of any collected pattern of scores. In those assessments in which the focus is on identifying and diagnosing learning disabilities, there is little if any consensus as to what constitutes appropriate criteria for making decisions regarding the presence or absence of any such weaknesses or deficits. Practitioners will no doubt be required to supplement clinical judgment with experience, current theoretical and empirical research, and knowledge of the quantitative and qualitative characteristics of many tests of cognitive ability when interpreting performance on the tests selected for CHC Cross-Battery assessments (McGrew & Flanagan, 1998; see Chapters 4 and 5).

The iterative process that integrates assessment and interpretation and guides supplemental or focused investigations of intellectual functioning in CHC Cross-Battery assessment is extremely valuable in situations in which unusual or unexpected findings emerge or whenever there is a need to test a posteriori hypotheses. The information contained in this book and other sources (viz., Flanagan, McGrew, et al., 2000; McGrew & Flanagan, 1998) provides practitioners with an extensive arsenal of cognitive ability tests that may be used as required by the iterative nature of assessment in general and within the context of the CHC Cross-Battery approach, in particular.

SUMMARY

This chapter provided specific guidelines to assist practitioners in properly evaluating CHC Cross-Battery data and for drawing appropriate inferences and making accurate interpretations on the basis of the patterns evident in the data. The process of interpretation within the context of CHC Cross-Battery assessments is both systematic and integrated and represents a method of test interpretation that is highly defensible and grounded in contemporary intelligence theory.

CHC Cross-Battery assessment incorporates an hypothesis-driven framework that serves to reduce the possibility of confirmatory bias. Practitioners are advised to follow the guidelines for specifying both a priori and a posteriori hypotheses carefully and not to circumvent the protections offered by the use of an hypothesis-generation and -testing framework.

The manner in which inter- and intracognitive analyses of individual ability clusters provides greater diagnostic and prescriptive information than is ordinarily obtained with traditional methods of individual subtest analysis was also explained, as were the advantages and disadvantages of each interpretive method. Practitioners were instructed to distinguish carefully between relative and normative strengths and weaknesses so as not to generate inappropriate interpretations of functioning or performance. On the whole, the interpretive process with respect to both relative and normative comparisons represents a balance between the practitioners need for clinically meaningful data and the need to make decisions as objectively as possible.

Because CHC Cross-Battery assessment is supported by a growing body of research on the relationships between cognitive abilities (as specified by CHC theory) and academic achievement, the process can ensure that the abilities most closely related to academically oriented referrals are well represented in the assessment. In addition, when applied in a selective manner (S-CB), such assessment provides a means for significantly reducing or eliminating the evaluation of abilities that are unrelated to the achievement skill(s) in question, and is particularly useful in all types of special education evaluations.

Investigations regarding the predictive utility of CHC Cross-Battery assessment over traditional assessment are available (see Chapter 1 for a summary); however, the diagnostic and treatment validity of the approach, just as with any new and innovative assessment approach, is not yet well developed. Traditional assessment approaches have not fared well in this respect. This is most evident in research involving the Wechsler Intelligence Scales, which have for decades demonstrated convincingly that "it is impossible to predict specific disabilities and areas of cognitive competency or dysfunction from the averaged ability test scores" (i.e., IQs; Lezak, 1995). In keeping with the overall structure of the approach, CHC Cross-Battery data are grounded in contemporary theory and research and may eventually prove to yield more clinically meaningful and diagnostically relevant information than has historically been obtained via the ubiquitous IQ.

The next chapter deals specifically with the continued need to include global measures of ability in assessment, particularly for use in ability-achievement discrepancy formulas. Suggestions are offered that allow for measurement of the breadth of broad CHC abilities and the calculation of global ability scores within the context of the CHC Cross-Battery approach.

REFERENCES

American Heritage Dictionary. (1994). *The American Heritage Dictionary–Third Edition*. New York: Dell Publishing.

Anastasi, A., & Urbina, S. (1997). *Psychological testing* (7th ed.). Upper Saddle River, NJ: Prentice Hall.

Atkinson, L. (1991). On WAIS-R difference scores in the standardization sample. *Psychological Assessment, 3,* 292–294.

Brouerman, D. M. (1961). Effects of score transformations in the Q and R factor analysis techniques. *Psychological Review, 68,* 68–80.

Daniel, M. H. (1997). Intelligence testing: Status and trends. *American Psychologist, 52,* 1038–1045.

Flanagan, D. P., Andrews, T. J., & Genshaft, J. L. (1997). The functional utility of intelligence tests with special education populations. In D. P. Flanagan, J. L. Genshaft, & P. L. Harrison (Eds.), *Contemporary intellectual assessment: Theories, tests, and issues* (pp. 457–483). New York: Guilford.

Flanagan, D. P., McGrew, K. S., & Ortiz, S. O. (2000). *The Wechsler intelligence scales and CHC theory: A contemporary approach to interpretation*. Boston: Allyn & Bacon.

Glutting, J. J., McDermott, P. A., & Konold, T. R. (1997). Ontology, structure, and diagnostic benefits of a normative subtest taxonomy from the WISC-III standardization sample. In D. P. Flanagan, J. L. Genshaft, & P. L. Harrison (Eds.), *Contemporary intellectual assessment: Theories, tests, and issues* (pp. 349–372). New York: Guilford.

Kamphaus, R. W. (1998). Intelligence test interpretation: Acting in the absence of evidence. In A. Prifitera & D. Saklofske (Eds.), *WISC-III clinical use and interpretation*. San Diego: Academic.

Kamphaus, R. W., Petoskey, M. D., & Morgan, A. W. (1997). A history of intelligence test interpretation. In D. P. Flanagan, J. L. Genshaft, & P. L. Harrison (Eds.), *Contemporary intellectual assessment: Theories, tests, and issues* (pp. 32–51). New York: Guilford.

Kaufman, A. S. (1979). *Intelligent testing with the WISC-R*. New York: Wiley.

Kaufman, A. S. (1990). *Assessing adolescent and adult intelligence*. Boston: Allyn & Bacon.

Kaufman, A. S. (1994). *Intelligent testing with the WISC-III*. New York: Wiley.

Keith, T. Z. (1988). Research methods in school psychology: An overview. *School Psychology Review, 17,* 502–520.

Lezak, M. D. (1976). *Neuropsychological assessment*. New York: Oxford University Press.

Lezak, M. D. (1995). *Neuropsychological assessment* (3rd ed.). New York: Oxford University Press.

McDermott, P. A., & Glutting, J. J. (1997). Informing stylistic learning behavior, disposition, and achievement through ability subtests: Or, more illusions of meaning? *School Psychology Review, 26,* 163–175.

McDermott, P. A., Fantuzzo, J. W., Glutting, J. J., Watkins, M. W., & Baggaley, R. A. (1992). Illusions of meaning in the ipsative assessment of children's ability. *Journal of Special Education, 25,* 504–526.

McGrew, K. S. (1994). *Clinical interpretation of the Woodcock-Johnson Tests of Cognitive Ability–Revised.* Boston: Allyn & Bacon.

McGrew, K. S., & Flanagan, D. P. (1998). *The intelligence test desk reference (ITDR):* Gf-Gc *cross-battery assessment.* Boston: Allyn & Bacon.

McGrew, K. S., Flanagan, D. P., Keith, T. Z., & Vanderwood, M. (1997). Beyond *g:* The impact of *Gf-Gc* specific cognitive abilities research on the future use and interpretation of intelligence tests in the schools. *School Psychology Review, 26*(2), 189–210.

McGrew, K. S., Werder, J. K., & Woodcock, R. W. (1991). *Woodcock-Johnson Psycho-Educational Battery–Revised technical manual.* Chicago: Riverside.

Messick, S. (1989). Validity. In R. Linn (Ed.), *Educational Measurement* (3rd ed., pp. 131–104). Washington, DC: American Council on Education.

Paik, M., & Nebenzahl, E. (1987). The overall percentile rank versus the individual percentile ranks. *The American Statistician, 41,* 136–138.

Reschly, D. J., & Grimes, J. P. (1995). Intellectual assessment. In A. Thomas & J. Grimes (Eds.), *Best practices in school psychology* (Vol. 3, pp. 763–774). Washington, DC: The National Association of School Psychologists.

Sandoval, J., Frisby, C. L., Geisenger, K. F., Scheuneman, J. D., & Grenier, J. R. (Eds.). (1998). *Test interpretation and diversity: Achieving equality in assessment.* Washington, DC: American Psychological Association.

Vanderwood, M., McGrew, K. S., Flanagan, D. P., & Keith, T. Z. (2000). *Examination of the contribution of general and specific cognitive abilities to reading achievement.* Manuscript submitted for publication.

Watkins, M. W., & Kush, J. C. (1994). Wechsler subtest analysis: The right way, the wrong way, or no way? *School Psychology Review, 23,* 640–651.

Woodcock, R. W. (1994). Measures of fluid and crystallized intelligence. In R. J. Sternberg (Ed.), *The encyclopedia of intelligence* (pp. 452–456). New York: Macmillan.

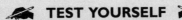

👈 TEST YOURSELF 👉

1. **Meaningful and defensible interpretation of CHC Cross-Battery data includes an understanding of which of the following:**

   (a) literature on the relations between cognitive abilities specified by CHC theory and specific academic and occupational outcomes.

   (b) principles and philosophies underlying the CHC Cross-Battery approach to assessing cognitive functioning.

   (c) network of validity evidence that exists in support of the structure and nature of abilities within CHC theory.

   (d) all of the above

2. **Which of the following situations might warrant additional assessment within a broad ability domain?**

   (a) A statistically significant difference is found between narrow abilities in a broad domain, and the lower score is more than 1 SD below the normative mean.

   (b) Both narrow abilities within the broad domain are discrepant from one another and significantly below that of most other CHC domains.

   (c) Detailed analysis of the narrow ability (or abilities within the domain) is deemed useful in understanding the individual's presenting difficulties.

   (d) all of the above

3. **The most common situation in which a posteriori hypotheses and additional assessment will be used occurs when there is a significant difference between two measures of a particular cognitive ability that fail to converge as expected.** True or False?

4. **In CHC Cross-Battery assessment, the basic criterion for rejecting the null hypothesis is set at the level of**

   (a) $> \pm.5$ SD of the mean.

   (b) $> \pm 1$ SD of the mean.

   (c) $> \pm 2$ SD of the mean.

   (d) $> \pm 3$ SD of the mean.

5. **If the confidence bands for any two test scores or clusters touch or overlap, practitioners can assume that any observed difference between ability scores being compared is significant.** True or False?

(continued)

6. **Which of the following is a reason that scores on similar measures may not converge as expected in accordance with the theory underlying CHC Cross-Battery assessment?**

   (a) inherent differences in an individual's narrow abilities

   (b) differences in the demands required by one task versus another

   (c) anomalous or extraneous influences that affect the administration or performance

   (d) cultural or linguistic factors

   (e) all of the above

7. **Which of the following is not true of traditional subtest (or ipsative) analysis?**

   (a) Ipsative scores have near-zero (and typically negative) intercorrelations.

   (b) Ipsative scores tend not to be stable over time.

   (c) Ipsative scores have properties that make attempts at remediation a no-win situation (e.g., their sum equals zero).

   (d) Ipsative scores have average to high levels of construct and predictive validity.

8. **According to CHC Cross-Battery interpretive guidelines, proper interpretation at the narrow ability level requires at least two qualitatively different narrow ability indicators.** True or False?

9. **Confirmatory bias occurs when an examiner begins with preconceived notions regarding expected performance on a test.** True or False?

10. **When a statistically significant difference exists between two qualitatively different narrow ability indicators, the broad ability cluster score**

    (a) is likely a misleading estimate of the broad ability.

    (b) should not be interpreted.

    (c) should be considered an approximate estimate of the broad ability.

    (d) both (a) and (b)

11. **The primary level of analysis in CHC Cross-Battery interpretation is**

    (a) the narrow (stratum I) ability level.

    (b) the broad (stratum II) ability level.

    (c) neither (a) nor (b)—there is no primary level of analysis in CHC Cross-Battery interpretation.

12. When functioning within a broad ability domain cannot be interpreted, practitioners can take which of the following actions?

(a) Administer two additional measures (one for each of the corresponding narrow abilities).

(b) Administer one additional narrow ability measure that corresponds to the *weakest* ability.

(c) Leave the broad ability cluster uninterpreted.

(d) All of the above are potentially appropriate actions, depending on the context of the assessment.

Answers: 1. d; 2. d; 3. True; 4. b; 5. False; 6. e; 7. d; 8. False; 9. True; 10. d; 11. b; 12. d

Four

Although the preceding chapters outlined the complete set of procedures involved in CHC Cross-Battery assessment and interpretation, additional considerations may arise that can influence various aspects of the approach. Probably the most common among such considerations involves the need to derive a global ability score, related primarily to compliance with various legal mandates. Specifically, an additional and important consideration in the use of CHC Cross-Battery assessment concerns its relationship to the "ability-achievement discrepancy" component embedded in most legal definitions of and criteria for diagnosing learning disability (see Appendix F for the prevailing definitions of learning disability).

Legislative requirements, in particular special education law (Individuals with Disabilities Act of 1997 [IDEA]), typically create a need to frame the results of any assessment approach, including a cross-battery assessment, within a context that allows for the determination and calculation of ability-achievement discrepancies. Such a need is often codified at the state level into legal mandates that specify particular methods that must be followed in order to establish this discrepancy. This is unfortunate because there is much research demonstrating the limited utility of the ability-achievement discrepancy model and indeed the *invalidity* of this method (e.g., "severe" discrepancy) as the *sole* criterion for identifying and diagnosing learning disability (see Flanagan, McGrew, & Ortiz, 2000, for a summary of this literature). Nonetheless, practitioners are often required by law to include an ability-achievement discrepancy component in their evaluations of individuals suspected of having learning disability. Because CHC Cross-Battery assessment yields multiple cognitive ability clusters for the purpose of examining underlying cognitive strengths and weaknesses, it does not incorporate a global ability score. Therefore, practitioners who use the CHC Cross-Battery approach are often at a loss when deciding on the most time-efficient way to incorporate and calculate a global ability score in their cross-battery-based assessments, particularly for use in ability-achievement discrepancy formulas. This chapter will provide information necessary to make informed decisions regarding: (a) the utility of the ability-achievement discrepancy model in (cross-battery) assessment of learning disability; (b) the manner in which a global ability score can be derived within the context of CHC Cross-Battery assessments; and (c) how to meaningfully interpret the results of an ability-achievement discrepancy analysis within the context of the CHC Cross-Battery approach.

THE ABILITY-ACHIEVEMENT DISCREPANCY
MODEL IN PERSPECTIVE

There are probably few things more noxious to practitioners involved in psychological assessment than the need to integrate myriad legal mandates, school-based policies, statistical formulas, and conflicting theoretical perspectives into a defensible framework for identifying learning disabilities. The lack of precision found in each of these arenas notwithstanding, the need to establish a discrepancy between ability and achievement through the many varied and far-ranging prescriptions proffered from every corner of the psychoeducational realm creates a significant problem for many practitioners.

Ninety-eight percent of the states incorporate the notion of *discrepancy* in their translations of the federally based special education definition of learning disability contained in IDEA (PL 105-17). Two-thirds of states provide criteria for determining how large a discrepancy must exist between ability and achievement before it is considered severe (Mercer, Jordan, Allsop, & Mercer, 1995). The *Diagnostic and Statistical Manual of Mental Disorders–Fourth Edition* (*DSM-IV;* American Psychiatric Association, 1994) includes in its criteria for diagnosing a learning disorder, "... achievement, as measured by individually administered standardized tests ... [that is] substantially below that expected [i.e., more than 2 standard deviations below IQ {p. 46}] given the person's chronological age, measured intelligence, and age-appropriate education" (p. 50). It is clear that the "driving clinical force" in diagnosing learning disability (Gridley & Roid, 1998, p. 250) involves a discrepancy between ability (aptitude or potential) and achievement (Lyons, 1995; Mather & Roberts, 1994). In spite of the abundance of well-reasoned and empirically supported arguments *against* using ability-achievement discrepancy criteria to diagnose learning disability, "the fact remains that many clinicians are obligated by laws and regulations to determine such discrepancies on a daily basis" (Gridley & Roid, 1998, p. 252).

It is beyond the scope of this chapter to provide a detailed discussion of the problems associated with the use of or sole reliance on ability-achievement discrepancy formulas in the evaluation of learning disability. Clearly, there are several false assumptions and beliefs surrounding the utility of various ability-achievement discrepancy approaches (see Flanagan, McGrew, et al., 2000, for a comprehensive discussion). The most common misconceptions related to the ability-achievement discrepancy approach are summarized for the reader in Table 4.1 in a "common beliefs/clarifications" format.

After reviewing the information in Table 4.1, it should be apparent that the meaning of an ability-achievement discrepancy is largely dependent upon: (a) the content (i.e., specific cognitive ability mix) of the general-ability measure (i.e., score) that is used in an ability-achievement discrepancy formula; and (b) the relations between the cognitive abilities that comprise the general-ability score and the achievement domain in question. The information in this table highlights the fact that ability-achievement *discrepancies,* in and of themselves, do not provide much insight into the nature of a learning disability. Nevertheless, the current criteria for documenting a learning disability have not caught up to (i.e., do not reflect) the current research that argues strongly against the use of or reliance on an ability-achievement discrepancy model.

Given the degree to which the concept of ability-achievement discrepancies has been codified into various federal and state statutes, it is unlikely to disappear from the practical reality of psychoeducational assessment anytime soon. We recognize that this endeavor, however precarious it may be, remains a fact of life for applied psychologists. With this reality in mind, the following sections of this chapter provide examples and guidelines regarding how to conduct a Comprehensive Cross-Battery (C-CB) assessment, while at the same time addressing the need to generate a global ability score for use in ability-achievement discrepancy formulas. It is important to realize that the recommendations offered herein are based mainly on three important conditions: (a) the need to derive a global ability estimate in C-CB assessment; (b) the manner in which a given intelligence battery can be supplemented via CHC Cross-Battery principles and procedures to ensure coverage of the major CHC

Common Beliefs	Clarifications
As long as I use a formula for determining significant ability-achievement discrepancies, my diagnostic decisions based on such discrepancies are supported	Numerous formulas and methods for determining significant ability-achievement discrepancies exist; only a few are technically valid (see McGrew, 1994). For example, the commonly used methods of deviation from grade level and scatter analysis are technically *invalid*. Predicted-achievement methods using regression formulas are technically *valid*. Notwithstanding, a finding of a significant difference between ability and achievement provides evidence for a learning disability only when several other sources of data (e.g., behavioral observations, work samples, educational history and nature of instruction, etc.) corroborate the diagnosis, especially an underlying or *intrinsic* deficit(s) that is/are empirically or logically linked to the academic skill deficit(s).
Ability-achievement discrepancy analysis and *aptitude*-achievement discrepancy analysis are the same thing,	*Ability* and *aptitude* are not synonymous. "An ability is a power to perform some specified act or task, either the physical or mental" (Snow, 1994, p. 3). The general, broad, and narrow abilities specified in CHC theory are important aspects of ability. *Aptitude* "includes any enduring personal characteristics that are propaedeutic to successful performance in some particular situation . . . [C]ognitive abilities are a particularly important source of aptitude for learning and performance in many school and work situations" (Snow, 1994, p. 4). Aptitude measures are validated for a particular purpose through demonstrating that they predict important external criteria (e.g., specific academic skills). For example, the WJ-R yields a Broad Cognitive Ability cluster as well as Scholastic Aptitude clusters. The WJ-R Aptitude Clusters consist of only four cognitive-ability tests each and predict their respective outcome criterion (e.g., reading achievement, math achievement, etc.) better than both the 7-test and 14-test Broad Cognitive Ability clusters. Because aptitude measures, like those on the WJ-R, predict academic criteria better than do global ability measures (simply because they were validated for this purpose), they will provide different results than ability measures when used in ability/aptitude-achievement discrepancy formulas.
The Wechsler Full Scale IQ and similar general intelligence index scores are the best scores to use in ability-achievement discrepancy formulas.	The ability-achievement discrepancy model is a *model of prediction*. Therefore, aptitude measures (such as the WJ-R Scholastic Aptitude clusters) are the best measures to use when calculating ability-achievement discrepancies. This is because aptitude measures are better predictors than general ability measures (e.g., FSIQ) of the outcome criteria (which they were designed to predict). Because aptitude measures are designed for the purpose of prediction, they are better than global ability measures for use in discrepancy formulas (see McGrew, 1994, for a discussion).

(continued)

Table 4.1 (continued)

Common Beliefs	Clarifications
A significant ability-achievement discrepancy must be present to support a diagnosis of learning disability	If an individual demonstrates a cognitive ability deficit(s) in an area with an established relation to the academic difficulty, and if the individual had an *ability-* or *aptitude-achievement consistency* (i.e., there was no significant discrepancy between aptitude and achievement), then the cognitive ability deficit together with the aptitude-achievement consistency may provide evidence of an underlying learning problem. In other words, it is expected that an individual with an academic skill deficit that is the result of *intrinsic* cognitive factors would have a measured aptitude (consisting of only those abilities that significantly predict that academic skill) that is consistent with measured achievement. The finding of an aptitude-achievement consistency coupled with a cognitive-ability deficit in one or more areas associated with the academic deficit(s) provides stronger evidence for an underlying disability than either an aptitude- or ability-achievement discrepancy, in and of itself.
All total test scores are created equal. In other words, it does not matter which global score one plugs into an ability-achievement discrepancy formula, the result will be the same.	A significant amount of variation exists across intelligence batteries in terms of what CHC abilities are included in their respective total test composites (see Table 4.2 in this chapter). For example, the Full Scale IQ of a Wechsler battery consists of mainly Gv and Gc abilities, while the WJ-R Broad Cognitive Ability cluster consists of an equally weighted combination of Gf, Gc, Gv, Ga, Glr, Gsm, and Gs abilities. The global ability scores of other major intelligence batteries consist of some differentially weighted combination of at least two or more of the broad CHC cognitive abilities. Because the cognitive ability content of total test composites is different for different batteries, the results of ability-achievement discrepancy analyses depend, in part, on the ability measure used. Differences in content across predictor variables (i.e., global ability scores) *will* result in differing amounts of variance explained in the criterion variable (i.e., academic achievement). It seems clear that this condition alone undermines the utility and validity of the ability-achievement discrepancy as either the sole or most salient criterion in learning disability diagnosis.
Ability and achievement are mutually exclusive. In other words, they represent two distinct constructs.	The difference between ability and achievement is a popular *verbal* distinction. Cognitive and academic abilities lie on a continuum with those abilities that develop largely through formal education, direct learning, and instruction at one end (e.g., Grw, Gq) and those that develop as a result of informal and indirect learning and instruction at the other end (e.g., Gf).

Common Beliefs	Clarifications
We should pay attention to the controversies surrounding whether ability *or* achievement tests should be used to understand the source of specific academic problems (e.g., Siegel, 1998).	Both intelligence and achievement tests provide useful information. The controversy regarding what type of test ought to be used in the assessment of learning problems appears to have been sparked by a lack of understanding of what IQ and achievement tests measure, as well as a lack of knowledge of comprehensive and validated models of the structure of human cognitive abilities. Because of the continuous (rather than dichotomous) nature of cognitive and academic abilities, advocating for either ability or achievement measures to assess individuals with learning difficulties is unfounded. Instead, practitioners should review referral information, decide what skills and abilities ought to be evaluated, and then choose the best instruments for measuring these skills and abilities, be they cognitive tests, achievement tests, or some combination thereof.
Because in many cases we are mandated by law to report a significant ability-achievement discrepancy as part of a comprehensive learning disability evaluation, the finding of a severe discrepancy between ability and achievement is a diagnostic criterion of learning disability that is supported by research.	The research shows unequivocally that a significant ability-achievement discrepancy, in and of itself, is an *invalid* method of identifying or diagnosing a learning disability. For example, there is overwhelming evidence to support the conclusion that the method of separating poor readers on the sole basis of a severe ability-achievement discrepancy is of questionable significance. Likewise, Siegel (1998) concluded, "the IQ-achievement discrepancy score serves no useful purpose in defining or understanding reading disabilities" (p. 131). Unfortunately, current criteria for documenting a learning disability has not caught up to the research that fails to support the reliance on an ability-achievement discrepancy model.

Note. From *The Wechsler intelligence scales and Gf-Gc Theory: A Contemporary approach to interpretation*, by D. P. Flanagan, K. S. McGrew, and S. O. Ortiz, 2000, Boston: Allyn & Bacon. Copyright 2000 by the publisher. Adapted with permission of Allyn & Bacon.

broad abilities in assessment; and (c) the manner in which practitioners can achieve the previous two objectives without increasing testing time. Practitioners can use the recommendations in this chapter with information about the nature of the referral, the nature of the individual being tested, and the psychometric, qualitative, and theoretical characteristics of the cognitive ability tests at their disposal to guide their selection of both the core battery and supplemental batteries used in C-CB assessment (McGrew & Flanagan, 1998).

The "Need" for a Full Scale IQ

Many practitioners emphasize the *need* to generate a Full Scale IQ (very often a Wechsler Full Scale IQ in particular), stating that it is mandated by their state regulations or school district policy, for use in ability-achievement discrepancy formulas required to document a learning disability. Requirements like these only emphasize the often ludicrous restrictions and constraints placed on practitioners. Such blind endorsement of a Wechsler Full Scale IQ (and the need to document a significant FSIQ-achievement discrepancy) negates flexibility in assessment approaches and hinders the use of a more clinically based assessment model (Brackett & McPherson, 1996). In some cases, the lack of flexibility in choice and usage of assessment instruments and the inability to exercise a more clinically based model in diagnostic decision making (due to various mandates) has the unfortunate result of encouraging practitioners to literally search for significant discrepancies to support otherwise sound, data-based judgments about disability that are grounded in psychometric theory and research.

The very need to document a significant discrepancy between ability and achievement, and hence the process of searching for discrepancies using various IQs (e.g., FSIQ, VIQ, PIQ), often results in failure to gather more pertinent information necessary to support a diagnosis of learning disability (e.g., an intrinsic cognitive processing deficit). According to Reynolds (1984–1985), "an astute diagnostician can qualify between 50% and 80% of a random sample of the population as having a learning disability that requires special education services" by using various discrepancy formulas espoused by the states (p. 454; cited in Brackett & McPherson, 1996). Many practitioners who have gathered sufficient data that support a diagnosis of learning disability (e.g., specific and circumscribed cognitive-processing deficits, in an otherwise above-average or better profile of cognitive performance, that are linked to the academic skill deficits; multiple sources of corroborating data; documentation showing that the impairment is longstanding and not the result of external factors; etc.) cannot secure the appropriate services for the individual without first finding and documenting a discrepancy between ability and achievement. Conversely, it is often easier to secure services for the individual who demonstrates an ability-achievement discrepancy, even in the absence of evidence for an intrinsic impairment or deficit. These two scenarios highlight one of the inherent frailties of the ability-achievement discrepancy model.

Reliance on an IQ score in diagnostic decision-making also ignores the fact that "it is impossible to predict specific disabilities and areas of cognitive competency or dysfunction from the averaged ability test scores" (Lezak, 1995, p. 691). In that light, the *mandated* use of IQ scores appears rather indefensible. Lezak further argued:

> [It] has been suggested that examiners retain IQ scores in their reports to conform to the current requirements of . . . various other administrative agencies . . . [T]his is not merely a case of the tail wagging the dog but an example of how outdated practices may be perpetuated even when their invalidity and potential harmfulness has been demonstrated. Clinicians have a responsibility not only to maintain the highest—and most current—practice standards, but to communicate these to the consumer agencies. If every clinician who understands the problems inherent in labeling people with IQ scores ceased using them, then agencies would soon cease asking for them. (p. 691)

The problems associated with over-reliance on a Full Scale IQ and the ability-achievement discrepancy model aside, the purpose here is to provide guidelines for practitioners who must operate within such narrow guidelines in accordance with whatever misguided administrative requirements that might exist and bind clinical judgment or decision making. Given the perilous nature of the practice of using or relying on analysis of ability-achievement discrepancies, practitioners are strongly advised to continue in efforts to substantiate the diagnosis of learning disability with information and data from multiple, convergent sources. The guidelines presented in this chapter will, nevertheless, allow for the inclusion of ability-achievement discrepancy analyses within the context of the contemporary theory-based, psychometrically defensible CHC Comprehensive Cross-Battery (C-CB) approach, irrespective of the limited utility, defensibility, and interpretability of such discrepancy analyses.

LEARNING DISABILITY AND C-CB ASSESSMENT

Briefly, after the need for standardized assessment is established, the C-CB approach outlined in Chapter 2 places primary emphasis on the intracognitive and intercognitive components of assessment. Typically, intracognitive cross-battery data are evaluated simultaneously with intra-achievement data to determine whether meaningful relationships exist between cognitive and academic functions, particularly those that have emerged as deficient relative to people of the same age or grade in the general population. Following the evaluation of cognitive and academic performance, if a meaningful connection is made between weak cognitive performance in one or more areas and the academic skill area(s) in question, then reexamination of potential exclusionary criteria is necessary in an effort to completely rule out external factors and influences that may explain manifest deficit performance. Of course, application of exclusionary criteria (e.g., cultural and linguistic factors, environmental influences, etc.) begins at or before the time of referral (e.g., in prereferral consultation with teachers, through a formal process of evaluating prereferral difficulties, or during implementation and evaluation of systematic educational interventions, etc.) and continues throughout the assessment process (see Chapters 3 and 5). However, particular and careful emphasis should be placed on exclusionary criteria at this stage, precisely because a cognitive deficit has been preliminarily identified and should be assumed to be *extrinsic* until all reasonable external factors have been ruled out.

When it has been determined that an identified cognitive ability deficit(s) can be reasonably linked to the academic skill deficit(s) (e.g., through supporting research and other corroborative data sources), and, when exclusionary criteria have been ruled out as potential *primary* causes for deficit performance, then there is little need to advance further in the assessment process with respect to testing. Rather, the focus should turn to intervention and to developing methods to link cognitive and academic *intra-individual* strengths to specific strategies for the individual in an effort to improve identified skill deficiencies. Yet, because many practitioners operate under mandates that require them to report a significant ability-achievement discrepancy when documenting a learning disability (e.g., to receive federal funding for special education services), additional evaluation activities may have to be performed. In this regard, it is imperative that the importance or *meaningfulness* of a significant or nonsignificant ability-achievement discrepancy be emphasized within the context of a comprehensive learning disability evaluation. Prior to the discussion of the meaningfulness of ability-achievement discrepancies, however, it is important to examine the ways in which core intelligence batteries can be used in C-CB assessments when a global ability measure is necessary for the purpose of conducting ability-achievement discrepancy analyses.

C-CB Assessment and Global Ability Scores

The most obvious method for ensuring that a global ability score is obtained in the course of CHC Cross-Battery assessment is to administer the tests that comprise a global score from the core battery used in the assessment (e.g., tests that comprise the Wechsler FSIQ or the WJ-R BCA). Following the administration of these tests, practitioners can augment or supplement them with tests from other batteries as may be needed to broaden the assessment. Depending on the core battery used in assessment, however, the drawback of this method is that in some cases it may increase average testing time. Nevertheless, whenever the need for a global score is deemed necessary or is in fact legally required in an assessment, it can be readily integrated into a cross-battery framework. Several examples of assessment that incorporate a global score within the context of CHC Cross-Battery assessment follow.

WISC-III–based CHC Cross-Battery Assessments and Global Ability Measures

WISC-III: Full Scale IQ
The most popular core batteries used by practitioners in the evaluation of individuals with a variety of cognitive deficits or learning problems are the Wechsler Intelligence Scales (Wechsler, 1989, 1991, 1997). When practitioners who use these scales routinely are mandated by law or other administrative regulations to obtain global IQ scores, they would need to administer the subtests from these respective batteries that comprise the FSIQ irrespective of the considerations

that may have guided a cross-battery assessment in the first place. In the case of the Wechsler Intelligence Scale for Children–Third Edition (WISC-III; Wechsler, 1991; see Rapid Reference 4.1), 10 subtests would need to be administered: five from the Verbal Scale (Information, Vocabulary, Similarities, Comprehension, Arithmetic) and five from the Performance Scale (Block Design, Object Assembly, Picture Completion, Picture Arrangement, Coding). This combination of WISC-III tests is depicted in Figure 4.1. Specifically, the solid arrows pointing from the FSIQ oval in this figure to the Gc/VIQ and Gv/PIQ ovals (which represent composites) as well as to the Coding rectangle (or subtest) depict the combination of WISC-III tests that constitute the FSIQ.

When evaluated from the CHC theoretical perspective, Figure 4.1 shows that the tests that comprise the FSIQ (i.e., tests printed in the white rectangles) measure mainly Gc and Gv abilities. This is denoted in the figure by the arrows pointing from the FSIQ oval to the Gc/VIQ and Gv/PIQ ovals, which in turn have arrows pointing to five rectangles or WISC-III subtests each. Gs (Coding) and Gq (Arithmetic) are measured to a much lesser extent by the tests that make up the FSIQ. Thus, the WISC-III core battery of tests together measures a very

---

⚏Rapid Reference 4.1

Wechsler Intelligence Scale for Children–Third Edition

Author: David Wechsler

Publication Date: 1949–1991

Age Range: 6:0 to 16:11

Publisher: The Psychological Corporation

Further Information: For information on the psychometric, theoretical, and qualitative characteristics of the individual tests in this battery, see:

Flanagan, D. P., McGrew, K. S. & Ortiz, S. O. (2000). *The Wechsler intelligence scales and Gf-Gc theory: A contemporary approach to interpretation.* Boston: Allyn & Bacon.

Kaufman, A. S. (1994). *Intelligent testing with the WISC-III.* New York: Wiley.

Kaufman, A. S., & Lichtenberger, E. O. (2000). *Essentials of WPPSI-R and WISC-III Assessment.* New York: Wiley.

McGrew, K. S., & Flanagan, D. P. (1998). *The intelligence test desk reference (ITDR): Gf-Gc cross-battery assessment.* Boston: Allyn & Bacon.

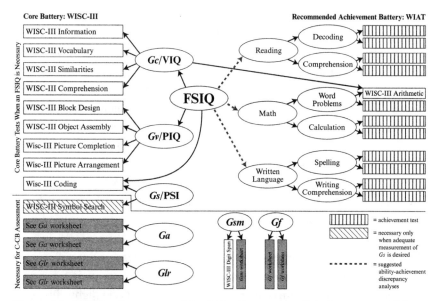

Figure 4.1 Abilities Represented (and Not Represented) in Assessment When a WISC-III FSIQ is Derived

limited number of CHC abilities. The implications that this relatively poor FSIQ-CHC theory match has for C-CB assessment are essentially twofold.

First, when the WISC-III is selected as the core battery in C-CB assessment and it has been deemed necessary to determine the FSIQ, then the assessment will consist of unnecessary *redundancy* in measurement of both *Gc* and *Gv* abilities. For instance, if neither *Gc* nor *Gv* are areas of particular or selective concern in a given evaluation, but it is still considered necessary to sample functioning in these areas, then only *two* (rather than four) qualitatively different indicators of each would be appropriate. From the perspective of a typical, initial C-CB assessment, in which the purpose is to gather baseline information about cognitive functioning across a comprehensive range of broad abilities, the need to calculate an FSIQ results in the administration of essentially five unnecessary tests (i.e., two extra *Gc* tests, two extra *Gv* tests, and a *Gq* test). The time allocated to the administration of redundant *Gc* and *Gv* measures, for example, could be used more meaningfully to assess abilities not measured by the WISC-III (e.g., abilities that are important in the explanation of academic skill development), such as *Ga, Glr,* and *Gf.*

Second, when the 10 core battery subtests of the WISC-III are used to calculate the FSIQ within the context of CHC Cross-Battery assessment, the result is an underrepresentation of two potentially important abilities, *Gs* and *Gq*. However, adequate measurement of both abilities can be achieved with relative ease and efficiency. That is, if practitioners are interested in an individual's broad *Gs* ability, then the Symbol Search test can be administered as an additional test. The combination of Symbol Search and Coding (depicted in Figure 4.1 as the CHC *Gs* cluster or WISC-III Speed of Processing Index) will provide the basic information necessary to evaluate functioning in this area. If practitioners are interested in *Gq*, then it is most appropriate to evaluate an individual's performance on a variety of math tests from standardized achievement batteries. In other words, because *Gq* (and by association, the abilities underlying the WISC-III Arithmetic subtest) is measured sufficiently by standardized achievement batteries, it is not necessary to measure this ability when conducting C-CB assessments. The placement of the Arithmetic test on the right side of Figure 4.1 with other math achievement tests highlights this point. In the event that the WISC-III Arithmetic test was administered, however, practitioners may have reason to hypothesize that performance on this test (a test of primarily math achievement) was attenuated by difficulties in Working Memory. If practitioners are interested in testing this hypothesis, then it would be most appropriate to examine and administer tests from the Working Memory section of the *Gsm* worksheet (in Appendix A) and evaluate and compare Arithmetic performance with *Gsm*-MW performance, within the context of other background information and behavioral data.

Indeed, there are many occasions when practitioners are interested in measuring a broader range of abilities than that assessed by the WISC-III. In these situations, practitioners should follow the CHC Cross-Battery principles and procedures (from Chapter 2) and systematically augment the WISC-III core battery tests with tests from other batteries to ensure that all necessary cognitive ability components of the assessment are well represented. The cognitive ability domains that are either not assessed or not assessed adequately by the WISC-III core battery tests are presented below the heavy, solid horizontal line in the bottom half of Figure 4.1.

A review of the lower portion of Figure 4.1 shows that four CHC broad abilities are not measured by the WISC-III *core battery* tests (i.e., *Gsm, Ga, Glr, Gf*), despite the fact that these abilities have been found to contribute significantly to the explanation of academic skill development in a number of areas and, to different degrees, at different developmental levels (e.g., Flanagan, 2000; Keith, 1999; McGrew, 1993; McGrew, Flanagan, Keith, & Vanderwood, 1997; Vanderwood, McGrew, Flanagan, & Keith, 2000). Therefore, measurement of these abilities will likely be appropriate to test a variety of hypotheses generated from referral information, especially those embedded within the psychoeducational realm. The reader is referred to Chapter 2, where an example of a WISC-III–based C-CB assessment was presented in Table 2.3.

Figure 4.1 also shows dotted arrows pointing from the oval depicting the FSIQ to the ovals that represent Reading, Math, and Written Language. These arrows demonstrate the most frequently made ability-achievement discrepancy calculations in assessments of individuals suspected of having a learning disability. The ovals for Reading, Math, and Written Language (or general-achievement composites) have arrows, each pointing to two other ovals. These ovals represent academic subskill composites of the respective general-achievement domains. For example, general reading achievement in Figure 4.1 is composed of reading decoding and reading comprehension. The arrows pointing from these subskill ovals to the striped rectangles (which represent academic achievement tests) demonstrates that at least two tests should be used to represent each academic subskill, especially when subskill composites are used in ability-achievement discrepancy analyses. Like CHC-specific cognitive abilities, specific academic skills should be summarized in a composite that is composed of at least two measures of the skill in question. Following this recommendation will improve upon reliability and validity in measures of these academic skills.

In short, when both the calculation of a WISC-III FSIQ as well as adequate measurement of *Gsm, Ga, Glr, Gs,* and *Gf* abilities (or some combination thereof) are desired, then WISC-III–based C-CB assessment will likely increase average testing time. There are, however, two alternative solutions to ensure that a Wechsler-based global ability score is included in C-CB assessments—solutions that are both more time-efficient and practical than administering the 10 WISC-III core battery tests; these options are discussed in the following sections.

WISC-III: General Ability Index

An alternative composite score, called the *General Ability Index* (GAI), was provided recently by Prifitera, Weiss, and Saklofske (1998). As depicted in Figure

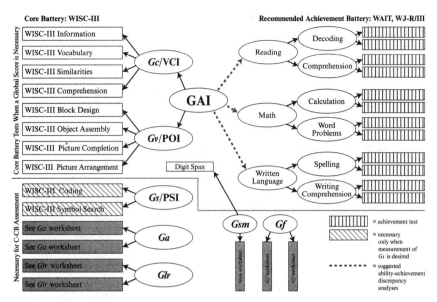

Figure 4.2 Abilities Represented (and Not Represented) in Assessment When a WISC-III GAI is Derived

4.2, the GAI is composed of the four WISC-III subtests that make up the Verbal Comprehension Index (or VCI: Information, Vocabulary, Similarities, and Comprehension) and the four subtests that make up the Perceptual Organization Index (or POI: Block Design, Object Assembly, Picture Completion, and Picture Arrangement). What distinguishes the GAI from the FSIQ is its *exclusion* of the Arithmetic and Coding subtests. The benefit of the GAI over the FSIQ in C-CB assessment is that practitioners can derive a global score through the administration of 8 rather than 10 subtests. Therefore, derivation of the GAI is slightly more time-efficient than calculation of the FSIQ.

In addition, the GAI does not include math achievement (i.e., the WISC-III Arithmetic subtest). Therefore, it is a more appropriate index than the FSIQ in ability–math achievement discrepancy analyses, simply because it does not use math achievement to predict math achievement (see McGrew, 1994, for a discussion). Essentially, the GAI is derived from *purer* measures of *Gc* abilities (i.e., VCI) and *Gv* abilities (i.e., POI) than the FSIQ is. This is because the FSIQ includes, in addition to the VCI and POI tests, Arithmetic and Coding, tests that are not as highly correlated with *Gc* and *Gv* abilities, respectively, as are the other tests that make up these composites (Prifitera et al., 1998).

According to Prifitera and colleagues (1998), the GAI may be reported under the following conditions:

1. When interpretation of verbal abilities focuses on the VCI rather than the VIQ. In other words, when Arithmetic is significantly different than the mean of the student's five Verbal subtest scaled scores.
2. When POI is interpreted over the PIQ. That is, when Coding is significantly different than the mean of the student's five Performance subtests.
3. When both VIQ and PIQ are abandoned in favor of interpreting VCI and POI. (p. 19)

From the perspective of traditional approaches to Wechsler test interpretation (i.e., psychometric profile analysis), the recommendations of Prifitera and colleagues (1998) provide well-reasoned and rational interpretive procedures. Likewise, the use of the GAI in lieu of the FSIQ whenever it is deemed necessary to calculate a global ability score in C-CB organized assessments is also recommended. The rationale for use of the GAI is twofold. First, the GAI includes fewer subtests than the FSIQ and, therefore, requires less time in test administration. The time saved can be better used to assess additional abilities related to referral issues—abilities not represented in the GAI. Second, although the use of the GAI in C-CB assessments (like the use of the FSIQ) is characterized by redundancy in the measurement of *Gc* and *Gv* abilities, these abilities are measured more *cleanly* in GAI-based assessments (using the VCI and POI) than in FSIQ-based assessments (using VIQ and PIQ). Specifically, the VIQ and PIQ contain construct-irrelevant variance (i.e., Arithmetic and Coding, respectively), which compromises the validity of interpretations drawn from these global ability estimates (see Chapter 1 for a discussion), whereas the GAI does not.

According to Prifitera and colleagues (1998), when the GAI is calculated, it can be used in ability-achievement discrepancy analyses for the purpose of determining eligibility for services for learning disabilities in the same way as the FSIQ can be used. The use of the GAI in this way is depicted in Figure 4.2 by the dotted arrows pointing from the oval representing the GAI to the ovals representing reading, math, and written language. The norms for calculating a GAI were derived using the standardization data of the WISC-III and are provided in Table 4.2. This table should be used in the following manner, according to Prifitera and colleagues:

Table 4.2 General Ability Index Equivalents of Sums of Scaled Scores

Sum of Scaled Scores	GAI	Percentile rank	Confidence interval 90%	95%	Sum of scaled scores	GAI	Percentile rank	Confidence interval 90%	95%
8	50	< .1	47–58	46–59	51	78	7	74–84	73–85
9	50	< .1	47–58	46–59	52	79	8	75–85	74–86
10	50	< .1	47–58	46–59	53	79	8	75–85	74–86
11	50	< .1	47–58	46–59	54	80	9	76–86	75–87
12	50	< .1	47–58	46–59	55	81	10	77–87	76–88
13	50	< .1	47–58	46–59	56	81	10	77–87	76–88
14	50	< .1	47–58	46–59	57	82	12	78–88	77–89
15	50	< .1	47–58	46–59	58	83	13	79–89	78–90
16	50	< .1	47–58	46–59	59	84	14	80–90	79–91
17	51	0.1	48–59	47–60	60	84	14	80–90	79–91
18	52	0.1	49–60	48–61	61	85	16	80–91	80–92
19	53	0.1	50–61	49–62	62	86	18	81–92	80–93
20	54	0.1	51–62	50–63	63	87	19	82–93	81–94
21	55	0.1	52–63	51–63	64	88	21	83–94	82–95
22	56	0.2	53–63	52–64	65	88	21	83–94	82–95
23	57	0.2	54–64	53–65	66	89	23	84–95	83–96
24	58	0.3	55–65	54–66	67	90	25	85–96	84–97
25	58	0.3	55–65	54–66	68	91	27	86–97	85–98
26	59	0.3	56–66	55–67	69	91	27	86–97	85–98
27	60	0.4	57–67	56–68	70	92	30	87–98	86–99
28	61	0.5	58–68	57–69	71	93	32	88–99	87–100
29	62	1	59–69	58–70	72	94	34	89–100	88–101
30	63	1	60–70	59–71	73	94	34	89–100	88–101
31	63	1	60–70	59–71	74	95	37	90–101	89–101
32	64	1	61–71	60–72	75	96	39	91–101	90–102
33	64	1	61–71	60–72	76	97	42	92–102	91–103
34	65	1	61–72	61–73	77	98	45	93–103	92–104
35	66	1	62–73	61–74	78	98	45	93–103	92–104
36	67	1	63–74	62–75	79	99	47	94–104	93–105
37	67	1	63–74	62–75	80	100	50	95–105	94–106
38	68	2	64–75	63–76	81	101	53	96–106	95–107
39	69	2	65–76	64–77	82	102	55	97–107	96–108
40	70	2	66–77	65–78	83	103	58	98–108	97–109
41	70	2	66–77	65–78	84	103	58	98–108	97–109
42	71	3	67–78	66–79	85	104	61	99–109	98–110
43	72	3	68–79	67–80	86	105	63	99–110	99–111
44	73	4	69–80	68–81	87	106	66	100–111	99–112
45	74	4	70–81	69–82	88	107	68	101–112	100–113
46	75	5	71–82	70–82	89	107	68	101–112	100–113
47	75	5	71–82	70–82	90	108	70	102–113	101–114
48	76	5	72–82	71–83	91	109	73	103–114	102–115
49	77	6	73–83	72–84	92	109	73	103–114	102–115
50	77	6	73–83	72–84	93	110	75	104–115	103–116

Sum of Scaled Scores	GAI	Percentile rank	Confidence interval 90%	Confidence interval 95%	Sum of scaled scores	GAI	Percentile rank	Confidence interval 90%	Confidence interval 95%
94	111	77	105–116	104–117	124	138	99	131–141	130–142
95	112	79	106–117	105–118	125	139	99.5	132–142	131–143
96	112	79	106–117	105–118	126	140	99.6	133–143	132–144
97	113	81	107–118	106–119	127	141	99.7	134–144	133–145
98	114	82	108–119	107–120	128	142	99.7	135–145	134–146
99	115	84	109–120	108–120	129	143	99.8	136–146	135–147
100	116	86	110–120	109–121	130	143	99.8	136–146	135–147
101	117	87	111–121	110–122	131	144	99.8	137–147	136–148
102	118	88	112–122	111–123	132	145	99.9	137–148	137–149
103	119	90	113–123	112–124	133	146	99.9	138–149	137–150
104	119	90	113–123	112–124	134	147	99.9	139–150	138–151
105	120	91	114–124	113–125	135	148	99.9	140–151	139–152
106	121	92	115–125	114–126	136	149	99.9	141–152	140–153
107	122	93	116–126	115–127	137	150	> 99.9	142–153	141–154
108	122	93	116–126	115–127	138	150	> 99.9	142–153	141–154
109	123	94	117–127	116–128	139	150	> 99.9	142–153	141–154
110	124	95	118–128	117–129	140	150	> 99.9	142–153	141–154
111	125	95	118–129	118–130	141	150	> 99.9	142–153	141–154
112	126	96	119–130	118–131	142	150	> 99.9	142–153	141–154
113	127	96	120–131	119–132	143	150	> 99.9	142–153	141–154
114	128	97	121–132	120–133	144	150	> 99.9	142–153	141–154
115	129	97	122–133	121–134	145	150	> 99.9	142–153	141–154
116	130	98	123–134	122–135	146	150	> 99.9	142–153	141–154
117	131	98	124–135	123–136	147	150	> 99.9	142–153	141–154
118	132	98	125–136	124–137	148	150	> 99.9	142–153	141–154
119	133	99	126–137	125–138	149	150	> 99.9	142–153	141–154
120	134	99	127–138	126–139	150	150	> 99.9	142–153	141–154
121	135	99	128–139	137–139	151	150	> 99.9	142–153	141–154
122	136	99	129–139	128–140	152	150	> 99.9	142–153	141–154
123	137	99	130–140	129–141					

Note. From *WISC-III Clinical Use and Interpretation* (p. 21), by A. Prifitera, L. G. Weiss, and D. Saklofske, 1998, San Diego: Academic. Data and table copyright 1997 by The Psychological Corporation. Reprinted by permission of the copyright holder. All rights reserved.

. . . [F]irst calculate the General Ability Sum of Scaled Scores (GASSS) by adding the scaled scores for the following eight subtests: Picture Completion, Information, Similarities, Picture Arrangement, Block Design, Vocabulary, Object Assembly, Comprehension. Find the resulting General Ability SSS in the column labeled Sum of Scaled Scores in Table [4.2] and read across the row to determine the GAI score, associated percentile rank, and confidence interval. (p. 19)

Prior to administering the tests that comprise the GAI, practitioners who are interested in a more comprehensive assessment should decide which additional cognitive ability measures would help clarify and illuminate the referral concerns (e.g., see Table 2.1 in Chapter 2). A review of Figure 4.2 shows that five broad cognitive abilities are not represented in the GAI (*Gs, Ga, Glr, Gsm,* and *Gf*). These are the abilities that fall below the solid horizontal line in the bottom half of Figure 4.2. If measurement of *Gs* or *Gsm* is desired, then additional WISC-III tests can be administered. Unlike *Gs,* however, adequate coverage of *Gsm* would require the administration of at least one test (preferably a Working Memory test) from another battery in a manner consistent with the guiding principles of the CHC Cross-Battery approach (see Chapters 1 and 2). Because the GAI consists of 8 subtests (compared to the WISC-III full battery, which consists of 13 subtests), it is possible to administer the GAI tests in addition to tests that adequately represent 2 to 3 cognitive abilities other than *Gc* and *Gv* in roughly the same time as it would take to administer a complete WISC-III battery. In such cases, a GAI-based cross-battery assessment would provide more information than an FSIQ-based cross-battery assessment without the expenditure of any additional time or effort, and possibly even with less. Nevertheless, it is still likely that in order to represent all the major broad CHC abilities in an assessment, additional testing time beyond that typically required for a complete WISC-III battery (for example) would be required.

WISC-III: WASI FSIQ-4

A second alternative to the use of the FSIQ involves the Wechsler Abbreviated Scale of Intelligence (WASI; The Psychological Corporation, 1999; see Rapid Reference 4.2). The WASI offers a means of deriving a valid and reliable estimate of global ability, called the Full Scale IQ–4 (FSIQ-4). The FSIQ-4 is composed of four subtests: Vocabulary, Similarities, Block Design, and Matrix Reasoning. This abbreviated global ability index is highly reliable at ages 6 to 16 years (.96)[1] and is highly correlated with the WISC-III FSIQ. Its correlation with the WISC-III FSIQ (.87) is similar in magnitude to the correlations that were reported between the WISC-R FSIQ and WISC-III FSIQ (i.e., .81 to .90;

---

[1] .96 is the average reliability of the FSIQ-4 for children ages 6 to 16 in the WASI standardization sample (The Psychological Corporation, 1999, p. 125).

≣*Rapid Reference 4.2*

Wechsler Abbreviated Scale of Intelligence

Author: The Psychological Corporation
Publication Date: 1999
Age Range: 6 to 89
Publisher: The Psychological Corporation
Further Information: For information on the psychometric, theoretical, and qualitative characteristics of the individual tests in this battery, see:

Flanagan, D. P., McGrew, K. S., & Ortiz, S. O. (2000). *The Wechsler intelligence scales and Gf-Gc theory: A contemporary approach to interpretation.* Boston: Allyn & Bacon.

Wechsler, 1991). Therefore, according to the publisher, the WASI FSIQ-4 appears to provide a reasonably good estimate of global ability (The Psychological Corporation, 1999).

Within the context of Wechsler-based C-CB assessment, the WASI FSIQ-4 represents perhaps the most practical solution to the mandated use of global ability scores in ability-achievement discrepancy analyses, when it is used *solely* for the purpose of providing support for existing evidence of a learning disability. As stated earlier, the primary focus of C-CB assessment is the examination of intracognitive and intercognitive strengths and weaknesses across the major CHC abilities specified in contemporary theory. In the assessment of learning disabilities in particular, the results of C-CB intracognitive and intercognitive analyses are important for the documentation of cognitive processing or ability deficits (related to the intrinsic component of most definitions of learning disability).

The documentation of a significant ability-achievement discrepancy is regarded as less important in C-CB assessment of learning disability, primarily because of its limited usefulness in understanding, identifying, and diagnosing this disorder (see Table 4.1 for a review). Therefore, when there exist sufficient corroborating data that support a relationship between (a) cognitive deficits, intrinsic to the individual (i.e., cannot be primarily explained by external factors); and (b) specific, manifest academic skill deficits (in an otherwise average or better profile of cognitive and academic capabilities),[2] then a significant discrepancy between some global ability score and the academic skill(s) in question only serves to corroborate or support what essentially amounts to a learning disability by most definitions (see Appendix F). Therefore, under certain circumstances, there appear to be sufficiently defensible grounds for using the WASI FSIQ-4 as the global ability estimate in ability-achievement discrepancy formulas. Rapid Reference 4.3 lists the criteria that *must* be met prior to interpreting the WASI FSIQ-4 in an ability-achievement discrepancy analysis.

If the criteria listed in Rapid Reference 4.3 are satisfied, it appears appropriate to report the results of an FSIQ-4–achievement discrepancy analysis and to use the finding of a significant discrepancy as further evidence in support of an underlying learning disability. However, even when criteria 1 through 6 are satisfied, the difference between the FSIQ-4 and the achievement area in question may not be significant. This finding, however, does not preclude a diagnosis of learning disability. That is, it may be the case that one of the tests comprising the WASI FSIQ-4 attenuated this index. For example, a significantly low score on Matrix Reasoning compared to the other FSIQ-4 tests will attenuate the global score. In this case, if a significant *Gf* weakness or deficit was identified as a contributing factor to poor performance in the academic skill area in question, then the finding of a WASI/FSIQ-4–achievement *consistency* provides further evidence in support of an underlying learning disability. These issues, particularly those related to the distinctions between the notions of discrepancy and consistency, are discussed further in the last section of this chapter.

---

[2] In this example, "in an otherwise average or better profile" refers to cases where (a) one or perhaps two broad abilities are identified as normative deficits [i.e., < 85; more than 1 SD below the normative mean of 100]; (b) the remainder of the measured broad abilities are identified as being within or above the average range [i.e., ≥ 85]; and (c) there is a logical relationship and consistency between these identified cognitive deficits and identified academic skills deficits. In such cases, a learning disability is evident, irrespective of the presence of any ability-achievement discrepancy. However, in cases where there are several cognitive abilities identified as deficiencies (e.g., a low to low average profile), practitioners will need to use clinical judgment and other data (e.g., information on adaptive behavior) in order to differentiate between one or more learning disabilities and possible mental retardation.

≡ Rapid Reference 4.3

Conditions for Appropriate Use of WASI FSIQ-4

The WASI FSIQ-4 is appropriate to use in ability-achievement discrepancy analysis within the context of a learning disability evaluation only when the following conditions are met:

1. The tests that comprise the WASI FSIQ-4 have been administered within the context of a Wechsler-based CHC Comprehensive Cross-Battery (C-CB) approach.

2. The difference between the examinee's WASI VIQ and PIQ is *not* statistically significant or unusual, rendering the FSIQ-4 the best estimate of global ability (see Tables B.3 and B.4 in the *WASI Manual*, The Psychological Corporation, 1999).

3. Intercognitive analysis of the Wechsler-based C-CB data (from item 1, above) revealed one or more specific cognitive-processing or -ability deficits (i.e., the confidence band for one or more CHC cluster averages fell greater than 1 SD below the mean) within an otherwise average or better profile of cognitive capabilities (i.e., standard scores that are generally ≥ 85).

4. A clear empirical (or logical) connection between the cognitive ability deficit(s) (from item 2, above) and the manifest academic-skill deficit(s) was documented.

5. Other sources of data were gathered or are available to support the cognitive and academic deficits identified through C-CB assessment.

6. A comprehensive review of case-history data (including educational records, medical history, language and cultural factors, behavioral observations, etc.) demonstrated that the cognitive and academic deficits are not the result of external factors or influences.

Use of the WASI FSIQ-4 as a global ability estimate in a WISC-III–based C-CB assessment seems to offer a viable alternative to the FSIQ and GAI for the following reasons. First, the four subtests comprising the WASI FSIQ-4 fit well within the CHC Cross-Battery framework. That is, the Similarities and Vocabulary subtests represent two qualitatively different indicators of *Gc*, thereby allowing for adequate representation of this ability in assessment. Block Design provides a strong measure of *Gv* and Matrix Reasoning provides a strong measure of *Gf*. Following the CHC Cross-Battery principles and procedures (outlined in Chapter 2), tests from the WISC-III (and perhaps other batteries) can be used to augment the WASI FSIQ-4 subtests to allow for adequate rep-

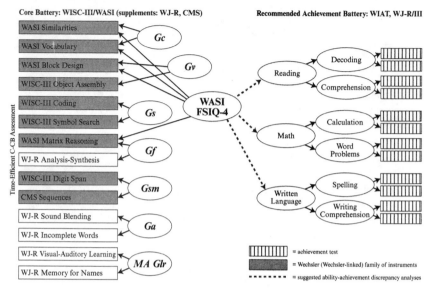

Figure 4.3 Time-efficient C-CB Assessment with WISC-III/WASI Using WJ-R and CMS as Supplements

resentation of the major CHC abilities. This combination of tests is depicted in Figure 4.3.

As can be seen in Figure 4.3, in addition to the adequate representation of *Gc* by two WASI subtests, the WASI Block Design test can be combined with the WISC-III Object Assembly test to ensure adequate representation of *Gv*. Moreover, the WISC-III Symbol Search and Coding tests can be used to represent *Gs* adequately. Thus, when the WASI and selected WISC-III subtests are used together, practitioners can readily obtain broad ability estimates of *Gc, Gv,* and *Gs* as well as a global ability estimate (WAIS FSIQ-4). However, in order to provide for adequate measurement of *Gf, Gsm, Glr,* and *Ga,* the WASI and WISC-III tests need to be augmented with tests from other batteries.

Perhaps the most logical choice of batteries for the purpose of supplementing the WASI and WISC-III is the WJ-R (presented later in this chapter); this is because the WJ-R currently provides the broadest measurement of CHC abilities of all the major intelligence batteries. Thus, in addition to the WASI and WISC-III tests presented in Figure 4.3, the WJ-R can be used to measure *Ga* and *Glr.* Also, by combining the WJ-R Analysis-Synthesis test with the WASI Matrix Reasoning test, adequate representation of *Gf* is achieved.

As may be seen in Figure 4.3, the WISC-III/WASI/WJ-R cross-battery provides for adequate measurement of *Gc, Gv, Gs, Gf,* and *Ga.* That is, each of these abilities is measured by two qualitatively different indicators (i.e., subtests that measure different aspects of these broad abilities) following the first guiding principle of the CHC Cross-Battery approach (see Chapter 1). *Glr* was not represented broadly in this cross-battery because neither the WISC-III nor WASI measures this ability, and the WJ-R only measures one narrow aspect of *Glr*—namely, Associative Memory (MA). Therefore, the two tests that are used to represent *Glr* in Figure 4.3 are best interpreted as MA, not *Glr.*

Similarly, an examination of the CHC classifications of the *Gsm* tests of the WISC-III (Digit Span) and WJ-R (Memory for Words, Memory for Sentences) shows that these tests are primarily measures of Memory Span (MS). As such, the WISC-III Digit Span test could be combined with the WJ-R Memory for Words test (a purer measure of MS than Memory for Sentences) to provide for adequate measurement of MS. Within the context of the current cross-battery example, all the broad abilities are represented adequately, except *Glr* and *Gsm,* using the WISC-III/WASI/WJ-R cross-battery.[3] Of the options presented thus far, this particular combination provides the most efficient means of obtaining adequate measurement of a wide range of broad cognitive abilities as well as the derivation of a global ability score when use of the Wechsler instrument is desirable. However, depending on the reason for referral, it may be necessary to measure *Glr* and *Gsm* more broadly.

In Figure 4.3, the Children's Memory Scale (CMS; Cohen, 1997; see Rapid Reference 4.4), which is psychometrically linked to the WISC-III, was used to provide for broader measurement of *Gsm.* Specifically, the CMS Sequences test (a measure of Working Memory) was combined with the WISC-III Digit Span test. Following the same guiding principle of two qualitatively different indicators for broad ability representation, one of the WJ-R's Associative Memory tests could have been combined (in Figure 4.3) with a qualitatively different measure of *Glr* from the CMS to provide for broad representation

---

[3] The WJ III contains tests that measure qualitatively different aspects of both *Glr* and *Gsm.* The WJ-R was used in this example because the WJ III was not available for use at the time this book was written.

Rapid Reference 4.4

Children's Memory Scale

Author: Morris Cohen

Publication Date: 1997

Age Range: 5:0 to 16:0

Publisher: The Psychological Corporation

Further Information: For information on the psychometric, theoretical, and qualitative characteristics of the individual tests in this battery, see:

Flanagan, D. P., McGrew, K. S., & Ortiz, S. O. (2000). *The Wechsler intelligence scales and Gf-Gc theory: A contemporary approach to interpretation.* Boston: Allyn & Bacon.

of this ability. Alternatively, two qualitatively different measures of *Glr* from the CMS could have been used to represent this ability in assessment. For example, the CMS Stories and Stories 2 tests measure mainly Meaningful Memory, and the CMS Word Lists and Word Lists 2 tests measure mainly Free Recall Memory (Flanagan, McGrew, et al., 2000). Therefore, while the WISC-III/WASI/WJ-R cross-battery results in narrow measurement of *Gsm* (i.e., Memory Span) and *Glr* (i.e., Associative Memory), the CMS, whether used alone or in combination with this cross-battery (shown in Figure 4.3), allows for broad measurement of *Gsm* and *Glr* because it contains qualitatively different indicators of each broad ability.

WISC-III–Based CHC Cross-Battery Assessments and Global Ability Measures in Perspective

An examination of Figures 4.1 through 4.3 shows that there are different ways to achieve compliance with whatever legal mandates necessitate the calculation of global ability scores (or IQs) for use in ability-achievement discrepancy formulas. Figure 4.1 showed that when a Wechsler FSIQ must be used (and calculated from the 10 core WISC-III subtests), measurement of many broad cognitive abilities, such as *Gf, Ga, Gsm, Glr,* and *Gs,* would require additional testing time. Given a minimum of two subtests for each broad ability, the result would be a 19-subtest battery whenever the goal is a Comprehensive CHC Cross-Battery assessment. Decisions related to the manner in which a WISC-III FSIQ ought to be supplemented to measure abilities that are not measured by the core WISC-III tests should follow directly from the referral concerns and should be consistent with the principles and procedures of CHC Cross-Battery assessment.

Figure 4.2 showed that the calculation of the WISC-III GAI is a more viable alternative to the FSIQ when a global ability measure is desired in cross-battery assessments, primarily because it serves the same purpose as the FSIQ but consists of 8 rather than 10 subtests. Therefore, practitioners can allocate the time saved in calculating a GAI instead of an FSIQ to the administration of measures of abilities related to referral issues but that are not represented by the GAI. Due to the redundancy in measurement of Gv and Gc abilities in the calculation of the GAI, GAI-based cross-batteries, like FSIQ-based cross-batteries, will require additional testing time to measure certain abilities germane to referral questions or desired in C-CB assessment.

The CHC Cross-Battery assessment depicted in Figure 4.3 can be thought of as representing the best of both worlds. Essentially, the cross-battery shown in Figure 4.3 is both consistent with contemporary CHC theory and allows for the calculation of a global ability score. As such, practitioners can achieve broad measurement of the major CHC abilities (*Gf, Gc, Gv, Gsm, Glr, Ga, Gs*) as well as a global ability estimate (FSIQ-4) in approximately the same amount of time that it would take to administer a complete WISC-III battery. However, it is important to remember that when using an FSIQ-4–based cross-battery, intracognitive and intercognitive analyses of the CHC abilities should always be the *primary* components of assessment (particularly learning-disability assessment), along with ongoing examination of exclusionary criteria. Because the FSIQ-4 is used primarily as a screening measure for level of general ability or intelligence, the results of FSIQ-4–achievement discrepancy analyses should be used *only to support* already existing evidence of an underlying learning disability. Significant FSIQ-4 achievement-discrepancies should *never* be used in isolation to diagnose a learning disability.

WAIS-III–Based CHC Cross-Battery Assessments and Global Ability Measures

WAIS-III: *Full Scale IQ*

When the core battery selected for C-CB assessment is the Wechsler Adult Intelligence Scale—Third Edition (WAIS-III; Wechsler, 1997; see Rapid Reference 4.5) and the derivation of an FSIQ is necessary, then the following 11 WAIS-III subtests will need to be administered: Information, Vocabulary, Similarities, Comprehension, Block Design, Picture Completion, Picture

≡ Rapid Reference 4.5

Wechsler Adult Intelligence Scale–Third Edition

Author: David Wechsler

Publication Date: 1997

Age Range: 16 to 89

Publisher: The Psychological Corporation

Further Information: For information on the psychometric, theoretical, and qualitative characteristics of the individual tests in this battery, see:

Flanagan, D. P., McGrew, K. S., & Ortiz, S. O. (2000). *The Wechsler intelligence scales and Gf-Gc theory: A contemporary approach to interpretation.* Boston: Allyn & Bacon

Kaufman, A. S., & Lichtenberger, E. O. (1999). *Essentials of WAIS-III assessment.* New York: Wiley.

McGrew, K. S., & Flanagan, D. P. (1998). *The intelligence test desk reference (ITDR): Gf-Gc cross-battery assessment.* Boston: Allyn & Bacon.

Arrangement, Digit Span, Digit-Symbol Coding, Arithmetic, and Matrix Reasoning. This combination of WAIS-III tests that comprise the FSIQ is depicted by the white rectangles in Figure 4.4.

When evaluated from the CHC theoretical perspective, Figure 4.4 shows that the WAIS-III tests that comprise the FSIQ, like the tests that comprise the WISC-III FSIQ, measure *Gc* and *Gv* abilities adequately. That is, each of these broad abilities is measured by at least two narrow ability indicators (i.e., subtests) that, in part, define these domains. The WAIS-III FSIQ also contains one measure of *Gsm* (Digit Span), one measure of *Gf* (Matrix Reasoning), one measure of *Gs* (Digit Symbol Coding), and one measure of *Gq* (Arithmetic). When compared to the tests that comprise the WISC-III FSIQ, the WAIS-III FSIQ contains a broader range of CHC abilities. However, the abilities of *Gf, Ga,* and *Glr* remain either unmeasured or measured inadequately by both batteries.

When measurement of *Gf* (one of the abilities not measured adequately by the WAIS-III), is deemed necessary vis-à-vis referral information, practitioners will need to supplement the Matrix Reasoning test with another *Gf* measure following the CHC Cross-Battery principles and procedures (see Chapter

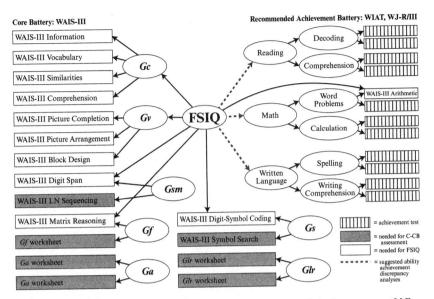

Figure 4.4 Abilities Represented (and Not Represented) in Assessment When a WAIS-III FSIQ is Derived

2). Likewise, when measurement of *Ga* and *Glr* (two additional abilities inadequately measured by the WAIS-III) is a necessary component of assessment, practitioners will need to augment the core WAIS-III battery with tests from another battery to ensure adequate representation of these abilities. Although the WAIS-III measures *Gsm* and *Gs* adequately, the FSIQ contains only one measure of each of these abilities. Therefore, when measurement of *Gsm* and *Gs* is required, practitioners should administer the Letter-Number Sequencing and Symbol Search tests, respectively, to provide for adequate measurement of these abilities. In short, when C-CB assessment is the goal and derivation of an FSIQ is necessary, practitioners will need to supplement the WAIS-III core battery with seven additional tests (one test each for adequate measurement of *Gf, Gsm,* and *Gs,* as well as two tests each for adequate measurement of *Ga* and *Glr*), resulting in an 18-subtest battery. These additional tests are depicted by the gray shaded boxes in Figure 4.4.

The administration of 18 subtests will seldom be viewed as practical in light of the often rigid time constraints under which many practitioners operate. As with the WISC-III, the primary reason for the excessive amount of additional testing required to measure a broad range of cognitive abilities (when the

WAIS-III is selected as the core battery in assessment) is redundancy in measurement of *Gc* and *Gv* abilities, as well as measurement of *Gq* (which is more appropriately and adequately measured by achievement batteries). Much in the same way as was described in the previous section concerning use of the WISC-III, one way to achieve the goal of measuring the broad range of CHC abilities and obtaining a global ability score in a time-efficient manner is to use an abbreviated intelligence scale for the purpose of deriving a global ability index. This time-efficient alternative to WAIS-III–based C-CB assessment is described in the next section.

It is noteworthy that the WAIS-III, unlike the WISC-III, measures *Gsm* adequately (through the tests that comprise the Working Memory Index [WMI]), and perhaps better than most currently available intelligence batteries. This is because it includes measures of both Memory Span and Working Memory. However, performance on the WMI of the WAIS-III is dependent, in part, on math knowledge and math achievement due to the inclusion of the Arithmetic subtest in the calculation of this index. Therefore, it is important to evaluate *Gq* abilities separately from memory abilities in the initial phase of interpreting the *Gsm*/WMI on the WAIS-III, in order to determine the extent to which extreme performance on *Gq* tasks (very high or very low) may spuriously inflate or attenuate the WMI, respectively.

Although Working Memory is believed to be involved when solving problems on the Arithmetic subtest, from the CHC perspective it has been found to relate more strongly with other measures of *Gq* than with measures of *Gsm* (for a more detailed discussion, see Flanagan, McGrew, et al., 2000). As such, the Arithmetic subtest is included on the right side of Figure 4.4 with other tests of math achievement. Regardless of the placement of the Arithmetic subtest in assessment (i.e., with other measures of *Gq* or with measures of Working Memory), additional research is necessary to achieve a better understanding of the Working Memory construct, in particular, within the CHC theoretical model.

Like the previously presented WISC-III figures, Figure 4.4 shows dotted arrows pointing from the oval depicting the FSIQ to the ovals that represent Reading, Math, and Written Language. These arrows demonstrate the most frequently made ability-achievement discrepancy calculations in assessment of individuals suspected of having a learning disability. It should be noted that ability-achievement comparisons also are made between the FSIQ and more specific academic (as opposed to global) skills, such as reading decoding, math calculation, spelling, and so forth.

WAIS-III: WASI FSIQ-4

The WAIS-III and WASI can be used in C-CB assessment to ensure time-efficient measurement of a wide range of broad cognitive abilities, including a global ability score, in much the same way as the WISC-III was used with the WASI previously (see Figure 4.3). That is, the four subtests that comprise the WASI FSIQ-4 should be organized first in the CHC Cross-Battery assessment, followed by select WAIS-III subtests as shown in Figure 4.5. Specifically, the WASI Similarities and Vocabulary tests provide adequate measurement of *Gc*. The WASI Block Design test provides a measure of *Gv* and the WASI Matrix Reasoning test provides a measure of *Gf*. The latter two tests should be supplemented with other tests to ensure that these abilities are represented adequately in assessment. Together, the four WASI subtests combine to yield a global ability score or FSIQ-4. This global ability score correlates highly with the WAIS-III FSIQ (i.e., .92) and, therefore, can be used confidently as a *screening* measure used to estimate general ability.

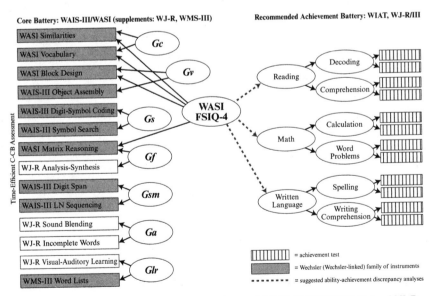

Figure 4.5 Time-efficient C-CB Assessment with WAIS-III/WASI Using WJ-R and WMS-III as Supplements

Within the context of C-CB assessment, the WASI Block Design (BD) test can be combined with a strong measure of *Gv* (which represents a qualitatively different aspect of *Gv* than does BD) to provide for adequate measurement of this broad ability. Research has shown consistently that the Object Assembly test provides just such a qualitatively different and strong measure of *Gv* (see McGrew & Flanagan, 1998). Therefore, this test was used in Figure 4.5 along with BD to represent the *Gv* domain. The Picture Completion test typically displays a secondary loading on *Gc* and, therefore, is considered a mixed measure of *Gv* and *Gc* abilities. As such, it is not recommended over the Object Assembly test for inclusion in the *Gv* cluster. Although the Matrix Reasoning test is included in the POI on the WAIS-III, it is primarily a measure of *Gf* (see Woodcock, McGrew, & Mather, 2001). Therefore, it should not be used in the calculation of the *Gv* cluster in C-CB assessments until research suggests otherwise.

The WAIS-III Digit-Symbol Coding and Symbol Search tests together provide for adequate measurement of *Gs* (see Figure 4.5). To this point, the combination of WAIS-III and WASI tests allows for adequate measurement of *Gc*, *Gv*, *Gs*, and *Gsm*. *Gf* is underrepresented, and *Ga* and *Glr* are not measured by this combination of tests. Therefore, in order to ensure adequate representation of *Gf*, *Ga*, and *Glr* in this WAIS-III/WASI cross-battery assessment, the practitioner will need to cross another battery.

As in the case of the options presented with the WISC-III, perhaps the most logical choice of batteries for supplementing the WAIS-III and WASI is the WJ-R due to its broad measurement of CHC abilities. Specifically, the WJ-R Analysis-Synthesis test can be combined with WASI Matrix Reasoning to ensure adequate measurement of *Gf*. Likewise, the WJ-R Sound Blending and Incomplete Words tests can be combined to provide for adequate measurement of *Ga*. However, as stated previously, the WJ-R includes only Associative Memory measures of *Glr*. Therefore, when broader measurement of *Glr* is necessary, tests from the Wechsler Memory Scale—Third Edition (WMS-III; The Psychological Corporation, 1997; see Rapid Reference 4.6), which was co-normed with the WAIS-III, can be used and are recommended in these situations.[4] Figure 4.5 shows that the WMS-III Word

---

[4] The WJ III contains tests that measure qualitatively different aspects of *Glr*. The WJ-R was used in this example because the WJ III was not available for use at the time this book was written.

Lists test (a measure of Free Recall Memory) was used in combination with the WJ-R Visual-Auditory Learning test to provide for adequate measurement of *Glr*. Alternatively, tests from only the WMS-III can be used to represent *Glr* adequately in assessment (see Flanagan, McGrew, et al., 2000). Overall, when use of the Wechsler instrument is desirable, the systematic combining of WAIS-III, WASI, WMS-III, and WJ-R tests (or WAIS-III, WASI, and WJ III tests) results in a time-efficient C-CB assessment of seven broad CHC abilities as well as a global ability score (FSIQ-4) that can be used in ability-achievement dis-

> ≡*Rapid Reference 4.6*
>
> ### Wechsler Memory Scale– Third Edition
>
> **Author:** David Wechsler
> **Publication Date:** 1945–1997
> **Age Range:** 16:0 to 89:0
> **Publisher:** The Psychological Corporation
> **Further Information:** For information on the psychometric, theoretical, and qualitative characteristics of the individual tests in this battery, see:
> Flanagan, D. P., McGrew, K. S., & Ortiz, S. O. (2000). *The Wechsler intelligence scales and Gf-Gc theory: A contemporary approach to interpretation.* Boston: Allyn & Bacon.

crepancy analysis. Again, given the rather precarious nature and use of brief intelligence scores, practitioners must ensure that *all* criteria listed in Rapid Reference 4.3 are met before interpreting the WASI FSIQ-4 in ability-achievement discrepancy analyses.

WAIS-III–Based CHC Cross-Battery assessments and global ability measures in perspective

An examination of Figures 4.4 and 4.5 shows that there are at least two viable ways to comply with various legal mandates that necessitate the calculation of global ability scores (or IQs) for use in ability-achievement discrepancy formulas within the context of CHC C-CB assessment. Figure 4.4 shows the more traditional approach of calculating a WAIS-III FSIQ. This calculation requires the administration of 11 core WAIS-III subtests and, from a CHC theoretical perspective, results in adequate measurement of *Gc* and *Gv* only. Thus, once the tests that comprise the WAIS-III FSIQ are administered, an additional seven subtests (minimum) will need to be given to measure other important broad CHC abilities (viz., *Gf, Ga, Glr, Gsm, Gs*). Figure 4.5 shows an alternative approach that places primary emphasis on measurement of the major CHC abilities in a manner consistent with CHC Cross-Battery assessment while still allowing for the calculation of a global ability estimate.

Following a review of referral information, WAIS-III users may determine that more in-depth measurement of *Gf, Ga, Gsm, Gs,* and *Glr* (or some combination thereof) is necessary to test initial hypotheses regarding an individual's level of functioning in addition to a global ability measure. Under these circumstances, the WAIS-III user has two options.

First, the *entire* WAIS-III battery can be administered, followed by the supplemental tests chosen to represent *Gf, Ga,* and *Glr.* The worksheets in Appendix A are most useful in the selection of supplemental tests, especially when used in conjunction with the CHC Cross-Battery procedures. The calculation of the WAIS-III FSIQ as well as the additional *Gf, Ga, Glr, Gs,* and *Gsm* composites in this cross-battery example require the administration of a minimum of 18 subtests (see Figure 4.4).

Second, the WASI subtests that comprise the FSIQ-4 can be administered and then systematically supplemented with tests from the WAIS-III and another battery (or batteries) to ensure that the breadth of CHC abilities is represented adequately in assessment. An example of this WAIS-III/WASI–based C-CB assessment is depicted in Figure 4.5. In this example, a set of conormed WASI and WAIS-III subtests were supplemented with tests from the WMS-III and WJ-R to provide for adequate representation of seven CHC abilities following the CHC Cross-Battery principles and procedures (in Chapter 2). This cross-battery requires the administration of only 14 subtests (see Figure 4.5) and is, therefore, much more time-efficient than the previous example, and is approximately equal to the average time required to administer just about any individual intelligence battery.

The latter cross-battery produces an abbreviated global ability estimate (i.e., the WASI FSIQ-4). Although this score correlates highly with the WAIS-III FSIQ, it should be used with significantly more caution until research is available that suggests otherwise. Therefore, when the FSIQ-4 is used in ability-achievement discrepancy formulas, as part of a comprehensive Wechsler-based CHC Cross-Battery, it is recommended that the results of discrepancy analyses be used *only to support* already existing evidence of a learning disability (an academic-skill deficit that is related to an underlying cognitive ability or processing deficit [as determined through intracognitive and intercognitive discrepancy analyses and examination of exclusionary criteria in a manner consistent with the criteria listed in Rapid Reference 4.3).

WPPSI-R–Based CHC Cross-Battery Assessment and Global Ability Measures

WPPSI-R: Full Scale IQ

When the core battery for C-CB assessment is the Wechsler Preschool and Primary Scale of Intelligence—Revised (WPPSI-R; Wechsler, 1989; see Rapid Reference 4.7) and the derivation of an FSIQ is necessary, then the following 10 subtests will need to be administered: Information, Comprehension, Vocabulary, Similarities, Arithmetic, Mazes, Object Assembly, Geometric Designs, Block Design, and Picture Completion. This combination of WPPSI-R tests that comprise the FSIQ is depicted by the white rectangles in Figure 4.6. Specifically, the solid arrows pointing from the oval depicting the FSIQ in this figure to the ovals that represent *Gc*/VIQ and *Gv*/PIQ (composites) illustrate the combination of WPPSI-R tests that constitute the FSIQ.

≋Rapid Reference 4.7

Wechsler Preschool and Primary Scale of Intelligence–Revised

Author: David Wechsler

Publication Date: 1949–1989

Age Range: 2:11 to 7:3

Publisher: The Psychological Corporation

Further Information: For information on the psychometric, theoretical, and qualitative characteristics of the individual tests in this battery, see:

Flanagan, D. P., McGrew, K. S., & Ortiz, S. O. (2000). *The Wechsler intelligence scales and Gf-Gc theory: A contemporary approach to interpretation.* Boston: Allyn & Bacon.

Kaufman, A. S., & Lichtenberger, E. O. (2000). *Essentials of WPPSI-R and WISC-III Assessment.* New York: Wiley.

McGrew, K. S., & Flanagan, D. P. (1998). *The intelligence test desk reference (ITDR): Gf-Gc cross-battery assessment.* Boston: Allyn & Bacon.

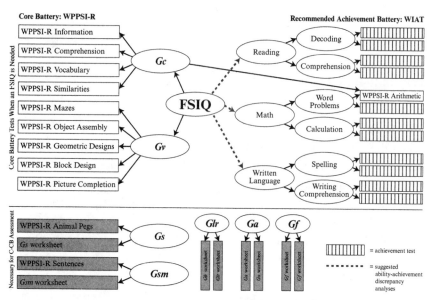

Figure 4.6 Abilities Represented (and Not Represented) in Assessment When a WPPSI-R FSIQ is Derived

When evaluated from the CHC theoretical perspective, Figure 4.6 shows that the tests that comprise the WPPSI-R FSIQ (tests printed in the white rectangles) measure mainly *Gc* and *Gv* abilities, similar to the composition of the WISC-III and WAIS-III FSIQs described earlier. As such, the WPPSI-R core battery of tests measures a narrow range of CHC abilities. Measurement of additional abilities requires the crossing of two or more batteries following the CHC Cross-Battery approach.

Figure 4.6 shows that when an FSIQ is desired within the context of C-CB assessment, it is necessary to administer 10 additional subtests in order to sample functioning in seven CHC cognitive ability domains, resulting in a 20-test battery! The gray shaded boxes in Figure 4.6 represent these additional tests. The significant time that is necessary to supplement the WPPSI-R FSIQ adequately to gain additional information is due to the poor WPPSI-R FSIQ–CHC theory match. More specifically, the additional testing is the result of the significant redundancy in measurement of *Gc* and *Gv* abilities. For example, in order to calculate the WPPSI-R FSIQ, Figure 4.6 shows that five subtests that measure mainly *Gv* abilities and four subtests that measure mainly

Gc abilities must be administered. In C-CB assessment, wherein two tests are required to represent each broad ability, two to three additional abilities could be assessed in the same amount of time that it takes to administer the redundant (or extra) measures of *Gc* and *Gv* abilities on the WPPSI-R. In other words, in approximately the same time it takes to administer the core battery of WPPSI-R tests, which, albeit provides good estimates of *Gc* and *Gv* abilities, a WPPSI-R–based C-CB assessment (such as the one outlined in Table 2.3 in Chapter 2) yields estimates of seven (as opposed to only two) CHC abilities. Therefore, unless it is absolutely necessary to calculate a WPPSI-R FSIQ *within the context of C-CB assessment,* practitioners should explore other options (or batteries) that result in adequate measurement of the wide range of CHC abilities in a more time-efficient manner (such as the option described in the next section).

As in Figures 4.1 through 4.5, the dotted arrows pointing from the global ability score (in this case, from the WPPSI-R FSIQ) to the academic-achievement ovals (i.e., Reading, Math, Written Language) in Figure 4.6 demonstrate the most frequently made ability-achievement discrepancy calculations in the assessment of individuals suspected of having a learning disability. This type of discrepancy analysis is discussed in detail in the last section of this chapter.

Use of a cross-battery approach in the assessment of preschool children may seem inconsistent with the bulk of extant factor-analytic research that supports an underlying dichotomous model of ability (e.g., Verbal/Nonverbal) at the preschool age range (see Flanagan, McGrew, et al., 2000, for a review). However, when the current universe of preschool cognitive ability tests is evaluated (through both empirical and logical analyses within the CHC framework), it is evident that aspects of eight broad CHC cognitive abilities (i.e., essentially, the full range) can be assessed at the preschool age range (see Flanagan, Mascolo, & Genshaft, 2000, for a review). Nevertheless, there are some notable limitations to the measurement of CHC abilities at this age range.

First, when one considers that broad abilities are interpreted most confidently when they are represented by at least two qualitatively different indicators (or measures of the broad ability), the lack of available tests for this age range means that it is possible to represent only five broad CHC abilities well (i.e., *Gc, Gf, Gv, Gq, Glr*) in any given assessment of preschool children (see

Flanagan, Mascolo, et al., 2000). Moreover, in order to represent these five abilities adequately in assessment, practitioners will need to have access to more than two or three preschool intelligence tests. Second, *in-depth* assessment, (i.e., assessment of three or more qualitatively different indicators of a broad cognitive ability) is possible only in the areas of Gc and Gv with currently available preschool assessment tools. That is, Gc and Gv are the only cognitive constructs that are represented by more than three qualitatively different indicators across current preschool intelligence batteries (Flanagan, Mascolo, et al., 2000). The range of abilities that can be assessed adequately at the preschool age range will likely increase, perhaps significantly, when the next editions of the WJ-R and WPPSI-R are published in the near future (e.g., Woodcock et al., 2001).

WPPSI-R: WASI FSIQ-4 (ages 6 to 7 only)

The WASI can be used with the WPPSI-R in C-CB assessment of 6- and 7-year-old children to ensure time-efficient measurement of seven CHC abilities, as well as the calculation of a global ability estimate, in a manner similar to that already described for the WISC-III (Figure 4.3). The WASI FSIQ-4 was found to be a highly reliable estimate of general intelligence for 6- and 7-year-olds (i.e., $r = .95$ at both age levels; The Psychological Corporation, 1999, p. 125). In particular, the WASI tests that comprise the FSIQ-4 can be combined with select WPPSI-R, WJ-R, and CMS tests to allow for calculation of Gc, Gv, Gs, Gf, Gsm, Ga, and Glr composites for use in intracognitive and intercognitive discrepancy analysis (see Chapter 3) as well as a global ability estimate (i.e., WASI FSIQ-4) for use in ability-achievement discrepancy analysis. The WPPSI-R/WASI-based C-CB cross-battery is depicted in Figure 4.7. As in every case in which the use of a brief intelligence score is being considered for use in the evaluation of cognitive ability, especially within the context of diagnosing learning disabilities, practitioners must ensure that all six criteria listed in Rapid Reference 4.3 are met prior to interpreting the WASI FSIQ-4 as the global ability estimate in ability-achievement discrepancy formulas.

WPPSI-R–Based CHC Cross-Battery Assessments and Global Ability Measures in Perspective

It is clear that the need to calculate a WPPSI-R FSIQ within the context of C-CB assessment is neither time-efficient nor practical. Due to excessive redundancy in the measurement of Gc and Gv abilities needed to derive the FSIQ,

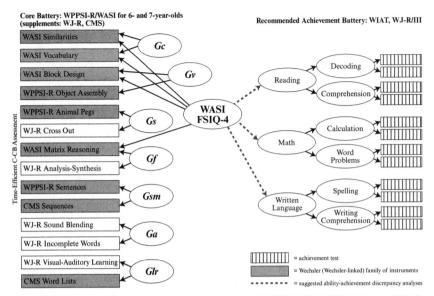

Figure 4.7 Time-efficient C-CB Assessment with WPPSI-R/WASI Using WJ-R and CMS as Supplements (6- and 7-year-olds)

the length of time required to assess other abilities that might be important with respect to specific referral concerns would be considered unreasonable and impractical by most practitioners. Therefore, when the goal of assessment at the preschool age range is to "touch *all* of the major cognitive areas, with emphasis on those most suspect on the basis of history, observation, and on-going test findings" (Wilson, 1992, p. 382, emphasis added), practitioners are encouraged to use a battery other than the WPPSI-R in their C-CB assessments. For example, a much more practical alternative to the WPPSI-R is the Differential Abilities Scale (DAS; Elliott, 1991) which is described in the next section.

When the goal of assessment is to evaluate functioning in all the major CHC cognitive ability domains and at the same time derive an estimate of global ability, administration of the core WPPSI-R subtests in particular is not recommended for children at the upper end of the preschool age range (i.e., 6- to 7-year-olds). Instead, a WPPSI-R/WASI–based C-CB assessment is recommended for 6- to 7-year-olds whereby a *select* combination of Wechsler tests is supplemented systematically with tests from other batteries. Note that this type of assessment remains distinct from S-CB assessment, in which the focus is on only a select subset of cognitive abilities, not on comprehensive assessment of such abilities. In fact, this type of C-CB assessment, depicted in Figure 4.7, results in the derivation of seven CHC ability composites as well as a global-ability index in a time-efficient and theoretically and psychometrically defensible framework. Nevertheless, because of the length of time necessary to administer the subtests that make up the WPPSI-R FSIQ and the limitations associated with using an abbreviated global-ability estimate (i.e., WASI FSIQ-4) for certain purposes, practitioners may wish to select an intelligence battery other than the WPPSI-R as their core battery in C-CB assessment.

DAS-Based CHC Cross-Battery Assessments and Global Ability Measures

DAS General Conceptual Ability (GCA)

Of the major intelligence batteries with norms for children ages 3 years, 6 months to 5 years, 11 months, the Differential Ability Scales (DAS; Elliott, 1991, see Rapid Reference 4.8) appears to have emerged as the overall best available "tool of choice" (Flanagan & Alfonso, 1995). When the DAS is used as the core battery for C-CB assessment and derivation of a global ability score is necessary, six subtests (as opposed to 10 on the WPPSI-R) need to be administered. The DAS subtests that comprise the global ability composite, called *General*

≡*Rapid Reference 4.8*

Differential Ability Scales

Author: Colin D. Elliott

Publication Date: 1990

Age Range: 2:6 to 17:11

Publisher: The Psychological Corporation

Further Information: For information on the psychometric, theoretical, and qualitative characteristics of the individual tests in this battery, see:

Elliot, C. D. (1997). The differential ability scales. In D. P. Flanagan, J. L. Genshaft, & P. L. Harrison (Eds.), *Contemporary intellectual assessment: Theories, tests, and issues* (pp. 183–208). New York: Guilford.

McGrew, K. S., & Flanagan, D. P. (1998). *The intelligence test desk reference (ITDR): Gf-Gc cross-battery assessment.* Boston: Allyn & Bacon.

Conceptual Ability (GCA), include Verbal Comprehension, Naming Vocabulary, Copying, Pattern Construction, Picture Similarities, and Early Number Concepts. These tests are represented by the white rectangles in Figure 4.8. Specifically, the solid arrows pointing from the oval depicting the GCA to the ovals representing *Gc*/Verbal Ability and *Gv*/Nonverbal Ability (composites) as well as to the rectangles denoting Picture Similarities and Early Number Concepts (i.e., subtests) illustrate the combination of DAS tests that constitute the GCA.

When evaluated from the CHC theoretical perspective, Figure 4.8 shows that the tests that comprise the GCA, like the tests that make up the WPPSI-R FSIQ, measure mainly *Gc* and *Gv* abilities. However, the DAS assesses *Gc* and *Gv* in a much more time-efficient manner (i.e., through two qualitatively different indicators of each broad ability as opposed to four [for *Gc*] and five [for *Gv*] tests on the WPPSI-R). In addition to its tests of *Gc* and *Gv* ability, the GCA also includes one test of *Gf* (Picture Similarities) and one test of *Gq* (Early Number Concepts). Each of the latter two broad ability domains can be represented adequately in assessment when combined with another test that measures a qualitatively different aspect of the respective broad ability via the CHC Cross-Battery approach. As was the case with the Wechsler Arithmetic subtest, however, the DAS Early

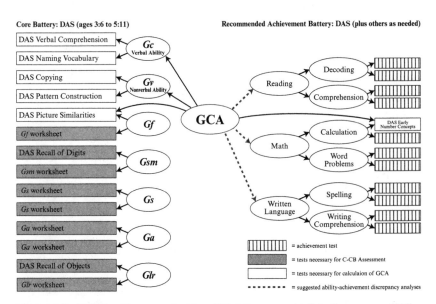

Figure 4.8 Abilities Represented (and Not Represented) in Assessment When a DAS GCA is Derived (ages 3:6 to 5:11)

Number Concepts test measures aspects of *Gq* that are typically assessed adequately by individual academic achievement batteries. Therefore, the Early Number Concepts test was placed on the right side of Figure 4.8.

The gray shaded boxes in Figure 4.8 represent the additional tests that would need to be administered in order to represent all the major CHC broad abilities adequately in the assessment. Unlike the WPPSI-R, the DAS is not characterized by redundancy in assessment. Therefore, even when the full range of CHC abilities is deemed necessary to measure and a global ability score is required, systematic supplementation of the DAS in order to achieve a C-CB assessment is roughly equivalent to the time required to administer a complete WPPSI-R battery. The DAS-based cross-battery, however, yields *substantially more* information than the individual WPPSI-R battery.

The benefits of using the DAS instead of the WPPSI-R for upper-level preschool-aged children are similar to those associated with using the DAS instead of the WISC-III for a school-aged population (6 years, 0 months to 17 years, 11 months). When the core battery for C-CB assessment of school-aged children is the DAS and the derivation of a global ability score is necessary, then only six subtests (as opposed to 10 on the WISC-III) would need to be administered. The DAS subtests that comprise the GCA for school-aged children include Word Definitions, Similarities, Recall of Designs, Pattern Construction, Sequential and Quantitative Reasoning, and Matrices. These tests are represented by the white rectangles in Figure 4.9.

When evaluated from contemporary assessment perspectives, Figure 4.9 shows that the DAS is likely a better core battery selection in C-CB assessment than the WISC-III for three important reasons. First, the tests that comprise the GCA are not only fewer in number than those that comprise the WISC-III FSIQ (i.e., 6 vs. 10), but they result in adequate representation of three CHC broad abilities (i.e., *Gc, Gv,* and *Gf*) as opposed to only two on the WISC-III (*Gc* and *Gv*). Second, the DAS assesses *Gc* and *Gv* in a much more time- and psychometrically-efficient manner (i.e., through two qualitatively different indicators of each broad ability as opposed to four for each of these abilities on the WISC-III). Third, whereas the WISC-III does not measure *Gf,* the DAS measures this broad domain adequately.

The gray shaded boxes in Figure 4.9 represent the additional tests that would need to be administered, over and above the tests that comprise the DAS GCA, in order to represent all the major CHC broad abilities adequately

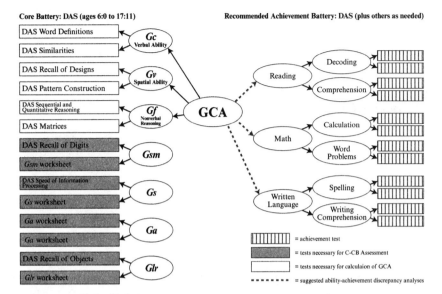

Figure 4.9 Abilities Represented (and Not Represented) in Assessment When a DAS GCA is Derived (ages 6:0 to 17:11)

in assessment. Again, unlike the WISC-III, the DAS is not characterized by redundancy in assessment. Therefore, even when the full range of CHC abilities is to be measured and a global ability score is required, use of the DAS with systematic supplementation via cross-battery principles and procedures requires an approximately equal amount of time to achieve a C-CB assessment as that required to administer a complete WISC-III battery. The DAS-based cross-battery (Figure 4.9), however, has the significant added benefit of yielding substantially more information than that which is derived from administration of an individual WISC-III battery.

As was the case with all previously presented figures, the dotted arrows pointing from the ovals that represent global ability (in this case, the GCA) to the ovals that depict academic achievement in Figures 4.8 and 4.9 show the most frequently made ability achievement discrepancy calculations. It is recommended that practitioners use the DAS achievement tests to augment their DAS cognitive assessments because the achievement and cognitive ability tests of this battery are co-normed (see Flanagan, McGrew, et al., 2000, for a discussion of the benefits of using co-normed tests). However, because the range of academic skills assessed by the DAS achievement tests is relatively limited, practitioners who desire a more thorough assessment of academic skills may want to supplement the DAS tests with tests from other achievement batteries or simply administer a more comprehensive achievement battery.

DAS-Based CHC Cross-Battery Assessments and Global Ability Measures in Perspective

In comparison to the Wechsler-based cross-battery assessments described earlier, when the global ability score *of the core battery* must be calculated within the context of C-CB assessment, the DAS is recommended over the Wechsler batteries for several reasons. First, the composition of tests that comprise the GCA score on the DAS is smaller in number than that comprising the FSIQ on the Wechsler batteries (i.e., WISC-III and WPPSI-R) and, as such, results in more time-efficient measurement of global ability. Second, the breadth of abilities represented by the GCA is greater than that represented by the FSIQ. Third, the DAS is not characterized by redundancy in measurement of certain abilities; the Wechsler batteries are characterized by considerable redundancy in measurement of *Gc* and *Gv* abilities, in particular. Fourth, practitioners can measure seven broad CHC abilities *and* derive a global ability score in a *time-efficient manner* by augmenting the DAS-GCA tests via C-CB assessment procedures. In order to achieve the same goal using a Wechsler Scale as the core battery in assessment, the global ability measure must be derived from the WASI (i.e., the FSIQ-4), an abbreviated intelligence battery. Although the WASI FSIQ-4 is highly reliable across its age range, it is nevertheless an abbreviated set of tests. Therefore, the DAS GCA is likely a more reliable and better estimate of global ability than is the WASI FSIQ-4. In short, within the context of CHC Cross-Battery assessment, the DAS fits within the CHC framework better than do the Wechsler batteries. Therefore, the application of cross-battery principles and procedures is made easier when the DAS is used as the core battery in assessment rather than a Wechsler Scale, especially when the derivation of a global ability score is warranted.

KAIT: Composite IQ

When the core battery selected for C-CB assessment is the Kaufman Adolescent and Adult Intelligence Test (KAIT; Kaufman & Kaufman, 1993; see

Rapid Reference 4.9) and the derivation of a global ability score (or IQ) is necessary, then the following six subtests must be administered: Definitions, Auditory Comprehension, Double Meanings, Logical Steps, Mystery Codes, and Rebus Learning. The combination of subtests that comprise the KAIT Composite IQ is depicted by the white rectangles in Figure 4.10.

When evaluated from the CHC perspective, Figure 4.10 shows that the KAIT tests that comprise the Composite IQ measure mainly *Gc* and *Gf* abilities adequately. That is, each of these broad abilities is measured by at least two narrow ability

≡Rapid Reference 4.9

Kaufman Adolescent and Adult Intelligence Test

Authors: Alan S. Kaufman and Nadeen L. Kaufman

Publication Date: 1993

Age Range: 11:0 to 85+

Publisher: American Guidance Service

Further Information: For information on the psychometric, theoretical, and qualitative characteristics of the individual tests in this battery, see:

McGrew, K. S., & Flanagan, D. P. (1998). *The intelligence test desk reference (ITDR): Gf-Gc cross-battery assessment.* Boston: Allyn & Bacon.

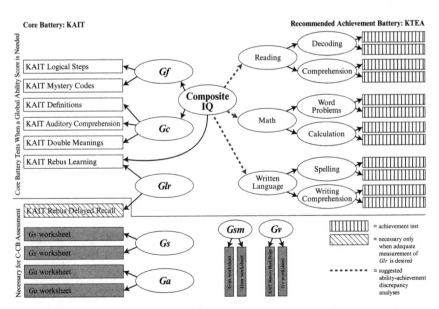

Figure 4.10 Abilities Represented (and Not Represented) in Assessment When a KAIT Composite IQ is Derived

indicators (i.e., subtests) that, in part, define these domains. In addition to *Gc* and *Gf* abilities, the Composite IQ also includes a measure of *Glr* (i.e., Rebus Learning). Note that the combination of tests that makes up the global ability score for the KAIT is different from the combination of tests that makes up the WAIS-III FSIQ, which consists largely of *Gc* and *Gv* abilities. Although the KAIT Composite IQ–CHC match does not appear to be much better than the Wechsler Scale FSIQ–CHC match, selecting the KAIT over the WAIS-III as the core battery in C-CB assessment (particularly when derivation of a global ability score is necessary) is considered a better choice for the following reasons.

First, in order to derive a global ability measure using the KAIT, only six subtests (as opposed to 11 subtests on the WAIS-III) need to be administered. Second, the KAIT core battery subtests are characterized by less redundancy in measurement of CHC abilities than the WAIS-III. For example, the WAIS-III includes four measure of *Gc* in its global ability composite (i.e., FSIQ) whereas the KAIT includes three. Third, the KAIT Composite IQ consists of tests that measure two important abilities that predict a variety of academic and occupational outcomes (i.e., *Gf* and *Gc*). The Wechsler FSIQ consists largely of measures of *Gc* and *Gv*, the latter of which has been found to be the *least* important (as compared to *Gf, Gc, Ga, Glr, Gsm,* and *Gs*) in explaining academic achievement (see McGrew & Flanagan, 1998). Therefore, depending on referral concerns, the KAIT may be more relevant than the WAIS-III. Fourth, when a *C-CB* assessment is desired in addition to the global ability estimate of the core battery, CHC Cross-Battery procedures require that the WAIS-III FSIQ (an 11-subtest composite) be supplemented with seven additional tests, for a total of 18 tests overall. In contrast, the KAIT Composite IQ (a 6-subtest composite) needs to be supplemented with nine additional tests, resulting in a total of only 15. Thus, in order to achieve the broadest measurement of abilities as well as derive the global ability estimate, choosing the KAIT is slightly more time-efficient.

Although the choice of a KAIT C-CB assessment likely results in more testing time than is typically required to administer an entire WAIS-III battery (15 vs. 13 subtests, respectively), the amount of information gained from a KAIT-based C-CB approach versus that gained from an individual WAIS-III battery outweighs the implications of approximately 15 to 20 minutes of additional testing time. Likewise, because the information gained from a KAIT-based C-CB assessment (Figure 4.10) is essentially the same as the information gained from a WAIS-III-based C-CB assessment (Figure 4.4), in order to achieve measurement of the major CHC abilities *and* the global ability score of the core battery, the former is recommended because it is more time-efficient. It should be noted, of course, that a WAIS-III/WASI–based C-CB assessment (Figure 4.5; a better alternative than the single WAIS-III battery) yields essentially the same type of information in the same amount of time as a KAIT-based C-CB assessment.

Figure 4.10 also shows the most frequently made ability-achievement discrepancy analyses in assessments of individuals suspected of having a learning disability. These comparisons are represented by the dotted arrows in the figure and will be discussed in detail at the end of this chapter.

K-ABC: Mental Processing Composite (MPC)

When the core battery for C-CB assessment is the Kaufman Assessment Battery for Children (K-ABC; Kaufman & Kaufman, 1983; see Rapid Reference 4.10) and the derivation of a global ability score from this core battery is necessary, then eight subtests must be administered for individuals aged 5 years, 0 months to 12 years, 5 months. The K-ABC subtests that comprise the global ability score, called the *Mental Processing Composite* (MPC), include Gestalt Closure, Triangles, Spatial Memory, Photo Series, Hand Movements, Number Recall, Word Order, and Matrix Analogies. These tests are represented by the white rectangles in Figure 4.11.

≡*Rapid Reference 4.10*

Kaufman Assessment Battery for Children

Authors: Alan S. Kaufman and Nadeen L. Kaufman

Publication Date: 1983

Age Range: 2:6 to 12:6

Publisher: American Guidance Service

Further Information: For information on the psychometric, theoretical, and qualitative characteristics of the individual tests in this battery, see:

McGrew, K. S., & Flanagan, D. P. (1998). *The intelligence test desk reference (ITDR): Gf-Gc cross-battery assessment.* Boston: Allyn & Bacon.

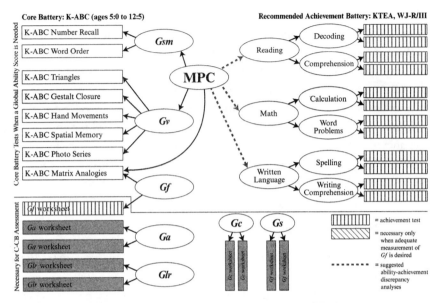

Figure 4.11 Abilities Represented (and not Represented) in Assessment When a K-ABC MPC is Derived (ages 5:0 to 12:5)

When evaluated from the CHC theoretical perspective, Figure 4.11 shows that the tests that comprise the MPC measure mainly *Gv* and *Gsm*. The MPC also contains one measure of *Gf*. Among the abilities represented by the MPC, *Gv* is the only *broad* ability that is measured adequately. This is because the K-ABC, like the WPPSI-R, contains five measures that represent qualitatively different aspects of *Gv*. Conversely, although Figure 4.11 shows that the K-ABC contains two measures of *Gsm,* both are measures of Memory Span. In order to represent the CHC ability of *Gsm* in assessment adequately, measures of Memory Span *and* Working Memory would need to be administered. Likewise, when using the K-ABC, in order to provide adequate coverage of *Gf,* practitioners would need to supplement the Matrix Analogies test (a mixed measure of *Gf* and *Gv* abilities), in particular, with another measure (or measures) that represents an aspect of *Gf* that is qualitatively different than that represented by Matrix Analogies. The worksheets in Appendix A are useful for the purpose of selecting the most appropriate supplemental tests (see also Table 2.3 for a K-ABC cross-battery example).

Because the K-ABC provides relatively limited coverage of the major CHC abilities, practitioners who choose the K-ABC as their core battery in assessment will need to supplement it extensively with tests from other batteries following cross-battery principles and procedures, especially when measurement of *Gc, Ga, Glr, Gf, Gsm,* and *Gs* (or some combination thereof) is deemed necessary. The gray shaded boxes in Figure 4.11 represent the tests that would need to be administered in addition to those comprising the MPC in order to represent all the major CHC broad abilities adequately. Specifically, in order to conduct a K-ABC–based C-CB assessment that allows for the calculation of the K-ABC global ability score, 17 tests would need to be administered (8 for the calculation of the MPC and 9 for the calculation of *Gf, Ga, Glr, Gs,* and *Gc* clusters). In order to achieve the same broad measurement of CHC abilities and derive a global ability estimate with the WPPSI-R, 20 tests are needed (see Figure 4.6). However, when the DAS is used as the core battery in C-CB assessment only 15 tests are necessary. Thus, DAS-based C-CB assessment (Figures 4.8 and 4.9) allows for adequate measurement of seven broad CHC abilities and calculation of the core battery global ability score in a more time-efficient manner than either WPPSI-R FSIQ–based (Figure 4.6) or K-ABC MPC–based (Figure 4.11) C-CB assessment.

WJ-R: Broad Cognitive Ability (BCA)

When the Woodcock-Johnson Psycho-Educational Battery–Revised (WJ-R; Woodcock & Johnson, 1989; see Rapid Reference 4.11) is selected as the core battery in C-CB assessment and the derivation of a global ability estimate is deemed necessary, then the following seven subtests must be administered: Picture Vocabulary, Visual Closure, Visual Matching, Analysis-Synthesis, Memory for Sentences, Incomplete Words, and Memory for Names. Each of these tests measures a particular aspect of the major CHC broad abilities, including *Gc, Gv, Gs, Gf, Gsm, Ga,* and *Glr,* respectively. Together, these tests comprise the standard *Broad Cognitive Ability* (BCA-Std.) cluster from the WJ-R Standard Battery (Woodcock & Johnson, 1989), which is interpreted as an estimate of general ability or intelligence. These tests are printed in the white rectangles in Figure 4.12.

It is no surprise that the WJ-R BCA–CHC theory match is good. The WJ-R

≡Rapid Reference 4.11

Woodcock-Johnson Psycho-Educational Battery–Revised

Author: Richard W. Woodcock

Publication Date: 1977–1991

Age Range: 2:0 to 90+

Publisher: The Riverside Publishing Company

Further Information: For information on the psychometric, theoretical, and qualitative characteristics of the individual tests in this battery, see:

McGrew, K. S. (1994). *Clinical interpretation of the Woodcock-Johnson Tests of Cognitive Ability–Revised.* Boston: Allyn and Bacon.

McGrew, K. S., & Flanagan, D. P. (1998). *The intelligence test desk reference (ITDR): Gf-Gc cross-battery assessment.* Boston: Allyn & Bacon.

was intentionally developed to operationalize the CHC theoretical model (see McGrew, 1994, and McGrew & Flanagan, 1998, for details). However, in order to measure the seven broad CHC abilities represented by the BCA tests adequately, at least one additional measure of each ability, assessing a qualitatively different aspect of the ability than that already represented by the respective BCA tests, would need to be administered. Adequate measurement of Gs, Gf, Gv and Ga can be achieved by supplementing the standard battery of tests that measure these abilities with their counterparts from the WJ-R supplemental battery of cognitive tests. These tests include Cross Out, Concept Formation, Picture Recognition and Sound Blending, respectively. Unlike with Gs, Gf, Gv and Ga, however, practitioners cannot measure Gc, Gsm, and Glr adequately by selecting tests from the WJ-R supplemental battery of cognitive tests (i.e., tests 8–14). This is because the supplemental tests of these CHC abilities measure qualitatively *similar*, rather than different, aspects of the respective broad abilities.[5]

---

[5] Unlike the WJ-R, the WJ III contains tests that measure qualitatively different aspects of Gc, Gsm, and Glr. Therefore, the WJ III would not require supplementing unless, for example, in-depth assessment of a particular broad ability was warranted or hypothesis testing and evaluation of significant differences between narrow abilities were necessary, and so forth.

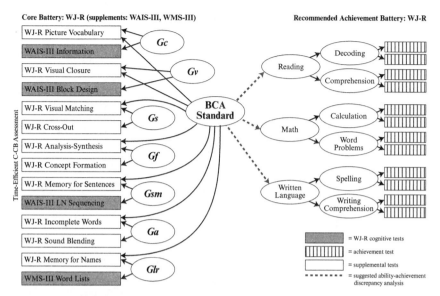

Figure 4.12 Time-efficient C-CB Assessment with WJ-R (BCA Std tests) Using WAIS-III and WMS-III as Supplements

Following Guiding Principle 1 of the CHC Cross-Battery approach for adequate representation of broad abilities in assessment, it is possible to augment the WJ-R standard battery *Gc, Gsm,* and *Glr* tests with tests from the Wechsler Scales to achieve broad representation of these abilities in assessment. An example of a WJ-R/Wechsler–based C-CB assessment is presented in Figure 4.12. In this figure, measurement of the broad *Gc* ability is achieved by supplementing the WJ-R Picture Vocabulary test with the Information test from the WAIS-III. Likewise, adequate representation of *Gsm* was achieved by supplementing the WJ-R Memory for Sentences test with the Letter-Number Sequencing test from the WAIS-III. However, adequate representation of *Glr* requires that practitioners cross a third battery.

In the area of *Glr,* the WJ-R only measures Associative Memory whereas the WAIS-III does not measure any aspect of this broad ability. Therefore, in addition to the WAIS-III tests just mentioned, the WJ-R can be augmented with tests from the WMS-III to provide for adequate measurement of *Glr* (see Figure 4.12).

Because the WAIS-III and WMS-III are co-normed, they can be used in a psychometrically defensible manner to augment the WJ-R in C-CB assessment (see Flanagan, McGrew, et al., 2000 for a discussion).

In contrast to the previous batteries mentioned in this chapter, the WJ-R not only measures aspects of seven CHC broad cognitive abilities, but it does so in a time-efficient manner (through one or two measures of each CHC broad ability). Unfortunately, approximately half of the broad CHC abilities measured by the WJ-R (extended battery [tests 1–14]) are underrepresented. Much as with all previously mentioned batteries, it must be supplemented in order to achieve a C-CB assessment of seven broad cognitive abilities. However, because the WJ-R is not characterized by redundancy in measurement, practitioners who select it as the core battery in their cognitive evaluations can achieve a C-CB assessment using only 14 subtests (see Figure 4.12). Thus, use of the WJ-R can provide an extremely efficient means for obtaining a broad ability score within the context of C-CB assessment and with a negligible increase in time. In addition, use of the WJ-R has added benefits that cannot be accomplished to date when other tests are used as the core battery in CHC Cross-Battery assessment. One of these benefits relates to the use of aptitude scores and is described in the following section.

WJ-R: Scholastic Aptitude Clusters

According to McGrew (1994), differential scholastic aptitude clusters, such as those included on the WJ-R, are the best scores to use in ability-achievement discrepancy analyses for two main reasons. First, because aptitude measures were designed for a specific purpose (e.g., to predict some outcome), they predict certain outcomes better than global ability measures (see Table 4.1 for details). Second, because the ability-achievement (or aptitude-achievement) discrepancy model is a model of *prediction,* the best predictor variables of a particular outcome (e.g., specific academic skills) should be used. Because the WJ-R Scholastic Aptitude Clusters, for example, predict their respective outcomes (e.g., Reading, Math, etc.) better than the WJ-R BCA Clusters (standard or extended), McGrew (1994) argued logically that they are the most appropriate scores to use in ability-achievement discrepancy formulas. Thus, when aptitude measures are used, it is expected that an individual who is deficient in basic reading skills (for example) will have a reading aptitude score that is consistent with the measured level of reading skills, *if such academic-skill deficits are re-*

lated to or can be explained in part by deficits in one or more of the cognitive processes and abilities that comprise the aptitude measure. On the other hand, when an individual who has demonstrated deficient reading skills, for example, demonstrates a Reading Aptitude–Reading Achievement discrepancy (in which measured aptitude is higher than measured achievement), it is unlikely that the manifest reading skills are related to those cognitive processes and abilities that comprise the aptitude measure. This latter situation suggests the need to evaluate performance in other cognitive processes and abilities that are related to reading achievement but that are not measured by the tests that comprise the aptitude measure. For example, the WJ-R Reading Aptitude measure does not include tests of Rapid Automatic Naming (RAN, or Naming Facility as specified in the CHC model). Because RAN has been found to predict basic reading skills to a significant degree, it is an important area to assess in reading-related referrals in addition to the areas represented by the Reading Aptitude Cluster. Additionally, the finding of a Reading Aptitude–Reading Achievement discrepancy in an individual with deficient reading skills suggests the need to explore further factors that are extrinsic to the individual (see Flanagan, McGrew, et al., 2000, for a discussion of these issues).

When evaluated within the context of current legal mandates and various other regulatory requirements, the need to document a significant ability-achievement discrepancy appears to limit or negate the use of aptitude measures in ability-achievement discrepancy formulas. The limitation, however, is an artificial one based on misconceptions involving the relationship between latent cognitive abilities and manifest academic skills. Consider for example, that when individuals demonstrate cognitive-processing or ability deficits in one or more areas that are closely related to the academic-skill deficit (e.g., reading), the finding of a *consistency* (rather than discrepancy) between Reading Aptitude and measured level of Reading Achievement is logical and expected. It is precisely this consistency that provides support for the existence of an underlying cognitive processing or ability deficit, especially when such deficits have been identified and established through CHC Cross-Battery intracognitive and intercognitive discrepancy analyses. The finding of a *discrepancy* between Reading Aptitude and Reading Achievement is illogical and unexpected and provides evidence to suggest that there may not be an intrinsic learning disability (i.e., the specific cognitive abilities comprising the aptitude cluster are not deficient), and that the manifest reading difficulty may be attributable to other factors (e.g., variables extrinsic to the individual).

When assessments are conducted and assessment data are evaluated within the context of contemporary theory and research on the structure of abilities and their relation to specific academic skills, the ability-achievement discrepancy model takes on a new and different dimension in terms of meaning. Specifically, depending on the nature and composition of the global ability index used in an ability-achievement discrepancy formula, findings of significantly discrepant as well as non-discrepant performance may provide support for an underlying learning disability. In short, if all existing data (including background information, educational history, observations, work samples, results of intracognitive and intercognitive analyses, evaluation of exclusionary factors, etc.) *converge on* an underlying learning disability, then use of an aptitude-achievement consistency as further evidence in support of a learning disability is far more defensible than use of an ability-achievement discrepancy as one of the primary criteria (or the sole criterion) in diagnostic decision making. Figures 4.13 and 4.14 demonstrate examples of WJ-R–based C-CB assessments that are organized around Reading and Math Aptitude, respectively,

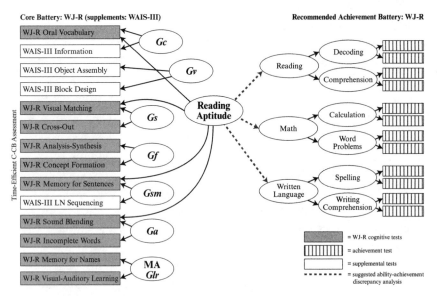

Figure 4.13 Time-efficient C-CB Assessment with WJ-R (Reading Apt Tests) Using WAIS-III as a Supplement

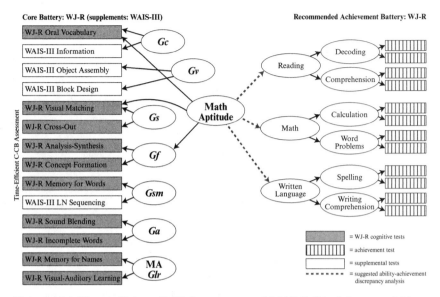

Figure 4.14 Time-efficient C-CB Assessment with WJ-R (Math Apt tests) Using WAIS-III as a Supplement

in addition to the major CHC broad cognitive abilities.[6] For example, Figure 4.13 shows that the Reading Aptitude cluster is comprised of four cognitive ability tests, namely Memory for Sentences, Visual Matching, Sound Blending, and Oral Vocabulary, which measure aspects of *Gsm, Gs, Ga,* and *Gc,* respectively. Of all the WJ-R cognitive ability tests, this subset was found to explain the most variance in reading achievement (see McGrew, 1994; McGrew, Werder, & Woodcock, 1991). Likewise, Figure 4.14 shows that tests of *Gf* (Analysis Synthesis and Concept Formation), *Gs* (Visual Matching) and *Gc* (Oral Vocabulary) comprise the Math Aptitude Cluster on the WJ-R. Of all the WJ-R cognitive ability tests, this subset was found to explain the most variance in math achievement (McGrew, 1994; McGrew et al., 1991).

Because the WJ-R Scholastic Aptitude Clusters explain substantially more variance in academic achievement than that explained by most global ability

---

[6] *Gv* is represented by WAIS-III Object Assembly and Block Design in Figures 4.13 and 4.14 because these tests have typically yielded stronger factor loadings in CHC-driven joint confirmatory factor analysis studies than have WJ-R Visual Closure and Picture Recognition (see Flanagan, McGrew, & Ortiz, 2000).

measures (e.g., Wechsler FSIQ), when used in ability (aptitude)-achievement discrepancy analysis it is reasonable to assume that aptitude and corresponding achievement performance will be *consistent* (not discrepant) for individuals who have weaknesses or deficits in one or more cognitive processes or abilities represented in the aptitude cluster for the reasons just mentioned.

SB:IV: Total Test Composite

The Stanford-Binet Intelligence Scale—Fourth Edition (SB:IV; Thorndike, Hagen, & Sattler, 1986; see Rapid Reference 4.12) measures a broader range of CHC abilities than all the current intelligence batteries except the WJ III. For example, Figure 4.15 shows a combination of SB:IV tests that measure four CHC abilities, namely, *Gc, Gv, Gf,* and *Gsm.* Of these broad cognitive abilities, all can be measured adequately through two or more qualitatively different indicators (or subtests) for the SB:IV except *Gsm,* which includes measures of Memory Span only. The eight SB:IV subtests that measure these four CHC abilities are presented in the white rectangles in Figure 4.15. For illustrative purposes, eight SB:IV tests were used to demonstrate an appropriate battery for a 9-year-old who obtained an average score on the SB:IV Vocabulary (routing) subtest (Delaney & Hopkins, 1987).

Figure 4.15 also shows that the SB:IV subtests that contribute to each of the four CHC abilities (*Gc, Gv, Gf, Gsm*) can be combined to yield a global ability score, called the *Total Test Composite* on the SB:IV. Unlike most other batteries, the SB:IV is not characterized by redundancy in measurement of any broad CHC cognitive abilities. Although the SB:IV contains more than two measures of certain CHC abilities (e.g., *Gv*), its *selective-testing* format provides the practitioner with the flexibility to organize

---

≡ Rapid Reference 4.12

Stanford-Binet Intelligence Scale–Fourth Edition

Authors: Robert L. Thorndike, Elizabeth P. Hagen, and Jerome M. Sattler

Publication Date: 1916–1986

Age Range: 2:0 to 24

Publisher: The Riverside Publishing Company

Further Information: For information on the psychometric, theoretical, and qualitative characteristics of the individual tests in this battery, see: McGrew, K. S., & Flanagan, D. P. (1998). *The intelligence test desk reference (ITDR): Gf-Gc cross-battery assessment.* Boston: Allyn & Bacon.

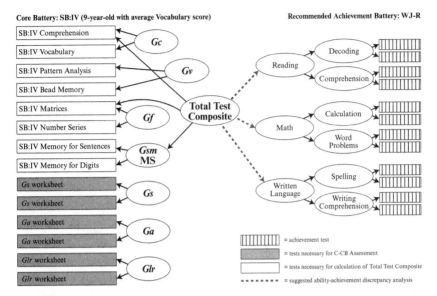

Figure 4.15 Abilities Represented (and Not Represented) in Assessment When a SB:IV Total Test Composite is Derived (9-year-old as example)

a battery of SB:IV subtests to meet the specialized needs of a referral. Moreover, the calculation of the SB:IV Total Test Composite follows directly from the selected subtests in a given evaluation.

For example, although the SB:IV subtests are organized according to the CHC model in Figure 4.15, two were selected from the Verbal Reasoning Area (Vocabulary and Comprehension), three were selected from the Abstract Visual Reasoning Area (Pattern Analysis, Copying, and Matrices), one was selected from the Quantitative Reasoning Area (Number Series), and two were selected from the Short-Term Memory Area (Memory for Sentences and Memory for Digits). Because the test format of the SB:IV allows for this type of selective testing, practitioners can calculate a Total Test Composite based on tests that measure only those abilities considered most germane to the referral.

When abilities not measured by the SB:IV are important to represent in assessment, the practitioners can follow the CHC Cross-Battery principles and procedures to augment this battery, particularly in the areas of *Gs, Ga,* and *Glr.* As may be seen in Figure 4.15, the CHC Cross-Battery Worksheets (Appendix A) can be used to guide the selection of supplemental tests in these areas. In short, within the context of the cross-battery approach, and the need to derive a global ability score, the SB:IV represents one of the best instruments available for two main reasons. First, a total test score can be calculated easily, flexibly, and appropriately within the CHC framework. Second, flexibility in test selection allows for an overall time-efficient assessment of global ability and of seven CHC broad cognitive abilities because it minimizes unnecessary redundancy for any given ability.

CAS: Full Scale Score

The Cognitive Assessment System (CAS; Riverside Publishing, 1997) is another test battery that practitioners may consider useful within the context of conducting comprehensive CHC Cross-Battery assessments. Although the CAS was developed with the express purpose of operationalizing the Planning-Attention-Simultaneous-Successive (PASS) Model of information processing (Naglieri, 1997; Naglieri & Das, 1997), recent research has demonstrated that the factor structure underlying the standardization data of the CAS (Das & Naglieri, 1997; see Rapid Reference 4.13) is perhaps explained better by the CHC theoretical model than the PASS model (e.g., Keith, Kranzler, & Flanagan, in press; Kran-

---

≡Rapid Reference 4.13

Cognitive Assessment System

Authors: J. P. Das and Jack A. Naglieri
Publication Date: 1997
Age Range: 5:0 to 17:11
Publisher: The Riverside Publishing Company
Further Information: For information on the psychometric, theoretical, and qualitative characteristics of the individual tests in this battery, see:

McGrew, K. S., & Flanagan, D. P. (1998). *The intelligence test desk reference (ITDR): Gf-Gc cross-battery assessment.* Boston: Allyn & Bacon.

Naglieri, J. A. (1997). Planning, attention, simultaneous, and successive theory and the Cognitive Assessment System: A new theory-based measure of intelligence. In D. P. Flanagan, J. L. Genshaft, & P. L. Harrison (Eds.), *Contemporary intellectual assessment: Theories, tests, and issues* (pp. 247–267). New York: Guilford.

Naglieri, J. A. (1999). *Essentials of CAS Assessment.* New York: Wiley.

zler & Keith, 1999; Kranzler, Keith, & Flanagan, in press). Accordingly, the CAS will be discussed within the context of CHC Cross-Battery Assessment.

When the core battery for C-CB assessment is the CAS and the derivation of the CAS global ability score is necessary or desired, 12 subtests must be administered (for individuals ages 8–17 years): Matching Numbers, Planned Codes, Planned Connections, Expressive Attention, Number Detection, Receptive Attention, Nonverbal Matrices, Verbal-Spatial Relations, Figure Memory, Word Series, Sentence Repetition, and Sentence Questions. These tests are represented by the white rectangles in Figure 4.16.

As can be seen in Figure 4.16, in order to calculate the Full Scale score on the CAS, practitioners will need to administer six measures of *Gs*, three measures of primary *Gv* abilities, and three measures of *Gsm* (mainly Memory Span). The major drawback in using the CAS as the core battery in C-CB assessment, especially when derivation of the CAS global ability score is desired, is this redundancy in measurement of *Gs*. Compared to *Gs*, *Gv* and *Gsm* are measured in a much more time-efficient manner on the CAS. However, *Gsm* is underrepresented on the CAS because it is measured by tests of Memory Span only.

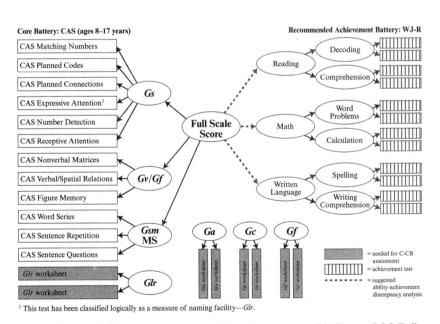

[1] This test has been classified logically as a measure of naming facility—*Glr*.

Figure 4.16 Abilities Represented (and Not Represented) When a CAS Full Scale Score is Derived

The gray shaded boxes in Figure 4.16 represent the additional subtests that would need to be administered in order to ensure that all the major CHC broad abilities are measured adequately in a CAS Full Scale Score-based C-CB assessment. As depicted in Figure 4.16, when a CAS Full Scale score is required and measurement of the seven CHC broad cognitive abilities is desirable, 20 subtests would need to be administered, at a minimum! As in the case with the WPPSI-R FSIQ–based C-CB assessment (see Figure 4.6), the minimum number of subtests necessary to achieve a CAS Full Scale score–based C-CB assessment is not very practical. For this reason, it is recommended that the CAS be used as a supplemental instrument in C-CB assessment, especially when derivation of a global ability score is necessary. The CAS would be particularly useful, for example, as a supplement to other batteries that either do not measure or do not measure adequately the CHC broad ability of *Gs*.

THE MAJOR INTELLIGENCE TESTS, GLOBAL ABILITY SCORES, AND C-CB ASSESSMENT: PUTTING IT ALL TOGETHER

The previous discussion of organizing assessments around the contemporary CHC theoretical model highlighted the current theory-measurement gap that exists in assessment-related fields. Specifically, in order to ensure adequate measurement of the major CHC broad cognitive abilities in assessment, all current intelligence batteries, including the Wechsler Scales, DAS, KAIT, K-ABC, WJ-R, SB:IV, CAS, and so forth, need to be supplemented with tests from other batteries following the CHC Cross-Battery principles and procedures. This was especially evident in the assessment of preschool-aged children, in which case the lack of available tests greatly limits and constrains the choices for practitioners. Moreover, although practitioners can typically assess the major CHC broad cognitive abilities in a time-efficient manner using the CHC Cross-Battery approach (Flanagan, McGrew, et al., 2000; McGrew & Flanagan, 1998), C-CB assessment time is compromised by the need to derive a global ability score.

When a global ability score must be derived for use in ability-achievement discrepancy analyses or for other purposes, within the context of C-CB assessment, the average time spent in assessment may increase depending on the core battery selected for this purpose. Rapid Reference 4.14 provides a summary of the number of tests necessary to administer when a global ability score from a given intelligence battery is derived within the context of C-CB assessment. For example,

≡ *Rapid Reference 4.14*

Summary of Number of Tests Necessary for C-CB Assessments by Battery and Global Ability Score

Core Battery Used in C-CB Assessment	Global Score	Minimum No. of Subtests Required[1]	Example
WISC-III	FSIQ	19	Figure 4.1
WISC-III	GAI	18	Figure 4.2
WISC-III	WASI FSIQ-4	14	Figure 4.3
WAIS-III	FSIQ	18	Figure 4.4
WAIS-III	WASI FSIQ-4	14	Figure 4.5
WPPSI-R	FSIQ	20	Figure 4.6
WPPSI-R (6- and 7-year-olds)	WASI FSIQ-4	14	Figure 4.7
DAS (3:6 to 5:11)	GCA	15	Figure 4.8
DAS (6:0 to 17:11)	GCA	14	Figure 4.9
KAIT	Composite IQ	15	Figure 4.10
K-ABC (5:0 to 12:5)	MPC	17	Figure 4.11
WJ-R	BCA (Standard)	14	Figure 4.12
WJ-R	Reading Scholastic Aptitude	14	Figure 4.13
WJ-R	Math Scholastic Aptitude	14	Figure 4.14
SB:IV	Total Test Composite	14	Figure 4.15
CAS	Full Scale Score	20	Figure 4.16

Note. All CHC Cross-Battery assessments in this table include measures of *Gf, Gc, Ga, Gv, Gsm, Glr,* and *Gs.*

[1]This number of subtests will need to be administered *only when* the global ability score from the core battery (or column 2) is desired *in addition to* the seven major CHC broad abilities.

Rapid Reference 4.14 shows that when the DAS, WJ-R, or SB:IV is selected as the core battery in C-CB assessment, practitioners can calculate both a global ability score and seven cluster scores in the areas of *Gf, Gc, Ga, Gv, Gsm, Glr,* and *Gs* by administering only 14 subtests. However, when a Wechsler FSIQ is required, practitioners will need to administer 18 to 20 tests to achieve the same result (i.e., a global ability score or FSIQ and seven CHC broad cognitive ability clusters). When one of the Wechsler Scales is chosen as the core battery in C-CB assessment and a global ability score is needed, guidelines for using and interpreting the WASI FSIQ-4 were presented in an effort to reduce the number of tests (from 18–20 subtests to 14 subtests), and thus testing time, without significantly jeopardizing the psychometric rigor behind the CHC Cross-Battery approach.

Given the range of global ability scores that can be derived from the major intelligence batteries (see Rapid Reference 4.14), it is reasonable to assume that these scores may differ from one another in some qualitative way. An examination of Figures 4.1 through 4.16 demonstrates, for example, that the total test scores of each intelligence battery are composed of a different cognitive ability mix of subtests. The different cognitive ability compositions of the global ability scores included in Figures 4.1 through 4.16 are summarized in Table 4.3. This table shows that no two total test scores are exactly alike. Although *group* data show that these global ability scores predict various outcomes (academic achievement) similarly, *individual* data may vary as a function of intra-individual strengths and weaknesses. For example, a school-aged child with poor *Gf* ability may demonstrate a lower DAS GCA as compared to his or her WISC-III FSIQ, simply because the GCA is based in part on *Gf* performance, whereas the FSIQ is not (see Table 4.3).

The fact that no two global ability scores are created equal has implications for how such scores are used to make diagnostic and educational-placement decisions. For example, if the child in the previous example also demonstrated poor reading comprehension and math achievement (two academic skill domains that are explained, in part, by *Gf* abilities), his or her GCA may be more consistent with academic performance in these areas than his or her FSIQ. In these situations practitioners will typically opt for the FSIQ in ability-achievement discrepancy analyses simply out of legal necessity—that is, the need to demonstrate a discrepancy between ability and achievement when documenting a learning disability. The guidelines that follow demonstrate how practitioners can relegate the ability-achievement discrepancy component of

Table 4.3 CHC Narrow (Stratum I) Abilities Measured by Cognitive Battery Test Composites

CHC Ability	WPPSI-R FSIQ	WISC-III FSIQ	WISC-III GAI	WAIS-III FSIQ	WASI FSIQ-4	DAS GCA (preschool)	DAS GCA (school-age)	KAIT Composite IQ	K-ABC (MPC; ages 5:0–12:5)	WJ-R BCA (7 subtests)	WJ-R Reading Aptitude Cluster	WJ-R Math Aptitude Cluster	CAS Full Scale
Gf													
RG						✓		✓	✓	✓		✓	✓
I				✓	✓	✓	✓	✓	✓			✓	✓
RQ						✓							
Gq													
A3	✓	✓		✓	✓	✓							
KM						✓			✓				
Gc													
LD	✓	✓	✓	✓	✓	✓	✓	✓		✓	✓	✓	
VL	✓	✓	✓	✓	✓	✓	✓	✓			✓	✓	
LS			✓			✓		✓					
KO	✓	✓			✓	✓							
Gsm													
MS				✓		✓	✓		✓	✓	✓		✓
MV (*Gv*)									✓				✓
Gv													
Vz	✓	✓	✓	✓	✓	✓	✓		✓	✓			
SR	✓	✓	✓	✓		✓			✓				
CS	✓	✓	✓										✓
CF	✓	✓	✓	✓									✓
SS	✓												✓
PI											✓		
Ga													
PC-S										✓			
PC-A													

(continued)

Table 4.3 (continued)

CHC Ability	WPPSI-R FSIQ	WISC-III FSIQ	WISC-III GAI	WAIS-III FSIQ	WASI FSIQ-4	DAS GCA (preschool)	DAS GCA (school-age)	KAIT Composite IQ	K-ABC MPC; (ages 5:0–12:5)	WJ-R BCA (7 subtests)	WJ-R Reading Aptitude Cluster	WJ-R Math Aptitude Cluster	CAS Full Scale
Glr													
MA								✓		✓			
MM								✓					
NA													✓
Gs													
P		✓		✓									✓
R9										✓	✓	✓	✓
N										✓	✓	✓	✓
Gt													
R4													✓
R7													
Grw													
RD								✓					
V								✓					
SG								✓					

Note. Table includes primary and secondary abilities as well as "probable" and "possible" classifications in a manner consistent with the *ITDR* (McGrew & Flanagan, 1998). Some tests may measure psychomotor abilities that are not reported in this table.

most learning-disability definitions to the back burner in favor of a research-based method of uncovering underlying cognitive processing and ability strengths and weaknesses that are related to manifest academic skills performance. When multiple sources of data are available that converge on a diagnosis of learning disability, practitioners can use this method as well as their knowledge of the cognitive ability composition of global ability scores and the relations between these cognitive abilities and academic achievements to interpret more appropriately the results of ability-achievement analyses within a comprehensive framework for assessing learning difficulties.

Guidelines for Interpreting Ability-Achievement Discrepancies

It may be helpful to follow along with the flowchart depicted in Figure 4.17, which provides an illustration of the points to be described herein. First, practitioners should determine whether there is a significant ability-achievement discrepancy. Many test manuals contain critical-value tables that provide the values necessary for determining whether a given ability-achievement standard-score difference is significant (at either the .05 or .01 level of confidence). Some computer software scoring and report-writing programs also include a set of functions for determining statistically significant ability-achievement discrepancies. Rapid Reference 4.15 provides the information necessary to locate the appropriate sources necessary to determine whether a given ability-achievement discrepancy is significant depending on the measure and global ability score used.

Second, in addition to statistical significance, some test manuals provide information regarding whether the magnitude of the ability-achievement difference is *unusual*. This is accomplished typically by examining base-rate data. For example, if it is found that the magnitude of an individual's ability-achievement discrepancy occurred in less than 5% of same-age peers in the standardization sample, then the difference is considered unusual and may be clinically meaningful (see Sattler, 1992). Recall, however, that a significant and meaningful ability-achievement discrepancy, in and of itself, neither supports nor fails to support the presence of a learning disability (see Table 4.1; Flanagan, McGrew, et al., 2000).

Third, it is necessary to consider whether the cognitive abilities that have been found in the extant literature to predict the academic skill identified as problematic in the referral were included in the derivation of a total test-ability score (Table 2.1 provides a summary of this literature; see also McGrew &

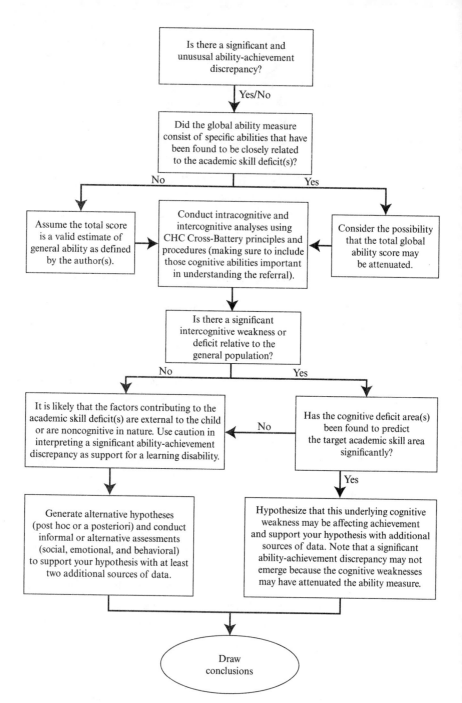

Figure 4.17 Flowchart for Interpretation of Ability-Achievement Discrepancies

Relevant Sources for the Determination of Significant Ability-Achievement Discrepancies

Predictor Variable (Ability)	Criterion Variable	Critical Values for Determining Difference between Predicted and Actual Achievement
WAIS-III FSIQ	WIAT	*WAIS-III/WMS-III Technical Manual:* Table B.13 "Differences Between Predicted and Obtained WIAT Subtest and Composite Scores Required for Statistical Significance (Predicted-Difference Method—WAIS-III FSIQ)" p. 280
WAIS-III VIQ	WIAT	*WAIS-III/WMS-III Technical Manual:* Table B.14 "Differences Between Predicted and Obtained WIAT Subtest and Composite Scores Required for Statistical Significance (Predicted-Difference Method—WAIS-III VIQ)" p. 281
WAIS-III PIQ	WIAT	*WAIS-III/WMS-III Technical Manual:* Table B.15 "Differences Between Predicted and Obtained WIAT Subtest and Composite Scores Required for Statistical Significance (Predicted-Difference Method—WAIS-III PIQ)" p. 282
WPPSI-R FSIQ	WIAT	*WIAT Manual:* Table C.4 "Ability-Achievement Discrepancies: Differences Between Predicted and Actual Subtest Standard Scores and Between Predicted and Actual Composite Standard Scores Required for Statistical Significance (Predicted-Achievement Method)" p. 352

(continued)

Predictor Variable (Ability)	Criterion Variable	Critical Values for Determining Difference between Predicted and Actual Achievement
WISC-III FSIQ	WIAT	*WIAT Manual:* Table C.4 "Ability–Achievement Discrepancies: Differences Between Predicted and Actual Subtest Standard Scores and Between Predicted and Actual Composite Standard Scores Required for Statistical Significance (Predicted-Achievement Method)" p. 352
WISC-III VIQ	WIAT	Flanagan and Alfonso (1993a, b)
WISC-III PIQ	WIAT	Flanagan and Alfonso (1993a, b)
CAS	WJ-R Achievement	*CAS Administration and Scoring Manual:* Appendix F "Comparisons with the Woodcock-Johnson-Revised Tests of Achievement" pp. 209–274
WJ-R BCA-Standard	WJ-R Achievement	Appendix G of this text
WJ-R Scholastic Aptitude Clusters	WJ-R Achievement	*WJ-R Manual:* Woodcock Scoring and Interpretive Program (Schrank & Woodcock, 1997)
WASI	WIAT	Appendix G of this text

Flanagan, 1998). If these abilities were assessed and performance on tests of these abilities was reflected in the global ability score used in the discrepancy analysis, then the total test score may be attenuated. Conversely, if these abilities were not assessed (and thus, performance on tests of these abilities was not reflected in the total test score), then it is assumed that the total test score is a valid estimate of general intelligence as defined by its cognitive ability constituents, provided there were not any individual/situational or background/environmental factors that inhibited performance (Flanagan, McGrew, et al., 2000).[7]

Fourth, conduct intracognitive and intercognitive discrepancy analyses using the CHC Cross-Battery principles and procedures (detailed in Chapters 2 and 3). Prior to conducting these analyses, the examiner should ensure that the cognitive abilities that are most predictive of the presenting academic skill deficit(s) are represented in the assessment. If an intercognitive deficit was not found based on this method, then it is assumed that factors contributing to the academic skill deficit(s) identified in the referral may be external to the individual or that they are most likely *noncognitive* in nature. Therefore, the fundamental *a priori* hypothesis (i.e., that the individual is not disabled) cannot be rejected and alternative explanations (e.g., factors extrinsic to the individual) for any observed manifest difficulties must be carefully reconsidered. In sum, it is best practice to exercise considerable caution when interpreting a significant ability-achievement discrepancy as support for a learning-disability diagnosis.

Guidelines for interpreting deficient performance based on the results of intracognitive and intercognitive analyses were presented in Chapter 3 (see Figure 8.12). If one or more cognitive weaknesses or deficits is found, it is necessary to determine whether the identified cognitive ability deficit(s) is related to the academic skill deficit(s). As may be seen in Figure 4.17, if the cognitive ability deficit(s) is closely associated with the academic skill deficit(s), then it is logical and reasonable to hypothesize that an underlying deficit in this cognitive domain(s) is affecting academic achievement adversely. If measures of abilities within the cognitive domain identified as an area of deficit are part of

---

[7] It is also important to examine whether aberrant scores artificially inflated or attenuated the global ability composite. In such instances, the global score may not represent an accurate estimate of general ability or intelligence. Most test manuals and intelligence test resources provide guidelines for interpretation of global ability scores.

the ability measure, then it is important to realize that a significant ability-achievement discrepancy may not emerge because the cognitive deficit(s) may have attenuated the ability measure (total test score) in the ability-achievement discrepancy analysis. This is the main reason why primary emphasis should be placed on intracognitive and intercognitive analyses rather than on ability-achievement or aptitude-achievement discrepancy analyses in learning disability identification and diagnostic procedures. Figure 4.17 shows that identified cognitive deficits should always be corroborated by other sources of data prior to drawing conclusions.

SUMMARY

This chapter highlighted the major limitations of the ability-achievement discrepancy model for the purpose of identifying and diagnosing learning disability. In spite of its many limitations and, indeed, of its invalidity as a method in and of itself to diagnose learning disability, practitioners are often mandated by law to conduct an ability-achievement discrepancy analysis as part of a comprehensive learning disability evaluation (e.g., in special education–related evaluations). Consequently, this chapter offered guidelines to assist practitioners in conducting comprehensive CHC Cross-Battery assessments that allow for the generation of a global ability score for such purposes in a practical and time-efficient manner. The purpose in offering these guidelines was threefold:

1. To encourage the use of a more theoretically and psychometrically defensible method of evaluating multiple cognitive abilities that incorporates an efficient means of deriving a global ability score
2. To encourage examination of intracognitive, intercognitive and, intra-achievement discrepancy analyses as the preferred and primary method for establishing whether an individual demonstrates cognitive deficits that are empirically (or logically) related to manifest academic skill deficits
3. To provide guidelines that assist practitioners in evaluating and interpreting significant and nonsignificant ability (or aptitude)-achievement discrepancies appropriately with respect to the decision-making process involved in documenting and supporting the presence of a learning disability.

It is hoped that the information presented herein will allow practitioners to understand more clearly the nature of and meaning behind ability-achievement discrepancy analysis to the extent that it will represent an appropriate and defensible *secondary or tertiary* (rather than the primary or sole) component of future learning disability evaluations.

To summarize, it is clear that the meaning of an ability-achievement discrepancy is largely dependent upon the content (i.e., cognitive mix) of the general ability measure and upon the relations among the cognitive abilities that comprise the general ability score and the achievement domain in question. Ability-achievement discrepancies, in and of themselves, do not provide much insight into the nature of a learning disability. Unfortunately, much of the current legal and regulatory criteria for documenting a learning disability has not caught up with and does not reflect the current research that argues strongly against reliance on an ability-achievement discrepancy model. Until the appropriate agencies and constituencies that are responsible for defining and developing the criteria for identifying and documenting learning disability understand the often dangerous and misguided decisions that have resulted from uninformed interpretations of significant ability-achievement discrepancies—indeed, interpretations that are made out of legal necessity rather than in the context of scientific evidence—practitioners will continue to be forced to couch these largely meaningless ability-achievement discrepancy results within a defensible framework that allows for responsible clinical and educational decision making (e.g., in accordance with IDEA criteria, *DSM-IV* criteria, the Americans with Disabilities Act, etc.). Practitioners who follow the guidelines presented in this chapter should gain a greater appreciation and understanding of the arbitrary nature of the ability-achievement discrepancy approach. They will then be in a better position to defend their choices of global ability estimates for this purpose, to defend their interpretations of selected ability-achievement discrepancy comparisons, and to defend their use of ability-achievement discrepancy findings (be they significant or nonsignificant) in decisions regarding learning disability determination.

REFERENCES

American Psychiatric Association. (1994). *Diagnostic and Statistical Manual of Mental Disorders* (4th ed.). Washington, DC: Author.

Brackett, J., & McPherson, A. (1996). Learning disabilities diagnosis in postsecondary students: A comparison of discrepancy-based diagnostic models. In N. Gregg, C. Hoy, & A. F. Gay (Eds.), *Adults with learning disabilities: Theoretical and practical perspectives* (pp. 68–84). New York: Guilford.

Cohen, M. (1997). *Children's memory scale.* San Antonio, TX: Psychological Corporation.

Das, J. P., & Naglieri, J. A. (1997). *Cognitive Assessment System.* Itasca, IL: Riverside.

Delaney, E. A., & Hopkins, T. E. (1987). *Examiner's handbook: An expanded guide for fourth edition users.* Chicago, IL: Riverside.

Elliott, C. D. (1990). *Differential ability scales.* San Antonio, TX: Psychological Corporation.

Flanagan, D. P., & Alfonso, V. C. (1995). A critical review of the technical characteristics of new and recently revised intelligence tests for preschool children. *Journal of Psychoeducational Assessment, 13,* 66–90.

Flanagan, D. P., Mascolo, J., & Genshaft, J. L. (2000). A conceptual framework for interpreting preschool intelligence tests. In B. A. Bracken (Ed.), *The psychoeducational assessment of preschool children* (pp. 428–473). Boston: Allyn & Bacon.

Flanagan, D. P., McGrew, K. S., & Ortiz, S. O. (2000). *The Wechsler intelligence scales and Gf-Gc theory: A contemporary approach to interpretation.* Boston: Allyn & Bacon.

Flanagan, D. P. (in press). Wechsler-based CHC cross-battery assessment and reading achievement: Strengthening the validity of interpretations drawn from Wechsler test scores. *School Psychology Quarterly.*

Gridley, B. E., & Roid, G. H. (1998). The use of the WISC-III with achievement tests. In A. Prifitera & D. Saklofske (Eds.), *WISC-III clinical use and interpretation: Scientist-practitioner perspectives* (pp. 249–288). San Diego: Academic.

Individuals with Disabilities Education Act of 1997 (IDEA), 20 U.S.C. §§ 1400 *et seq.* (West, 1997).

Kaufman, A. S., & Kaufman, N. L. (1983). *Kaufman Assessment Battery for Children.* Circle Pines, MN: American Guidance Service.

Kaufman, A. S., & Kaufman, N. L. (1993). *The Kaufman Adolescent and Adult Intelligence Test.* Circle Pines, MN: American Guidance Service.

Keith, T. Z. (1999). Effects of general and specific abilities on student achievement: Similarities and differences across ethnic groups. *School Psychology Quarterly.*

Keith, T. Z., Kranzler, J., & Flanagan, D. P. (in press). What does the Cognitive Assessment System (CAS) measure? Joint confirmatory factory analysis of the CAS and the Woodcock-Johnson Tests of Cognitive Ability–Third Edition (WJ III). *School Psychology Review.*

Kranzler, J. H., & Keith, T. Z. (1999). Independent confirmatory factor analysis of the Cognitive Assessment System (CAS): What does the CAS measure? *School Psychology Review, 28,* 117–144.

Lezak, M. D. (1995). *Neuropsychological assessment* (3rd ed.). New York: Oxford University Press.

Lyon, G. R. (1995). Toward a definition of dyslexia. *Annals of Dyslexia, 45,* 3–27.

Mather, N., & Roberts, R. (1994). Learning disabilities: A field in danger of extinction? *Learning Disabilities Research & Practice, 9*(1), 49–58.

McGrew, K. S. (1993). The relationship between the WJ-R *Gf-Gc* cognitive clusters and reading achievement across the lifespan. *Journal of Psychoeducational Assessment, Monograph Series: WJ-R Monograph,* 39–53.

McGrew, K. S. (1994). *Clinical interpretation of the Woodcock-Johnson Tests of Cognitive Ability–Revised.* Boston: Allyn & Bacon.

McGrew, K. S., & Flanagan, D. P. (1998). *The intelligence test desk reference (ITDR):* Gf-Gc cross-battery assessment. Boston: Allyn & Bacon.

McGrew, K. S., Flanagan, D. P., Keith, T. Z., & Vanderwood, M. (1997). Beyond *g:* The impact of *Gf-Gc* specific cognitive abilities research on the future use and interpretation of intelligence tests in the schools. *School Psychology Review.*

McGrew, K. S., Werder, J. K., & Woodcock, R. W. (1991). *Woodcock-Johnson Psycho-Educational Battery–Revised technical manual.* Chicago: Riverside.

Mercer, C. D., Jordan, L., Allsopp, D. H., & Mercer, A. R. (1999). *Learning disabilities definitions and criteria used by state education departments.* Manuscript submitted for publication.

Naglieri, J. A. (1997). Planning, attention, simultaneous, and successive theory and the Cognitive Assessment System: A new theory-based measure of intelligence. In D. P. Flanagan, J. L. Genshaft, & P. L. Harrison (Eds.), *Contemporary intellectual assessment: Theories, tests, and issues* (pp. 247–267). New York: Guilford.

Naglieri, J. A., & Das, J. P. (1997). *Cognitive Assessment System: Interpretive handbook.* IL: Riverside.

Prifitera, A., Weiss, L. G., & Saklofske, D. (1998). *WISC-III clinical use and interpretation.* San Diego: Academic.

Psychological Corporation. (1999). *Wechsler Abbreviated Scale of Intelligence.* San Antonio, TX: Psychological Corporation.

Reynolds, C. R. (1984–1985). Critical measurement issues in learning disabilities. *Journal of Special Education, 18,* 451–475.

Sattler, J. (1992). *Assessment of children* (Rev. 3rd ed.). San Diego: Sattler.

Siegel, L. S. (1998). The discrepancy formula: Its use and abuse. In B. K. Shapiro, P. J. Accardo, & A. J. Capute (Eds.), *Specific reading disability: A view of the spectrum* (pp. 123–136). Timonium, MD: York.

Snow, R. E. (1994). Abilities and aptitudes. In R. J. Sternberg (Ed.), *Encyclopedia of human intelligence* (pp. 3–5). New York: Macmillan.

Thorndike, R. L., Hagen, E. P., & Sattler, J. M. (1986). *Stanford-Binet Intelligence Scale: Guide for administering and scoring the fourth edition.* Chicago: Riverside.

Vanderwood, M., McGrew, K. S., Flanagan, D. P., & Keith, T. Z. (2000). *Examination of the contribution of general and specific cognitive abilities to reading achievement.* Manuscript submitted for publication.

Wechsler, D. (1989). *Wechsler Preschool and Primary Scale of Intelligence–Revised.* San Antonio, TX: Psychological Corporation.

Wechsler, D. (1991). *Wechsler Intelligence Scale for Children* (3rd ed.). San Antonio, TX: Psychological Corporation.

Wechsler, D. (1997). *Wechsler Adult Intelligence Scale–Third Edition.* San Antonio, TX: Psychological Corporation.

Wilson, B. C. (1992). The neuropsychological assessment of the preschool child: A branching model. In I. Rapm & S. I. Segalowitz (Eds.), *Handbook of neuropsychology: Child neuropsychology* (Vol. 6, pp. 377–394).

Woodcock, R. W., & Johnson, M. B. (1989). *Woodcock-Johnson Psycho-Educational Battery–Revised.* Chicago: Riverside.

Woodcock, R. W., & Mather, N. (1989). WJ-R tests of cognitive ability—Standard and supplemental batteries: Examiner's manual. In R. W. Woodcock & M. B. Johnson (Eds.), *Woodcock-Johnson Psycho-Educational Battery* (Rev. ed.). Chicago: Riverside.

Woodcock, R. W., & McGrew, K. S. (in press). *Woodcock-Johnson Psycho-Educational Battery* (3rd ed.). Chicago: Riverside.

🖋 TEST YOURSELF 🖋

1. **Within the context of an *initial* Comprehensive CHC Cross-Battery assessment, redundancy in measurement of cognitive abilities is characterized by**

   (a) the use of two subtests that purport to measure a particular cognitive ability.

   (b) the use of three or more subtests that purport to measure a particular cognitive ability.

2. **In CHC Cross-Battery assessment, cognitive abilities should be summarized in a cluster that is composed of at least two measures of the ability in question.** True or False?

3. **Which of the following distinguishes the WISC-III GAI from the FSIQ?**

   (a) The GAI does not include Arithmetic and Coding; the FSIQ does.

   (b) The FSIQ does not include Arithmetic and Coding; the GAI does.

   (c) It takes more time to administer the tests that comprise the GAI compared to those that comprise the FSIQ.

   (d) The FSIQ includes measures of Gc and Gv, whereas the GAI includes measures of Gc, Gv, Gq, and Gs.

4. **Which battery provides the broadest measurement of CHC abilities?**

   (a) WISC-III

   (b) WAIS-III

   (c) CAS

   (d) DAS

   (e) WJ-R/III

   (f) KAIT

   (g) SB:IV

5. **When conducting an *in-depth* assessment (i.e., administering three or more qualitatively different indicators of a broad cognitive ability), how many CHC broad cognitive abilities can be assessed in preschool-aged children (age 3 to 5 years) using currently available preschool assessment tools?**

   (a) 10

   (b) 8

   (c) 5

   (d) 2

6. **The SB:IV is considered a good instrument to use as the core battery in Comprehensive Cross-Battery (C-CB) assessment when the derivation of a global ability score is warranted because**

   (a) it incorporates flexibility in regard to the organization and selection of the tests that comprise the Total Composite.

   (b) it includes many tests that fit well within the CHC framework.

   (c) it provides adequate measurement of all the major CHC broad abilities.

   (d) it is not a good instrument to use in C-CB assessment.

   (e) both (a) and (b)

   (f) both (a) and (c)

7. **The WPPSI-R is considered a good instrument to use as the core battery in Comprehensive Cross-Battery (C-CB) assessment when the derivation of a global ability score is warranted because**

   (a) the FSIQ is the best index of global ability.

   (b) it includes many tests that fit well within the CHC framework.

   (c) it provides adequate measurement of all the major CHC broad abilities.

   (d) no reason; it is not a good instrument to use in C-CB assessment when derivation of a global ability score is warranted.

   (e) both (a) and (b)

   (f) both (a) and (c)

(continued)

8. **When a Wechsler Scale is selected as the core battery in Comprehensive Cross-Battery assessment and derivation of a global ability score is warranted, the WASI FSIQ-4 is recommended over the FSIQ because**

(a) it takes less time to administer the tests that make up the FSIQ-4 compared to the FSIQ.

(b) the FSIQ-4 is a reasonably good estimate of global ability and therefore can be used in lieu of the FSIQ under certain circumstances.

(c) the FSIQ is characterized by redundancy in measurement of certain abilities (e.g., *Gc*, *Gv*) and therefore is unnecessarily time consuming when an assessment of a broad range of abilities is desired.

(d) all of the above

(e) none of the above

9. **The WASI FSIQ-4 may be used as the ability score in ability-achievement discrepancy analysis when which of the following criteria is/are met?**

(a) The tests that comprise the WASI FSIQ-4 have been administered within the context of a Wechsler-based comprehensive CHC Cross-Battery (C-CB) approach.

(b) Intercognitive analysis of the Wechsler-based C-CB data reveals one or more specific cognitive-processing or -ability deficits within an otherwise average or better profile of cognitive capabilities.

(c) A clear empirical (or logical) connection between the cognitive ability deficit(s) and the manifest academic skill deficit(s) was documented.

(d) Other sources of data are available to support the cognitive and academic deficits identified through C-CB assessment.

(e) A comprehensive review of case history data demonstrates that the cognitive and academic deficit(s) are not the result of external factors or influences.

(f) none of the above

(g) all of the above

10. **The finding of a significant ability-achievement discrepancy, in and of itself, is sufficient evidence to support a diagnosis of learning disability.** True or False?

11. **There are times when a *nonsignificant* difference between ability (or aptitude) and achievement can be used to support existing evidence of an underlying learning disability.** True or False?

Answers: 1. b; 2. True; 3. a; 4. e; 5. d; 6. e; 7. d; 8. d; 9. g; 10. False; 11. True

Five

HOW TO APPLY CHC CROSS-BATTERY ASSESSMENT TO CULTURALLY AND LINGUISTICALLY DIVERSE INDIVIDUALS

Working with culturally and linguistically diverse individuals presents unique challenges to practitioners, especially in the use of standardized tests of intelligence or cognitive ability. In recognition of the need to consider the many variables that may influence the manner in which psychological services should be delivered to diverse individuals, the American Psychological Association (APA) published *Guidelines for Providers of Psychological Services to Ethnic, Linguistic, and Culturally Diverse Populations* (1990). The guidelines emphasized the need for psychologists to acknowledge the influences of language and culture on behavior and to consider those factors when working with diverse groups, particularly in regard to the validity of the methods and procedures used for assessment and interpretation.

Unfortunately, the manner in which language and culture affect test performance, let alone interpretation of test results, remains very poorly understood. Training programs do not routinely provide such training and few standards exist that specify precisely what which practitioners should know when working with individuals from one particular culture or another (Ortiz & Flanagan, 1998). Moreover, there is a tendency to view cultural differences as primarily a language difference, which in turn leads to neglect of factors that are extremely important in understanding the nature of test results. Practitioners should remember "mere possession of the capacity to communicate in an individual's native language does not ensure appropriate, nondiscriminatory assessment of that individual. Traditional assessment practices and their inherent biases can be easily replicated in any number of languages" (Flanagan, McGrew, & Ortiz, 2000, p. 291). Finally, the lack of a comprehensive, systematic framework for nondiscriminatory assessment in the literature leaves practitioners frantically searching for guidance on what constitutes best practices for diverse individuals. These factors have resulted in situations

213

DON'T FORGET

Assessment Bias and Cultural Diversity

"[The] mere possession of the capacity to communicate in an individual's native language does not ensure appropriate, nondiscriminatory assessment of that individual. Traditional assessment practices and their inherent biases can be easily replicated in any number of languages" (Flanagan, McGrew, & Ortiz, 2000, p. 291).

in which there may be untrained or poorly trained individuals, with varying levels of language proficiency, who are attempting to evaluate equitably the abilities of diverse individuals with procedures and methods that do not take into account the attenuating effects of culture or language differences. As such, issues in instrument selection, instrument administration, and instrument interpretation (not to mention referral and the entire decision-making process as well) remain problematic at best for the vast majority of practitioners using standardized tests (Ysseldyke, 1979).

The entire breadth and depth of the issues involved in bilingual, cross-cultural, nondiscriminatory assessment are far beyond the scope of this chapter and book. There are no simple answers, prescriptions, or shortcuts for this rather complex topic. Practitioners are often concerned primarily with trying to determine which standardized tools are considered best and which are not, but this represents only a very small part of what is a much broader process. In fact, there are many occasions in which standardized tests may not be used at all for the purposes of assessment. The CHC Cross-Battery assessment procedures to be discussed in this chapter must not be viewed as the answer to the broad range of difficulties encountered in the comprehensive assessment of diverse individuals. Rather, CHC Cross-Battery assessment should, as with the use of standardized tests in any comprehensive evaluation, be seen as only one component that is integrated together with multiple sources of data into a larger framework that uses the individual's cultural and linguistic history as the appropriate context from which to draw meaning and conclusions from the data. Figure 5.1 provides an example of how CHC Cross-Battery assessment should be viewed as representing only one element within the structure of a broad approach to nondiscriminatory assessment. The steps outlined in Figure 5.1 were developed by Ortiz (2000) and represent the various stages of assessment that would comprise a comprehensive, systematic approach to

1. Develop culturally- and linguistically-based hypotheses.
2. Assess language history, development, and proficiency.
3. Assess effects of cultural and linguistic differences.
4. Assess environmental and community factors.
5. Evaluate, revise, and re-test hypotheses.
6. Determine appropriate languages of assessment.
7. Reduce bias in traditional practices.
8. Utilize authentic and alternative assessment practices.
9. Apply cultural-linguistic context to all data.
10. Link assessment to intervention.

Figure 5.1   A Model for Comprehensive Nondiscriminatory Assessment

reducing bias and discrimination in the assessment of diverse individuals. Note that in the overall structure of this approach, CHC Cross-Battery assessment is utilized primarily in only one of the ten stages depicted (the shaded area). As such, it represents only a portion of the entire assessment process, emphasizing the fact that CHC Cross-Battery assessment (even with the cultural and linguistic extensions to be described) is insufficient to represent the totality of what might constitute current best practices in the assessment of culturally and linguistically diverse children. To accomplish such an undertaking properly would entail the application of a broad framework that is well beyond the scope of this chapter. However, as a beginning point to understanding the issues in-

CAUTION

CHC Cross-Battery Assessment as Part of a Larger Whole

CHC Cross-Battery assessment procedures must not be viewed as the answer to the broad range of difficulties encountered in the comprehensive assessment of diverse individuals. Rather, CHC Cross-Battery assessment is only one component that is integrated together with multiple sources of data into a larger framework that uses the individual's cultural and linguistic history as the appropriate context from which to draw meaning and conclusions from the data.

volved in the use of standardized tests with diverse individuals, the following discussion and approach is offered.

This chapter begins with a section that discusses the manner in which culture and language typically affect the assessment process. This discussion is crucial in order to allow practitioners to gain a firm appreciation of what factors constitute bias or discrimination and those that do not. This discussion also highlights the need and rationale behind the extensions of the CHC Cross-Battery method to culturally and linguistically diverse populations. The next section in this chapter describes the basis for cognitive ability test classifications according to cultural and linguistic dimensions. The information contained in this section serves as a new frame of reference from which tests can be both selected and interpreted in accordance with principles directly relevant in the assessment of diverse individuals. The final section of this chapter covers specific methods and procedures involved in the application of CHC Cross-Battery methods in the assessment of diverse individuals. Guidelines for both test selection and interpretation of data are also presented. As will become evident, CHC Cross-Battery assessment methods and procedures can be extended in ways that can assist in reducing bias or the discriminatory aspects related primarily to test selection and interpretation. The reader is referred to Flanagan, McGrew, and colleague (2000, Chapter 8) and McGrew and Flanagan (1998, Chapter 14) for details and an extensive discussion of issues related to the use of the CHC Cross-Battery approach with culturally and linguistically diverse individuals.

CULTURE, LANGUAGE, AND TESTS OF COGNITIVE ABILITY

Because their training may not have provided the essential knowledge needed for the assessment of culturally and linguistically diverse individuals, practitioners have often been forced to utilize procedures and tests that may not be suitable or appropriate for measuring the cognitive abilities or intellectual functioning of such individuals (Flanagan & Miranda, 1995; Lopez, 1997). According to Ochoa, Powell, and Robles-Pina (1996), the most commonly used instruments with culturally and linguistically diverse students include a Wechsler Scale (generally administered completely in English), the Bender Visual-Motor Gestalt test, the Draw-A-Person test, and the Leiter. Generally speaking, given the inadequate psychometric properties, inappropriate norms and comparison groups, unidimensional assessments, linguistic and cultural confounds, and so forth, that characterize many of these tests, such a combination or battery is rather problematic. Moreover, the problems associated with the use of such tests on diverse populations is not entirely solved when native-language tests are used or when interpreters are used for the process of administration (Lopez, 1997; McCallum & Bracken, 1997). But perhaps the greatest problem associated with the use of any set of tests or any test battery lies in the fact that they are often selected, administered, and then interpreted in a manner that is not systematic or guided by the literature on how culture or language influence test performance of individuals from various cultures or with various linguistic backgrounds. Decisions and conclusions based on such data are rather haphazard and largely indefensible. Clearly, in order to derive meaningful information from the use of standardized tests with individuals who are culturally and linguistically diverse, the nature and process of bias and discrimination need to be well understood.

Culture Bias versus Culture Loading

An extensive review of the question and nature of bias in psychometric procedures is not practical, given the practitioner-oriented focus of this book. The reader is referred to Valdés and Figueroa (1994) for perhaps the best discussion available on the subject, as well as to Flanagan, McGrew, and colleague (2000) and Ortiz and Flanagan (1998) for limited but detailed treatment. Nevertheless, it is necessary to provide some explanation of how bias operates in the psychometric approach that underlies testing.

In order to begin clarifying the nature of bias, it is necessary to recognize the extent to which culture and cultural values have played a part in the construction and development of intelligence batteries from their very origins. According to Kamphaus (1993), "the traditions of Galton, Binet, Wechsler, Cattell, and others underlie all modern tests of intelligence. These tests emanated from French, British, German, North American, and

> **DON'T FORGET**
> ....
> ### The Nature and Process of Bias and Discrimination
>
> In order to derive meaningful information from the use of standardized tests with individuals who are culturally and linguistically diverse, the nature and process of bias and discrimination need to be well understood.

other similarly European cultures" (p. 441). Perhaps the best illustration of this notion comes from Kaufman (1994), who provides a very poignant recollection of his "collaborative" work with David Wechsler on decisions regarding item deletion for the revision of the WISC. Kaufman wrote:

> From that point on, I never held back anything. He would usually respond calmly but occasionally I'd strike a raw nerve, and his grandfatherly smile would evaporate. His temples would start to pulse, and his entire face and scalp would turn crimson. I'd unconsciously move my chair back in self-protection, the way I did when I tested hard-core prisoners on the old WAIS and had to ask the question, "Why should we keep away from bad company?" I struck that exposed nerve when I urged him to eliminate the Comprehension item about walking away from a fight if someone much smaller starts to fight with you. The argument that you can't walk away from any fight in a black ghetto just added fuel to his rage. When I suggested, at a later meeting, that he just *had* to get rid of the item, "Why should women and children be saved first in a shipwreck?" or incur the wrath of the new wave of militant feminists, his response was instant. With red face and pulsing head, he stood up, leaned on his desk with extended arms, and said as if he were firing a semiautomatic, "Chivalry may be dying. Chivalry may be dead. *But it will not die on the WISC.*" (p. x; emphasis in original)

As is evident in the WISC-R, the fight item was retained whereas the shipwreck item was eventually deleted. Kaufman's battles with Wechsler illustrate the degree to which test content, at the most fundamental level, is often a very real reflection of the attitudes and beliefs of the individuals who create them. Clearly, it is essential that practitioners understand that all tests of intelligence and cognitive ability reflect the culture from which they emanated and are based on the culturally bound values and beliefs of their authors. Neisser and colleagues (1996) stress that "it is obvious that the cultural environment—how people live, what they value, what they do—has a significant effect on the intellectual skills developed by individuals" (p. 86). In order to assess individuals from diverse cultures in a more equitable manner, practitioners will need to come to terms with the fact that "intelligence cannot be tested independently of the culture that gives rise to the test" (Cole & Cole, 1993, p. 502) and that "intelligence tests are not tests of intelligence in some abstract, culture-free way. They are measures of the ability to function intellectually by virtue of knowledge and skills in the culture of which they sample" (Scarr, 1978, p. 339).

Yet the vast majority of research into the nature of bias in intelligence tests has failed to find any evidence of bias. Study after study has examined and re-examined test items (including content and novelty), test structure (sequence, order, difficulty), test reliability (measurement error or accuracy), factor structure (theoretical structure, cluster or composite scores), and prediction (academic success or achievement), without any significant findings of bias (Flanagan, McGrew, et al., 2000; Valdés & Figueroa, 1994). It would seem that if cultural background were a variable that differentially affected performance it would be readily identified in such studies. The answer to this seeming dilemma lies in the fact that bias is all too often inappropriately defined. Culture (and in effect, cultural bias) has historically been viewed as a unitary, monolithic construct that is expected to interact with performance in some way that might systematically differentiate one group of people from another (Figueroa, 1990a, b; Valdés & Figueroa, 1994). However, this view represents an inaccurate and unrealistic perspective of the attenuating influence of cultural differences. This is because intelligence tests and tests of cognitive ability measure quite well the degree to which *anyone* has acquired and can access the culturally specific information reflected in and inherent in their structures. It is not culture per se that acts as a biasing factor; rather, it is an individual's exposure to and familiarity with (or lack thereof) the test's underlying culture that affects performance on such tests (Cummins, 1984; Figueroa, 1990b; Matsumoto, 1994; Valdés & Figueroa, 1994).

The process of acquiring culture (i.e., acculturation) is invariant. The simpler, more common elements of the culture are learned first; the more complex elements of the culture follow later in predictable and measurable ways. According to Salvia and Ysseldyke (1991), the very process of acculturation represents a fundamental principle within test development known as the *assumption of comparability*. They wrote,

When we test students using a standardized device and compare them to a set of norms to get an index of their relative standing, we assume that the students we test are similar to those on whom the test was standardized; that is, we assume their acculturation is comparable, but not necessarily identical, to that of the students who made up the normative sample for the test. (p. 18)

Therefore, the structure and design of intelligence and cognitive ability tests are actually based on the notion that there is an equivalent level of acculturation across the variables of age or grade for individuals on whom the test was standardized and on whom the test will be used. This assumption can be far from reality when such tests are used on individuals from other cultures. Salvia and Ysseldyke (1991) make this point clear as well:

When a child's general background experiences differ from those of the children on whom a test was standardized, then the use of the norms of that test as an index for evaluating that child's current performance or for predicting future performances may be inappropriate. (p. 18)

The biasing effect from the use of psychometric instruments, therefore, operates whenever tests of intelligence and cognitive ability (developed and normed in the United States) are given to individuals whose cultural backgrounds, experiences, and exposures are not similar to or consistent with those of the individuals comprising the norm group against whom performance will be compared. In these cases, such tests will likely measure a lower range of ability in diverse individuals because the test samples only the cultural content related to mainstream experience and not the full or entire range of cultural content possessed by the individual (Valdés & Figueroa, 1994). This biasing influence is best construed as involving *cultural loading* and is distinctly different from definitions that are based on culture, race, or ethnicity as unitary, monolithic interacting variables that should somehow disrupt performance. Thus, although there is considerable research evidence suggesting that many intelligence and cognitive ability tests are technically sound and appropriately normed, and are not culturally *biased,* they are, nevertheless, culturally *loaded* (Sattler, 1992; Valdés & Figueroa, 1994).

Given the preceding discussion, practitioners who seek to increase the validity of results obtained in the assessment of individuals from diverse cultural backgrounds should attempt to acquire two important and interrelated pieces of information: (a) the individual's level of acculturation, and (b) the degree to which performance on any given test is contingent upon culture-specific knowledge. Mercer (1979), Valdés and Figueroa (1994), and others have addressed the few studies that attempted to measure the former issue. The cultural extensions to the CHC Cross-Battery approach presented in this chapter involve the latter.

Language Bias versus Linguistic Demands

Practitioners have paid much more attention than researchers to the issue of language differences in testing. No doubt this is because the practical implications of working with individuals who may not be fully proficient in English is a matter of greater importance to the applied psychologist than the theoretical one. There appears to be an intuitive understanding among practitioners

≡ *Rapid Reference 5.1*

Information Needed to Increase Validity in the Assessment of Culturally Diverse Individuals

Practitioners who seek to increase the validity of results obtained in the assessment of individuals from diverse cultural backgrounds should attempt to acquire two important and interrelated pieces of information:

(a) the individual's level of acculturation, and

(b) the degree to which performance on any given test is contingent upon culture-specific knowledge.

that an examiner who is a monolingual English speaker is going to have significant problems in conducting an assessment on an individual who does not speak or comprehend English well or at all, particularly in the use of standardized tests. Nevertheless, the specific manner in which such communicative obstacles may affect test performance is not clearly understood, and it becomes extremely cloudy in those situations in which the individual being assessed knows some English, but may not be fully proficient as compared to other individuals of the same age or grade.

The effect that language difference has on test performance is quite similar to that just described for acculturation. Valdés and Figueroa (1994) noted "empirically established difficulty levels in psychometric tests are not altered by cultural differences. Neither are they because of proficiencies in the societal language" (p. 101). In other words, development of language (English or otherwise) is just as experientially based and follows just as invariant a developmental course as acculturation. Given the developmental structure and sequence of items on standardized tests, the attenuating effect of language development or language proficiency is not manifest in comparisons of performance within any single subtest. Rather, it is the lack of concurrence between constructs that are measured through different channels (i.e., a set of verbal subtests versus a set of nonverbal subtests) that begins to reveal the nature of language bias in tests (Cummins, 1984; Valdés & Figueroa, 1994). There exist only a few scientific studies that have examined linguistic bias in tests using this comparative manner. However, they have been strikingly consistent in their findings that tasks that are primarily language-based do not measure incidental learning equally well compared to tasks that are more visual or perceptual in nature (Cummins, 1984; Jensen, 1974, 1976).

Tests of intelligence or cognitive ability are constructed in ways that presume that a given level of language proficiency is present in the average individual that is sufficient to comprehend the instructions, formulate and verbalize responses, or otherwise use language ability in completing the expected task. As in the case of acculturation, there may be times when an individual's language proficiency is not developmentally commensurate with the language proficiency of the individuals comprising the norm group against whom performance will be compared (Cummins, 1984; Figueroa, Delgado, & Ruiz, 1984). In some cases in which the focus is on evaluating language-related disabilities, this is precisely the point. However, when individuals who are not language disabled but are in fact limited in English proficiency or, for whatever reasons, are not developmentally equivalent in language proficiency with the norm group against whom performance will be compared, the result will be bias. In similar fashion to the discussion on acculturation, tests may be linguistically biased, not because of any inherent structural defect, but because of the expectations and assumptions regarding the comparability of language proficiency. The assumption of comparability regarding language development and proficiency for such individuals is very often invalid. Figueroa (1990b) strongly cautions practitioners to remember "language *background,* not just language proficiency, must be taken into account in every facet of assessment such as test development, selection, administration, and interpretation" (p. 94).

With respect to language differences in assessment, the evidence seems abundantly clear that tests that carry high linguistic demands (e.g., vocabulary tests) tend to "degenerate in unknown degrees into tests of English language proficiency" whenever they are used with individuals who are linguistically different (Figueroa, 1990a, p. 93). In order to improve upon current use of tests of intelligence and cognitive ability, practitioners should continue to strive for the collection of at least two key factors that will affect the path of assessment. These factors include the individual's level of proficiency in English and any other language he or she has acquired or has been exposed to (no matter how little the exposure may be), and the degree or level of language required by any test or tests that will be used to evaluate the individual's functioning. The former is ordinarily accomplished through the use of any one of the various English language proficiency tests available on the market today (e.g., Woodcock Language Proficiency Battery—Revised, Woodcock-Muñoz Language Survey, etc.). These tests are sufficient to gauge the general degree to which an individual may differ in proficiency from age-related peers. Collection of data related to the latter factor (linguistic characteristics of tests) may be accomplished via the linguistic extensions of the CHC Cross-Battery approach, to be discussed in the following sections. As will be explained, the combination of these sources of information provides practitioners with perhaps a more systematic and defensible basis for evaluating performance of dual-language learners in a more fair and equitable manner than is ordinarily achieved using current methods.

> # DON'T FORGET
> ....
> ### Presumed Language Proficiency
>
> Tests of intelligence or cognitive ability are constructed in ways that require or presume that a given level of language proficiency is present in the average individual that is sufficient to comprehend the instructions, formulate and verbalize responses, or otherwise use language ability in completing the expected task.

> # DON'T FORGET
> ....
> ### English-Language Proficiency and Bias
>
> In cases in which individuals are limited in English proficiency or, for whatever reasons, are not developmentally equivalent in language proficiency with the norm group against whom performance will be compared, the result will be bias.

A Comment on Nonverbal Methods of Assessment

Practitioners may wonder whether the issues related to language differences (and to a lesser degree, cultural differences) in assessment are effectively answered by the use of so-called nonverbal tests. In fact, the advertising literature disseminated by many publishers of such tests often touts them as being both culture-free and language-free because they contain a protocol for administration that is entirely nonverbal (e.g., UNIT, Leiter-R). Unfortunately, the representation of any test as culture- or language-free is, at best, very misleading. Reducing the oral or spoken language requirements in any given test does not completely eliminate potential linguistic bias and does little, if anything, to reduce bias related to acculturation. Certainly, when tests are given that utilize little or no oral language demands, they can greatly assist in generating results that are less discriminatory for individuals from diverse backgrounds (Figueroa, 1990b; McCallum & Bracken, 1997). In fact, the extensions to the CHC Cross-Battery approach to be presented in the next section are based, in part, on this notion.

Practitioners are well advised, however, to recognize that although some commonly accepted nonverbal tests (e.g., Wechsler Block Design or WJ-R Analysis-Synthesis) may not require any oral or expressive language ability per se, they often do demand from the examinee a high level of nonverbal receptive language skill in order to comprehend the examiner's instructions and expectations. Similarly, tests that are often thought of as representing verbally reduced functioning (e.g., Wechsler performance tests) may contain lengthy and possibly confusing verbal directions, which can affect an individual's ability to comprehend what is expected or to provide an appropriate response (e.g., Block Design). In such cases, whenever the individual being tested does not possess the minimum required or expected level of receptive language (as may be the case for linguistically diverse individuals), performance will be directly affected in an adverse manner. Moreover, even tests that effectively eliminate most, if not all, oral (expressive or receptive) language demands are not free of the communicative requirement. Test performance, even with tests administered entirely with gestures or in pantomime, continues to remain very dependent upon the level of nonverbal communication between the examiner and examinee and

> # CAUTION
>
> ## Elimination of Spoken-Language Requirements
>
> Reducing the oral or spoken language requirements in any given test does not completely eliminate potential linguistic bias and does little, if anything, to reduce bias related to acculturation.

their ability to interact effectively in a nonverbal manner. Such tests continue to require that the examiner clearly and correctly convey the nature of a given task and its expected response to the examinee, and they continue to require that the examinee comprehend that communication and accurately re-convey an acceptable response to the examiner. To say that a test requires no language is misleading because, in fact, some type of communication is still necessary in order to conduct the test process. If such communication were unnecessary and the test truly required no language then we might effectively generate valid IQs for a wide range of inarticulate and even inanimate objects. It is, therefore, somewhat an exaggeration to portray nonverbal tests as being completely language-free and thus free of bias. The significant reduction in communicative demand does greatly reduce the possible effects of bias, but it does not eliminate it entirely. In addition, the type of nonverbal communication that may be required for administration in such tests often carries more culturally based implications than does verbal communication (Ehrman, 1996). There is an emerging body of research that suggests that nonverbal tasks may actually carry as much if not more cultural content than that found in verbal tests (Greenfield, 1998). Moreover, because of the extreme redundancy found in many nonverbal tests with respect to the measurement of the broad and narrow abilities specified in CHC theory, interpretation can be quite confusing, is often much less defensible, and does not necessarily provide more valid assessment data (McCallum & Bracken, 1997).

A Comment on Culture Loading, Linguistic Demands, and Norms

Over the last half century, test developers have seen both the merit and the need for the development of

---

DON'T FORGET

Elimination of Language from Tests

Test performance, even with tests administered entirely with gestures or in pantomime, continues to remain very dependent upon the level of nonverbal communication between the examiner and examinee and their ability to interact effectively in a nonverbal manner. Such tests continue to require that the examiner clearly and correctly convey the nature of a given task and its expected response to the examinee, and continue to require that the examinee comprehend that communication and accurately re-convey an acceptable response to the examiner.

CAUTION

Cultural Bias in Nonverbal Communication

The type of nonverbal communication that may be required for administration of nonverbal tests often carries more culturally based implications than does verbal communication (Ehrman, 1996).

norm groups that more accurately reflect the composition of individuals living in the United States so that comparisons of performance can be made even more validly and accurately. The result has been that norm samples over the years have become increasingly more representative. Virtually all of the major intelligence or cognitive ability batteries available today have more than adequate national norms and meet the strictest criteria with respect to the technical aspects of norm sample development. The emphasis on representing diversity, which has slowly crept into the psychometric arena, is clearly reflected in the composition of these modern norm groups. To meet the stringent demands of modern-day practitioners, test developers have made it rather common practice to stratify their standardization samples along several important variables, including age, sex, race, ethnicity, education level, and geographic location. One of the primary goals for the inclusion of such a broad range of variables is the creation of a norm sample that minimizes and equalizes any systematic variation that might be due to differences along any one of (or a combination of) these dimensions. In essence, a standardization sample that contains these variables allows for valid comparisons of performance that are no more or less biased against any single individual for whom the sample is representative.

For practitioners, the difficulty with norms in the assessment of culturally and linguistically diverse individuals lies in some of the assumptions related to the stratification process. The question becomes one concerning the notion of exactly what constitutes *representative*. It was discussed previously that there exists an assumption of comparability that, when true, allows for valid conclusions about relative performance to be drawn. Conversely, when the assumption is false, conclusions and interpretation of performance are questionable at best. Salvia and Ysseldyke (1991) noted that in any case in which testing is conducted on an individual whose general background experiences are different from the experiences of the individuals on whom the test was standardized, the use of those norms for performance comparisons or prediction may be inappropriate. They further emphasized that

[i]ncorrect educational decisions may well be made. It must be pointed out that acculturation is a matter of experiential background rather than of gender, skin color, race, or ethnic background. When we say that a child's acculturation differs from that of the group used as a norm, we are saying that the *experiential background* differs, not simply that the child is of different ethnic origin, for example, from the children on whom the test was standardized. (1991, p. 18, emphasis in original)

In the case of culturally or linguistically diverse individuals, Salvia and Ysseldyke's comments make it clear that skin color, race, or ethnicity should not be equated with cultural differences, and that it is the difference in experiential background (related to differences in cultural background) that adversely affects test performance. These differences in experience (which are based on cultural differences) represent a variable that is not stratified in any norm sample available today. Therefore, no matter how much a test developer might want to emphasize the fairness of a given test by illustrating the inclusion of racially or ethnically diverse individuals (e.g., in accordance with their frequency in the general population), claims about equity are highly misleading and inaccurate (Valdés & Figueroa, 1994). Practitioners should thus be careful not to fall prey to the assumption that stratification in the norm sample on the basis of race is equivalent to stratification on the basis of culture. Not only is this not true, but it is not even culture itself that is the crucial variable, but the *level of acculturation* that should be controlled.

The implications of the lack of adequate representation due to varying levels of acculturation in modern-day standardization samples creates an important implication for practitioners. Until and unless publishers of intelligence and cognitive ability tests provide norm samples that adequately stratify along the dimension of acculturation, performance of individuals reared either completely or partly outside the U.S. mainstream culture cannot be compared validly against existing norm samples (Cummins, 1984; Figueroa, 1990a; Samuda,

CAUTION

Stratification on Race versus Culture

Practitioners should be careful not to fall prey to the assumption that stratification in the norm sample on the basis of race is equivalent to stratification on the basis of culture.

Kong, Cummins, Pascual-Leone, & Lewis, 1991; Valdés & Figueroa, 1994). Accomplishing such a feat in the development of a norm sample may well prove impossible from a practical point of view, especially considering the difficulties inherent in stratifying a variable that is by nature continuous, and considering the broad range and number of variables that might be needed even to measure acculturation accurately. Nevertheless, until the culturally based experiences that are sampled by standardized tests (and established by the performance of the norm group) are comparable to the cultural experiences of the individual being tested, fair and equitable interpretation of performance will remain difficult and elusive.

Representation within existing standardization samples along the dimension of language proficiency is an issue similar to that of acculturation. The fundamental goal of the U.S. educational system is English literacy. Therefore, regardless of the manner or specific program used to achieve this goal (research indicates that two-way bilingual or dual-immersion programs appear to provide the best results, followed by late-exit programs), each pupil who enters the system as a non-English or limited-English speaker will, by default, become a circumstantial bilingual speaker (i.e., by force of circumstance as opposed to choice). As was discussed previously, language proficiency and history are variables that can greatly attenuate results obtained from the use of standardized tests. This consequence of the educational system alone would seem to make it prudent on the part of test developers to provide norms that include individuals according to their respective levels of language proficiency. Unfortunately, such dual-language learners or bilingual individuals have not been systematically incorporated into the design and composition of any extant norm samples.

Even when a sample is established in a language other than English (e.g., WISC-RM, WISC-R-PR, Bateria-R, BVAT, etc.), the issue of control through proper stratification of language proficiency remains a concern. For example, the WISC-RM norm sample is composed almost exclusively of monolingual Spanish speakers, just as the norm samples for its English-language counterpart is composed of monolingual English speakers. Monolingual Spanish speakers offer no more an appropriate comparison group for the many bilingual individuals residing in the United States than does the monolingual-English norm group. Both are unrepresentative of individuals who are bilingual. There are some tests, such as the Bateria-R and the BVAT, that do include dual-language individuals in the norm sample. Unfortunately, their inclusion is not accomplished in any systematic manner or for purposes of controlling differences among individuals on the basis of dual-language proficiency.

As with the acculturation variable, stratifying a sample on the basis of dual-language or bilingual ability is an extremely daunting task. Creation of a truly representative sampling of bilingual individuals faces many of the same difficulties encountered by publishers who seek to create special norm groups (e.g., individuals who are deaf, who have learning disabilities, ADD, etc.). The issue would not be settled simply by evaluating individual language proficiency alone, but would need to include consideration of variables involving length of time learning each language, amount of formal instruction received in each language, proficiency in the language or languages spoken by parents and siblings in the home, and so forth. Problems with norm groups notwithstanding, it is important to recognize that tests such as the BVAT represent an emerging and distinct research and development tradition. From the inception of standardized tests of intelligence, the vast majority of research and test development conducted to evaluate the effect of bilingualism on performance has been accomplished with intelligence tests given in English, not in the native language. The unwavering and consistent findings regarding the biasing effect of testing bilinguals with monolingual tests (see Valdés & Figueroa, 1994) is the research tradition that forms the basis for the culture and linguistic extensions of the CHC Cross-Battery approach, which are presented in the following section. This is because the patterns of expected performance of bilinguals on monolingual tests are very well known. On the other hand, the BVAT is an innovative test that sits at the forefront of a new research tradition, which seeks to test bilinguals with bilingual tests in a manner much more consistent with theory concerning bilingual development and second language acquisition than anything ever accomplished with monolingual tests. Although the BVAT represents a significant advancement in this practice and will no doubt help to encourage and push related research further along, there is at present very little known about the performance of bilinguals on bilingual tests. The difference between these two veins of research has important practical implications and highlights the fact that bilingual assessment is not the same as assessment of bilinguals. Whereas the BVAT is a prime example of developments in the former, the culture and linguistic extensions of the CHC Cross-Battery approach to assessment and interpretation described in the next section fall within the context of the latter.

In the absence of any appropriate norm group, measuring the cognitive or intellectual performance of linguistically diverse individuals with standardized tests, whether in English or the native language, amounts to a measure of language proficiency more than to any reflection of actual cognitive ability (Cummins, 1984; Valdés & Figueroa, 1994). This conclusion is shared by a number of researchers (e.g., Bialystok, 1991; Figueroa, 1990a; Samuda et al., 1991) who reinforce the notion that there are no tests of intelligence or cognitive ability containing suitable norms for use with bilingual individuals. The implications for practitioners are critical. "Tests developed without accounting for language differences are limited in their validity and on how they can be interpreted" (Figueroa, 1990b, p. 94).

The vast array of complex variables involved in the assessment of diverse individuals can give even the most experienced practitioner considerable pause. Completely culture-free or truly equitable evaluation seems a rather lofty and unattainable goal. Perhaps a more realistic approach to the assessment of diverse individuals lies not in attempts to eliminate all bias or find unbiased tests (which is unlikely and impractical), but rather in efforts to reduce bias in their use to the maximum extent possible while maintaining as much accuracy as possible in construct measurement. The cultural and linguistic extensions of the CHC Cross-Battery approach are designed with this philosophy in mind. In the final analysis, there is no such thing as a completely nondiscriminatory or unbiased assessment. However, use of CHC Cross-Battery assessment along with the cultural and linguistic extensions provides a systematic and defensible method for greatly reducing the discriminatory aspects inherent in the use of cognitive ability tests with diverse individuals.

To summarize, practitioners who need to assess individuals who are culturally or linguistically diverse using standardized, norm-referenced instruments should remain well aware

DON'T FORGET

A Realistic Approach to Assessing Diverse Individuals

A more realistic approach to the assessment of diverse individuals lies not in attempts to eliminate all bias or even find unbiased tests (which is unlikely and impractical), but rather in efforts to reduce bias in their use to the maximum extent possible while maintaining as much accuracy as possible in construct measurement.

≡ Rapid Reference 5.2

Summary of Points to Consider in Assessing Culturally and Linguistically Diverse Individuals

Practitioners who need to assess individuals who are culturally or linguistically diverse using standardized, norm-referenced instruments should remain well aware of four essential points:

1. All tests are culturally loaded and reflect the values, beliefs, and knowledge that are deemed important within the culture in which the tests were developed—for example, U.S. mainstream culture.

2. All tests require some form of language (or communication) on the part of both the examiner and the examinee, and such factors can affect administration, comprehension, and performance on virtually any test, including nonverbal ones.

3. Tests vary significantly on both dimensions—the degree to which they are culturally loaded and the degree to which they require language.

4. Interpretation of results from standardized tests using existing norm groups for performance comparisons may be invalid for diverse individuals.

of four essential points. (These points are also enumerated in Rapid Reference 5.2.) In general terms, these points include recognition that: (a) All tests are culturally loaded and reflect the values, beliefs, and knowledge that are deemed important within the culture in which the tests were developed (e.g., U.S. mainstream culture); (b) all tests require some form of language (or communication) on the part of both examiner and examinee, and such factors can affect administration, comprehension, and performance on virtually any test (including nonverbal ones, albeit to a lesser extent than on verbal ones); (c) tests vary significantly on both dimensions (the degree to which they are culturally loaded and require language); and (d) interpretation of results from standardized tests using existing norm groups for performance comparisons may be invalid for diverse individuals.

CULTURAL AND LINGUISTIC EXTENSIONS OF THE CHC CROSS-BATTERY APPROACH

For practitioners engaged in applied work settings, the standardized, norm-referenced instrument represents one of the most important and valuable tools in the assessment repertoire. When such instruments are brought out for use with diverse individuals, practitioners need to be aware of how cultural and linguistic factors may affect both the results and the subsequent interpretations they may make. The manner in which cultural or linguistic bias may operate in these cases has been discussed briefly in the previous sections. The implications of such bias have been formally operationalized in the development of extensions to the basic CHC Cross-Battery approach, providing a rather new frame of reference from which to understand and interpret performance on tests of intelligence and cognitive ability that may be of significant benefit and utility to practitioners.

In 1990, Figueroa recommended the application of defensible theoretical frameworks in the assessment of culturally and linguistically diverse individuals and admonished practitioners to pay particular attention to cultural and linguistic dimensions. The cultural and linguistic extensions to the CHC Cross-Battery approach are in line with these recommendations. The extensions described herein are also consistent with the propositions for testing bilinguals contained in Chapter 13 of the *Standards for Educational and Psychological Tests* (American Educational Research Association, American Psychological Association, & American Council on Measurement, 1985), especially the notions that idiosyncratic variations in cultural and linguistic background can lower test performance. Similarly, these extensions, as well as the basic CHC Cross-Battery approach, remain in full accordance with APA's *Guidelines for Providers of Psychological Services to Ethnic, Linguistic, and Culturally Diverse Populations* (1990).

Culture and Language Classification

The test classifications based on CHC theory presented in Chapter 2 (and contained in Appendix B) serve as the foundation for extending the CHC Cross-Battery approach. In addition to their theory-based classifications, these tests can be classified according to inherent cultural and linguistic dimensions. Table 5.1 illustrates these extensions through the creation of a matrix that organizes tests of cognitive ability and special-purpose tests according to three important test characteristics: (a) stratum I and stratum II abilities measured according to CHC theory; (b) degree of cultural loading; and (c) degree of linguistic demand. Table 5.1 retains the essential information necessary for

Table 5.1 Test Classification by Degree of Cultural Loading and Linguistic Demand

		DEGREE OF CULTURAL LOADING—LOW		
	Battery	Age	Subtest	CHC Ability
	CTONI	6–18	Geometric Sequences	Gf (I, RG)
	LEITER-R	5–18+	Design Analogies	Gf (I)
	LEITER-R	2–18+	Repeated Patterns	Gf (I)
	LEITER-R	2–18+	Sequential Order	Gf (I)
	LEITER-R	11–18+	Paper Folding	Gv (Vz)
	LEITER-R	11–18+	Figure Rotation	Gv (Vz, SR)
	UNIT	5–17	Cube Design	Gv (SR, Vz)
	UNIT	5–17	Mazes	Gv (SS)
DEGREE OF LINGUISTIC DEMAND: LOW	UNIT	5–17	SPATIAL MEMORY	Gv (MV)
	DAS	6–17	MATRICES	Gf (I)
	DAS	6–17	SEQUENTIAL & QUANTITATIVE REASONING	Gf (RQ, I)
	DTLA-4	6–17	SYMBOLIC RELATIONS	Gf (I)
	CAS	5–17	Nonverbal Matrices	Gf (I)
	WAIS-III	16–89	MATRIX REASONING	Gf (I, RG)
	Raven's	5–18+	Raven's Progressive Matrices	Gf (I)
	TONI-3	5–85	Test of Nonverbal Intelligence-3rd Edition	Gf (I)
	CAS	5–17	Expressive Attention	Glr (NA)
	DAS	3–17	Pattern Construction	Gv (SR)
	DAS	2–3	Block Building	Gv (Vz)

(continued)

Table 5.1 (continued)

	Battery	Subtest	Age	CHC Ability
DEGREE OF CULTURAL LOADING—LOW				
DEGREE OF LINGUISTIC DEMAND: LOW	DAS	Matching Letter-Like Forms	4–5	*Gv* (Vz)
	DAS	**RECALL OF DESIGNS**	6–17	*Gv* (MV)
	K-ABC	**TRIANGLES**	4–12	*Gv* (SR)
	KAIT	**MEMORY FOR BLOCK DESIGNS**	11–85+	*Gv* (MV)
	SB:IV	**PATTERN ANALYSIS**	2–24	*Gv* (SR)
	WPPSI-R	Geometric Designs	3–7	*Gv* (Vz, P2)
	CAS	**FIGURE MEMORY**	5–17	*Gv* (CF, MV)
	DTLA-4	Design Sequences	6–17	*Gv* (MV)
	DTLA-4	Design Reproduction	6–17	*Gv* (MV)
	TOMAL	Facial Memory	5–19	*Gv* (MV)
	TOMAL	Abstract Visual Memory	5–19	*Gv* (MV)
	TOMAL	Manual Imitation	5–19	*Gv* (MV)
	TOMAL	Delayed Recall of Visual Selective Reminding	5–19	*Gv* (MV)
	WJ-R/III	**SPATIAL RELATIONS**	4–85+	*Gv* (Vz,SR)
	WMS-III	Visual Reproduction I	16–89	*Gv* (MV)
DEGREE OF LINGUISTIC DEMAND: MODERATE	DAS	Recall of Digits	3–17	*Gsm* (MS)
	K-ABC	**NUMBER RECALL**	2–12	*Gsm* (MS)
	SB:IV	**MEMORY FOR DIGITS**	7–24	*Gsm* (MS, MW)
	WAIS-III	**DIGIT SPAN**	16–89	*Gsm* (MS, MW)

		DEGREE OF CULTURAL LOADING—LOW	
Battery	Age	Subtest	CHC Ability
WISC-III	6–16	**DIGIT SPAN**	Gsm (MS, MW)
K-SNAP	11–85	Number Recall	Gsm (MS)
LAMB	20–60	Digit Span	Gsm (MS)
TOMAL	5–19	Digits Forward	Gsm (MS)
TOMAL	5–19	Letters Forward	Gsm (MS)
WMS-III	16–89	Digit Span	Gsm (MS, MW)
CMS	5–16	Dot Locations	Gv (MV)
CMS	5–16	Numbers	Gsm (MS, MW)
WRAML	5–17	Number/Letter Memory	Gsm (MS)
WJ-R	2–85+	**MEMORY FOR NAMES**	Glr (MA)
WJ-R	4–85+	**DELAYED RECALL–MEMORY FOR NAMES**	Glr (MA)
WRAML	5–17	Sound Symbol	Glr (MA)
DAS	6–17	Speed of Information Processing	Gs (N, R9)
DTLA-4	6–17	Word Sequences	Gsm (MS)
TOMAL	5–19	Word Selective Reminding	Glr (M6)
TOMAL	5–19	Delayed Recall of Word Selective Reminding	Glr (M6)
SB:IV	7–24	**MATRICES**	Gf (I)
SB:IV	2–24	**Bead Memory**	Gv (MV)
WISC-III	6–16	Mazes	Gv (SS)

DEGREE OF LINGUISTIC DEMAND: MODERATE

(continued)

Table 5.1 (continued)

		DEGREE OF CULTURAL LOADING—LOW		
	Battery	Age	Subtest	CHC Ability
	WPPSI-R	3–7	Mazes	Gv (SS)
	WECHSLERS	3–74	**BLOCK DESIGN**	Gv (SR, Vz)
	LAMB	20–60	Simple Figure	Gv (MV)
	LAMB	20–60	Complex Figure	Gv (MV)
	WRAML	5–17	Design Memory	Gv (MV)
DEGREE OF LINGUISTIC DEMAND: MODERATE	CAS	5–17	**MATCHING NUMBERS**	Gs (N, R9)
	CAS	5–17	**NUMBER DETECTION**	Gs (N, R9)
	CAS	5–17	**PLANNED CODES**	Gs (R9)
	WISC-III	6–16	**SYMBOL SEARCH**	Gs (P, R9)
	WAIS-III	16–89	**DIGIT SYMBOL-CODING**	Gs (R9)
	WISC-III	6–16	**CODING**	Gs (R9)
	WJ-R/III	4–85+	**NUMBERS REVERSED**	Gsm (MW)
	WJ-R/III	4–85+	**VISUAL MATCHING**	Gs (P, R9)
	WJ-R	4–85+	**CROSS OUT**	Gs (P)
	SB:IV	7–24	Number Series	Gf (RQ)
DEGREE OF LINGUISTIC DEMAND: HIGH	WJ-R/III	4–85+	**CONCEPT FORMATION**	Gf (I)
	WJ-R/III	4–85+	**ANALYSIS-SYNTHESIS**	Gf (RG)
	WMS-III	16–89	Letter-Number Sequencing	Gsm (MW)
	WJ III	4–85+	**AUDITORY WORKING MEMORY**	Gsm (MW)

	DEGREE OF CULTURAL LOADING—LOW		
	Battery	Subtest	CHC Ability
DEGREE OF LINGUISTIC DEMAND: HIGH	WJ-R	**SOUND PATTERNS**	*Ga* (US/U3)
	CAS	**VERBAL SPATIAL RELATIONS**	*Gv* (PI)
	LAMB	Supraspan Digit	*Gsm* (MS)

	DEGREE OF CULTURAL LOADING–MODERATE		
	Battery	Subtest	CHC Ability
	LEITER-R	Visual Coding	*Gf* (RG)
	LEITER-R	Matching	*Gv* (Vz)
	LEITER-R	Attention Sustained	*Gs* (P, R9)
	DAS	Picture Similarities	*Gf* (I)
	DAS	Recognition of Pictures	*Gv* (MV)
	K-ABC	Face Recognition	*Gv* (MV)
DEGREE OF LINGUISTIC DEMAND: LOW	SB:IV	**Memory for Objects**	*Gv* (MV)
	WECHSLERS	**OBJECT ASSEMBLY**	*Gv* (CS, SR)
	WJ-R/III	**Picture Recognition**	*Gv* (MV)
	UNIT	**SYMBOLIC MEMORY**	*Gv* (MV)
	K-ABC	**WORD ORDER**	*Gsm* (MS)
	CAS	**RECEPTIVE ATTENTION**	*Gs* (P, R4)
	K-ABC	Magic Window	*Gv* (PI)
	K-ABC	**Gestalt Closure**	*Gv* (CS)

(continued)

Table 5.1 (continued)

	Battery	Age	Subtest	CHC Ability
DEGREE OF CULTURAL LOADING—MODERATE				
DEGREE OF LINGUISTIC DEMAND: LOW	WJ-R	2–85+	**Visual Closure**	*Gv* (CS)
	DAS	4–17	Recall of Objects	*Glr* (M6)
	TOMAL	5–19	Paired Recall	*Glr* (MA)
	CAS	5–17	**WORD SERIES**	*Gsm* (MS)
	CAS	5–17	**PLANNED CONNECTIONS**	*Gs* (P,R9)
	KAIT	11–85+	**REBUS LEARNING**	*Glr* (MA)
	KAIT	11–85+	**REBUS DELAYED RECALL**	*Glr* (MA)
	WJ-R/III	4–85+	**VISUAL-AUDITORY LEARNING**	*Glr* (MA, MM)
	WJ-R/III	4–85+	**Delayed Recall–Visual Auditory Learning**	*Glr* (MA, MM)
	KAIT	11–85+	**MYSTERY CODES**	*Gf* (I)
DEGREE OF LINGUISTIC DEMAND: MODERATE	K-SNAP	11–85	Four-letter Words	*Gf* (I)
	CMS	5–16	Word Pairs	*Glr* (MA)
	CMS	5–16	Word Pairs 2	*Glr* (MA)
	WMS-III	16–89	Verbal Paired Associates I	*Glr* (MA)
	WMS-III	16–89	Verbal Paired Associates II	*Glr* (MA)
	WPPSI-R	3–7	Animal Pegs	*Gs* (R9)
	KAIT	11–85+	**LOGICAL STEPS**	*Gf* (I)
	LAMB	20–60	Word Pairs	*Glr* (MA, FI)
	DAS	3–5	Early Number Concepts	*Gq* (A3, KM)

	Battery	Age	Subtest	CHC Ability
DEGREE OF CULTURAL LOADING—MODERATE				
DEGREE OF LINGUISTIC DEMAND: MODERATE	SB:IV	2–4	QUANTITATIVE	*Gq* (A3)
	WJ III	4–85+	RETRIEVAL FLUENCY	*Glr* (FI, FA)
	WJ III	4–85+	RAPID PICTURE NAMING	*Glr* (NA)
	WECHSLERS	3–74	ARITHMETIC	*Gq* (A3)
DEGREE OF LINGUISTIC DEMAND HIGH	WJ-R/III	2–85+	INCOMPLETE WORDS	*Ga* (PC:A)
	WJ-R/III	4–85+	SOUND BLENDING	*Ga* (PC:S)
	TOPA	5–8	Test of Phonological Awareness	*Ga* (PC:A)
	SB:IV	12–24	EQUATION BUILDING	*Gf* (RQ)
	WPPSI-R	3–7	Sentences	*Gsm* (MS)
	WJ-R/III	4–85+	MEMORY FOR WORDS	*Gsm* (MS)
	CAS	5–17	SENTENCE REPETITION	*Gsm* (MS)
	CAS	5–17	SENTENCE QUESTIONS	*Gsm* (MS)
	CMS	5–16	Sequences	*Gsm* (MW)
	CMS	5–16	Word Lists	*Glr* (M6)
	CMS	5–16	Word Lists 2	*Glr* (M6, MA)
	WMS-III	16–89	Word Lists I	*Glr* (M6)
	WJ III	4–85+	AUDITORY ATTENTION	*Ga* (US/U3, UR)
	WJ III	4–85+	DECISION SPEED	*Gs* (N)
	WRAML	5–17	Verbal Learning	*Glr* (M6)

(continued)

Table 5.1 (continued)

			DEGREE OF CULTURAL LOADING—HIGH	
	Battery	**Age**	**Subtest**	**CHC Ability**
DEGREE OF LINGUISTIC DEMAND: LOW	LEITER-R	2–6	Classification	Gf (I)
	LEITER-R	2–10	Picture Context	Gf (RG)
	UNIT	5–17	**ANALOGIC REASONING**	Gf (I)
	UNIT	5–17	**OBJECT MEMORY**	Gv (MV)
	LEITER-R	2–18+	Form Completion	Gv (Vz, SR)
	LEITER-R	4–10	Immediate Recognition	Gv (MV)
	LEITER-R	2–18+	Forward Memory	Gv (MV)
	LEITER-R	2–18+	Figure Ground	Gv (CF)
	LEITER-R	4–10	Delayed Recognition	Glr (MA)
	LEITER-R	2–18+	Associated Pairs	Glr (MA, MM)
	LEITER-R	6–18+	Delayed Pairs	Glr (MA, MM)
	K-BIT	4–90	Matrices	Gf (I)
DEGREE OF LINGUISTIC DEMAND: MODERATE	DAS	2–5	Verbal Comprehension	Gc (LD, LS)
	WRAML	5–17	Picture Memory	Gv (MV)
	DAS	2–5	Naming Vocabulary	Gc (VL, LD)
	KAIT	11–85+	**FAMOUS FACES**	Gc (K2)
	WJ-R	4–85+	**ORAL VOCABULARY**	Gc (VL, LD)
	WJ-R	4–85+	**PICTURE VOCABULARY**	Gc (VL, K0)
	DTLA-4	6-17	Word Opposites	Gc (LD)

		DEGREE OF CULTURAL LOADING—HIGH		
	Battery	**Age**	**Subtest**	**CHC Ability**
DEGREE OF LINGUISTIC DEMAND: MODERATE	K-BIT	4–90	Expressive Vocabulary	*Gc* (VL, K0, LD)
	DTLA-4	6–17	Picture Fragments	*Gv* (CS)
	K-SNAP	11–85	Gestalt Closure	*Gv* (CS)
	WMS-III	16–89	Mental Control	*Gsm* (MW)
DEGREE OF LINGUISTIC DEMAND: HIGH	CMS	5–16	Stories 2	*Glr* (MM)
	DAS	6–17	**SIMILARITIES**	*Gc* (LD)
	DAS	6–17	**WORD DEFINITIONS**	*Gc* (VL, LD)
	SB:IV	2–24	**VOCABULARY**	*Gc* (VL, LD)
	SB:IV	2–14	Absurdities	*Gc* (LD)
	WECHSLERS	3–74	**SIMILARITIES**	*Gc* (VL, LD)
	WECHSLERS	3–74	**VOCABULARY**	*Gc* (VL, LD)
	WECHSLERS	3–74	**INFORMATION**	*Gc* (K0)
	DTLA-4	6–17	Story Construction	*Gc* (LD)
	DTLA-4	6–17	Basic Information	*Gc* (K0)
	PPVT-3	2–85	Peabody Picture Vocabulary Test–Third edition	*Gc* (VL, K0, LD)
	WJ-R	4–85+	**LISTENING COMPREHENSION**	*Gc* (LS, LD)
	WJ III	2–85+	**VERBAL COMPREHENSION**	*Gc* (VL, LD)
	WJ III	2–85+	**GENERAL INFORMATION**	*Gc* (K0)
	EVT	2–85	Expressive Vocabulary Test	*Gc* (VL, LD)

(continued)

Table 5.1 (continued)

| | | DEGREE OF CULTURAL LOADING—HIGH | | |
	Battery	Age	Subtest	CHC Ability
DEGREE OF LINGUISTIC DEMAND: HIGH	LAMB	20–60	Wordlist	*Glr* (M6, MA)
	SB:IV	12–24	**VERBAL RELATIONS**	*Gc* (LD)
	SB:IV	2–24	**Comprehension**	*Gc* (LD, K0)
	WECHSLERS	3–74	**COMPREHENSION**	*Gc* (LD, K0)
	WMS-III	16–89	Logical Memory II	*Glr* (MM)

Note. See Appendix B for test descriptions.

Tests printed in bold, uppercase letters are strong measures as defined empirically; tests printed in bold, lowercase letters are moderate measures as defined empirically; tests printed in regular type lowercase letters are classified logically (see Flanagan, McGrew, & Ortiz, 2000; McGrew & Flanagan, 1998). In the case in which tests have two narrow ability classifications, the second classification is reported in parentheses following the test description. Tests of the major batteries that were classified either empirically or logically as mixed measures are not included in this table.

appropriate test selection in accordance with CHC Cross-Battery guiding principles (i.e., broad ability measured, narrow ability measured, strong vs. moderate vs. logical classification, etc.) while adding information regarding cultural loading and linguistic demand. With proper care and caution, Table 5.1 can assist practitioners in compiling a selective set of measures that may be less discriminatory and thus more valid for use with individuals who are culturally and linguistically diverse. The following is a brief description of the manner in which these specific characteristics of cognitive ability tests are indicated in Table 5.1.

Readers will notice that Table 5.1 continues to provide information regarding the CHC theory–based broad (stratum II) and narrow (stratum I) abilities measured by each test. Essentially, the tests listed in Table 5.1 are the same as those in Appendix B, and are consistent with the CHC Cross-Battery Worksheets contained in Appendix A. Table 5.1 also utilizes the same conventions for classification along these lines as used in other parts of this book. That is, tests printed in bold, uppercase letters represent empirically strong measures of the respective broad CHC abilities; tests printed in bold, lowercase letters represent those tests with moderate loadings on these abilities; tests printed in regular-face, lowercase letters were classified logically (i.e., there is no or insufficient research available to establish empirical classification). Table 5.1 also continues to provide the name of the parent battery to which the test belongs in addition to the specified age range for which the test is appropriate. Practitioners should note that classification along the dimensions just described does not actually represent any particular accommodation to issues concerning the assessment of culturally or linguistically diverse individuals. Retention of the CHC theoretical framework emphasizes that the basis of valid assessments, including assessments conducted on diverse individuals, must first and foremost rest on the best available and most solid theoretical and empirical grounds.

Cultural-Loading Classification

Although the tests listed in Table 5.1 maintain their links to classification according to CHC theory, one of the two principal dimensions along which they are organized relates to *Degree of Cultural Loading,* which represents the degree to which a given test requires specific knowledge of or experience with mainstream U.S. culture. The tests included in Table 5.1 are classified in terms of several characteristics, including emphasis on process, content, and nature of response. Specifically, tests were categorized along dimensions that related to process or product (process-dominant vs. product-dominant) and stimuli (use of abstract or novel stimuli vs. use of culture-specific stimuli)—although attention was also given to aspects of the communicative relationship between examinee and examiner (i.e., culturally specific elements apart from actual oral language, such as affirmative head nods, pointing, etc.; see McCallum & Bracken, 1997). These characteristics are in accordance with the findings of various researchers (e.g., Jensen, 1974; Valdés & Figueroa, 1994) who suggest that tests that are more process oriented and that contain more novel, culture-reduced stimuli and communicative requirements might yield scores that are fairer estimates of ability or skill, since they would be less subject to attenuating influences from an individual's level of exposure to mainstream culture. Classification of tests utilizes a simple, three-category system (high, moderate, and low), which reflects the fact that the nature of these dimensions is better represented by a continuum than by a dichotomy. These categories can be found in Table 5.1 and are arranged in order of increasing cultural loading.

Careful selection of tests listed in the table with respect to this dimension can help practitioners reduce the distance between an individual's familiarity with mainstream culture and the cultural demands of the test. Given the findings that demonstrate that individuals who are not fully acculturated tend to score lower on standardized tests than individuals who are fully acculturated (i.e., those who fall within the parameters of the assumption of comparability), the information provided in Table 5.1 begins to offer practitioners a systematic method for selecting tests that may be more fair for use with such individuals and for establishing a basis for interpretation.

Linguistic-Demand Classification

As discussed previously, test performance can also be adversely affected on the basis of an individual's language proficiency. In short, those who are not fully English-proficient (i.e., those individuals whose language development skills do not meet the age-appropriate expectations built into tests) may score lower on a wide variety of tests, not because of lower ability but because of linguistic barriers that impede comprehension and communication. Thus, there is a need for practitioners to understand the inherent language demands placed on an individual as a function of any given test selected for administration. Table 5.1 provides this information in the form of test classifications based on Degree of Linguistic Demand, which can be used by practitioners to assist in determining the amount of linguistic skill required by the various tests of intelligence and cognitive ability they may choose to use with any given individual.

Three main factors were considered in the classification of tests in Table 5.1, including verbal versus nonverbal language requirements on the part of the examiner (in administration of the test), receptive-language requirements on the part of the examinee, and expressive-language requirements on the part of the examinee. These distinctions are important because all three relate to issues of language proficiency on the part of the examinee and all three bear directly on an individual's performance on such tests. With respect to the language requirements on the part of the examiner, it is important to note that some tests have lengthy, verbose instructions (e.g., WJ-R Analysis-Synthesis), including some that are commonly accepted to be relatively nonverbal (e.g., Wechsler Block Design). On the opposite end of the spectrum are tests that require virtually no written or oral language on the part of the examiner (albeit effective communication is still required as explained before) and that can be given using simple gestures (e.g., UNIT, Leiter-R, etc.).

There are other tests in which an individual's actual language proficiency becomes central to performance, as with the Wechsler Vocabulary and Similarities tests. Such tests place significant demands on language development and rely heavily on the assumption that an individual's language proficiency is comparable to that of age- or grade-related peers. The linguistic demands operate in both the receptive and expressive realms for the examinee. For example, some tests utilize linguistic conventions that are part of the necessary structure for an individual's response (e.g., WJ-R Concept Formation: "round or yellow or red"); some simply are lengthy, requiring significant receptive-language ability in order to comprehend the administrator's instructions fully. In addition, certain tests require the individual to rely directly on expressive-language skills in order to provide an appropriate or correct response (e.g., Wechsler Vocabulary and Comprehension), whereas some tests need no actual spoken response (e.g., K-ABC Triangles). Similar to the structure for classifications based on degree of cultural loading, tests in Table 5.1 have been organized according to a system that uses "high," "moderate," and "low" categories, again emphasizing the continuous nature of these variables. These categories can be found on the left side of Table 5.1 and are arranged in order of increasing language demands corresponding to each of the three levels of cultural loading previously described.

Once again, practitioners may use the linguistic-demand information contained in this table as a way of assisting in the deliberate selection of tests that best match an individual's language development and proficiency with the linguistic demands of the test. Because research has indicated that individuals whose linguistic backgrounds are at significant variance with the linguistic backgrounds of individuals who comprise the norm group, the former will tend to score lower on standardized tests as a function of their reliance on language. Moreover, as in the case of degree of cultural loading, the language information provided in Table 5.1 begins to offer practitioners a systematic method for selecting tests that may be fairer for use with such individuals and may help to establish a defensible basis for interpretation.

CHC Test-Specific Culture-Language Matrices

The classification of tests in Table 5.1 may appear rather daunting at the outset. Although there are only nine categories total (3 levels of cultural loading × 3 levels of linguistic demand), the breadth of tests listed makes the table somewhat unwieldy at first. In addition, the organization of the table does not lend itself readily to attempts that seek to evaluate specific test batteries as a whole. Because practitioners may be interested in seeing what the relative classifications of all the tests in one test battery might be or how the collected tests from one battery compare to another battery, additional CHC Test-specific Culture-Language Matrices are included here as a convenience. Figures 5.2 through 5.10 provide this information for the Wechsler Scales, WJ-R/III, DAS, Leiter-R, K-ABC, CAS, UNIT, KAIT, and SB:IV. It is important to note that tests from these individual intelligence batteries that were classified either empirically or logically as *mixed* measures of abilities were not included in these figures. This is because mixed measures of ability are psychologically ambiguous and, therefore, difficult to interpret. Moreover, the tests listed in these figures are consistent with the tests recommended for use in CHC Cross-Battery assessment (i.e., tests that are relatively pure measures of their respective underlying CHC abilities).

Degree of Linguistic Demand

		Low	Moderate	High
Degree of Cultural Loading	**Low**	**MATRIX REASONING** (*Gf*-I) Geometric Designs (*Gv*-Vz)	**BLOCK DESIGN** (*Gv*-SR, Vz) **SYMBOL SEARCH** (*Gs*-P, R9) **DIGIT SPAN** (*Gsm*-MS, MW) **DIGIT SYMBOL-CODING** (*Gs*-R9) **CODING** (*Gs*-R9)	**LETTER-NUMBER SEQUENCING** (*Gsm*-MW)
	Moderate	**OBJECT ASSEMBLY** (*Gv*-CS, SR) Mazes (*Gv*-SS)	**ARITHMETIC** (*Gq*-A3) Animal Pegs (*Gs*-R9)	
	High			**INFORMATION** (*Gc*-K0) **SIMILARITIES** (*Gc*-LD, VL) **VOCABULARY** (*Gc*-VL, LD) **COMPREHENSION** (*Gc*-LD, K0)

Figure 5.2 Matrix of Cultural Loading and Linguistic Demand Classifications of the Wechsler Scales

Note. Tests printed in bold, uppercase letters are strong measures as defined empirically; tests printed in bold, lowercase letters are moderate measures as defined empirically; tests printed in regular type, lowercase letters are classified logically. Tests that are classified either empirically or logically as mixed measures are not included in this table (see Flanagan, McGrew, & Ortiz, 2000; McGrew & Flanagan, 1998).

Figures 5.2 through 5.10 each contain the respective tests from a single battery arranged in a simple 3 × 3 matrix that can be viewed all at once and that contains the essential information regarding classification according to degree of linguistic demand, degree of cultural loading, and CHC broad and narrow ability classifications. These matrices provide an easy-to-use, graphical representation of how the tests that comprise each of the major cognitive ability batteries are arranged when classified according to these dimensions. The three categories (low, moderate, and high) for degree of linguistic demand span across the matrix from left to right and the similar categories for degree of cultural loading run down the matrix from top to bottom.

The CHC Test-specific Culture-Language Matrices offer practitioners an efficient means for sorting through the information contained in Table 5.1 in

Degree of Linguistic Demand

		Low	Moderate	High
Degree of Cultural Loading	**Low**	SPATIAL RELATIONS (*Gv*-Vz, SR)*	VISUAL MATCHING (*Gs*-P, R9)* NUMBERS REVERSED (*Gsm*-MW)* MEMORY FOR NAMES (*Glr*-MA) DELAYED RECALL— MEMORY FOR NAMES (*Glr*-MA) CROSS OUT (*Gs*-P)	CONCEPT FORMATION (*Gf*-I)* ANALYSIS SYNTHESIS (*Gf*-RG)* AUDITORY WORKING MEMORY (*Gsm*-MW)** SOUND PATTERNS (*Ga*-US/U3)
	Moderate	Picture Recognition (*Gv*-MV)* Visual Closure (*Gv*-CS)	VISUAL-AUDITORY LEARNING (*Glr*-MA, MM)* Delayed Recall—Visual-Auditory Learning (*Glr*-MA, MM)* RETRIEVAL FLUENCY (*Glr*-FI, FA)** RAPID PICTURE NAMING (*Glr*-NA)**	MEMORY FOR WORDS (*Gsm*-MS)* INCOMPLETE WORDS (*Ga*-PC:A)* SOUND BLENDING (*Ga*-PC:S)* AUDITORY ATTENTION (*Ga*-US/U3, UR)** DECISION SPEED (*Gs*-N)**
	High		ORAL VOCABULARY (*Gc*-VL, LD) PICTURE VOCABULARY (*Gc*-VL, K0)	LISTENING COMPREHENSION (*Gc*-LS, LD) VERBAL COMPREHENSION (*Gc*-VL, LD)** GENERAL INFORMATION (*Gc*-K0)**

Figure 5.3 Matrix of Cultural Loading and Linguistic Demand Classifications of the WJ-R/WJ III

*Indicates tests that appear on the WJ-R and WJ III.

**Indicates tests that appear on the WJ III only. Tests with no mark appear on the WJ-R only.

Note. Tests printed in bold, uppercase letters are strong measures as defined empirically; tests printed in bold, lowercase letters are moderate measures as defined empirically; tests printed in regular type, lowercase letters are classified logically. Tests that are classified either empirically or logically as mixed measures are not included in this table (see Flanagan, McGrew, & Ortiz, 2000; McGrew & Flanagan, 1998).

order to guide assessment decisions related to test selection and interpretation. Knowledge of the cultural loading and linguistic demands of test and of their CHC broad- and narrow-ability loadings allows practitioners to select tests that are most appropriate to the referral questions while giving due consideration to the experiential factors unique to the individual. In addition, because the classifications provide relative positions of the tests—that is, distinctions between tests are made on the bases of cultural-loading and linguistic-demand differences—results from testing can be interpreted within the context of expected patterns for diverse individuals (this concept will be discussed in more detail in the next section). This is not to say, however, that the information in

Degree of Linguistic Demand

	Low	Moderate	High
Low	**MATRICES** (*Gf*-I) **SEQUENTIAL AND QUAN- TITATIVE REASONING** (*Gf*-I, RQ) Pattern Construction (*Gv*-SR) Block Building (*Gv*-Vz) Matching Letter-like Forms (*Gv*-Vz) **RECALL OF DESIGNS** (*Gv*-MV)	Recall of Digits (*Gsm*-MS) Speed of Information Processing (*Gs*-N, R9)	
Moderate	Picture Similarities (*Gf*-I) Recognition of Pictures (*Gv*-MV) Recall of Objects (*Glr*-M6)	Early Number Concepts (*Gq*-A3, KM)	
High		Verbal Comprehension (*Gc*-LD, LS) Naming Vocabulary (*Gc*-VL, LD)	**SIMILARITIES** (*Gc*-LD) **WORD DEFINITIONS** (*Gc*-*VL*, LD)

Degree of Cultural Loading (left axis label)

Figure 5.4   Matrix of Cultural Loading and Linguistic Demand Classifications of the DAS

Note. Tests printed in bold, uppercase letters are strong measures as defined empirically; tests printed in bold, lowercase letters are moderate measures as defined empirically; tests printed in regular type, lowercase letters are classified logically. Tests that are classified either empirically or logically as mixed measures are not included in this table (see Flanagan, McGrew, & Ortiz, 2000; McGrew & Flanagan, 1998).

Table 5.1 or the CHC Test-specific Culture-Language Matrices should be solely relied upon for decisions related to test selection and interpretation. It should be noted that the culture and language classifications of culture and language cognitive ability tests in Table 5.1 and the CHC Test-specific Culture-Language Matrices are not definitive and therefore, may change as a result of new research.

The classifications in Table 5.1 do not establish (and are not intended to establish) a comprehensive basis for the assessment of diverse individuals. The information provided in Table 5.1 and Figures 5.2 through 5.10 are meant primarily to supplement the assessment process in both the diagnostic and interpretive arenas within the context of a broader, defensible system of multilingual, nondiscriminatory, cross-cultural assessment (see Figure 5.1). Their limitations notwithstanding, these classifications offer practitioners a viable, sys-

Degree of Linguistic Demand

		Low	Moderate	High
Degree of Cultural Loading	**Low**	Design Analogies (*Gf*-I) Repeated Patterns (*Gf*-I) Sequential Order (*Gf*-I) Paper Folding (*Gv*-Vz) Figure Rotation (*Gv*-Vz, SR)		
	Moderate	Visual Coding (*Gf*-RG) Matching (*Gv*-Vz) Attention Sustained (*Gs*-P, R9)		
	High	Classification (*Gf*-I) Picture Context (*Gf*-RG) Form Completion (*Gv*-Vz, SR) Immediate Recognition (*Gv*-MV) Forward Memory (*Gv*-MV) Figure Ground (*Gv*-CF) Delayed Recognition (*Glr*-MA) Associated Pairs (*Glr*-MA, MM) Delayed Pairs (*Glr*-MA, MM)		

Figure 5.5 Matrix of Cultural Loading and Linguistic Demand Classifications of the Leiter-R

Note. Tests printed in bold, uppercase letters are strong measures as defined empirically; tests printed in bold, lowercase letters are moderate measures as defined empirically; tests printed in regular type, lowercase letters are classified logically. Tests that are classified either empirically or logically as mixed measures are not included in this table (see Flanagan, McGrew, & Ortiz, 2000; McGrew & Flanagan, 1998).

tematic, and defensible method by which certain important decisions regarding culturally fair assessment can be made. When used in conjunction with other relevant assessment information (e.g., direct observations, review of records, interviews, language-proficiency testing, socioeconomic status, developmental data, family history, etc.), these classifications may well prove to be of significant practical value in decreasing bias related to the selection and interpretation of tests.

CONDUCTING CHC CROSS-BATTERY ASSESSMENT WITH DIVERSE INDIVIDUALS

The decision to engage in CHC Cross-Battery assessment represents a decision to use norm-referenced standardized tests. Although such tests are not necessarily essential or required in the assessment of diverse individuals, there

Degree of Linguistic Demand

	Low	Moderate	High
Low	TRIANGLES (*Gv*-SR)	NUMBER RECALL (*Gsm*-MS)	
Moderate	Face Recognition (*Gv*-MV) WORD ORDER (*Gsm*-MS) Magic Window (*Gv*-PI) Gestalt Closure (*Gv*-CS)		
High			

Degree of Cultural Loading

Figure 5.6 Matrix of Cultural Loading and Linguistic Demand Classifications of the K-ABC

Note. Tests printed in bold, uppercase letters are strong measures as defined empirically; tests printed in bold, lowercase letters are moderate measures as defined empirically; tests printed in regular type, lowercase letters are classified logically. Tests that are classified either empirically or logically as mixed measures are not included in this table (see Flanagan, McGrew, & Ortiz, 2000; McGrew & Flanagan, 1998).

are doubtless many occasions in which practitioners will find themselves faced with the need to exercise this option in evaluation. When in the professional judgment of practitioners it becomes clear that the use of standardized tests is warranted, every effort should be made to utilize them in ways that are specifically designed to reduce bias. The selection, administration, and interpretation of any results from standardized test results with diverse individuals must be systematic and defensible, and guided by research and best practices.

Tests selected for the purposes of CHC Cross-Battery assessment should be administered in accordance with the instructions provided by publishers of the tests as described in Chapter 2. In the case of linguistically diverse individuals, questions about the language(s) of assessment often arise, especially in light of legal mandates regarding evaluation in the primary language. Therefore, it is necessary to draw a distinction between bilingual assessment (evalu-

Degree of Linguistic Demand

	Low	Moderate	High
Low	**FIGURE MEMORY** (*Gv*-CF, MV) Expressive Attention (*Glr*-NA) Nonverbal Matrices (*Gf*-I)	**MATCHING NUMBERS** (*Gs*-N, R9) **NUMBER DETECTION** (*Gs*-N, R9) **PLANNED CODES** (*Gs*-R9)	**VERBAL SPATIAL RELATIONS** (*Gv*-PI)
Moderate	**RECEPTIVE ATTENTION** (*Gs*-P, R4)	**WORD SERIES** (*Gsm*-MS) **PLANNED CONNECTIONS** (Gs-P, R9)	**SENTENCE REPETITION** (*Gsm*-MS) **SENTENCE QUESTIONS** (*Gsm*-MS)
High			

(row labels at left: Degree of Cultural Loading)

Figure 5.7 Matrix of Cultural Loading and Linguistic Demand Classifications of the CAS

Note. Tests printed in bold, uppercase letters are strong measures as defined empirically; tests printed in bold, lowercase letters are moderate measures as defined empirically; tests printed in regular type, lowercase letters are classified logically. Tests that are classified either empirically or logically as mixed measures are not included in this table (see Flanagan, McGrew, & Ortiz, 2000; McGrew & Flanagan, 1998).

ation of a bilingual individual, by a bilingual examiner, in a bilingual manner) and assessment of bilingual individuals (evaluation of a bilingual individual, by an English-speaking examiner, in English only). The former requires a practitioner who is knowledgeable and familiar with the examinee's culture; who has the prerequisite training and education in nondiscriminatory assessment, including knowledge about how culture and language differences affect test performance; and who speaks the examinee's language fluently enough to evaluate functioning properly. The rarity of such highly skilled practitioners often limits the viability of this method of evaluation. Conversely, the latter situation represents the most common scenario by far. Given the relative lack of psychological professionals who are *both* culturally competent and linguistically proficient *and* who have received specific training and preparation in methods of nondiscriminatory assessment and interpretation, it seems likely

Degree of Linguistic Demand

	Low	Moderate	High
Low	**SPATIAL MEMORY** (*Gv*-MV) Cube Design (*Gv*-SR, Vz) **Mazes** (*Gv*-SS)		
Moderate	**SYMBOLIC MEMORY** (*Gv*-MV)		
High	**OBJECT MEMORY** (*Gv*-MV) **ANALOGIC REASONING** (*Gf*-I)		

Degree of Cultural Loading

Figure 5.8 Matrix of Cultural Loading and Linguistic Demand Classifications of the UNIT

Note. Tests printed in bold, uppercase letters are strong measures as defined empirically; tests printed in bold, lowercase letters are moderate measures as defined empirically; tests printed in regular type, lowercase letters are classified logically. Tests that are classified either empirically or logically as mixed measures are not included in this table (see Flanagan, McGrew, & Ortiz, 2000; McGrew & Flanagan, 1998).

that such rare professionals will not perform the vast majority of assessments conducted on diverse individuals. Given the problems inherent in the use of interpreters to assist in the assessment practice, as well as the lack of any research to guide appropriate interpretation of results generated from their use, the need for more equitable methods of assessment that are within the immediate reach of every practitioner is obvious.

Practitioners should recognize that although linguistic (e.g., use of an interpreter) accommodations may serve to reduce the language barriers to test administration, they are not strictly necessary in CHC Cross-Battery assessment. The reason is that the cultural and linguistic extensions provided herein are specifically designed to account for bias that may arise when practitioners are forced to use tests of cognitive ability in English with individuals whose cultural and linguistic experiential histories differ from the norm groups for these

Degree of Linguistic Demand

	Low	Moderate	High
Low	**MEMORY FOR BLOCK DESIGNS** (Gv-MV)		
Moderate		**REBUS LEARNING** (Glr-MA) **REBUS DELAYED RECALL** (Glr-MA) **MYSTERY CODES** (Gf-I) **LOGICAL STEPS** (Gf-I)	
High		**FAMOUS FACES** (Gc-K2)	

Degree of Cultural Loading (vertical axis label)

Figure 5.9 Matrix of Cultural Loading and Linguistic Demand Classifications of the KAIT

Note. Tests printed in bold, uppercase letters are strong measures as defined empirically; tests printed in bold, lowercase letters are moderate measures as defined empirically; tests printed in regular type, lowercase letters are classified logically. Tests that are classified either empirically or logically as mixed measures are not included in this table (see Flanagan, McGrew, & Ortiz, 2000; McGrew & Flanagan, 1998).

tests. Use of an interpreter may in fact result in additional confusion regarding the nature and meaning of test results, primarily because there will be a tendency to discount the influence of language proficiency on performance, and because the performance of bilinguals on native-language tests has not been systematically researched. All too often, matching individuals with practitioners solely on the basis of language or culture is believed sufficient to eliminate bias. As was made clear before, mere possession of the capacity to communicate with an individual in his or her native-language does not automatically imbue the practitioner with the necessary knowledge or skills with which to engage in nondiscriminatory assessment. Additionally, the lack of available research with which to guide the use of native-language tests with bilingual individuals makes reliable interpretation extremely difficult.

Much as with language matching, appropriate cross-cultural skills are not an

Degree of Linguistic Demand

	Low	Moderate	High
Low	PATTERN ANALYSIS (*Gv*-SR)	MEMORY FOR DIGITS (*Gsm*-MS, MW) MATRICES (*Gf*-I) Bead Memory (*Gv*-MV)	Number Series (*Gf*-RQ)
Moderate	Memory for Objects (*Gv*-MV)	QUANTITATIVE (*Gq*-A3)	EQUATION BUILDING (*Gf*-RQ)
High			VOCABULARY (*Gc*-VL, LD) VERBAL RELATIONS (*Gc*-LD) Absurdities (*Gc*-LD) Comprehension (*Gc*-LD, K0)

(Left axis: Degree of Cultural Loading)

Figure 5.10 Matrix of Cultural Loading and Linguistic Demand Classifications of the SB:IV

Note. Tests printed in bold, uppercase letters are strong measures as defined empirically; tests printed in bold, lowercase letters are moderate measures as defined empirically; tests printed in regular type, lowercase letters are classified logically. Tests that are classified either empirically or logically as mixed measures are not included in this table (see Flanagan, McGrew, & Ortiz, 2000; McGrew & Flanagan, 1998).

inherent part of a practitioner's assessment repertoire simply because there is a cultural match with the individual being evaluated. Knowledge regarding the manner in which culture influences such things as test performance, classroom behavior, interpersonal skills, adaptive behavior, and so forth, as well as professional skill and expertise in using the cultural context to interpret such data, must be taught and learned directly. Therefore, in many cases, practitioners who possess the requisite cross-cultural assessment skills, as well as knowledge of how second-language acquisition or bilingual development affect test performance, are able to perform a much less discriminatory and much less biased evaluation than practitioners who merely match the child in terms of language and culture, but have none of these skills or knowledge.

CHC Cross-Battery assessment in English in no way precludes CHC Cross-Battery assessment in the native language. The major limitations in attempting to conduct such assessment, however, revolve around the lack of available appropriate assessment instruments and the fact that they have not yet been strictly classified according to CHC theory. It is possible, however, to derive *logical* classifications for such tests as the Bateria-R, BVAT, WISC-R-PR, and other tests with different language versions by matching the respective subtests with their English counterparts as classified in Appendix B. In cases in which the tests are virtually identical, in English and the other language, it is reasonable to assume that there would be relatively good correspondence in the constructs measured by each, but this assumption awaits empirical validation and should be used cautiously. The following sections provide a reasonable illustration of the process of CHC Cross-Battery assessment with diverse individuals when English is the language in which the assessment is conducted.

Test Selection

Application of CHC Cross-Battery assessment methods with diverse individuals rests on the premise that an empirically based selection of a set of tests known to assess a particular construct, combined with consideration of the relevant cultural and linguistic dimensions of such tests, can provide more reliable, valid, and interpretable assessment data than that ordinarily obtained using traditional methods. Careful and deliberate selection of tests, based on factors relevant to the background of the individual being assessed, creates a unique test battery that is responsive to the particular referral questions. In this way, practitioners can develop custom batteries for any given individual that will differ as a function of both the specific language competencies and cultural experiences of the examinee, and the specific nature of the referral concerns. With respect to issues of bias related to test selection, the basic goal in constructing a CHC Cross-Battery–based set of tests for use with diverse individuals is to ensure a balance between empirical issues and considerations related to cultural and linguistic factors. This is accomplished primarily through the use of the information contained in Table 5.1 and Figures 5.2 through 5.10.

The initial step in constructing an appropriate CHC Cross-Battery for use with a particular diverse individual is essentially identical to the steps already described in Chapter 2, especially application of hypothesis generation and testing. Because the realm of potential extrinsic factors that may be primarily related to any observed or suspected difficulties is expanded with diverse individuals, the hypothesis generation and testing process becomes significantly more important. Practitioners should continue to use the CHC theory and research knowledge base and link any presenting problems or patterns of learning difficulties to specific cognitive abilities that may be logically related. This step provides a basis for selecting tests in accordance with the known relationships between manifest skill deficits and cognitive dysfunction. This step also reinforces the notion that valid assessment begins with the selection of tests that have been demonstrated empirically to be reliable and accurate measures of the constructs of interest. Although this step represents the selective (S-CB) approach because of its focus on a few select cognitive abilities, it does not preclude use of the comprehensive (C-CB) approach. Use of C-CB makes this step rather simple in that practitioners have made a decision to measure a wide range of cognitive abilities, irrespective of whether there are any concerns with functioning in specific areas.

Once the constructs to be measured within the parameters of the assessment have been identified (whether a few or a wide range), practitioners will need to select the tests that are most suitable for measuring them. As in the case of the general approach to CHC Cross-Battery assessment described in Chapter 2, practitioners need to consider many factors in the selection process, including age of the individual, availability of tests, and so on. However, in the case of assessment with diverse individuals, practitioners must now add two additional considerations—the cultural and linguistic dimensions of the tests being considered for selection. Test selection will become slightly more complicated as practitioners try to balance the guiding principles of CHC Cross-Battery assessment (primarily, crossing the fewest batteries, providing adequate representation of the broad constructs, selecting strong empirical measures, etc.) with decision issues related to individual variables (language proficiency, cultural experience, etc.). For the most part, the guiding principles of CHC Cross-Battery assessment should be adhered to as much as possible and then supplemented with decisions regarding the cultural and linguistic characteristics of the tests. Although there will be individual considerations, given the variation in experience and proficiency among individuals, *in general, tests with the lowest cultural loadings and lowest linguistic demands should be selected over tests that are classified higher.*

As described previously, application of this guideline helps to reduce the discriminatory aspects involved in the selection of standardized tests related to acculturation level and language proficiency. Note that in some cases, however, there will be very little (if any) choice available when making decisions along these dimensions, such as in the case of Gc, where most tests of this construct (by nature and definition) tend to fall in the high culture–high language category. Likewise, the majority of tests that fall in the low culture–low language category tend to be measures of Gv. Therefore, there will be times when concessions will need to be made regarding adherence to the guiding principles. At the most basic level, tests must first be selected according to the broad constructs they measure (e.g., Gv, Gc, Gs, etc.). After that, practitioners have much more latitude in being able to select tests that are most appropriate given the various needs in assessment. It is recommended that practitioners use their best judgment in deciding the final balance among all factors involved in decisions related to test selection. Once the customized CHC Cross-Battery has been developed, the practitioner merely follows the procedures for administration and scoring offered in Chapter 2.

Test Interpretation

Much as with test selection, application of CHC Cross-Battery assessment methods with diverse individuals also rests on the premise that proper and systematic consideration of the relevant cultural and linguistic characteristics of such tests provides a framework for interpretation that is more valid and reliable than that ordinarily obtained using traditional methods. Based on knowledge of the manner in which cultural and linguistic variables attenuate performance, coupled with information regarding an individual's experiential background, analysis of the patterns contained in test data derived from CHC Cross-Battery assessment provides a reasonable and defensible basis for interpretation. By combining the methods regarding normative and intracognitive analysis and interpretation, described in Chapter 3, with comparisons of performance against hypotheses related to cultural and linguistic factors, practitioners have the means with which to achieve less discriminatory interpretation and perhaps draw more valid inferences from collected data. With respect to issues of bias related to test interpretation, the basic goal is to reframe the manner in which data are typically evaluated so that the potential attenuating effects of cultural and linguistic factors are much more clear and evident.

The initial step in interpreting results generated from CHC Cross-Battery assessment on diverse individuals remains wholly consistent with the process of interpretation described in Chapter 3 of this book. Practitioners should continue to use the CHC Cross-Battery Worksheets located in Appendix A and the CHC Cross-Battery Summary Sheet found in Appendix E. These graphic organizers assist practitioners in documenting the collected data and greatly facilitate interpretation. Practitioners should also follow the guidelines listed in Chapter 3 regarding intercognitive (normative) and intra-cognitive (relative) analysis. Of course, given the preceding discussion on the problems associated with the use of norm groups with diverse individuals, practitioners should not place absolute faith in the significance of any unusual patterns. Whether indications of normatively-based weaknesses are to be believed rests upon joint consideration of the data viewed in this manner and in an alternative manner (to be discussed next).

Because intra-cognitive analysis is person-relative, it is theoretically no more discriminatory in and of itself with individuals who are diverse or otherwise. Recall, however, that this type of analysis rests on assumptions unsupported by research, especially in the context of profiles. In addition, because the cultural and linguistic characteristics of the tests used in assessment can differentially affect the performance of diverse individuals, even person-relative scatter and deviation are exceedingly difficult, if not impossible, to interpret within this framework. Nevertheless, the data generated within the context of a CHC Cross-Battery assessment with diverse individuals should be made available because it can serve to highlight apparent patterns that may be spurious or illusory when evaluated from an alternative perspective.

The first sections of this chapter provided a discussion related to the effects that differences in cultural or linguistic background could have on individual performance on standardized tests, in particular tests of intelligence and cognitive ability. In both cases, culture (or level of acculturation) and language (or language proficiency) operate as attenuating variables—that is, the greater the difference between an individual's cultural or linguistic background and the cultural or linguistic background of the individuals comprising the norm group, the more likely the test will measure lower performance as a function of this *experiential* difference as opposed to being due to actual lower ability. When an individual's background is commensurate with the background of the individuals comprising the norm group, differences in performance can be more reliably interpreted as the result of true differences in ability. Therefore, we know that, in general, cultural and linguistic differences serve to artificially *depress* the scores of diverse individuals. The more different the individual is, the greater the score is attenuated.

If we draw upon an understanding of this relationship and combine it with a blank matrix similar to the ones used for classifying test batteries in Figures 5.2 through 5.10, we can create a pattern within the matrix that describes a logical and expected pattern of performance for diverse individuals. Figure 5.11 pro-

DON'T FORGET

Performance Measurement and Experiential Difference

Culture (or level of acculturation) and language (or language proficiency) operate as attenuating variables—that is, the greater the difference between an individual's cultural or linguistic background and the cultural or linguistic background of the individuals comprising the norm group, the more likely the test will measure lower performance as a function of this *experiential* difference as opposed to being due to actual lower ability.

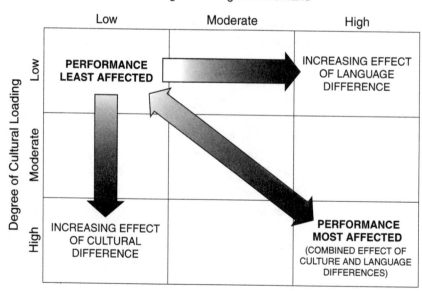

Figure 5.11 Pattern of Expected Test Performance for Diverse Individuals

vides this illustration. There are two small shaded arrows and one large shaded arrow depicted in the figure. The smaller arrow at the top, pointing from left to right, represents the increasing effect that language differences are likely to have on test performance as a function of the increasing linguistic demands of the tests. When practitioners use tests that have relatively heavy language demands (i.e., classified in the "high linguistic demand" cells), performance of diverse individuals is likely to be adversely affected to a relatively large degree. When the tests are more language-reduced (i.e., classified in the "low linguistic demand" cells), then performance is likely to be relatively less adversely affected. Likewise, the small arrow on the left side pointing from top to bottom represents the increasing effect that cultural differences are likely to have on test performance as a function of the increasing cultural loadings of the tests. When practitioners use tests that are classified as being culturally loaded to a relatively high degree (i.e., classified in the "high cultural loading" cells), performance of diverse individuals is also likely to be adversely affected to a relatively large degree. When the tests used are more culturally reduced (i.e., classified in the "low cultural loading" cells), then performance is likely to be relatively less adversely affected. The double-headed arrow in Figure 5.11 shows the overall effect that cultural *and* language differences have on performance across tests categorized along the dimensions of cultural loading and linguistic demand. Generally speaking, performance of diverse individuals on standardized tests is least likely to be affected by tests that are classified more to the left and top of the matrix and most likely to be affected by tests that are classified closer to the right and bottom of the matrix. In essence, the matrix provides a graphical representation of the patterns of expected performance for diverse individuals from the perspective of the tests' cultural and linguistic characteristics rather than from the perspective of constructs measured.

In order to utilize this alternative frame of reference for test results, practitioners must group the tests they selected for use in CHC Cross-Battery assessment according to their respective cultural and linguistic dimensions. Given the 3 × 3 construction of the classifications, there are nine possible groups formed from the permutation of the high, moderate, and low categories for each of the two dimensions. Practitioners should take care to group and classify the tests used in assessment accurately. In addition, numerical data can be used to provide a means for comparisons across such groups. For the purposes of CHC Cross-Battery assessment, this is accomplished through use of the converted standard score obtained for each individual test administered. These values can be taken directly from the second column (labeled "SS 100 ± 15") of the CHC Cross-Battery Worksheets. For each set of tests grouped together according to their degree of cultural loading and degree of linguistic demand, an overall mean or average can be calculated.[1] This score will be called the *Cell Average* and is the score that will be used to assist interpretation. In order to facilitate the process of grouping the tests in accordance with their respective characteristics as well as the process of deriving the Cell Average, practitioners may use the CHC Culture-Language Matrix Worksheet provided in Figure 5.12. Once all of the information has been entered on this worksheet, practitioners can begin the process of comparative evaluation and interpretation of performance.

Note also that the Cell Average score itself has *no meaning* beyond an *arithmetical representation of average performance* on a set of tests grouped together according to both cultural and linguistic characteristics. Beyond this, there is no inherent meaning or implied construct for this score and it should not be interpreted as such. Rather, the Cell Averages are meant to offer only an easy way for practitioners to evaluate the pattern of scores revealed by the data when viewed from this perspective. Calculation of a Cell Average score for each group begins to approximate a variation of the person-relative approach to analysis. However, although it would be possible to apply intracognitive methods or even other methods of analysis to the data when organized in this fashion, doing so may create additional complexities that could obscure the simple nature of basic pattern analysis. Given the existing difficulties associated with integrating considerations related to culture and language on test performance; the use of an alternative and unfamiliar frame of reference (for most practitioners); the primary need to distinguish difference from dysfunction; and perhaps the limited benefits of any such additional statistical analysis, it seems

---

[1] Although the CHC Culture-Language Matrix was expressly designed to help address issues related to test selection and performance patterns *in general,* the authors would like to point out that the idea of taking mathematical averages within each cell to facilitate actual pattern comparisons belongs to J. Ryan Burke, MEd, a school psychologist with the Washington Elementary School District. His contribution to the development of this work and his original thinking in this area are worthy of individual recognition and are greatly appreciated.

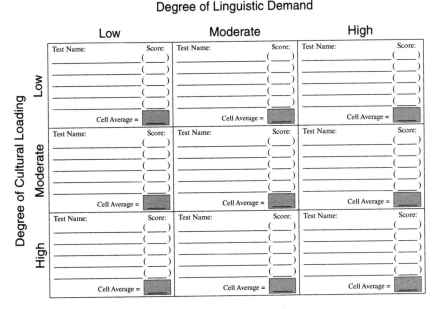

Figure 5.12 CHC Culture-Language Matrix Worksheet

prudent to limit such explorations until practitioners have developed a high level of comfort and familiarity with this type of analysis.

When the data are calculated, practitioners should examine the Cell Averages as recorded on the CHC Culture-Language Matrix Worksheet and compare them both across cells, from left to right, and down cells, from top to bottom. What is important to note is not the normative positions of the scores (average, low average, etc.), but rather the relationships between the scores and the degree to which they form a pattern that is either consistent or inconsistent with the pattern of performance predicted by the matrix (as specified in Figure 5.11). In general, when the overall pattern of scores obtained for a given individual approximates the general predicted patterns, practitioners may interpret such results as being a reflection of cultural or linguistic differences rather than of true ability.

As depicted in Figure 5.11, there are three general patterns that may emerge: (a) effect of cultural loading only—scores decrease as they move down the cells in the matrix; (b) effect of linguistic demand only—scores decrease as they move across the cells from left to right in the matrix; and (c) overall effect of culture and language—scores in or near the upper left corner of the matrix tend to be higher than scores at or near the bottom right corner of the matrix. All three patterns are important because levels of acculturation and language proficiency are not perfectly correlated. Consequently, it is possible that only one of these variables may be at variance with the experiential backgrounds of the norm group; thus performance may be affected in only one way, along only one dimension. In addition, there may be times when cultural or linguistic differences do not produce significant, *individual* adverse effects on performance, but do affect performance negatively when *combined* (e.g., on tests classified as high on both cultural loading and linguistic demand).

Once again, patterns that emerge when the data are organized in this way and that are consistent with the expected general patterns of performance outlined previously tend to provide support for the notion that the individual's scores are more a reflection of cultural or linguistic differences (or both), than they are a reflection of actual ability or skill. In such cases, interpretation of the data should remain at this level and be based accordingly. Notions regarding performance derived previously from intercognitive and intra-cognitive analysis will be of only secondary importance. When the patterns that emerge from the data are not consistent with the expected general patterns of performance for diverse individuals, then practitioners should revert to the inter- and intra-cognitive analyses conducted previously and base interpretation on results at that level. This is not to say that results from such analysis are fully valid because no demonstrable effects of culture or language differences were found. Although that is one possible interpretation, it is also equally possible that the effects from these variables were distributed in a manner that was not captured or revealed by this interpretive organization. Thus interpretations of dysfunction or disability should remain bolstered by a wide range and multiple sources of evidence that converge and support opinion and inference. Practitioner conclusions must not rest solely on the presence or absence of expected patterns in the data from either intercognitive, intracognitive, or culture-language analysis.

SUMMARY

The cultural and linguistic extensions to the CHC Cross-Battery approach described in this chapter do not offer a complete solution to all of the problems inherent in the process of fairly and equitably evaluating the cognitive abilities or intelligence of individuals who are culturally or linguistically diverse. It was made clear that this approach addresses only those issues involved in test selection and interpretation, and that there are numerous other sources of potential bias that can affect any given individual's performance on standardized tests. Nevertheless, with due consideration of these issues combined with well-reasoned application of the cultural and linguistic extensions to the approach outlined in the sections of this chapter, practitioners should be able to select an appropriate set of tests that, in addition to having a strong empirical base, can also reduce the potential discriminatory aspects involved in their use with diverse populations, and that provides a defensible, systematic framework for interpretation. Although the other potential sources of bias found throughout the assessment process (e.g., inappropriate cross-cultural transactions, failure to use culture as the context for framing behavior; see Figure 5.1) are not specifically attended to by this approach, use of CHC Cross-Battery assessment methods with the attendant cultural and linguistic extensions represents a significant advancement in the practice of bilingual, cross-cultural, nondiscriminatory assessment that is well within the professional reach of most practitioners.

The treatment in this chapter of the issues involved in the assessment of individuals from diverse backgrounds is admittedly brief and lacks much detail. The primary focus has been on issues related to test selection and interpretation, but there are numerous other substantive issues that simply fall beyond the limits of this chapter, including delineation of a comprehensive framework for nondiscriminatory assessment that addresses bias and discrimination on many levels. In short, fair and equitable assessment of individuals who are culturally and linguistically diverse rests primarily on a thorough knowledge and understanding of the manner in which tests of intelligence or cognitive ability may be affected by variables involving level of acculturation and language proficiency. Tests in the array of cognitive ability batteries and special purpose tests available to practitioners today, as well as those now emerging, tend in general to be very sophisticated and well designed. Nevertheless, their use with individuals from diverse backgrounds continues to be plagued by assumptions that tend to have discriminatory effects, in particular with issues involving level of acculturation and language proficiency. Practitioners are well advised to remain aware that the research that overwhelmingly supports the notion that such tests are not biased is based on definitions of bias that are either untenable or inaccurate. Bias is not a function simply of item content, factor structure, or racial differences. Bias is more a function of differences in experience that are due to factors involving many variables, including culture and language. Moreover, it was made clear in this chapter that tests possess cultural and linguistic characteristics to varying degrees that differentially affect the performance of individuals who are experientially different in ways that do not occur with individuals who are experientially comparable. According to Sattler:

> Probably no test can be created that will entirely eliminate the influence of learning and cultural experiences. The test content and materials, the language in which the questions are phrased, the test directions, the categories for classifying the responses, the scoring criteria, and the validity criteria are all culture bound. (1992, p. 579)

Whenever standardized, norm-referenced tests are used with individuals from diverse backgrounds, the possibility that what is actually being measured is acculturation or English-language proficiency, rather than ability, always exists. The information presented in the first part of this chapter provides assistance to practitioners by guiding decisions regarding test selection in the process of conducting CHC Cross-Battery assessment. Because this approach to assessment is built upon an empirical knowledge base of theory and research concerning the relationship between cognitive abilities and academic achievement, it allows practitioners to construct individualized test batteries that are more responsive to the unique demands of any given assessment. Application and use of the cultural and linguistic extensions of the CHC Cross-Battery approach represents a viable method for advancing assessment of diverse individuals in ways that seek to enhance the meaning of the collected data and that provide a mechanism for evaluation of the effects of cultural and linguistic differences on test performance.

REFERENCES

American Educational Research Association, American Psychological Association, & American Council on Measurement. (1985). *Standards for educational and psychological tests.* Washington, DC: American Psychological Association.

American Psychological Association. (1990). *Guidelines for providers of psychological services to ethnic, linguistic, and culturally diverse populations.* Washington, DC: Author.

Bialystok, E. (1991). *Language processing in bilingual children.* New York: Cambridge University Press.

Cole, M., & Cole, S. R. (1993). *The development of children.* New York: Scientific American Books.

Cummins, J. C. (1984). *Bilingual and special education: Issues in assessment and pedagogy.* Austin, TX: Pro-Ed.

Ehrman, M. E. (1996). *Understanding second language learning difficulties.* Thousand Oaks, CA: Sage.

Figueroa, R. A. (1990a). Assessment of linguistic minority group children. In C. R. Reynolds & R. W. Kamphaus (Eds.), *Handbook of psychological and educational assessment of children: Vol. 1: Intelligence and achievement.* New York: Guilford.

Figueroa, R. A. (1990b). Best practices in the assessment of bilingual children. In A. Thomas & J. Grimes (Eds.), *Best practices in school psychology* (Vol. 2). Washington, DC: National Association of School Psychologists, 93–106.

Figueroa, R. A., Delgado, G. L., & Ruiz, N. T. (1984). Assessment of Hispanic children: Implications for Hispanic hearing-impaired children. In G. L. Delgado (Ed.), *The Hispanic deaf: Issues and challenges for bilingual special education* (pp. 124–153). Washington, DC: Gallaudet College Press.

Flanagan, D. P., McGrew, K. S., & Ortiz, S. O. (2000). *The Wechsler intelligence scales and CHC theory: A contemporary approach to interpretation.* Boston: Allyn & Bacon.

Flanagan, D. P., & Miranda, A. H. (1995). Working with culturally different families. In A. Thomas & J. Grimes (Eds.), *Best practices in school psychology* (Vol. 3, pp. 1039–1060). Washington, DC: National Association of School Psychologists.

Greenfield, P. M. (1998). The cultural evolution of IQ. In U. Neisser (Ed.), *The rising curve: Long-term gains in IQ and related measures.* Washington, DC: American Psychological Association.

Jensen, A. R. (1974). How biased are culture-loaded tests? *Genetic Psychology Monographs, 90,* 185–244.

Jensen, A. R. (1976). Construct validity and test bias. *Phi Delta Kappan, 58,* 340–346.

Kamphaus, R. W. (1993). *Clinical assessment of children's intelligence.* Boston: Allyn & Bacon.

Kaufman, A. S. (1994). *Intelligent testing with the WISC-III.* New York: Wiley.

Lopez, E. C. (1997). The cognitive assessment of limited English proficient and bilingual children. In D. P. Flanagan, J. L. Genshaft, & P. L. Harrison (Eds.), *Contemporary intellectual assessment: Theories, tests, and issues* (pp. 506–516). New York: Guilford.

Matsumoto, D. (1994). *Cultural influences on research methods and statistics.* Pacific Grove, CA: Brooks/Cole.

McCallum, R. S., & Bracken, B. A. (1997). The Universal Nonverbal Intelligence Test. In D. P. Flanagan, J. L. Genshaft, & P. L. Harrison (Eds.), *Contemporary intellectual assessment: Theories, tests, and issues* (pp. 268–280). New York: Guilford.

McGrew, K. S., & Flanagan, D. P. (1998). *The intelligence test desk reference (ITDR): Gf-Gc cross-battery assessment.* Boston: Allyn & Bacon.

Mercer, J. R. (1979). *System of Multicultural Pluralistic Assessment: Technical manual.* New York: Psychological Corporation.

Neisser, U., Boodoo, G., Bouchard, T. J., Boykin, A. W., Brody, N., Ceci, S. J., Halpern, D. F., Loehlin, J. C., Perloff, R., Sternberg, R. J., & Urbina, S. (1996). Intelligence: Knowns and unknowns. *American Psychologist, 51,* 77–101.

Ochoa, S. H., Powell, M. P., & Robles-Pina, R. (1996). School psychologists' assessment practices with bilingual and limited-English-proficient students. *Journal of Psychoeducational Assessment, 14,* 250–275.

Ortiz, S. O. (2000). *Comprehensive assessment of culturally and linguistically diverse children: A systematic, practical approach to nondiscriminatory assessment.* Manuscript in preparation.

Ortiz, S., & Flanagan, D. P. (1998). Enhancing cognitive assessment of culturally and linguistically diverse individuals: Selective *Gf-Gc* cross-battery assessment. *The School Psychologist, 52*(1), 6–9.

Salvia, J., & Ysseldyke, J. (1991). *Assessment in special and remedial education* (5th ed.). Boston: Houghton-Mifflin.

Samuda, R. J., Kong, S. L., Cummins, J., Pascual-Leone, J., & Lewis, J. (1991). *Assessment and placement of minority students.* New York: C. J. Hogrefe/Intercultural Social Sciences.

Sattler, J. (1992). *Assessment of children* (Rev. 3rd ed.). San Diego: Author.

Scarr, S. (1978). From evolution to Larry P., or what shall we do about IQ tests? *Intelligence, 2,* 325–342.

Valdés, G., & Figueroa, R. A. (1994). *Bilingualism and testing: A special case of bias.* Norwood, NJ: Ablex.

Ysseldyke, J. E. (1979). Issues in psychoeducational assessment. In G. D. Phye & D. Reschly (Eds.), *School psychology: Methods and role.* New York: Academic.

🔖 TEST YOURSELF 🔖

1. **When an examiner matches the examinee in terms of both culture and language background, this is sufficient in order to ensure nondiscriminatory assessment.** True or False?

2. **Use of the cultural and linguistic extensions of the CHC Cross-Battery approach**

   (a) assists in reducing bias related to test selection.

   (b) assists in reducing bias related to test interpretation.

   (c) does not constitute a comprehensive framework for assessment.

   (d) all of the above

3. **Use of an interpreter during the administration of a test**

   (a) eliminates the problem with bias in language.

   (b) remains problematic even when the examiner and examinee are well trained.

   (c) represents best practices.

   (d) minimally affects the psychometric properties of the test.

   (e) none of the above

4. **Standardized, norm-referenced tests are biased because**

   (a) they don't predict equally well for different ethnic groups.

   (b) the factor structure changes as a function of race or ethnicity.

   (c) their item content differentially affects performance.

   (d) none of the above

5. **Cultural bias is the same as cultural loading, just as linguistic bias is the same as language loading.** True or False?

6. **Nonverbal tests**

   (a) despite their claims, are neither entirely culture-free nor language-free.

   (b) may be as culturally loaded or possibly more so than verbal tests.

   (c) do not circumvent issues related to communication between examiner and examinee.

   (d) have norm samples that remain problematic.

   (e) all of the above

7. **Which of the following is not true in selecting tests for CHC Cross-Battery assessment for culturally and linguistically diverse individuals?**

   (a) Tests with reduced language demands should be selected over equivalent tests with higher language demands.

   (b) Tests with reduced cultural loadings should be selected over equivalent tests with higher cultural loadings.

   (c) Tests should be selected only with respect to the broad abilities they measure.

   (d) Selection of tests represents striking a balance among CHC Cross-Battery guiding principles, specific referral concerns, and the unique background characteristics of the examinee.

8. **When using the CHC Culture-Language Matrix Worksheet, the expected pattern of performance for culturally and linguistically diverse individuals should, in general,**

   (a) decrease diagonally from the top left to the bottom right.

   (b) increase diagonally from the top left to the bottom right.

   (c) remain the same.

(continued)

9. **When using the CHC Culture-Language Matrix Worksheet, which of the following general interpretive statements is incorrect?**

   (a) When scores are consistent across all cells, this indicates a possible effect of both culture and language differences.

   (b) When scores decrease across cells from left to right, this indicates a possible effect of language difference.

   (c) When scores decrease across cells from top to bottom, this indicates a possible effect of cultural difference.

   (d) When scores decrease across cells from left to right and from top to bottom, this indicates a possible effect of both culture and language differences.

10. **The cultural and linguistic extensions to the CHC Cross-Battery approach described in this chapter offer a complete solution to all of the problems inherent in the process of fairly and equitably evaluating the cognitive abilities or intelligence of individuals who are culturally or linguistically diverse.** True or False?

Answers: 1. False, 2. d; 3. b; 4. d; 5. False; 6. e; 7. c; 8. a; 9. a; 10. False

Six

STRENGTHS AND WEAKNESSES OF CHC CROSS-BATTERY ASSESSMENT

All approaches to assessment and all assessment instruments have strengths and weaknesses. The CHC Cross-Battery approach is no exception. This chapter presents the most salient strengths and weaknesses of the CHC Cross-Battery approach (see Rapid Reference 6.1) and provides a brief question-and-answer–style discussion regarding common questions and possible misconceptions about this new method of assessment.

STRENGTHS OF THE CHC CROSS-BATTERY APPROACH

Empirically Validated Theory

The Cattell-Horn-Carroll (CHC) theory of cognitive abilities is the framework upon which the CHC Cross-Battery approach is based. Within the psychometric tradition, CHC theory is the most well-researched and best empirically established. Currently, it represents the culmination of six decades of systematic research on the structure of cognitive abilities. There is a network of validity evidence available to support CHC theory that includes structural evidence, developmental evidence, neurocognitive evidence, heritability evidence, and evidence of the relations between many CHC broad and narrow cognitive abilities and a variety of outcome criteria (e.g., specific academic and vocational skills). The research evidence available in support of CHC theory was summarized in Chapter 1 of this book and is presented in detail in Flanagan, McGrew, and Ortiz (2000) and McGrew and Flanagan (1998).

Because all the major intelligence tests (as well as numerous supplemental and special purpose tests of cognitive ability) have been empirically evaluated from the perspective of CHC theory, it represents a viable framework from which to organize assessments of cognitive functioning. The CHC Cross-

≡ *Rapid Reference 6.1*

Strengths and Weaknesses of the CHC Cross-Battery Approach

Strengths	Weaknesses
The CHC Cross-Battery approach:	The CHC Cross-Battery approach:
• Is based on a well-validated theory.	• Has no internal norm group.
• Facilitates communication.	• Requires a higher degree of examiner competency.
• Guards against invalidity in assessment.	• Requires additional time in scoring.
• Guards against unreliability in assessment.	• May require additional testing to obtain a global ability score.
• Is time-efficient.	
• Is consistent with best practices in assessment.	
• Fulfills various needs in assessment-related fields.	
• Has validity evidence.	
• Improves learning disabilities assessment.	
• Is systematic.	

Battery approach ensures that assessments are organized around and interpreted from this theoretical perspective so that practitioners can base their inferences about test performance on solid research rather than on clinical acumen alone.

Professional Communication

Most scientific disciplines have a standard nomenclature (a common set of terms and definitions) that facilitates communication among professionals and guards against miscommunication and misinterpretation. For example, the standard nomenclature in chemistry is reflected in the periodic table; in biology, it is reflected in the classification of animals according to phyla; in psychology and psychiatry, it is reflected in the *Diagnostic and Statistical Manual of Mental Disorders;* and in medicine, it is reflected in the *International Classification of Diseases.* Underlying the CHC Cross-Battery approach is a standard nomenclature or "table of human cognitive abilities" that includes classifications of more than 250 tests according to the broad and narrow CHC abilities they measure (Flanagan, McGrew, et al., 2000; McGrew & Flanagan, 1998). The classification system was developed, in part, to improve communication among practitioners, researchers, test developers, and scholars in the field of intelligence testing (McGrew & Flanagan, 1998).

The CHC classification system was also developed to bring consistency to intelligence-testing terminology and thereby improve interpretations that are drawn from test data. To illustrate, there are myriad interpretations associated with performance on a standard block design test that reflect the intelligence battery used and the test author's conception of what the test measures, rather than what the test may actually measure according to contemporary theory and research. For example, the Block Design test on the Wechsler Scales is often interpreted as a measure of nonverbal ability or perceptual organization ability and, in some cases, of fluid reasoning (e.g., Kaufman, 1994). Conversely, the block design test on the SB:IV, called Pattern Analysis, is interpreted as a measure of Abstract-Visual Reasoning following the test authors' guidelines (Thorndike, Hagen, & Sattler, 1986); and the DAS block design test, called Pattern Construction, is interpreted as a measure of spatial ability (Elliott, 1990). In yet another example, the Triangles subtest on the K-ABC, which involves essentially the same task demands as the other block design tests just mentioned, is interpreted as a measure of simultaneous processing (Kaufman & Kaufman, 1983). Despite the various interpretations that are associated with a standard block-design–type task, research shows that these tasks all measure a common underlying *Gv* ability (i.e., Spatial Relations, according to the CHC theory; e.g., Woodcock, 1990). Use of the CHC Cross-Battery approach ensures that test interpretation appropriately reflects empirically based similarities across instruments and specific cognitive ability tests. As a result, miscommunication and misinterpretation are minimized.

Protection Against Invalidity

Invalidity in assessment is ubiquitous among traditional assessment approaches. The most common types of invalidity in assessment are construct underrepresentation and construct-irrelevant variance (Messick, 1995; see

Chapter 1 of this book for detailed definitions). Briefly, traditional methods of assessment freely allow for the interpretation of individual subtests (e.g., subtest analysis or ipsative analysis; Sattler, 1992) despite the fact that an individual subtest score does not provide enough information to support an interpretation about functioning in the specific cognitive ability presumed to be measured by the test. Simply stated, individual subtests *underrepresent* the construct of interest.

According to Messick (1989), failure to represent constructs by more than one measure (or subtest) leads to *nomological noise*. That is,

> [b]ecause no single test is a pure exemplar of the construct but contains variance due to other constructs and method contaminants, there is no solid basis for concluding that an observed score relationship stems from that part of the test variance reflective of the construct. By using two or more tests to represent the construct ... one can disentangle shared variance from unshared variance and discern which aspects of construct meaning, if any, derive from the shared and unshared parts. (p. 48)

The CHC Cross-Battery approach specifies interpretation of clusters (aggregates of two or more subtests that reflect aspects of a common construct) only. By elevating test interpretation from the individual subtest level to the cluster level, the CHC Cross-Battery approach circumvents a common source of invalidity in assessment—construct underrepresentation.

The other major source of invalidity in traditional assessment methods—construct-irrelevant variance—occurs when clusters that include measures of *different* broad ability constructs (e.g., *Gf, Gc, Gsm, Glr,* etc.) are interpreted as measures of a unidimensional construct. The WAIS-III PIQ, for example, contains measures of *Gv, Gf,* and *Gs.* As such, it is difficult to discern the extent to which performance on the construct intended to be measured (viz., *Gv*) may have been influenced by measures that are *irrelevant* to that construct (viz., *Gf, Gs*). In this case, it may be difficult to determine whether aberrant performance on tests of *Gf* or *Gs* artificially inflated or attenuated the score representing the ability presumed to underlie the PIQ (i.e., *Gv*). By ensuring that only measures (i.e., subtests) that are *relevant to* the abilities of interest are included in the derivation of CHC clusters, the CHC Cross-Battery approach circumvents construct-irrelevant variance.

Protection Against Unreliability

Unreliability in assessment occurs when individual tests and subtests with low reliability are interpreted as diagnostically meaningful. According to Salvia and Ysseldyke (1991), tests with reliability coefficients below .80 are considered inadequate (i.e., unreliable) for making individual judgments about test performance. Unreliable test scores can contribute to misdiagnosis and inappropriate placement and treatment. In order to use the results of any given test diagnostically, it must be highly reliable (i.e., it must have a reliability coefficient of .90 or above). Tests with reliability coefficients between .80 and .89 (inclusive) may be used to aid in screening decisions only. The CHC Cross-Battery approach circumvents the problem of unreliability in assessment by recommending that only tests with high reliability be used in assessment whenever possible, and by combining individual tests into clusters and thereby increasing reliability. Information about the reliability of all the subtests of the major intelligence batteries is available in McGrew and Flanagan (1998) and Flanagan, McGrew, and colleagues (2000) as well as in the respective manuals of these instruments (also see Appendix C of this text).

Time-Efficiency

Two types of cross-battery assessments were described in this book: comprehensive and selective. Both are time-efficient. Comprehensive Cross-Battery (C-CB) assessment allows for an initial evaluation of performance across seven CHC broad cognitive abilities. A C-CB assessment can be conducted using a 14-subtest battery. The time required to administer 14 subtests is approximately the same as the time required to administer an entire Wechsler Scale or the extended battery of the WJ-R/III. Following a review of initial C-CB data (or data from any assessment method, for that matter), it may be necessary to administer additional measures either to gather more information to fully evaluate a priori hypotheses related to the referral or to test a posteriori hypotheses (as described in Chapter 3).

When a more focused assessment of cognitive ability is warranted, practitioners can conduct a Selective Cross-Battery (S-CB) assessment instead of a C-CB assessment. In S-CB assessment, in-depth evaluation of a select few cognitive abilities is typically the goal. This type of assessment is characterized by the administration of three to four qualitatively different indicators (i.e., sub-tests) for each of the cognitive ability domains of interest. Practitioners can conduct a thorough evaluation of approximately three or four broad cognitive abilities considered germane to a given referral in less than the time required to administer most of the major intelligence batteries in their entirety.

Consistency with Best Practices

The following best-practices assessment principles are true of the CHC Cross-Battery approach:

1. Assessment should be conducted only after other preassessment ac-tivities have been completed (e.g., preventive strategies, prereferral interventions, instructional alternatives and modifications, etc.).
2. Assessment of cognitive abilities should be pursued only when it is believed that results will have direct relevance to well-defined refer-ral questions.
3. Assessment should be embedded in a multifactored approach.
4. Assessment should be tailored to the unique needs of the individual case.
5. For cases in which a comprehensive assessment (e.g., C-CB assess-ment) is not considered necessary, a selective assessment approach should be implemented (e.g., S-CB assessment).

Intelligent Testing

Researchers, practitioners, and scholars in assessment-related fields have rec-ognized the need for cross-battery assessment methods. For example, in the field of neuropsychological assessment, Wilson (1992) stated that because there are no truly unidimensional measures in psychological assessment, there is a need to select subtests from standardized batteries that appear to reflect the neurocognitive function of interest. Therefore, in neuropsychological assess-ment the aim is to select those measures that, on the basis of careful task anal-ysis, appear mainly to tap a given construct (p. 380). Wilson reasoned that an eclectic approach was needed in the selection of measures, preferably *subtests* rather than the omnibus tests of cognitive abilities, in order to gain more specificity in the delineation of patterns of function and dysfunction (p. 381). The CHC Cross-Battery approach represents such an approach in that it guides practitioners in the selection of empirically and logically classified tests according to the cognitive abilities they measure, thereby allowing a more focused assessment of specific abilities presumed to be related to referral concerns.

Similarly, in clinical and school psychology, Kaufman (1994) has taught practitioners to use ingenuity, clinical sense, psychological theory and research, and *supplementary cognitive tests* to understand the dynamics of an individual's Wechsler scaled-score profile (p. 271). Indeed, the term *intelligent testing* belongs to him (e.g., Kaufman, 1979, 1994). Kaufman's pleas for practitioners to supplement the Wechsler Scales with tests from other instruments in an effort to gain a better understanding of cognitive capabilities is directly in line with the CHC Cross-Battery approach (see Flanagan, McGrew, & colleague, 2000). Therefore, it seems clear that professionals from many disciplines recognize the need to broaden the evaluation of cognitive functioning beyond the confines of a single battery and to focus assessment on the valid measurement of specific cognitive abilities. The CHC Cross-Battery approach is the first theoretically and psychometrically defensible method that is responsive to and addresses this need in assessment-related fields.

Validity Evidence

The CHC Cross-Battery approach is a new and innovative method of assessment and interpretation. Like any novel concept or idea, the promise of greater utility or benefit compared to traditional approaches, especially for the individuals on whom tests are used, emerges over time and emanates primarily from studies on its underlying validity. Although the entire CHC Cross-Battery approach rests on a solid research foundation (see Flanagan, McGrew, & colleague, 2000; Kaufman, 2000; McGrew & Flanagan, 1998), the validity of the approach itself was not evaluated until recently. The results of a series of preliminary investigations of the validity of the CHC Cross-Battery approach suggest that the CHC clusters that are derived through its recommended procedures are valid (e.g., Flanagan, in press; Flanagan, Keith, & Kranzler, 2000; Hanel, 2001; Mascolo, 2001). Furthermore, this line of research suggests that assessments organized according to the CHC Cross-Battery approach result in better prediction of academic skills than does a traditional Wechsler-based approach, and in more accurate descriptions of the specific cognitive abilities that contribute to the explanation of specific academic skills. The results of these studies were presented in Chapter 1. Although promising, the results of recent studies on the validity of CHC Cross-Battery assessment need further cross-validation, and additional research is necessary to examine the validity of this approach more fully.

Learning Disabilities Assessment

According to Brackett and McPherson (1996), "[a] major value of detecting severe discrepancies within and between areas of cognition is the focus on cognitive processing components of learning disabilities. However, the limited capacity of standardized instruments to assess isolated cognitive processes creates a major weakness in intracognitive discrepancy models" (p. 79). The CHC Cross-Battery approach addresses this limitation by providing a defensible set of procedures that allows for the calculation of intracognitive discrepancies among the major CHC broad cognitive abilities as well as among the narrow cognitive abilities selected to estimate each broad ability domain.

Brackett and McPherson also pointed out that "[a]lthough analyses of [Wechsler] subtests typically report measures of distinct cognitive abilities, such abilities may not emerge by individual subtests but rather in combination with other subtests" (p. 79). We agree with these researchers and have identified this problem as one of construct underrepresentation. As discussed earlier in this chapter and in Chapter 1, the CHC Cross-Battery approach circumvents this problem of invalidity in assessment by ensuring that all measured abilities are well represented.

In general, the CHC Cross-Battery approach represents an improvement in diagnostic intracognitive discrepancy models because it offers a theoretically and psychometrically defensible method of deriving a "greater range of information about the ways individuals learn—the ways individuals receive, store, integrate, and express information" (Brackett & McPherson, 1996, p. 80). When used in conjunction with case-history information, behavioral observations, convergent data sources, and careful attention to research on the relations between cognitive processes and abilities and specific academic outcomes, the cross-battery approach represents a much-needed alternative to existing diagnostic models for identifying learning disabilities.

Systematic Approach

It is important to understand that CHC Cross-Battery assessment is much more than simply picking and choosing subtests, precisely because it is based on empirical research and reasoning and not on haphazard guessing. Moreover, careful examination of referral concerns and other sources of data (e.g., specific needs of the examinee) also guide the selection of initial assessment instruments.

Not only is the CHC Cross-Battery approach systematic with regard to test selection, it is systematic with regard to test interpretation. That is, recommendations for test interpretation are grounded in a strong experimental method that requires the generation of a priori hypotheses, followed by a systematic and rigorous testing of those hypotheses as well as specification of a posteriori hypotheses. Within this systematic framework, assessment and interpretation are conceived of as iterative processes. For instance, an evaluation of cross-battery data determines whether additional assessment is needed to test initial hypotheses or to test hypotheses that were generated post hoc (after reviewing initial assessment data). Each phase of interpretation of cross-battery data is grounded in current theory and research and linked to well-defined referral questions. The systematic qualities of the CHC Cross-Battery approach to assessment are reflected in the detailed steps to test selection and interpretation, outlined in Chapters 2, 3, 4, and 5. These systematic elements are perhaps most evident in the guidelines offered in Chapter 5 related to the process of assessment and interpretation of individuals who are culturally and linguistically different. Within the broad spectrum of assessment-related endeavors, few areas of assessment are less organized, less cohesive, and less guided by research than are current practices seeking to measure the cognitive abilities of diverse individuals fairly and equitably. This is only one of the many arenas in which the systematic rigor provided by CHC Cross-Battery assessment represents a potentially significant improvement over existing methods.

WEAKNESSES OF THE CHC CROSS-BATTERY APPROACH

Lack of Norm Group

Because the CHC Cross-Battery approach involves using select tests from two or more cognitive batteries that were normed on different populations, a cross-battery norm group does not exist. Although this situation has the potential to lead to errors in interpretation, the CHC Cross-Battery approach incorporates several safeguards that serve to minimize or eliminate possible error associated with crossing batteries. First, the standard scores yielded by all subtests included in cross-battery assessments are converted to a common metric (having a mean of 100 and a standard deviation of 15) in order to allow for comparisons among tests. Second, the CHC Cross-Battery approach requires that all scores be reported with their corresponding confidence bands (see Chapter 3) to emphasize the inherent error in test scores and the need to view such scores only within the context of probability, not certainty. Third, the CHC Cross-Battery approach recommends that practitioners interpret clusters rather than individual subtests, thereby encouraging a focus on *common* or *shared variance* rather than on specific variance and error variance (Messick, 1989; see Flanagan, McGrew, et al., 2000, for details). Moreover, prior to interpreting clusters, practitioners must ensure that the subtests that comprise the cluster do not vary significantly from one another (see Chapter 3). This interpretation guideline allows practitioners to focus on the meaning of the construct underlying a convergence of indicators (i.e., subtests), rather than a single indicator.

Individuals who score at a particular level on a given test often score at roughly the same level on other purported indicators of the construct being measured. "[O]r, more precisely, persons high on the construct should score high on a variety of indicators of that construct" (Messick, 1989, p. 51). Thus, within each of the CHC broad ability domains, a convergence of indicators is expected. However, because a variety of factors may differentially influence indicators of the same construct (e.g., factors related to differences in norm groups), "it is usually desirable to take the notion of convergence of indicators quite literally and base inferences on *some combination of several indicators . . .*" (Messick, 1989, p. 51, emphasis added). The CHC Cross-Battery approach recommends that interpretations be based on a convergence of indicators.

Ideally, a comprehensive CHC assessment would be based on a single battery of tests normed on a single sample. However, currently this option neither exists nor is practical. For example, to operationalize CHC theory fully, a minimum of 70 subtests would need to be developed (one for every narrow ability currently specified in the integrated model) and normed on a representative sample of the U.S. population. Clearly, a battery of this size is not practical for a number of reasons (e.g., prohibitive costs, high potential for examiner and examinee fatigue, unreasonable length of time necessary to administer 70 tests, etc.). Therefore, if practitioners cannot derive the cognitive ability information considered most germane to the referral from a single intelligence battery, then crossing batteries via the CHC Cross-Battery approach is a viable and necessary endeavor. Indeed, the potential error that results from conducting an incomplete assessment of cognitive abilities through conventional methods is greater than that associated with the crossing of norm samples via cross-battery principles and interpretive procedures (see McGrew & Flanagan, 1998).

Competency Requirements

It is possible to organize and conduct a Comprehensive Cross-Battery (C-CB) assessment properly by using selected subtests from only two intelligence batteries. Access to additional batteries and tests may be required if more in-depth assessment in a given domain is necessary, or if it is necessary to derive a particular global ability score in C-CB assessment as described in Chapter 4. The CHC Cross-Battery Worksheets presented in Appendix A show that there is a variety of batteries from which to choose. It is recommended that practitioners review the worksheets to determine which batteries would be necessary to meet their needs (i.e., they may already have sufficient instrumentation and expertise to conduct C-CB assessments). The training of applied cognitive psychologists (e.g., school and clinical psychologists, neuropsychologists, etc.) in accredited programs routinely includes supervision and instruction in at least one or more major intelligence tests as well as exposure to others. Thus, the need for competency and expertise in at least two major cognitive batteries in order to gain maximum utility from the CHC Cross-Battery approach would not appear to represent an inordinate demand. Rather, it is very likely that the vast majority of practitioners already possess this level of expertise.

Scoring Requirements

Because the CHC Cross-Battery approach combines tests from different batteries, in addition to scoring the tests in the usual manner, practitioners must convert all test scores to a common metric prior to advancing to the interpretation process (see the standard score conversion table in Appendix D). Also, this approach requires practitioners to calculate CHC broad and narrow ability averages. These types of additional calculations are not usually necessary in single-battery assessments. However, a number of researchers have adapted the CHC Cross-Battery Worksheets and created computer-based spreadsheets that can be used by practitioners to automate the calculation process. The benefit of these spreadsheets is that they automatically convert all test standard scores to a common metric as well as calculate the broad and narrow ability averages. Examples of some of these spreadsheets are available via the Internet and can be found at and downloaded from various locations, including the following:

- The CHC Cross-Battery website (http://facpub.stjohns.edu/~ortizs/cross-battery/)
- The Institute for Applied Psychometrics (http://www.iapsych.com)
- Ron Dumont and John Willis's web pages (http://alpha.fdu.edu/~dumont/)
- The WWW School Psychology Homepage (http://facpub.stjohns.edu/~ortizs/spwww.html)

Global Ability Scores

The purpose of C-CB assessment is to sample functioning in a wide range of CHC broad cognitive abilities in an effort to uncover the unique cognitive strengths or weaknesses of the individual. The purpose of S-CB assessment is to conduct an in-depth evaluation of particular CHC broad cognitive abilities, presumably within cognitive domains that are deemed most important vis-à-vis referral concerns. In either case, practitioners can follow the CHC Cross-Battery principles and procedures for test selection and interpretation and engage in time-efficient assessment practices. However, practitioners are often mandated by law to obtain global ability estimates from their assessments for use in ability-achievement discrepancy formulas, particularly for individuals who are suspected of having a learning disability. Furthermore, many practitioners are required by various other administrative regulations to obtain a particular global ability score, such as a Wechsler FSIQ, for use in such formulas.

Under these circumstances, practitioners may well need to administer additional tests in a given domain (e.g., *Gv*) just to obtain the specific global ability estimate required, even when the domain is not particularly relevant to the referral. However, if practitioners are free to organize their assessments around a battery of tests of their choice, and can obtain a global ability estimate that complements the selection of tests, then the problem of redundancy in measurement of abilities, especially those not germane to the referral, is eliminated (see Chapter 4 for details).

COMMONLY ASKED QUESTIONS ABOUT THE CHC CROSS-BATTERY APPROACH

As with any new approach, especially one that differs markedly from traditional methods, a variety of questions and potential concerns (viz., practical, psychometric, theoretical, logistical, etc.) often arise with respect to its implementation. This section presents the most commonly asked questions about CHC Cross-Battery assessment. Answers to these questions are meant to clarify any misconceptions about cross-battery assessment and to provide practitioners with a better understanding of the utility of this approach in everyday practice.

Do CHC Cross-Battery assessments take longer to administer than single-battery assessments?   Not necessarily. Practitioners can conduct C-CB assessments in approximately the same amount of time required to administer any given intelligence battery in its entirety. However, if a *particular* global ability score is needed, such as a Wechsler FSIQ, then C-CB testing time may increase. Chapter 4 provides numerous examples of how to calculate a global ability score within the context of C-CB assessment. Many of these recommended C-CB assessment approaches could be administered in the same amount of time as an individual intelligence battery. Furthermore, the time required to conduct an S-CB assessment is often less than that required to administer completely almost all of the major intelligence batteries.

Is the CHC Cross-Battery approach complicated?   No. This approach to measuring cognitive abilities is characterized by an easy-to-follow set of steps that guides the practitioner through designing, scoring, and interpreting cross-battery assessments. (These steps were described in detail in Chapters 2 and 3.) In fact, it is likely that CHC Cross-Battery assessment can serve to make cognitive assessment even less complicated and confusing than it already is. By providing a guiding theoretical framework, a standard nomenclature for broad and narrow cognitive abilities, and straightforward interpretive guidelines, and by delineating relationships between cognitive abilities and academic skills, CHC Cross-Battery assessment may well prove to be more logical and easier to accomplish than what is now expected in the use and application of existing cognitive-assessment methods.

Why is it important to measure CHC abilities, such as Gs, if they do not correlate highly with g (or general intelligence)? The importance of assessing certain CHC abilities should be guided by referral concerns and by their established relations to outcome criteria (e.g., academic achievement). It is incorrect to assume that a low correlation between a specific ability and *g* means that the specific ability is unimportant. For example, it may be argued that the Wechsler Coding test is not important because it represents an ability (*Gs*) that is to the far right in Carroll's (1993) three-stratum model, meaning that it has a relatively low correlation with *g*. Abilities (and thus tests) may correlate relatively poorly with *g* but may correlate significantly with other criteria. For example, a review of the literature has shown that *Gs* abilities contribute to the explanation of reading, math, and writing skills during the elementary school years (see McGrew & Flanagan, 1998). Claims that certain abilities are not important because of lower internal validity (e.g., not a strong measure of *g*) fail to recognize that internal and external validity are different forms of evidence and that both are important for different reasons (Flanagan, McGrew, et al., 2000).

Is it inappropriate or invalid to combine tests from different intelligence batteries to derive CHC clusters? No. The cluster scores derived from a CHC Cross-Battery assessment are more valid than either individual subtests or most composites found on the major intelligence batteries, for two reasons. First, the CHC Cross-Battery clusters (as opposed to individual subtests) are based on the aggregate of two or more qualitatively different narrow ability indicators, which ensures that the underlying construct is represented adequately. Second, the cross-battery clusters (as opposed to many composites on intelligence batteries) are composed of tests that were classified empirically (through CHC theory–driven joint factor analyses) as relatively pure measures of a particular construct, which ensures that the constructs underlying cross-battery clusters are not contaminated by irrelevant variance. This makes the CHC Cross-Battery approach one of the best available procedures for conducting valid assessments of cognitive abilities.

Because the CHC Cross-Battery approach combines tests from different batteries, isn't there a problem associated with administering subtests out of sequence (i.e., out of the contexts of their respective batteries)?   No. In a wide variety of cases and historical contexts, individuals have routinely been given only a portion of certain batteries because other portions were deemed invalid or inappropriate for that individual (e.g., children who are culturally or linguistically diverse, blind, deaf, motor impaired, etc.). Giving only the Performance subtests of the Wechsler Scales to individuals who are bilingual or limited English-proficient, for example, has been a common practice for decades and remains so today. There are few, if any, published test manuals that explicitly state that the test is valid *only* when *every single* subtest is administered. Test publishers recognize that there are potential alternative uses of tests, and therefore rarely do anything to discourage exploration or adoption of such use. When alternative uses of tests are backed by empirical research, test developers and publishers seem to encourage such use, despite the fact that many alternatives are not always specifically endorsed in the test manual.

Given the lengthy history of psychometrics, it seems clear that if the sequence and context of test administration were critical to valid measurement of cognitive abilities, prohibitions against altering the sequence or context would be explicitly stated in the manuals of every major cognitive battery by now. In short, test developers do not often proscribe the use of tests in alternative ways. Instead, test developers seem merely to prescribe the manner in which the entire test is to be given in order to derive certain composite scores (e.g., a global ability score).

Because the administration and scoring procedures specified in the CHC Cross-Battery approach are entirely consistent with the procedures specified in the test manuals, cross-battery assessment does not violate any instructions set forth by the publishers. In cross-battery assessment, the combinations of subtests that are used may not be described by the tests' manuals, but they *are* supported by the empirical research upon which the CHC Cross-Battery approach is based.

Shouldn't I just use the test that includes the most comprehensive coverage of CHC abilities among the major intelligence batteries (e.g., WJ III) instead of the CHC Cross-Battery approach?   No, not necessarily. Upon publication, the WJ III will provide the most extensive coverage of broad and narrow abilities specified by CHC theory and will undoubtedly represent the most theoretically and perhaps psychometrically advanced test of cognitive ability available today. Given the extant validation and promise of CHC theory, other tests based on this theory are likely to follow in the future. Nevertheless, the fact remains that no single battery will ever measure the full range of CHC constructs, which thus far includes 10 broad abilities and over 70 narrow abilities. In addition, irrespective of how well any current or future test might follow CHC theory or the CHC Cross-Battery approach, it is important to recognize that operationalization (measurement) of the constructs specified by the theory represents only one component of the cross-battery approach. Other major components of the CHC Cross-Battery approach include flexibility in test choice and selection, responsiveness to the specific referral needs and purpose of assessment, and an interpretive framework to draw defensible meaning from whatever data may be generated. Clearly, factors related to the nature and purpose of referral will invariably influence the choice of tests used in assessment, at times even rendering issues related to precise measurement secondary, creating a need for a set of tests with particular characteristics that simply cannot be accommodated adequately by a single battery. There are simply too many variables and too many permutations of referral needs or purposes that preclude any test from being able to accommodate them all.

Suppose, for example, that a situation arises in which an examiner wishes to use two qualitatively different measures of a given broad ability but needs them both to be low in terms of culture loading and linguistic demand; or that the examiner needs to administer a second or even a third measure of a narrow ability for two or three different broad abilities. Although a well designed core battery that is based on CHC theory would certainly go a long way toward facilitating attainment of these particular assessment goals, the practical limitations inherent in the use of a single battery mean that the examiner will continue to benefit from the various components offered by the cross-battery approach. In sum, it is virtually impossible to operationalize the entire breadth of the CHC Cross-Battery approach effectively with any single test.

It is also important to reinforce the idea that the CHC Cross-Battery approach is not solely about measurement but also about interpretation. Current and future tests may well provide substantive operationalization of the broad and narrow ability constructs specified by CHC theory—but the CHC

Cross-Battery approach is intended to reflect the fourth wave of *interpretation* of intelligence tests (Kamphaus, Petoskey, & Morgan, 1997), not the fourth wave of *measurement* with intelligence tests. As such, it is the application of CHC theory to interpretation that represents the very essence of the approach as well as its major practical benefit. Even a test based on CHC theory still requires its users to have a clear understanding regarding the manner in which results are to be interpreted from the perspective of CHC theory. Thus, CHC Cross-Battery assessment should never be perceived simply as a collection of tests designed solely for measurement purposes, but should be seen as an interpretive framework designed more for inferential purposes.

As just described, there will be times when practitioners, for a variety of practical reasons, will have to make some concessions to the purity of measurement. This is the balance between science and practice that exists in much of what psychologists do. The one endeavor, however, in which compromise is not acceptable is in the application of theory to interpretation. This is, in fact, the hallmark of the CHC Cross-Battery approach—a method for scientifically deriving more valid (not necessarily the most valid, but more valid than with any other current framework) meaning and inference from data gathered across batteries or even within a single battery. The precision inherent in any test based on CHC theory or any other theory in no way precludes interpretation of its test data within the structure of CHC Cross-Battery assessment. Moreover, interpretation of data from within CHC theory or the CHC Cross-Battery approach does not preclude interpretation of results from a single battery as specified by the test's publisher in accordance with the theory underlying that test. As the unrelenting science of cognitive assessment edges forward, CHC theory will inevitably be supplanted and replaced by a different, more modern theory with greater promise. At that time, tests based on CHC theory will appear rather dated and will quickly become obsolete as new tests that operationalize new theory begin to emerge. This does not, however, herald the end of the Cross-Battery approach, because the majority of principles that guide the assessment and interpretive process can be readily applied to any new theory to provide, once again, a mechanism for modern interpretation of test data.

Is the CHC Cross-Battery approach defensible in a court of law?   Yes. Alternative uses of tests, whether with particular populations or through different theoretical foundations, is left up to the professional judgment of the examiner. In such cases, courts would hold practitioners responsible and liable for providing a suitable rationale for whatever decisions were made and actions taken with regard to any alternative use of tests, which includes the CHC Cross-Battery approach.

It is also noteworthy that the CHC Cross-Battery approach is not the first or only method that crosses batteries or takes subtests out of the contexts of their corresponding batteries. Standard methodology in neuropsychological evaluation has long crossed a wide variety of batteries and taken subtests out of context without any seeming legal or scientific ramifications. Although we may not know which subtests, if any, might be affected significantly by the context in which they are given, the advanced and defensible theoretical and psychometric context created by cross-battery assessment methods balances that concern as well as any other concerns that accompany the application of the method. As such, the CHC Cross-Battery approach not only is defensible but appears to be of equal (if not greater) value than the traditional alternative approaches, precisely because it is both systematic and specifically tailored to the unique aspects of the referral.

In short, the principles and procedures of the cross-battery approach outlined in this book and elsewhere (see Flanagan, McGrew, et al., 2000; McGrew & Flanagan, 1998) are entirely consistent with the regulations set forth in laws pertaining to the proper assessment of the intellectual capabilities of individuals (e.g., ADA, IDEA). In fact, the CHC Cross-Battery approach, unlike most traditional assessment approaches, is based on solid theory and research and is used to generate a test battery that is both unique to the individual's needs and specific to the referral concerns. Therefore, this approach to intellectual assessment is highly defensible in a court of law.

Can the CHC Cross-Battery cluster standard scores be entered into formulas to determine eligibility? No. The CHC Cross-Battery clusters should not be interpreted in the absence of their corresponding confidence bands. Therefore, they should not be entered into ability-achievement discrepancy formulas. Instead, when a global cognitive ability score is deemed necessary for the purpose of conducting ability-achievement discrepancy analyses within the context of cross-battery assessment, practitioners should follow the guidelines presented in Chapter 4 of this book. The CHC Cross-Battery clusters are used in inter- and intracognitive discrepancy analyses for the purpose of identifying cognitive ability and processing strengths and weaknesses.

Are data from CHC Cross-Battery assessments more difficult to interpret than data from traditional assessments (e.g., Wechsler-based assessments)? No. Cross-battery data are interpreted in much the same way as traditional assessment data. However, the cross-battery inter- and intracognitive discrepancy analysis procedures particular are far in advance of those associated with traditional batteries (e.g., ipsative analysis), mainly because they are defensible psychometrically and theoretically and are conducted as part of a systematic approach to assessment. CHC Cross-Battery assessment results may be plotted on a summary sheet (see Appendix E) that allows for a graphic depiction of normative and relative strengths and weaknesses.

Isn't the language of the CHC Cross-Battery approach more complex, and therefore more difficult to explain to teachers and parents, than the language of the more traditional Wechsler-based approach to intellectual assessment? No. The language used to report the results of CHC Cross-Battery assessments is no more confusing or difficult than that used in a standard Wechsler psychoeducational report. Although the former uses CHC terminology (as opposed to verbal/nonverbal terminology, for example), it is the responsibility of the practitioner to communicate the meaning of any psychological term. It is no more difficult to describe Visual Processing (a broad ability within the CHC framework) than it is to describe Simultaneous Processing or Nonverbal Ability. Simple and concise definitions of the broad and narrow CHC abilities as well as examples of the types of tests that measure these abilities can be found in Chapter 1 of his book, as well as in Flanagan, McGrew, and colleague (2000) and McGrew and Flanagan (1998). Furthermore, Chapter 7 of this book includes two comprehensive CHC Cross-Battery reports that incorporate the CHC terminology. As stated previously, the standard nomenclature provided by the CHC Cross-Battery approach allows for much more clarity among professionals in discussing cognitive ability constructs. This ease of com-munication transfers readily in helping parents and laypeople understand the relationship between test performance and practical manifestation. Moreover, the links specified by CHC Cross-Battery assessment between cognitive abilities and achievement provide practitioners with a clear and logical rationale that will greatly facilitate explanation in non-technical terms.

SUMMARY

This chapter provided a brief presentation of the most salient advantages and disadvantages of the CHC Cross-Battery approach. In addition, clarifications of some common misconceptions of the cross-battery method were discussed, many of which stem from actual practitioner experiences with implementing this assessment approach in school districts, training programs, and centers for psychological study and evaluation. Overall, it appears that the advantages of the CHC Cross-Battery approach are numerous and have the potential to elevate the practice of assessment and interpretation of cognitive functioning to a more psychometrically defensible and theoretically advanced level than that associated with most existing methods. It is clear that the advantages of CHC Cross-Battery assessment far outweigh its disadvantages. Moreover, it is noteworthy that the disadvantages highlighted in this chapter are not major and may be circumvented in a number of ways (many of which were discussed herein).

REFERENCES

Brackett, J., & McPherson, A. (1996). Learning disabilities diagnosis in postsecondary students: A comparison of discrepancy-based diagnostic models. In N. Gregg, C. Hoy, & A. F. Gay (Eds.), *Adults with learning disabilities: Theoretical and practical perspectives* (pp. 68–84). New York: Guilford.

Carroll, J. B. (1993). *Human cognitive abilities: A survey of factor-analytic studies*. Cambridge, UK: Cambridge University Press.

Elliott, C. D. (1990). *Differential Ability Scales: Introductory and technical handbook*. San Antonio, TX: Psychological Corporation.

Figueroa, R. A. (1990). Assessment of linguistic minority group children. In C. R. Reynolds & R. W. Kamphaus (Eds.), *Handbook of psychological and educational assessment of children: Vol. 1: Intelligence and achievement*. New York: Guilford.

Flanagan, D. P. (2000). Wechsler-based *Gf-Gc* cross-battery assessment: Strengthening the validity of interpretations drawn from Wechsler test scores. *School Psychology Quarterly*.

Flanagan, D. P., Keith, T. Z., & Kranzler, J. (2000). *The role of the Cognitive Assessment System in cross-battery assessment*. Manuscript in preparation.

Flanagan, D. P., McGrew, K. S., & Ortiz, S. O. (2000). *The Wechsler intelligence scales and CHC theory: A contemporary approach to interpretation*. Boston: Allyn & Bacon.

Hanel, C. (2001). *CHC Cross-Battery Assessment: Examining the relationship between specific cognitive abilities and reading, writing, and math achievement in a referred sample*. Unpublished doctoral dissertation, St. John's University.

Kamphaus, R. W., Petoskey, M. D., & Morgan, A. W. (1997). A history of intelligence test interpretation. In D. P. Flanagan, J. L. Genshaft, & P. L. Harrison (Eds.), *Contemporary intellectual assessment: Theories, tests, and issues* (pp. 32–51). New York: Guilford.

Kaufman, A. S. (1994). *Intelligent testing with the WISC-III.* New York: Wiley.

Kaufman, A. S. (2000). Foreword. In D. P. Flanagan, K. S. McGrew, & S. O. Ortiz, *The Wechsler intelligence scales and CHC theory: A contemporary approach to interpretation.* Boston: Allyn & Bacon.

Kaufman, A. S., & Kaufman, N. L. (1983). *Kaufman Assessment Battery for Children.* Circle Pines, MN: American Guidance Service.

Mascolo, J. (2001). *Interpreting cross-battery data from contemporary theory: Cross-validation of the CHC model in a referred sample.* Unpublished doctoral dissertation, St. John's University.

McGrew, K. S., & Flanagan, D. P. (1998). *The Intelligence Test Desk Reference (ITDR): Gf-Gc cross-battery assessment.* Boston: Allyn & Bacon.

Messick, S. (1989). Validity. In R. Linn (Ed.), *Educational Measurement* (3rd ed., pp. 131–104). Washington, DC: American Council on Education.

Messick, S. (1995). Validity of psychological assessment: Validation of inferences from persons' responses and performances as scientific inquiry into score meaning. *American Psychologist, 50,* 741–749.

Ortiz, S., & Flanagan, D. P. (1998). Enhancing cognitive assessment of culturally and linguistically diverse individuals: Selective *Gf-Gc* cross-battery assessment. *The School Psychologist, 52*(1), 6–9.

Sattler, J. (1992). *Assessment of children* (Rev. 3rd ed.). San Diego: Sattler.

Thorndike, R. L., Hagen, E. P., & Sattler, J. M. (1986). *Stanford-Binet Intelligence Scale: Guide for administering and scoring the fourth edition.* Chicago: Riverside.

Valdés, G., & Figueroa, R. A. (1994). *Bilingualism and testing: A special case of bias.* Norwood, NJ: Ablex.

Wilson, B. C. (1992). The neuropsychological assessment of the preschool child: A branching model. In I. Rapm & S. I. Segalowitz (Eds.), *Handbook of neuropsychology: Child neuropsychology* (Vol. 6, pp. 377–394).

Woodcock, R. W. (1990). Theoretical foundations of the WJ-R measures of cognitive ability. *Journal of Psychoeducational Assessment, 8,* 231–258.

🎣 TEST YOURSELF 🎣

1. **Which of the following is not considered a best-practices assessment principle?**

   (a) Assessment should be conducted before engaging in preventive activities or instructional modifications.

   (b) Assessment of cognitive abilities should be pursued only when it is believed that results will have direct relevance to well-defined referral questions.

   (c) Assessment should be embedded in a multifactored approach.

   (d) Assessment should be tailored to the unique needs of the individual case.

   (e) For cases in which a comprehensive assessment is not considered necessary, a selective assessment approach should be implemented.

(continued)

2. **Which of the following is not considered an advantage of the CHC Cross-Battery approach?**
   (a) The CHC Cross-Battery approach guards against invalidity in assessment.
   (b) The CHC Cross-Battery approach facilitates communication among professionals.
   (c) The CHC Cross-Battery approach requires less time to score than traditional methods.
   (d) The CHC Cross-Battery approach guards against unreliability in assessment.

3. **Which statement is false?**
   (a) The CHC Cross-Battery approach is more theoretically and empirically defensible than many typical assessment methods.
   (b) Within the context of CHC Cross-Battery principles and procedures, combining tests from different intelligence batteries into CHC clusters is defensible.
   (c) Data from CHC Cross-Battery assessments are no more difficult to interpret than data from traditional assessments (e.g., Wechsler-based assessments).
   (d) The language of the CHC Cross-Battery approach is more complex, and therefore more difficult to explain to teachers and parents, than the language of the more traditional Wechsler-based approach to intellectual assessment.
   (e) The CHC Cross-Battery approach is defensible in a court of law.

4. **Cognitive constructs (or abilities) that correlate highly with *g* are more important than those that have low correlations with *g*.** True or False?

5. **One way in which the CHC Cross-Battery approach guards against invalidity in assessment is that**
   (a) it requires that a minimum of four subtests be used to represent each CHC broad ability cluster.
   (b) it requires that every assessment include measures of at least seven different CHC broad cognitive abilities.
   (c) it requires that all interpretations at the broad and narrow ability levels be based on clusters, not on individual subtest scores.
   (d) all of the above
   (e) none of the above

6. **CHC Cross-Battery clusters should not be interpreted in the absence of their corresponding confidence bands.** True or False?

7. **The need for cross-battery assessment procedures has been expressed in which assessment-related field?**

    (a) neuropsychology

    (b) school psychology

    (c) clinical psychology

    (d) all of the above

    (e) none of the above

8. **The CHC Cross-Battery approach represents an improvement in intracognitive discrepancy models because**

    (a) when compared to existing models, it is more defensible from a theoretical standpoint.

    (b) when compared to existing models, it is more defensible from a psychometric standpoint.

    (c) when compared to existing models, it allows for the measurement of a wider range of cognitive abilities.

    (d) all of the above

    (e) (b) and (c) only

    (f) none of the above

9. **The CHC Cross-Battery approach requires practitioners to administer a minimum of two *complete* intelligence batteries.** True or False?

Answers: 1. a; 2. c; 3. d; 4. False; 5. c; 6. True; 7. d; 8. d; 9. False

Seven

ILLUSTRATIVE CHC CROSS-BATTERY ASSESSMENT CASE REPORTS

Strictly speaking, there is no single or correct way in which the results from CHC Cross-Battery assessment should be presented within the context of a psychological or psychoeducational report. CHC Cross-Battery assessment is essentially a method for engaging in cognitive assessment using standardized, norm-referenced tests and is insufficient to be considered a form of comprehensive assessment in and of itself. Evaluation of cognitive abilities, intellectual functioning, and relative strengths and weaknesses is typically only one component of psychological assessment that utilizes a wide perspective and that incorporates analysis of many other areas of functioning (e.g., academic achievement, social-emotional behavior, personality, adaptive behavior, sensory-motor integration, speech-language, etc.). Accordingly, the results of CHC Cross-Battery assessment may be easily worked into the section of any psychological report that discusses findings related to cognitive assessment. Practitioners should feel free to develop their own preferences regarding the manner in which such results are formatted in their own reports in accordance with the nature and style of report writing that is most familiar or convenient.

This chapter includes two sample reports on individuals who were referred for psychoeducational evaluation. These reports use different styles, have different formats, and present the entire range of collected data in very different ways. However, each report presents the relevant elements of the findings related to cognitive assessment (which utilized CHC Cross-Battery methods) in a relatively similar manner, and each utilizes the summary forms and worksheets described in the previous chapters and located in Appendix E. In addition, these reports reflect the key features of the administration, organization, and interpretive principles and procedures described in Chapters 1 through 5 of this book. Although there is no discussion surrounding the full context of the decision-making process involved in each assessment, the reports provide sufficient information to illustrate much of the process of CHC Cross-Battery assessment. As such, they are meant to serve primarily as guides for practitioners in the documentation of their procedures, decision rationales, and interpretations. Nevertheless, these reports do provide distinct illustrations regarding the various ways that the important facets related to the assessment process can be made evident to the potential readers of the reports.

The first case involves the psychoeducational assessment of a 9-year-old, fourth-grade, Caucasian student referred for difficulties in reading and mathematics. The format of the report is probably familiar to most practitioners and follows the traditional conventions for presenting psychological data. Because of the specific concerns regarding the presence of a learning disability, this case includes data on academic achievement and also provides an analysis of ability-achievement discrepancies. Note that analysis of ability-achievement discrepancies is not always included in every psychological report and the information is presented here mainly for illustrative purposes. Consequently, there is considerable discussion of results from both cognitive and achievement testing as they pertain to the decision-making process involved in the identification of learning disabilities.

The second case involves a 10-year-old, fifth-grade student of Hispanic heritage referred for slow progress and development in language arts. The format of this report is based on an alternative, thematic style in which conclusions and interpretation are presented in narrative form and the accompanying, convergent data listed in bullet form below the paragraphs. This report provides an illustration of the application of the cultural and linguistic extensions to the CHC Cross-Battery approach to help determine whether results should be interpreted in light of a difference or a disorder. This report does not include data on academic achievement, primarily because the results of cognitive assessment failed to support the presence of any deficits in intellectual functioning. Further analysis of the issue of learning disability was not warranted, and thus was not included in the final report.

Once again, practitioners are cautioned to remember that there is no standard CHC Cross-Battery report, and that results from the use of this method may be reported in any manner that is best suited to the needs and preferences of individual practitioners. Although the manner in which results are to be interpreted should remain strictly in accordance with the interpretive guidelines specified in this book (see Chapters 3, 4, and 5), the manner and mode of documentation of such interpretations remain at the discretion of the individual practitioner. The examples presented in this chapter are but two of the many possible ways in which results from CHC Cross-Battery assessment may be presented, and there is no reason that practitioners should not be able to incorporate easily such data and findings into their existing report formats.

CASE REPORT #1

Name: Melissa   Grade: 4th
D.O.B.: 2/15/90   Evaluator: Examiner A
Age: 9 years 11 months   Date of Evaluation: 1/12/00, 1/13/00
Home Language: English   Language of Instruction: English

Primary Referral Concerns

Melissa was referred for a psychoeducational evaluation by her teacher, Ms. Williams, due to concerns regarding Melissa's deficient performance in reading and mathematics. Specifically, Ms. Williams reported that Melissa is experiencing increasing frustration during in-class reading assignments and exams. She frequently pauses during oral reading assignments and often replaces the words she does not know with unrelated words. Additionally, Melissa has failed four out of five comprehension tests based on stories that were read and reviewed in class. In the area of mathematics, Melissa's primary difficulty has been with multistep problems. Although Ms. Williams has worked one-to-one with Melissa twice each week after school, there has been no improvement in her independent work. Because Melissa has not benefited from intervention, Ms. Williams requested that she be evaluated in order to determine both the specific nature of her difficulties and the types of intervention that may lead to improved academic performance.

Health and Developmental History

Melissa resides with her biological mother and father. Maternal report indicated that Melissa was the product of a normal, full-term pregnancy. Developmental milestones were achieved within normal limits. Melissa suffered from febrile seizures in infancy; however, no residual complications were experienced. Melissa is currently reported to be in good health and her medical history is otherwise unremarkable. Melissa's school health records indicated that the results of her recent vision and hearing tests were normal. In sum, there do not appear to be any physical factors to account for the academic difficulties that Melissa is experiencing currently.

Educational History

Referral information provided by Ms. Williams indicated that Melissa's current grades are 50 in Reading and 71 in Math (out of a possible 100 points in each domain). In mathematics, Ms. Williams reported that Melissa does very well during a class game called "around the world" in which children must provide a correct answer to a math problem presented on a flash card. She also indicated that Melissa memorized all of her times tables as quickly as the other children in the classroom. Given Melissa's apparent skills in math, Ms. Williams reported being "confused as to why Melissa is doing poorly now." According to Ms. Williams, Melissa's primary difficulty appears to be with multistep math problems that require regrouping. In the area of reading, Ms. Williams reported that Melissa can read fourth-grade material, but she experiences difficulty when she comes to an unknown word. Additionally, when Melissa is required to answer inferential questions regarding a passage just read, she experiences much difficulty and often provides incorrect responses.

Ms. Williams reported that she has been working individually with Melissa on reading comprehension and mathematics for approximately 10 weeks, but noted there has been "no real improvement." She also reported that Melissa's parents have been doing extra work with her at home, which, similar to the school-based efforts, has had "little to no impact." According to Ms. Williams, Melissa has told her that she understands what she reads but "the questions are too hard." In light of this information, Ms. Williams simplified the questions for Melissa's independent work, but reported "little improvement in comprehension." Based on a review of Melissa's educational records, the nature and failure of previous instructional interventions, observations by classroom teachers, and other information gathered through the referral process, further examination of cognitive abilities through standardized testing appeared to be warranted.

Tests Administered

Woodcock-Johnson Tests of Cognitive Ability–Revised (WJ-R COG; selected tests)

Wechsler Abbreviated Scale of Intelligence (WASI)

Wechsler Intelligence Scale for Children–Third Edition (WISC-III; selected tests)

NEPSY Neuropsychological Assessment (NEPSY; selected tests)

Children's Memory Scale (CMS; selected tests)

Wechsler Individual Achievement Test (WIAT)

Clinical and Behavioral Observations

Melissa was cooperative during testing and appeared to put forth her best effort on all tasks. Rapport was established and maintained throughout the testing session. Although Melissa indicated that some items were "hard to do," she persisted on difficult items. Melissa appeared very focused while completing tasks. At times when instructions were lengthy, Melissa requested that the instructions be repeated. When the instructions were being stated a second time, Melissa often repeated the instructions quietly as they were being said. On reading comprehension items, Melissa often paused for long intervals before answering, but appeared confident with her final response. Overall, the current test results appear to represent a reliable and valid estimate of Melissa's cognitive functioning.

Assessment of Cognitive Functioning

A carefully selected set of tests from the WISC-III, WASI, WJ-R, CMS, and NEPSY were combined via CHC Cross-Battery principles and procedures to yield seven broad cognitive ability clusters, including Crystallized Intelligence (*Gc*), Fluid Reasoning (*Gf*), Visual Processing (*Gv*), Short-term Memory (*Gsm*), Long-term Retrieval (*Glr*), Auditory Processing (*Ga*), and Processing Speed (*Gs*). Because Melissa reportedly experienced difficulties in reading and mathematics but had never been formally assessed, an extensive evaluation of cognitive functions was conducted. In addition to gathering baseline data across several major cognitive ability domains, particular emphasis was placed on closely examining those abilities that have an established or logical relation to Melissa's reported academic difficulties. In general, her performance across the cognitive ability clusters obtained in this evaluation ranged from *low* to *average*. A detailed summary of Melissa's performance within and across these cognitive ability domains follows.

Cross-Battery Assessment of Gc

Crystallized Intelligence (*Gc*) is a broad ability that involves an individual's breadth and depth of general and cultural knowledge, verbal communication, and reasoning with previously learned procedures. Melissa's *Gc* ability was assessed through tasks that required her to define orally presented words (Vocabulary, SS = 95 ± 7; *average*), and, when presented with a pair of common objects, identify how they are alike (Similarities, SS = 91 ± 7; *average*). More specifically, these tasks measured Melissa's knowledge of word meanings (*Lexical Knowledge*) as well as her understanding of words, sentences, and paragraphs requiring spoken native language skills (*Language Development*). Melissa's Crystallized Intelligence cluster score of 93 ± 5 is ranked at the 33rd percentile and is classified as *average*. The variation in scores Melissa earned in this area was not statistically significant, suggesting uniform ability within this domain. Overall, Melissa's ability to use her acquired knowledge and accumulated experiences to solve everyday problems is average. In other words, her ability to absorb and integrate the concepts, ideas, values, and knowledge of mainstream United States culture (as measured by the WASI) and to use this culturally based information meaningfully is within normal limits. Although Melissa's performance within this domain suggests that she ought to adapt, learn, and perform at an average level in a variety of environments, particularly academic, this is not the case in light of other specific cognitive ability weaknesses described in the following sections.

Cross-Battery Assessment of Gf

Fluid Intelligence (*Gf*) is the ability to reason, form concepts, and solve problems using unfamiliar information or novel procedures. Melissa's *Gf* ability was assessed through tasks that required her to identify a pattern within a set of geometric figures and to use that pattern to identify a missing piece (Matrix Reasoning, SS = 78 ± 7; *low*), as well as to analyze the parts of an incomplete logic puzzle and identify the missing parts (Analysis-Synthesis, SS = 84 ± 7; *low*). Specifically, these tasks primarily measure Melissa's ability to discover the underlying rule that governs a set of materials (*Inductive Reasoning*) and follow stated conditions to reach a solution to a problem (*General Sequential Reasoning* or *Deductive Reasoning*), respectively. Melissa's obtained scores on these reasoning tasks combined to yield a cluster score of 81 ± 5, which is ranked at the 11th percentile and is classified as *low*. The variation in Melissa's *Gf* test scores was not statistically significant, indicating that her ability to reason inductively is approximately the same as her ability to reason deductively.

Cross-Battery Assessment of Gv

Visual Processing (*Gv*) is defined as the ability to analyze and synthesize visual stimuli and involves perceptions and manipulations of visual shapes and forms, typically when figural or geometric in nature. Melissa's *Gv* ability was assessed through tasks that required her to copy designs using blocks (Block Design, SS = 90 ± 7; *average*) and assemble a series of puzzles (Object Assembly, SS = 100 ± 7; *average*). These tasks primarily assessed Melissa's ability to perceive and manipulate visual patterns quickly (*Spatial Relations*) and combine disconnected visual stimuli or patterns into a meaningful whole (*Closure Speed*), respectively. Because the standard score bands touch, Melissa's obtained scores on these *Gv* tests combined to yield a cluster score of 95 ± 5, which is ranked at the 38th percentile and is classified as *average*. The variation in scores Melissa earned in this area was not statistically significant, suggesting uniform ability within this domain.

Cross-Battery Assessment of Gsm

Short-term Memory (*Gsm*) is the ability to hold information in immediate awareness and then use it within a few seconds. Melissa's short-term memory was assessed through tasks that measure memory span and working memory. *Memory Span.* Memory span is the ability to recall temporally ordered elements in the correct order immediately following a single presentation. Melissa's memory span ability was assessed through tasks that required her to recall digits in a given order immediately (Digit Span, SS = 89 ± 7; *low average*) and repeat lists of unrelated words in a specified sequence (Memory for Words, SS = 90 ± 7; *average*). Melissa obtained a Memory Span cluster score of 90 ± 5, which is ranked at the 25th percentile and is classified as *average*. *Working Memory.* Working memory is the ability to store and manipulate stimuli prior to producing a response. Melissa's working memory ability was assessed through tasks that required her to perform simple tasks quickly, such as saying the days of the week forward and backward (Sequences SS = 70 ± 7; *low*), and repeating a series of random numbers backwards (Numbers Reversed, SS = 72 ± 7; *low*). Melissa obtained a Working Memory cluster score of 71 ± 5, which is ranked at the 3rd percentile and is classified as *low*.

The discrepancy observed within this memory domain suggests that Melissa's ability to order material temporally is within normal limits. However, when she is required to manipulate or transform such material prior to responding, her performance deteriorates significantly. Melissa's observed deficit in working memory is consistent with referral concerns, and therefore provides some insight into her difficulties in mathematics and reading.

Cross-battery Assessment of Glr

Long-term Storage and Retrieval (*Glr*) is the ability to store information and retrieve it fluently later through association. Melissa's *Glr* ability was assessed through tasks that required her to associate visual symbols with familiar words and translate a series of these symbols into verbal sentences when presented as a reading passage (Visual-Auditory learning, SS = 92 ± 7; *average*), and to name rapidly the color, size, and shape of a series of geometric shapes (Speeded Naming, SS = 90 ± 7; *average*). More specifically, these tasks measured Melissa's ability to recall one part of a previously learned but unrelated pair of items when the other part is presented (i.e., paired-associative learning, or *Associative Memory*) and her ability to produce names for concepts rapidly (*Naming Facility*), respectively. Melissa obtained a Long-term Retrieval cluster average of 91 ± 5, which is ranked at the 27th percentile and is classified as *average*. The variation in scores Melissa earned in this area was not statistically significant, indicating that the specific abilities assessed within this area are relatively equally developed.

Cross-Battery Assessment of Ga

Auditory Processing (*Ga*) is the ability to analyze and synthesize auditory stimuli. Melissa's *Ga* ability was assessed through tasks that required her to listen to a recorded word with one or more phonemes missing and identify the word (Incomplete Words, SS = 79 ± 7; *low*), as well as to integrate syllables and phonemes that were presented auditorily into whole words (Sound Blending, SS = 81 ± 7; *low average*). These tasks primarily measured Melissa's ability to analyze the individual sounds in words (*Phonetic Coding: Analysis*) and to synthesize individual sounds in words (*Phonetic Coding: Synthesis*), respectively. Melissa obtained a *Ga* cluster score of 80 ± 5, which is ranked at the 9th percentile and is classified as *low average*. Because these tasks involve the analysis and synthesis of sounds, it seems likely that Melissa's observed weakness in phonetic coding hindered the development of sound-symbol relationships, which is a core component of the reading process.

Cross-Battery Assessment of Gs

Processing Speed (*Gs*) is defined as one's ability to perform automatic cognitive tasks quickly, particularly when pressured to maintain focused concentration. Melissa's *Gs* ability was assessed through tasks that required her to draw quickly symbols that are paired with a series of simple shapes (Coding, SS = 90 ± 7; *average*), and to visually scan symbols to determine their presence or absence in a column (Symbol Search, SS = 100 ± 7; *average*). These tasks primarily measured Melissa's ability to search for and compare visual symbols presented side-by-side in a rapid manner (*Perceptual Speed*) as well as her ability to perform tasks rapidly that are relatively easy or require very simple decisions (*Rate-of-test-taking*). Melissa obtained a *Gs* cluster score of 95 ± 5, which is ranked at the 38th percentile and is classified as *average*. The variation in scores Melissa earned in this area was not statistically significant, indicating uniform ability on tests of processing speed.

Assessment of Academic Achievement

Melissa's performance on measures of academic achievement was variable. On the Wechsler Individual Achievement Test (WIAT), Melissa earned scores that ranged from *very low* to *average*.

Reading

Melissa's performance in the area of reading reflects her skill in identifying isolated words and letters on a page (Basic Reading, SS = 80 [73–87]; *low average*) and answering a series of questions based on previously read passages (Reading Comprehension, SS = 70 [61–79]; *very low*). Melissa obtained a Reading Composite score of 73 (67–79), which is ranked at the 4th percentile and is classified as *low*. Melissa demonstrated a significant ability-achievement discrepancy in this domain, indicating that her overall reading achievement is significantly below that which would be expected based upon her estimated level of intellectual functioning. Melissa's performance in this area is consistent with referral concerns. Specifically, while Melissa's basic reading skills are below those of same-age peers (i.e., SS = 80; 9th percentile), her most significant area of weakness is reading comprehension, or more specifically, her ability to apply her knowledge from what she has read to comprehend written discourse.

Written Language

Melissa's performance in the area of written language reflects her skill in writing the correct spelling of an orally presented word (Spelling, SS = 91 [83–99]; *average*) and writing a passage when given a combined oral and written prompt (Written Expression, SS = 92 [78–106]; *average*). Melissa obtained a Written Composite score of 88 (79–97), which is ranked at the 21st percentile and is classified as *low average*. Melissa's written language achievement was consistent with her estimated level of intellectual functioning.

Mathematics

In the area of mathematics, Melissa was required to perform basic mathematical operations (e.g., addition, subtraction) to solve problems (Numerical Operations, SS = 71 [61–81]; *low*) as well as to solve more involved word problems that were read to her (Mathematics Reasoning, SS = 70 [61–79]; *very low*). Melissa obtained a Mathematics Composite score of 66 (59–73), which is ranked at the 1st percentile and classified as *very low*. Melissa demonstrated a significant ability-achievement discrepancy in this domain, indicating that her mathematics achievement is significantly below that which would be expected based upon her estimated level of intellectual functioning. Melissa's overall performance was consistent with referral concerns, teacher reports, and school grades. Her difficulties with mathematics may be related, in part, to her low Fluid-Reasoning (*Gf*) and Working-Memory abilities.

Language

Melissa's performance in the area of language was variable. On a task measuring her skill to listen to an orally presented passage and answer questions about that passage (Listening Comprehension, SS = 88 [77–99]), she performed in the *low average* range. However, on a task designed to measure her ability to respond orally to questions (Oral Expression, SS = 107 [98–116]) she performed in the *average* range. Melissa obtained a Language Composite score of 100 (92–108), which is ranked at the 50th percentile and is classified as *average*. Her low average scores in Working Memory and Auditory Processing (*Ga*) may have negatively affected her listening ability. However, Melissa's overall performance in the area of language was consistent with her estimated level of intellectual functioning.

Data Integration and Interpretation

Data derived from the administration of select cognitive, achievement, and special-purpose tests suggest that Melissa demonstrates low to average functioning across the various cognitive and academic domains that were evaluated. Overall, Melissa's pattern of cognitive performance helps to explain the referral concerns. That is, the finding of specific and circumscribed cognitive deficits appears to underlie her reported difficulties in academic performance, particularly reading and mathematics achievement. For example, although Melissa appears to have a sufficient amount of information available to her (*Gc*) to read and understand age-appropriate reading passages, her inability to process sound-symbol relationships (*Ga*) adequately and to start with stated rules to reach a correct solution to novel problems (*Gf*) very likely contributes to her difficulties in reading. Moreover, her inability to manipulate information in short-term memory efficiently prior to producing a response (Working Memory [*Gsm*]), in conjunction with her fluid reasoning deficiencies, help explain her reported difficulties in mathematics.

Of particular relevance to Melissa's reading difficulty is her apparent deficit in phonetic coding (or phonological awareness). Melissa has considerable difficulty discriminating individual sounds in words. Phonetic coding difficulties (e.g., analyzing and interpreting sounds in words) hinder the development of sound-symbol relations, which, in turn, limits opportunities for success in reading. Thus, Melissa's performance on *Ga* tests of phonetic coding and on the Basic Reading test supports this conclusion. Although one might expect this phonological processing deficit to impact Melissa's spelling, her spelling ability (as measured by the WIAT) was estimated in the average range. Although Melissa's overall performance was average, an error analysis revealed that Melissa demonstrated significantly more errors when required to spell multisyllabic words versus monosyllabic words. This may be due in part to the fact that many of the monosyllabic words she was required to spell were already part of her sight-word vocabulary. That is, it is unlikely that Melissa actually applied phonemic strategies to spell such words.

Although a core phonological processing deficit helps to explain Melissa's difficulties in reading, her deficits in the areas of *Gsm* (namely, working memory) and *Gf* also likely contribute to her poor reading abilities. Specifically, her demonstrated deficit on tasks of working memory indicate that her capacity to store and manipulate relevant phonological information in memory is weak, especially if she is required to perform cognitive operations with the retained auditory information. This weakness can also negatively affect spelling skills, as spelling requires the ability to maintain words in short-term memory long enough to encode the complete phonetic string. Moreover, her deficits in fluid reasoning likely explain her difficulties with reading comprehension. Further analysis of Melissa's responses on reading comprehension tasks revealed that her primary difficulties surfaced when she was required to identify implied cause and effect, make predictions, and respond to questions requiring her to make inferences. Given that these tasks require a higher level of reasoning, it is likely that Melissa's severely deficient reasoning abilities greatly impact her performance.

Melissa's math difficulties may also be explained by her cognitive performance. Again, her deficits in fluid reasoning (*Gf*) and working memory (*Gsm*) make it difficult for her to apply previously learned procedures to novel problems and to perform multistep tasks, respectively. Melissa's performance on mathematics tasks revealed that although she demonstrated a limited knowledge of math facts, her ability to apply multiple rules within the context of a single problem, or to hold and manipulate information in memory, was severely limited. It appears as if her reasoning deficits largely impact her ability to decide which rule to apply, and, even if she knows the rule, her working memory deficits may preclude Melissa's retaining and manipulating the information long enough to solve the problem. Although Melissa's performance on tasks requiring basic application of math facts appears to be inconsistent with referral concerns (i.e., her teacher estimated her basic knowledge to be average), an analysis of Melissa's individual responses was consistent with her teacher's estimation. That is, Melissa responded correctly when required to multiply, add, or subtract single-digit responses. However, when multi-digit problems were presented, Melissa's responses were often incorrect. Thus, although Melissa may have average ability in terms of basic facts, when the material progresses from simple to more complex, her demonstration of such knowledge is impacted. This is likely due, in large part, to the fact that multistep problems require the involvement of working-memory abilities.

Melissa's specific cognitive weaknesses appear to be directly related to her academic difficulties and seem to be significantly impacting her ability to learn. Furthermore, the significant influences that Melissa's cognitive weaknesses have on her academic achievement do not appear to be related to external factors, such as language development, her environment, or cultural differences. Specifically, she exhibited significantly weak word recognition, comprehension, and mathematical skills. While she did exhibit average processing speed, crystallized intelligence, long-term storage and retrieval, and visual processing abilities, the remainder of her cognitive abilities (i.e., *Gf, Ga,* and *Gsm* [particularly working memory]), were in the *low* to *low average* range and were commensurate with her academic achievement difficulties in reading and mathematics.

Recommendations for Intervention

One of the primary purposes of psychoeducational assessment is to generate data that may be used to develop effective interventions. Regardless of the type of interventions that are developed, ongoing evaluation of their effectiveness must remain a part of whatever plans are developed to ameliorate the observed academic difficulties and concerns. The integration of collaborative information from standardized tests, teacher and parent reports, and prereferral data provided the basis for the following general education recommendations for Melissa:

1. Melissa's auditory processing deficit is related to her difficulty in decoding unfamiliar words. Therefore, it is recommended that Melissa receive training in phoneme segmentation and sound blending. Examples of these activities include identifying words beginning with the same sound (word matching), isolating individual sounds (e.g., recognizing the first sound in a word), identifying the numbers of phonemes in a word (phoneme counting), and identifying how the removal of a sound would change a given word (phoneme deletion). Additionally, teaching Melissa how to organize sounds to construct a word (sound blending) is recommended. Finally, working with Melissa on developing her sight-word vocabulary may also serve to aid her reading performance.
2. Melissa's deficit in working memory very likely affects both her

reading and math skills. To assist her in tasks requiring the retention and manipulation of information, memory strategies and techniques should be used. For example, her teachers may sequence material from simple to more complex. They can also provide frequent opportunities for practice and review, including systematic review within a few hours of learning. Melissa may further benefit from teacher-assisted reviews of each lesson, and could be taught to use mnemonic aids or strategies for retention, such as the use of verbal mediation or rehearsal (saying the information to be remembered while looking at it).

3. Melissa's demonstrated deficit in her ability to reason inductively and deductively appears to impact her math and reading comprehension skills adversely. In the area of reasoning, one of her most salient weaknesses involved her ability to detect patterns/rules/concepts. In order to help her with tasks requiring reasoning, some suggestions include engaging Melissa in demonstrations of the concept being taught, having her verbalize what she is being taught, and having her teach a concept to younger children. In addition, Melissa should have ample opportunity for repetition and review, and she should be taught strategies that may increase understanding and retention of a concept (e.g., verbalizing the steps of a task while it is being performed) and when and how to apply the strategies. She should be provided with a list of procedures to follow when working with tasks that involve problem solving. Specific to Melissa's reading comprehension difficulties, she should be provided with organizational strategies (e.g., story mapping) to use when reading a story. Imposing an organizational framework for Melissa during the process of reading may aid in increasing her comprehension.

Name: **Melissa**
Age: **9-11**   Grade: **4**
Examiner: **A**   Date: **1/13/00**

CHC Cross-Battery Summary Sheet
Part 1: Data Summary

Cluster	Test Battery	Subtest Name + (CHC ability code)	Standard Score	Standard Score Confidence Interval	Percentile Rank	Classification
Gf (Fluid Reasoning)		**Gf Cluster Average =**	81	76–86	11	Low
	WASI	Matrix Reasoning	78	71–85	8	Low
	WJ-R	Analysis-Synthesis	84	77–91	14	Low
Gc (Crystallized Intelligence)		**Gc Cluster Average =**	93	88–98	33	Average
	WASI	Similarities	91	84–98	27	Average
	WASI	Vocabulary	95	88–102	38	Average
Gv (Visual Processing)		**Gv Cluster Average =**	95	90–100	38	Average
	WASI	Block Design	90	83–97	25	Average
	WISC-III	Object Assembly	100	93–107	50	Average
Gsm (Short-Term Memory)		**Gsm Cluster Average =**				
		Memory Span Cluster Avg.=	90	85–95	25	Average
	WISC-III	Digit Span	89	82–96	23	Low Average
	WJ-R	Memory for Words	90	83–97	25	Average
		Working Memory Cluster Avg.=	71	66–76	3	Low
	CMS	Sequences	70	63–77	2	Low
	WJ-R	Numbers Reversed	72	65–79	3	Low
Glr (Long-Term Retrieval)		**Glr Cluster Average =**	91	86–96	27	Average
	WJ-R	Visual-Auditory Learning	92	85–99	29	Average
	NEPSY	Speeded Naming	90	83–97	25	Average
Ga (Auditory Processing)		**Ga Cluster Average =**	80	75–85	9	Low Average
	WJ-R	Incomplete Words	79	72–86	8	Low
	WJ-R	Sound Blending	81	74–88	11	Low Average
Gs (Processing Speed)		**Gs Cluster Average =**	95	90–100	38	Average
	WISC-III	Symbol Search	100	93–107	50	Average
	WISC-III	Coding	90	83–97	25	Average

Note. All standard scores are based on age norms. **Confidence Bands:** • Clusters = ±5 • Subtests = ±7

Name: **Melissa**
Age: **9–11**   Grade: **4**
Examiner: **A**   Date: **1/13/00**

CHC Cross-Battery Summary Sheet
Part 2: Normative Analysis Graph

Confidence Bands: • Clusters = ±5 • Subtests = ±7

–1 SEM ◄— 68% —► +1 SEM

Performance Classification	Very Low	Low	L. Avg.	Average	H.Avg.	Sup.	Very Superior
Percentile Ranks	≤ 2	3–8	9–24	25–75	76–97	92–97	98–99+

(CHC Code)   40   50   60   70   80   90   100   110   120   130   140   150   160

Broad/Narrow (**Gf**) Cluster
Matrix Reas. (**RG**) Test
Analysis-Syn. (**I**) Test
_____ (**I**) Test
_____ (**I**) Test
_____ (__) Test
_____ (__) Test

Broad/Narrow (**Gc**) Cluster
Similarities (**LD**) Test
Vocabulary (**VL**) Test
_____ (__) Test
_____ (__) Test
_____ (__) Test
_____ (__) Test

Broad/Narrow (**Gv**) Cluster
Block Design (**SR**) Test
Object Assemb. (**CS**) Test
_____ (__) Test
_____ (__) Test
_____ (__) Test
_____ (__) Test

Broad/Narrow (__) Cluster
MS Cluster (__) Test
Digit Span (**MS**) Test
Mem. for Word (**MS**) Test
MW Cluster (__) Test
Sequences (**MW**) Test
Num. Reversed (**MW**) Test

Broad/Narrow (**Glr**) Cluster
Vis. Aud. Lrng (**MA**) Test
Speed Naming (**NA**) Test
_____ (__) Test
_____ (__) Test
_____ (__) Test
_____ (__) Test

Broad/Narrow (**Ga**) Cluster
Inc. Words (**PCA**) Test
Sound Blending (**PCS**) Test
_____ (__) Test
_____ (__) Test
_____ (__) Test
_____ (__) Test

Broad/Narrow (**Gs**) Cluster
Symbol Search (**P**) Test
Coding (**R9**) Test
_____ (__) Test
_____ (__) Test
_____ (__) Test
_____ (__) Test

40   50   60   70   80   90   100   110   120   130   140   150   160

NORMATIVE RANGE CLASSIFICATION	Normative Deficit < 1 SD below mean	Normal Limits ±1 SD from mean	Normative Strength > 1 SD above mean

Name: __Melissa__

Age: __9-11__ Grade: __4__

Examiner: __A__ Date: __1/13/00__

CHC Cross-Battery Summary Sheet
Part 3: Intracognitive Analysis Graph

CHC FACTOR NAME	DIFF. SCORE	REL. S, W, or NS	Performance Classification and Corresponding Percentile Rank Ranges

Performance Classification and Corresponding Percentile Rank Ranges

	Very Low ≤ 2	Low 3–8	L. Avg. 9–24	Average 25–75	H. Avg. 76–97	Sup. 92–97	Very Superior 98–99+

Gf – __8__ (NS)

Gc + __4__ (NS)

Gv + __6__ (NS)

Gsm ± ___ ( )

Ga + __2__ (NS)

Glr – __9__ (NS)

Gs + __6__ (NS)

40   50   60   70   80   90   100   110   120   130   140   150   160

NORMATIVE RANGE CLASSIFICATION	Normative Weakness <1 SD below mean	Normal Limits ±1 SD from mean	Normative Strength >1 SD above mean

Calculation and Interpretation of Scores:

	(1) Cluster Averages		(5) Overall Average		(6) Difference Score	(7) Relative Interpretation Strength, Weakness, or NS	(8) Normative Interpretation Strength, Weakness, or NL.
Gf =	81	–	89	=	– 8	not significant	normative weakness
Gc =	93	–	89	=	+ 4	not significant	normal limits
Gv =	95	–	89	=	+ 6	not significant	normal limits
Gsm =		–		=	±		
Ga =	91	–	89	=	+ 2	not significant	normal limits
Glr =	80	–	89	=	– 9	not significant	normative weakness
Gs =	95	–	89	=	+ 6	not significant	normal limits

Sum of Averages = __535__ (2)

Number of factors = __6__ (3)

Overall Average = __89__ (4)

Relative Interpretation: SS Diff. ≥ –15 = Relative Weakness
SS Diff. ≥ +15 = Relative Strength
SS Diff. ≤ ±14 = Not Significant (NS)

Normative Interpretation: SS ≥ 116 = Normative Strength
SS ≤ 85 and ≥ 115 = Normal Limits (NL)
SS ≤ 84 = Normative Weakness

Achievement Test Normative Summary

Cluster	Battery	Test	Standard Score	Confidence Interval	Percentile Rank	Classification
Reading			**73**	**67–79**	**4**	**Low**
	WIAT	Basic Reading	80	73–87	9	Low Average
	WIAT	Reading Comp.	70	61–79	2	Very Low
Math			**66**	**59–73**	**1**	**Very Low**
	WIAT	Math Reasoning	70	61–79	2	Very Low
	WIAT	Numerical Ops.	71	61–81	3	Low
Language			**100**	**92–108**	**50**	**Average**
	WIAT	Listening Comp.	88	77–99	21	Low Average
	WIAT	Oral Expression	107	98–116	68	Average
Writing			**88**	**79–97**	**21**	**Low Average**
	WIAT	Spelling	91	83–99	27	Average
	WIAT	Written Expression	92	78–106	30	Average
Total			**79**	**75–83**	**8**	**Low**

Ability-Achievement Discrepancy Analysis

Subtest/Composite	WASI FSIQ-4	Predicted Achievement Score	Actual Achievement Score	Difference	Significance .05 Level	Strength or Weakness
Subtests						
Basic Reading	86	91	80	−11	13.58	NS
Mathematics Reasoning	86	91	70	−21	11.13	W
Spelling	86	92	91	−1	14.00	NS
Reading Comprehension	86	90	70	−20	9.55	W
Numerical Operations	86	92	71	−21	12.60	W
Listening Comprehension	86	92	88	−4	10.59	NS
Oral Expression	86	93	107	+14	15.39	NS
Written Expression	86	91	92	+1	5.91	NS
Composites						
Reading	86	90	73	−17	12.12	W
Mathematics	86	91	66	−25	13.30	W
Language	86	91	100	+9	12.16	NS
Writing	86	90	88	−2	9.22	NS

CASE REPORT #2

Report of Psycho-educational Evaluation

Name: Yuquita   Report Date: December 15, 2000
Evaluated by: Examiner B   Evaluation Dates: 22 Nov.–14 Dec. 2000
School: Anytown Middle   District: Anytown Union School District
Teacher: Smith   Grade: 5
Birth Date: 13 Aug. 1989   Chronological Age: 10:4
Ethnicity: Mexican   Instructional Language: English
First Language: Spanish   Second Language: English

Purpose of Evaluation

Yuquita was originally brought to the prereferral assistance team at the beginning of the school year by her fifth-grade teacher, who was concerned about her academic progress, in particular in the language arts. Yuquita was noted to be a very slow reader, with occasional difficulties in comprehension and a vocabulary well below that of her classroom peers. She was able to decode words that corresponded closely to their phonetic spelling, but had significantly more trouble in learning to pronounce words with irregular spellings. It was reported that Yuquita struggled even more with her basic writing skills, especially grammar, punctuation, and spelling, and she was evaluated by her teacher as being very far below the level of her same-grade peers. Generally speaking, these skills are most related to problems in *Ga* (auditory processing) and *Gc* (crystallized intelligence). However, given Yuquita's dual-language history and cultural difference, the team decided to attempt specific interventions rather than assume that an intrinsic deficiency was present. Accordingly, interventions were proposed and implemented, and included after-school tutoring in spelling, remedial reading assistance based on a phonetic approach, instructional modifications (shortened assignments, written instructions to supplement verbal instructions, and a work buddy to help with comprehension of assigned tasks), increased one-to-one attention and direct instruction from the teacher, and more involvement with small group instruction designed to increase engaged learning time. Unfortunately, the school lacked sufficient bilingual staff who could assist in making sure instruction was provided at the appropriate level for Yuquita and that information was made fully comprehensible to her. Thus, although progress was monitored carefully for approximately three months, it was noted at the follow-up meeting that Yuquita did not show significant progress as a result of these modifications in her educational program. Yuquita was subsequently referred for evaluation for special education to assess the possibility that she may have a learning disability.

Procedures of Evaluation

Procedures: Informative

1.	22 Nov.	Review of school records
2.	3 Dec.	Interview: Current teacher
		Interview: Parent(s)
3.	4 Dec.	Observation: Classroom
		Observation: Playground
4.	8 Dec.	Interview: Last year's teacher
		Interview: Student
5.	12 Dec.	Observation: Home
6.	13 Dec.	Review of student's Health and Developmental History Report

Procedures: Evaluative

8 Dec.   Woodcock-Johnson Psycho-educational Battery–Revised: Tests of Cognitive Ability (selected tests*)

10 Dec.   Wechsler Intelligence Scale for Children–Third Edition (selected tests*)

Leiter-R International Performance Scale (selected tests*)

*The primary concerns regarding Yuquita's functioning, described in the Purpose of Evaluation section, revolved around reading skills (mainly decoding and vocabulary, with some comprehension difficulties) and written language skills (including grammar, punctuation, and spelling). According to the literature, this pattern of academic difficulty is most likely related to deficiencies in *Ga* (auditory processing–phonetic coding: analysis and synthesis) and *Gc* (crystallized intelligence–lexical knowledge, language development, general information, etc.). Although a selective CHC Cross-Battery assessment targeting these particular abilities was contemplated, the ineffectiveness of the prior interventions created a need to uncover a broader picture of Yuquita's strengths and weaknesses in the hope that such information might inform future modifications and instructional planning irrespective of the presence of any disability. Consequently, tests selected from these batteries were integrated into a Comprehensive CHC Cross-Battery assessment.

Background Information

Educational and Family History

Yuquita was born near the town of Oaxaca, Mexico, and immigrated to the United States with her family when she was only 2 years old. She did not attend preschool in the United States but began her education at Anytown Elementary at the age of 5, and has remained enrolled continuously since that time. Although the Home Language Survey completed by Yuquita's parents indicated that her first language was Spanish and the primary language of the home is Spanish, Anytown Elementary did not offer any bilingual or native-language instructional programs, so she was given English immersion by default. There was some augmentation of her language education in the form of ESL assistance; however, records indicated that this was for only 15 min, approximately two or three times per week at the most, and very often not at all. Records also indicated that although Yuquita was considered for retention in second grade due to reported difficulties in language arts development, she was promoted to the next grade.

Yuquita's father currently works as a landscaper and her mother cares for Yuquita's younger sibling in the home. Yuquita's parents were both born in Mexico and reportedly did not have much formal schooling. Yuquita's mother reported that she completed only enough schooling to be equal to perhaps the third grade level, whereas her father reported that he completed the fifth grade before dropping out to assist his family economically. Yuquita has two brothers, one aged 21 who no longer lives at home, and the other aged 4. Yuquita's mother reported that Spanish is still the primary language in the home and that English is spoken only by Yuquita, usually when she is conversing with her younger brother.

Health and Developmental History

According to the information provided by Yuquita's mother, as well as by the nurse's screening results, Yuquita has vision and hearing that are within normal limits for successful learning in school. Although Yuquita was born about 25 miles away from her mother's village in a small community clinic and delivered by a midwife, her mother reported that she did not experience any complications during pregnancy and that labor and delivery were normal. Yuquita appears to have met all of her developmental milestones (walking, talking, toilet training, etc.) normally and without any delays. In sum, there do not appear to be any physical factors related to, or sufficient to account for, the educational problems that have been observed and reported in this case.

Thematic Discussion of Findings

Comment on Validity of Test Results

Because Yuquita is not a native English speaker, the area of most concern with respect to providing a fair and equitable assessment involves the use of norm-referenced tests. No tests are available with norms that are adequately representative of Yuquita's specific linguistic background and cultural experience. Thus, test results cannot be interpreted directly because the scores may not accurately reflect Yuquita's actual or true functioning. The procedures used in the course of this assessment are specifically intended to reduce potential bias and discrimination inherent in the interpretation of such test scores. In general, the following steps were used in order to increase the validity of the findings and provide a defensible basis for interpretation: (a) Tests were selected and interpreted in accordance with the guiding principles and cultural and linguistic extensions of the CHC Cross-Battery approach; (b) tests were augmented with ecological data (observations, records review, interviews, etc.); and (c) alternative methods of assessment were utilized (e.g., dynamic assessment, work samples, curriculum-based assessment). By adopting these procedures and gathering this type of information, an appropriate context was created in which to evaluate properly the meaning of the collected data in a manner that significantly reduces potential bias. In cases such as this one, in which there is evidence of cultural and linguistic difference, it is generally more appropriate to discuss the findings in terms of patterns that emerge from an integrative review of all available data. The following thematic descriptions are in keeping with this practice.

Language Arts Development is Partially Limited by Second Language Acquisition Factors

After careful evaluation and consideration of a broad range of factors, including school attendance, lack of school experience, cultural and linguistic differences, and environmental and economic disadvantages, some evidence was found indicating that Yuquita's suspected learning difficulties can be partially attributed to a language difference. The data suggest that the natural process of second language acquisition combined with a primarily English-only instructional history are factors that have contributed to Yuquita's current academic delays. However, although it is likely that at least some of Yuquita's current difficulties with language arts and written communication skills are the result of culture and language differences, additional information and evidence are needed to determine if they are in fact the primary reasons for her observed academic problems. The data that support these conclusions are presented in the following bulleted statements.

- Yuquita's cultural and linguistic experiences are different from those of children in the U.S. mainstream.
- Yuquita's mother reports that the first language Yuquita learned to speak was Spanish.
- There is no evidence of any English language development comparable to her peers prior to her entering kindergarten.
- Yuquita was not given the benefit of a primary language instructional (or bilingual) program.
- The amount of ESL given to Yuquita is inadequate to promote language proficiency to the level required for her to compete successfully with native English-speaking peers.
- Yuquita's current academic progress shows weaknesses only in heavily language-based tasks (reading and writing) but not in others such as math, where she is reportedly doing well.
- The pattern of results from school-based achievement testing also reinforces the influence of language differences (e.g., scores show high math skills, low language arts).

Direct Analysis of Test Data Suggests Patterns of Disorder

Normative (intercognitive) analysis (see attached CHC Cross-Battery Summary Sheet) appears to suggest that Yuquita has significant difficulties in at least two and possibly three areas of cognitive functioning. Interpretation of results from this analysis indicates normatively based weaknesses (i.e., SS ranges that fall below 85) in Crystallized Intelligence (*Gc*) and Auditory Processing (*Ga*). These scores indicate that her measured ability in these areas is > 1 SD below the general population mean of 100. Functioning in the area of Short-term Memory (*Gsm*) is also low but not sufficiently so to be characterized as a normative weakness. These findings suggest that Yuquita has limited breadth and depth of acquired knowledge or is unable to apply that knowledge effectively, and that her ability to perceive, analyze, and synthesize patterns among auditory stimuli is impaired. Data supporting these conclusions follow.

- The SS range for *Gc* = 72–82 (normative weakness).
- The SS range for *Ga* = 72–82 (normative weakness).
- The SS range for *Gsm* = 81–91 (not deficient, within normal limits).
- All other abilities (*Gf, Gv, Gs, Glr*) have SS ranges that fall within normal limits.

Relative (intracognitive) analysis (see attached summary and graph) provided additional information concerning Yuquita's apparent strengths and weaknesses that are consistent with the findings just mentioned. The patterns within the intracognitive analysis reveal relative weaknesses in the areas of *Gc* and *Ga* as well as a relative strength in the area of Visual Processing (*Gv*). Again, such a pattern indicates that Yuquita's *Gc* and *Ga* abilities are significantly different from and poorly developed in comparison to her other abilities. Conversely, her ability to work with (e.g., generate, perceive, analyze, synthesize, manipulate, transform) and think with visual patterns and stimuli is also significantly different than her other abilities, but in this case it represents an area of strength for her. The following data provide support for these conclusions.

- Difference between *Gc* mean (77) and overall mean (93) is −16 and is > 1 SD (relative and normative weakness).
- Difference between *Ga* mean (77) and overall mean (93) is −16 and is > 1 SD (relative and normative weakness).
- Difference between *Gv* mean (110) and overall mean (93) is +17 and is > 1 SD above the normative mean (relative strength).
- All other abilities (*Gf, Gsm, Gs, Glr*) do not deviate significantly from the overall mean.

Overall, this pattern of results appears to support the notion that Yuquita's cognitive functioning is impaired. However, these results were not interpreted within the context of culture or language differences. Therefore, these interpretations should not be considered valid estimates or completely reliable measures of Yuquita's true cognitive functioning or ability. Given that Yuquita's cultural and linguistic experiences are not comparable to those of the individuals on whom such tests were developed, standardized, and normed, interpretation is best conducted in a manner that reduces the potential discriminatory effects that such differences can have. The following section provides this analysis.

Nondiscriminatory Analysis of Test Data Suggests Patterns of Culture and Language Differences, Not Disorders

The data collected via standardized tests with Yuquita were arranged and grouped according to degree of cultural loading and degree of linguistic demand (see attached CHC Culture-Language Matrix Worksheet) to provide a graphical representation of the data. A careful review of the resulting patterns reveals the following conclusions: (a) Yuquita's scores tend to decrease as a function of the language demands of the tests; (b) Yuquita's scores tend to decrease as a function of the cultural loading of the tests; and (c) the overall pattern of Yuquita's scores tends to decrease the most as a function of the combination of language demands and cultural loading. A review of the data in this matrix suggests that as the cultural loading and linguistic demands of tests increase, Yuquita's performance decreases correspondingly, albeit overall performance remains within normal limits. The attenuating effect of these factors is greatest on tests that possess high levels of both of these characteristics, where performance is seen to fall within the normative weakness range. When viewed in this manner, the results provide support for interpretations that run counter to conclusions from direct analyses. That is, these results suggest that performance on these tests is more a function of Yuquita's not being fully acculturated and not being as English-proficient compared to her age- and grade-related peers. Because these tests appear to be *differentially and systematically* affected by these variables, strict normative and relative comparisons may not be entirely valid and do not necessarily offer the best hypothesis regarding the nature of Yuquita's observed academic difficulties. On the basis of the current analysis, nondiscriminatory interpretation suggests that Yuquita probably does not have any true cognitive impairments and that cultural and linguistic differences are the primary reasons for her low performance on the tests given to her and for her related academic skills deficits. The presence of a learning disorder or disability, therefore, is difficult to support. Moreover, nondiscriminatory interpretation of these data suggests that Yuquita may be able to perform well within the average range if not for the linguistic differences and cross-cultural barriers that have impeded her progress. Evidence to support these conclusions is based on the following.

- The pattern of scores declines as language demands increase (118–104–96 for low-culture cells; 105–78 for moderate-culture cells; 92–85–70 for high-culture cells).
- The pattern of scores declines as cultural loading increases (118–105–92 for low-language cells; 104–85 for moderate-language cells; 96–78–70 for high-language cells).
- The pattern of scores is highest in cells at or near the upper left side of the matrix and lowest for cells at or near the bottom right side of the matrix.

The conclusions regarding the direct attenuating effect of cultural and linguistic variables on Yuquita's measured performance are supported by the previous analyses. However, due to the fact that reorganization of the tests used in this evaluation for analysis within the CHC Culture-Language Matrix does not produce data in all cells of the matrix, some questions remained regarding notions of difference versus disorder. Therefore, in order to test further the hypothesis that cultural and linguistic factors were in fact adversely affecting Yuquita's cognitive performance, additional tests of Gf were given. In the original set of tests, Gf was measured with WJ-R Concept Formation and Analysis-Synthesis. Although these tests are low in terms of cultural loading, they are classified as high in terms of language demands. Thus, two additional tests of Gf were selected from the Leiter-R: Design Analogies and Repeated Patterns. These tests were chosen specifically because (a) They provide a means for comparing performance of tests that are expected to converge (with respect to Gf); (b) both are classified as low in terms of cultural loading and linguistic demand and thus provide data to fill in the upper-left-most cell of the matrix; and (c) they could be drawn from one of the batteries already used in the assessment. Results from this second iteration in testing demonstrated that these additional measures of *Gf* did not in fact converge with the indicators used initially. Design Analogies was significantly higher (SS bands do not touch or overlap) than both Concept Formation and Analysis-Synthesis, and Repeated Patterns was significantly higher than Concept Formation and only a few points away from being significantly higher than Analysis-Synthesis. Moreover, when viewed within the context of the other data contained in the CHC Culture-Language Matrix Worksheet, the patterns of interpretation regarding the attenuating effects of language were clearly evident. Therefore, based on this final analysis, it seems rather clear that Yuquita's cognitive abilities (especially with respect to *Gf*) are most likely higher than has been measured, and that her performance can be enhanced significantly when language factors are reduced. These conclusions are based on the following additional evidence.

- The SS range for Design Analogies (115–129) does not touch or overlap the SS range for Concept Formation (83–97) or Analysis-Synthesis (95–109).
- The SS range for Repeated Patterns (107–121) does not touch or overlap the SS range for Concept Formation (83–97) and only slightly overlaps the SS range for Analysis–Synthesis (95–109).
- The mean (SS = 96) for the initial set of high language demand tests of *Gf* (Analysis-Synthesis and Concept Formation) was lower than the mean (SS = 118) for the second set of low language demand tests of *Gf* (Design Analogies and Repeated Patterns).
- The average for the Low-Culture/High-Language cell (SS = 96) is lower than the mean for the Low-Culture/Moderate-Language cell (SS = 104) which is lower than the mean for the Low-Culture/Low-Language cell (SS = 118).

Conclusions

When examined from a less discriminatory framework, it seems reasonable to conclude that Yuquita's cognitive abilities are likely to be higher than what has been measured directly by this assessment, primarily because of factors related to cultural differences and second-language acquisition. Because Yuquita's education has been primarily English immersion, she has not been given an opportunity to develop the cognitive-academic language proficiency necessary for academic success at the appropriate grade level. Research on bilingual development and second-language acquisition has demonstrated consistently that it takes approximately 5 to 7 years to develop this level of proficiency. However, without the benefit of a primary-language program that facilitates development of such proficiency in both the native language and English, second-language learners such as Yuquita typically find themselves unable to keep up with the ever-advancing and developmentally based language demands of the curriculum; consequently, it is common for them to lag well behind native English speakers in language arts and related academic areas as was observed in Yuquita's case. In the case of intelligence or cognitive ability tests, lower performance demonstrated by individuals such as Yuquita may be interpreted incorrectly as deficient or dysfunctional, when in fact, culture and language differences are attenuating the results. Given Yuquita's cultural and linguistic background it appears that the most appropriate and least discriminatory conclusion that can be inferred from the data at this time is that Yuquita does not demonstrate any cognitive impairments and that her observed learning difficulties are the result of cultural and linguistic differences, not of disorders.

Recommendations

Given the findings just presented it is clear that modifications to Yuquita's learning environment are necessary to improve her academic success and provide an opportunity for greater success in the classroom. Yuquita's two greatest needs are: (a) ensuring that instruction provides input in a manner that is much more comprehensible for her; and (b) providing opportunities for enhancing her English-language development. Also, Yuquita appears to perform better when instruction caters to her visual processing (*Gv*) and fluid reasoning (*Gf*) abilities. These factors should be taken into consideration in the development of future instructional interventions designed to assist Yuquita. The following are some strategies that may serve as a starting point for discussion:

- Provide instruction using language strategies designed to facilitate greater comprehension by sheltering the language through the use of appropriate vocabulary level; use of physical materials, objects, and pictures to illustrate concepts; use of clear and distinct speech; reduced use of idioms and colloquialisms; and so forth.

- Closely monitor Yuquita's comprehension of tasks or lessons by asking her to repeat instructions for assignments that are given and posing brief, intermittent questions to her that relate to the current topic or discussion.

- Continue to facilitate English language development through ESL instruction that is tied directly to instruction within the main curriculum and that provides content-based learning experiences in English.

- Use an instructional strategy that previews the main concepts and key content vocabulary for lessons for Yuquita within the context of ESL instruction or with the assistance of a bilingual classroom aide.

- Begin teaching keyboard and computer word-processing skills to facilitate speed in production of written work assignments, and allow use of computerized or hand-held spelling aid/checker to assist with writing tasks.

- Allow for completion of assignments in alternative ways that capitalize on visual ability and do not rely as heavily on language or writing ability (e.g., creation of models, drawings, or dioramas as opposed to book reports or essays).

- Encourage and provide the opportunity for Yuquita and her family to become involved in school-sponsored literacy projects designed to provide English language–based learning experiences and access to high-interest literacy materials (e.g., books, tapes, videos, internet resources, etc.).

Name: **Yuquita**
Age: **10-4**   Grade: **5**
Examiner: **B**   Date: **12/15/00**

CHC Cross-Battery Summary Sheet
Part 1: Data Summary

Cluster	Test Battery	Subtest Name + (CHC ability code)	Standard Score	Standard Score Confidence Interval	Percentile Rank	Classification
Gf (Fluid Reasoning)		**Gf Cluster Average =**	**96**	**91–101**	**40**	**Average**
	WJ-R	Analysis-Synthesis	102	95–109	57	Average
	WJ-R	Concept Formation	90	83–97	25	Average
		Low Language Gf Average =	**118**	**113–123**	**88**	**High Average**
	Leiter-R	Design Analogies	122	115–129	92	Superior
	Leiter-R	Repeated Patterns	114	107–121	83	High Average
Gc (Crystallized Intelligence)		**Gc Cluster Average =**	**77**	**72–82**	**6**	**Low**
	WJ-R	Oral Vocabulary	84	77–91	14	Low Average
	WISC-III	Information	70	63–77	2	Low
Gv (Visual Processing)		**Gv Cluster Average =**	**110**	**105–115**	**75**	**Average**
	WJ-R	Visual Closure	105	98–112	65	Average
	WISC-III	Block Design	115	108–122	84	High Average
Gsm (Short-Term Memory)		**Gsm Cluster Average =**	**86**	**81–91**	**17**	**Low Average**
	WJ-R	Memory for Words	81	74–88	11	Low Average
	WISC-III	Digit Span	90	83–97	25	Average
Glr (Long-Term Retrieval)		**Glr Cluster Average =**	**92**	**87–97**	**29**	**Average**
	Leiter-R	Associated Pairs	94	87–101	35	Average
	Leiter-R	Delayed Pairs	89	82–96	23	Low Average
Ga (Auditory Processing)		**Ga Cluster Average =**	**77**	**72–82**	**6**	**Low**
	WJ-R	Sound Blending	70	63–77	2	Low
	WJ-R	Incomplete Words	83	76–90	13	Low Average
Gs (Processing Speed)		**Gs Cluster Average =**	**105**	**100–110**	**65**	**Average**
	WJ-R	Visual Matching	100	93–107	50	Average
	WISC-III	Coding	110	103–117	75	Average

Note. All standard scores are based on age norms. **Confidence Bands:** • Clusters = ±5 • Subtests = ±7

Name: **Yuquita**
Age: **10-4**   Grade: **5**
Examiner: **B**   Date: **12/15/00**

CHC Cross-Battery Summary Sheet
Part 2: Normative Analysis Graph

Confidence Bands: • Clusters = ±5 • Subtests = ±7

-1 SEM ← 68% → +1 SEM

Performance Classification	Very Low	Low	L. Avg.	Average	H.Avg.	Sup.	Very Superior
Percentile Ranks	≤ 2	3–8	9–24	25–75	76–97	92–97	98–99+

(CHC Code)   40   50   60   70   80   90   100   110   120   130   140   150   160

Broad/Narrow (**Gf**) Cluster
Analysis-Syn. (**RG**) Test
Concpt. Form. (**I**) Test
Design Anal. (**I**) Test
Repeated Pat. (**I**) Test
_____ (__) Test
_____ (__) Test

Broad/Narrow (**Gc**) Cluster
Oral Vocab. (**VL**) Test
Information (**K0**) Test
_____ (__) Test
_____ (__) Test
_____ (__) Test
_____ (__) Test

Broad/Narrow (**Gv**) Cluster
Visual Closure (**CS**) Test
Block Design (**SR**) Test
_____ (__) Test
_____ (__) Test
_____ (__) Test
_____ (__) Test

Broad/Narrow (**Gsm**) Cluster
Mem. for Words (**MS**) Test
Digit Span (**MS**) Test
_____ (__) Test
_____ (__) Test
_____ (__) Test
_____ (__) Test

Broad/Narrow (**Glr**) Cluster
Assoc. Pairs (**MA**) Test
Delayed Pairs (**MA**) Test
_____ (__) Test
_____ (__) Test
_____ (__) Test
_____ (__) Test

Broad/Narrow (**Ga**) Cluster
Sound Blend. (**PCS**) Test
Incom. Words (**PCA**) Test
_____ (__) Test
_____ (__) Test
_____ (__) Test
_____ (__) Test

Broad/Narrow (**Gs**) Cluster
Coding (**R9**) Test
Visual Match. (**P**) Test
_____ (__) Test
_____ (__) Test
_____ (__) Test
_____ (__) Test

40   50   60   70   80   90   100   110   120   130   140   150   160

NORMATIVE RANGE CLASSIFICATION	Normative Deficit < 1 SD below mean	Normal Limits ±1 SD from mean	Normative Strength > 1 SD above mean

Name: **Yuquita**
Age: **10-4** Grade: **5**
Examiner: **B** Date: **12/15/00**

CHC Cross-Battery Summary Sheet
Part 3: Intracognitive Analysis Graph

Performance Classification and Corresponding Percentile Rank Ranges

CHC FACTOR NAME	(6) DIFF. SCORE	(7) REL. S, W, or NS	Very Low ≤2	Low 3–8	L Avg. 9–24	Average 25–75	H. 76–97	Sup. 92–97	Very Superior 98–99+

Scale: 40 50 60 70 80 90 100 110 120 130 140 150 160

CHC Factor	Diff Score	Rel
Gf +	14	(NS)
Gc −	16	(W)
Gv +	17	(S)
Gsm −	7	(NS)
Ga −	16	(W)
Glr −	1	(NS)
Gs +	12	(NS)

Scale: 40 50 60 70 80 90 100 110 120 130 140 150 160

NORMATIVE RANGE CLASSIFICATION	Normative Weakness < 1 SD below mean	Normal Limits ±1 SD from mean	Normative Strength > 1 SD above mean

Calculation and Interpretation of Scores:

	(1) Cluster Averages		(5) Overall Average		(6) Difference Score	(7) Relative Interpretation Strength, Weakness, or NS	(8) Normative Interpretation Strength, Weakness, or NL.
Gf =	107	−	93	=	+ 14	not significant	normal limits
Gc =	77	−	93	=	− 16	relative weakness	normative weakness
Gv =	110	−	93	=	+ 17	relative strength	normal limits
Gsm =	86	−	93	=	− 7	not significant	normal limits
Ga =	77	−	93	=	− 16	relative weakness	normative weakness
Glr =	92	−	93	=	− 1	not significant	normal limits
Gs =	105	−	93	=	+ 12	not significant	normal limits

Sum of Averages = **654** (2)
number of factors = **7** (3)
Overall Average = **93** (4)

Relative Interpretation:
SS Diff. ≥ −15 = Relative Weakness
SS Diff. ≥ +15 = Relative Strength
SS Diff. ≤ ±14 = Not Significant (NS)

Normative Interpretation:
SS ≥ 116 = Normative Strength
SS ≤ 85 and ≥ 115 = Normal Limits (NL)
SS ≤ 84 = Normative Weakness

CHC Culture-Language Matrix Worksheet
Name of Examinee: __Yuquita__   Date: __12/15/00__

Degree of Linguistic Demand

Degree of Cultural Loading	Low	Moderate	High
Low	Test Name: / Score: Leiter-R Design Analogies (122) Leiter-R Repeated Patterns (114) Cell Average = **118**	Test Name: / Score: WISC-III Block Design (115) WISC-III Digit Span (90) WISC-III Coding (110) WJ-R Visual Matching (100) Cell Average = **104**	Test Name: / Score: WJ-R Analysis-Synthesis (102) WJ-R Concept Formation (90) Cell Average = **96**
Moderate	Test Name: / Score: WJ-R Visual Closure (105) Cell Average = **105**	Test Name: / Score: Cell Average =	Test Name: / Score: WJ-R Memory for Words (81) WJ-R Sound Blending (70) WJ-R Incomplete Words (83) Cell Average = **78**
High	Test Name: / Score: Leiter-R Associated Pairs (94) Leiter-R Delayed Pairs (89) Cell Average = **92**	Test Name: / Score: WJ-R Oral Vocabulary (85) Cell Average = **85**	Test Name: / Score: WISC-III Information (70) Cell Average = **70**

Appendix A

CHC Cross-Battery Worksheets

The following information pertains to all CHC Cross-Battery Worksheets included in this Appendix. These worksheets were adapted from McGrew and Flanagan (1998) and Flanagan, McGrew, and Ortiz (2000).

Tests printed in bold, uppercase letters are strong measures as defined empirically; tests printed in bold, lowercase letters are moderate measures as defined empirically; tests printed in regular-face, lowercase letters were classified logically. In the case of tests with two narrow ability classifications, the second classification is reported in parentheses. Tests that were classified either empirically or logically as mixed measures are not included on the worksheet. This classification system was described in Chapter 1 of this book; a description of how to use these worksheets appears in Chapters 2 and 3.

* If a test score is on a standard score scale other than 100 ± 15, record the score in the column marked by an asterisk. Then refer to the *Percentile-rank and Standard-score Conversion Table* (Appendix D) to convert the score to the scale of 100 ± 15. Record the new score in the next column.

* If the cluster includes two or more qualitatively different broad CHC indicators, then place a (✔) next to the word *Broad* and record the appropriate CHC code in the parentheses. If the cluster includes indicators from only one narrow ability subsumed by the broad CHC ability, then place a (✔) next to the word *Narrow* and record the respective narrow ability code in the parentheses.

For a more complete description of the tests included on these worksheets, see Appendix B.

Gf—COMPREHENSIVE FLUID INTELLIGENCE
CHC CROSS-BATTERY WORKSHEET

Battery or Test	Age	*Gf*—Fluid Intelligence Narrow Abilities Tests	SS*	SS (100 ± 15)
		Induction (I)		
WAIS-III	16–89	**MATRIX REASONING**		
DAS	6–17	**MATRICES**		
DAS	2–5	Picture Similarities		
KAIT	11–85+	**MYSTERY CODES**		
SB:IV	7–24	**MATRICES**		
WJ-R/III	2–85+	**CONCEPT FORMATION**		
DTLA-4	6–17	**SYMBOLIC RELATIONS**		
CTONI	6–18	Geometric Sequences (RG)		
K-BIT	4–90	Matrices		
KSNAP	11–85	Four-Letter Words		
Leiter-R	2–6	Classification		
Leiter-R	5–18+	Design Analogies		
Leiter-R	2–18+	Repeated Patterns		
Leiter-R	2–18+	Sequential Order		
CAS	5–17	Nonverbal Matrices		
Raven's	5–18+	Raven's Progressive Matrices		
TONI-3	5–85	Test of Nonverbal Intelligence–3rd Ed.		
UNIT	5–17	**ANALOGIC REASONING**		
Other				
		1. Sum of column		
		2. Divide by number of tests		
		3. Induction average		

Battery or Test	Age			
		General Sequential Reasoning (RG)		
KAIT	11–85+	**LOGICAL STEPS**		
WJ-R/III	4–85+	**ANALYSIS-SYNTHESIS**		
Leiter-R	2–10	Picture Context		
Leiter-R	6–18+	Visual Coding		
UNIT	5–17	**CUBE DESIGN**		
Other				
		1. Sum of column		
		2. Divide by number of tests		
		3. General Sequential Reasoning average		

Battery or Test	Age			
		Quantitative Reasoning (RQ)		
DAS	6–17	**SEQ & QUANT REASONING (I)**		
SB:IV	12–24	**EQUATION BUILDING**		
SB:IV	7–24	Number Series		
Other				
		1. Sum of column		
		2. Divide by number of tests		
		3. Quantitative Reasoning average		

Name: _____
Age: _____
Grade: _____
Examiner: _____
Date of Evaluation: _____

Fluid Intelligence: Mental operations that an individual may use when faced with a relatively novel task that cannot be performed automatically.

Induction: Ability to discover the underlying characteristic that governs a problem or set of materials.

General Sequential Reasoning: Ability to start with stated rules, premises, or conditions and to engage in one or more steps to reach a solution to a problem.

Quantitative Reasoning: Ability to reason inductively and deductively with concepts involving mathematical relations and properties.

Sum/No. of Narrow Ability Averages

Cluster Average**
__ Broad (__)
__ Narrow (__)

Note. From *The intelligence test desk reference (ITDR): Gf-Gc Cross-Battery Assessment* (p. 422), by K. S. McGrew and D. P. Flanagan, 1998, Boston: Allyn & Bacon. Copyright 1998 by the publisher. Adapted with permission of Allyn & Bacon.

Gc—COMPREHENSIVE CRYSTALLIZED INTELLIGENCE
CHC CROSS-BATTERY WORKSHEET

Battery or Test	Age	Gc—Crystallized Intelligence Narrow Abilities Tests	SS*	SS (100 ± 15)
Language Development (LD)				
WECH	3–74	**COMPREHENSION (K0)**		
WECH	3–74	**SIMILARITIES (VL)**		
DAS	6–17	**SIMILARITIES**		
DAS	2–5	Verbal Comprehension (LS)		
SB:IV	12–24	**VERBAL RELATIONS**		
SB:IV	2–24	**Comprehension (K0)**		
SB:IV	2–14	**Absurdities**		
DTLA-4	6–17	Word Opposites		
DTLA-4	6–17	Story Construction		
Other				
		1. Sum of column		
		2. Divide by number of tests		
		3. **Language Development** average		
Lexical Knowledge (VL)				
WECH	3–74	**VOCABULARY (LD)**		
DAS	6–17	**WORD DEFINITIONS (LD)**		
DAS	2–5	Naming Vocabulary (LD)		
SB:IV	2–24	**VOCABULARY (LD)**		
WJ-R	2–85	**ORAL VOCABULARY (LD)**		
WJ-R	2–85	**PICTURE VOCABULARY (K0)**		
WJ III	2–85	**VERBAL COMPREHENSION(LD)**		
NEPSY	3–4	Body Part Naming (K0)		
EVT	2–85	Expressive Vocabulary Test (LD)		
K-BIT	4–90	Expressive Vocabulary (K0, LD)		
PPVT-3	2–85	Peab Pic Voc Test–3rd ed. (K0, LD)		
Other				
		1. Sum of column		
		2. Divide by number of tests		
		3. **Lexical Knowledge** average		
Listening Ability (LS)				
WJ-R	4–85	**LISTENING COMP (LD)**		
NEPSY	3–12	Comp of Instructions (LD)		
Other				
		1. Sum of column		
		2. Divide by number of tests		
		3. **Listening Ability** average		
General Information (K0)				
WECH	3–74	**INFORMATION**		
DTLA-4	6–17	Basic Information		
WJ III	2–85+	**GENERAL INFORMATION**		
Other				
		1. Sum of column		
		2. Divide by number of tests		
		3. **General Information** average		
Information About Culture (K2)				
KAIT	11–85+	**FAMOUS FACES**		
Other				
		1. Sum of column		
		2. Divide by number of tests		
		3. **Information About Culture** average		

Name: _____
Age: _____
Grade: _____
Examiner: _____
Date of Evaluation: _____

Crystallized Intelligence: The breadth and depth of a person's acquired knowledge of a culture and the effective application of this knowledge.

Language Development: General development, or the understanding of words, sentences, and paragraphs (not requiring reading) in spoken native language skills.

Lexical Knowledge: Extent of vocabulary that can be understood in terms of correct word meanings.

Listening Ability: Ability to listen to and comprehend oral communications.

General Information: Range of general knowledge.

Information About Culture: Range of cultural knowledge (e.g., music, art).

Sum/No. of
Narrow Ability
Averages

Cluster
Average**
__ Broad (__)
__ Narrow (__)

Note. From *The intelligence test desk reference (ITDR): Gf-Gc Cross-Battery Assessment* (p. 422), by K. S. McGrew and D. P. Flanagan, 1998, Boston: Allyn & Bacon. Copyright 1998 by the publisher. Adapted with permission of Allyn & Bacon.

Gv—COMPREHENSIVE VISUAL PROCESSING
CHC CROSS-BATTERY WORKSHEET

Battery or Test	Age	Gv—Visual Processing Narrow Abilities Tests	SS*	SS (100 ± 15)
		Spatial Relations (SR)		
WECH	3–74	**BLOCK DESIGN (Vz)**		
DAS	3–17	Pattern Construction		
K-ABC	4–12	**TRIANGLES**		
SB:IV	2–24	**PATTERN ANALYSIS**		
Leiter-R	11–18+	Figure Rotation (Vz)		
UNIT	5–17	Cube Design (Vz)		
Other				
		1. Sum of column		
		2. Divide by number of tests		
		3. Spatial Relations average		
		Visualization (Vz)		
WPPSI-R	3–7	Geometric Designs (P2)		
DAS	2–3	**Block Building**		
DAS	4–5	Matching Letter-like Forms		
WJ-R/III	4–85+	**SPATIAL RELATIONS (SR)**		
Leiter-R	2–10	Matching		
Leiter-R	2–18+	Form Completion (SR)		
Leiter-R	11–18+	Paper Folding		
NEPSY	3–12	Block Construction		
Other				
		1. Sum of column		
		2. Divide by number of tests		
		3. Visualization average		
		Visual Memory (MV)		
WMS-III	16–89	Visual Reproduction I		
CMS	5–16	Dot Locations		
CMS	5–16	Dot Locations 2		
CMS	5–16	Picture Locations		
DAS	6–17	**RECALL OF DESIGNS**		
DAS	3–7	Recognition of Pictures		
K-ABC	2–4	Face Recognition		
KAIT	11–85+	**MEM. FOR BLOCK DESIGNS**		
SB:IV	2–24	**Bead Memory**		
SB:IV	7–24	**Memory for Objects**		
WJ-R/III	4–85+	**Picture Recognition**		
DTLA-4	6–17	Design Sequences		
DTLA-4	6–17	Design Reproduction		
Leiter-R	4–10	Immediate Recognition		
Leiter-R	2–18+	Forward Memory		
UNIT	5–17	**OBJECT MEMORY**		
UNIT	5–17	**SPATIAL MEMORY**		
UNIT	5–17	**SYMBOLIC MEMORY**		
NEPSY	3–12	Imitating Hand Positions		
LAMB	20–60	Simple Figure		
LAMB	20–60	Complex Figure		
WRAML	5–17	Picture Memory		
WRAML	5–17	Design Memory		
TOMAL	5–19	Facial Memory		
TOMAL	5–19	Abstract Visual Memory		
TOMAL	5–19	Manual Imitation		
TOMAL	5–19	Del Rec: Visual Sel. Reminding		
Other				
		1. Sum of column		
		2. Divide by number of tests		
		3. Visual Memory average		

Name: _____
Age: _____
Grade: _____
Examiner: _____
Date of Evaluation: _____

Visual Processing: The ability to generate, perceive, analyze, synthesize, manipulate, transform, and think with visual patterns and stimuli.

Spatial Relations: Ability to perceive and manipulate visual patterns rapidly or to maintain orientation with respect to objects in space.

Visualization: Ability to manipulate objects or visual patterns mentally and to "see" how they would appear under altered conditions.

Visual Memory: Ability to form and store a mental representation or image of a visual stimulus and then recognize or recall it later.

Closure Speed: Ability to combine disconnected, vague, or partially obscured visual stimuli or patterns quickly into a meaningful whole, without knowing in advance what the pattern is.

Spatial Scanning: Ability to survey a spatial field or pattern accurately and quickly and to identify a path through the visual field or pattern.

Flexibility of Closure: Ability to identify a visual figure or pattern embedded in a complex visual array, when knowing in advance what the pattern is.

Serial Perceptual Integration: Ability to identify a pictorial or visual pattern when parts of the pattern are presented rapidly in serial or successive order.

Note. From *The intelligence test desk reference (ITDR): Gf-Gc Cross-Battery Assessment* (p. 422), by K. S. McGrew and D. P. Flanagan, 1998, Boston: Allyn & Bacon. Copyright 1998 by the publisher. Adapted with permission of Allyn & Bacon.

Battery or Test	Age	Gv—Visual Processing Narrow Abilities Tests	SS*	SS (100 ± 15)
Closure Speed (CS)				
WECH	3–74	**OBJECT ASSEMBLY (SR)**		
K-ABC	2–12	Gestalt Closure		
WJ-R	2–85+	Visual Closure		
KSNAP	11–85	Gestalt Closure		
Other				
		1. Sum of column		
		2. Divide by number of tests		
		3. Closure Speed average		
Spatial Scanning (SS)				
WISC-III	6–16	Mazes		
WPPSI-R	3–7	Mazes		
UNIT	5–17	Mazes		
NEPSY	5–12	Route Finding		
Other				
		1. Sum of column		
		2. Divide by number of tests		
		3. Spatial Scanning average		
Flexibility of Closure (CF)				
CAS	5–17	**FIGURE MEMORY (MV)**		
Leiter-R	2–18+	Figure Ground		
Other				
		1. Sum of column		
		2. Divide by number of tests		
		3. Flexibility of Closure average		
Serial Perceptual Integration (PI)				
K-ABC	2–4	Magic Window		
CAS	5–17	**VERBAL SPATIAL RELATIONS**		
Other				
		1. Sum of column		
		2. Divide by number of tests		
		3. Serial Perceptual Integration average		

Sum/No. of Narrow Ability Averages

Cluster Average**
__ Broad (__)
__ Narrow (__)

Note. From *The intelligence test desk reference (ITDR): Gf-Gc Cross-Battery Assessment* (p. 422), by K. S. McGrew and D. P. Flanagan, 1998, Boston: Allyn & Bacon. Copyright 1998 by the publisher. Adapted with permission of Allyn & Bacon.

Gsm—COMPREHENSIVE SHORT-TERM MEMORY
CHC CROSS-BATTERY WORKSHEET

Battery or Test	Age	Gsm—Short-term Memory Narrow Abilities Tests	SS*	SS (100 ± 15)
		Memory Span (MS)		
WAIS-III	16–89	**DIGIT SPAN (MW)**		
WISC-III	6–16	**DIGIT SPAN (MW)**		
CMS	5–16	Numbers (MW)		
CMS	5–16	Stories*** (Gv-LS)		
WMS-III	16–89	Logical Memory I*** (Gv-LS)		
WMS-III	16–89	Digit Span (MW)		
DAS	3–17	Recall of Digits		
K-ABC	2–12	**NUMBER RECALL**		
K-ABC	4–12	**WORD ORDER**		
SB:IV	7–24	**MEMORY FOR DIGITS (MW)**		
WJ-R/III	4–85+	**MEMORY FOR WORDS**		
CAS	5–17	**WORD SERIES**		
CAS	5–17	**SENTENCE REPETITION**		
CAS	5–17	**SENTENCE QUESTIONS**		
WPPSI-R	3–7	Sentences		
KSNAP	11–85	Number Recall		
LAMB	20–60	Digit Span		
LAMB	20–60	Supraspan Digit		
TOMAL	5–19	Digits Forward		
TOMAL	5–19	Letters Forward		
WRAML	5–17	Number/Letter Memory		
NEPSY	5–12	Repetition of Nonsense Words		
NEPSY	3–12	Sentence Repetition		
Other				
		1. Sum of column		
		2. Divide by number of tests		
		3. **Memory Span** average		
		Working Memory (MW)		
WAIS-III	16–89	**LETTER-NUMBER SEQ.**		
WMS-III	16–89	Letter-Number Sequencing		
WMS-III	16–89	Mental Control		
CMS	5–16	Sequences		
WJ-R/III	4–85+	**NUMBERS REVERSED**		
WJ III	4–85+	**AUDITORY WORKING MEM**		
NEPSY	5–12	Knock and Tap		
Other				
		1. Sum of column		
		2. Divide by number of tests		
		3. **Working Memory** average		

Name: _____
Age: _____
Grade: _____
Examiner: _____
Date of Evaluation: _____

Short-Term Memory: The ability to apprehend and hold information in immediate awareness and then use it within a few seconds.

Memory Span: Ability to attend to and immediately recall temporally ordered elements in the correct order after a single presentation.

Working Memory: Ability to store temporarily and then perform a set of cognitive operations on information that requires divided attention and the management of the limited capacity of short-term memory.

Sum/No. of Narrow Ability Averages

Cluster Average**
__ Broad (__)
__ Narrow (__)

*** Although these tests are mixed measures of two CHC abilities (i.e., they involve Listening Ability in addition to Memory Span), they are included on this worksheet because they are necessary to administer prior to administering Stories 2 and Logical Memory II, respectively (measures of Glr-MM).

Note. From *The intelligence test desk reference (ITDR):* Gf-Gc *Cross-Battery Assessment* (p. 422), by K. S. McGrew and D. P. Flanagan, 1998, Boston: Allyn & Bacon. Copyright 1998 by the publisher. Adapted with permission of Allyn & Bacon.

Glr—COMPREHENSIVE LONG-TERM RETRIEVAL
CHC CROSS-BATTERY WORKSHEET

Battery or Test	Age	Glr—Long-term Retrieval Narrow Abilities Tests	SS*	SS (100 ± 15)
		Associative Memory (MA)		
WMS-III	16–89	Verbal Paired Associates I		
WMS-III	16–89	Verbal Paired Associates II		
CMS	5–16	Word Pairs		
CMS	5–16	Word Pairs 2		
KAIT	11–85+	REBUS LEARNING		
KAIT	11–85+	REBUS DELAYED RECALL		
WJ-R	2–85+	MEMORY FOR NAMES		
WJ-R/III	2–85+	VISUAL-AUD LEARNING (MM)		
WJ-R	4–85+	DEL REC: MEM FOR NAMES		
WJ-R/III	4–85+	Del Rec: Vis-Aud Learning (MM)		
Leiter-R	4–10	Delayed Recognition		
Leiter-R	2–18+	Associated Pairs (MM)		
Leiter-R	6–18+	Delayed Pairs (MM)		
NEPSY	5–12	Memory for Names		
TOMAL	5–19	Paired Recall		
LAMB	20–60	Word Pairs (FI)		
WRAML	5–17	Sound Symbol		
Other				
		1. Sum of column		
		2. Divide by number of tests		
		3. Associative Memory average		
		Ideational Fluency (FI)		
WJ III	4–85+	RETRIEVAL FLUENCY (FA)		
Other				
		1. Sum of column		
		2. Divide by number of tests		
		3. Ideational Fluency average		
		Figural Fluency (FF)		
NEPSY	5–12	Design Fluency		
Other				
		1. Sum of column		
		2. Divide by number of tests		
		3. Figural Fluency average		
		Naming Facility (NA)		
WJ III	4–85+	RAPID PICTURE NAMING		
CAS	5–17	Expressive Attention		
NEPSY	5–12	Speeded Naming		
Other				
		1. Sum of column		
		2. Divide by number of tests		
		3. Naming Facility average		

Name: _____
Age: _____
Grade: _____
Examiner: _____
Date of Evaluation: _____

Long-Term Retrieval: Ability to store information (e.g., concepts, ideas, items, names) in long-term memory and to retrieve it later fluently through association.

Associative Memory: Ability to recall one part of a previously learned but unrelated pair of items when the other part is presented (i.e., paired-associative learning).

Ideational Fluency: Ability to produce rapidly a series of ideas, words, or phrases related to a specific condition or object.

Figural Fluency: Ability to draw or sketch several examples or elaborations rapidly when given a starting visual stimulus.

Naming Facility: Ability to produce names for concepts rapidly.

Free Recall Memory: Ability to recall as many unrelated items as possible, in any order, after a large collection of items is presented.

Meaningful Memory: Ability to recall a set of items where there is a meaningful relation between items or the items create a meaningful story or connected discourse.

Note. From *The intelligence test desk reference (ITDR): Gf-Gc Cross-Battery Assessment* (p. 422), by K. S. McGrew and D. P. Flanagan, 1998, Boston: Allyn & Bacon. Copyright 1998 by the publisher. Adapted with permission of Allyn & Bacon.

Battery or Test	Age	*Glr*—Long-term Retrieval Narrow Abilities Tests	SS*	SS (100±15)
Free Recall Memory (M6)				
WMS-III	16–89	Word Lists I		
WMS-III	16–89	Word Lists II (MA)		
CMS	5–16	Word Lists		
CMS	5–16	Word Lists 2 (MA)		
DAS	4–17	Recall of Objects		
NEPSY	7–12	List Learning		
LAMB	20–60	Wordlist (MA)		
TOMAL	5–19	Word Selective Reminding		
TOMAL	5–19	Del Rec: Word Selective Reminding		
WRAML	5–17	Verbal Learning		
Other				
		1. Sum of column		
		2. Divide by number of tests		
		3. Free Recall Memory average		
Meaningful Memory (MM)				
WMS-III	16–89	Logical Memory II		
CMS	5–16	Stories 2		
Other				
		1. Sum of column		
		2. Divide by number of tests		
		3. Meaningful Memory average		

Sum/No. of Narrow Ability Averages

Cluster Average**
__ Broad (__)
__ Narrow (__)

Note. From *The intelligence test desk reference (ITDR): Gf-Gc Cross-Battery Assessment* (p. 422), by K. S. McGrew and D. P. Flanagan, 1998, Boston: Allyn & Bacon. Copyright 1998 by the publisher. Adapted with permission of Allyn & Bacon.

Ga—COMPREHENSIVE AUDITORY PROCESSING
CHC CROSS-BATTERY WORKSHEET

Battery or Test	Age	Ga—Auditory Processing Narrow Abilities Tests	SS*	SS (100 ± 15)
		Phonetic Coding: Analysis (PC:A)		
W-ADT	4–8	Wepman Aud Discrim Test		
GFW-TAD	3–70+	GFW Test of Aud Discrim		
G-FTA	2–16+	G-F Test of Articulation		
WJ-R/III	2–85+	INCOMPLETE WORDS		
TOPA	5–8	Test of Phonological Awareness		
TPAT	5–9	Segmentation		
TPAT	5–9	Isolation		
TPAT	5–9	Deletion		
TPAT	5–9	Rhyming		
NEPSY	3–12	Phonological Processing (PC:S)		
Other				
		1. Sum of column		
		2. Divide by number of tests		
		3. **Phonetic Coding: Analysis** average		

		Phonetic Coding: Synthesis (PC:S)		
WJ-R/III	4–85+	SOUND BLENDING		
TPAT	5–9	Substitution		
TPAT	5–9	Blending		
Other				
		1. Sum of column		
		2. Divide by number of tests		
		3. **Phonetic Coding: Synthesis** average		

		Speech/General Sound Discrimination (US/U3)		
WJ III	4–85+	AUDITORY ATTENTION (UR)		
WJ-R	4–85+	SOUND PATTERNS		
Other				
		1. Sum of column		
		2. Divide by number of tests		
		3. **Speech/General Sound Disc** average		

Name: _____
Age: _____
Grade: _____
Examiner: _____
Date of Evaluation: _____

Auditory Processing: Ability to perceive, analyze, and synthesize patterns among auditory stimuli.

Phonetic Coding (Analysis): Ability to segment larger units of speech sounds into smaller units.

Phonetic Coding (Synthesis): Ability to blend smaller units of speech together into larger units.

Speech/General Sound Discrimination: Ability to detect differences in speech sounds under conditions of little distraction or distortion.

Sum/No. of Narrow Ability Averages ÷

Cluster Average**
__ Broad (__)
__ Narrow (__)

Note. From *The intelligence test desk reference (ITDR): Gf-Gc Cross-Battery Assessment* (p. 422), by K. S. McGrew and D. P. Flanagan, 1998, Boston: Allyn & Bacon. Copyright 1998 by the publisher. Adapted with permission of Allyn & Bacon.

Gs—COMPREHENSIVE PROCESSING SPEED
CHC CROSS-BATTERY WORKSHEET

Battery or Test	Age	Gs—Processing Speed Tests	SS*	SS (100±15)
		Perceptual Speed (P)		
WAIS-III	16–74	**SYMBOL SEARCH (R9)**		
WISC-III	6–16	**SYMBOL SEARCH (R9)**		
WJ-R/III	2–85+	**VISUAL MATCHING (R9)**		
WJ-R	4–85+	**CROSS OUT**		
CAS	5–17	**RECEPTIVE ATTENTION (R4)**		
CAS	5–17	**PLANNED CONNECTIONS (R9)**		
Leiter-R	2–18+	Attention Sustained (R9)		
Other				
		1. Sum of column		
		2. Divide by number of tests		
		3. **Perceptual Speed** Average		
		Rate-of-test-taking (R9)		
WAIS-III	16–74	**DIGIT SYMBOL-CODING**		
WISC-III	6–16	**CODING**		
WPPSI-R	3–7	Animal Pegs		
CAS	5–17	**PLANNED CODES**		
Other				
		1. Sum of column		
		2. Divide by number of tests		
		3. **Rate-of-test-taking** average		
		Number Facility (N)		
DAS	6–17	Speed of Information Processing (R9)		
CAS	5–17	**NUMBER DETECTION (R9)**		
CAS	5–17	**MATCHING NUMBERS (R9)**		
WJ III	4–84+	**DECISION SPEED**		
Other				
		1. Sum of column		
		2. Divide by number of tests		
		3. **Mental Comparison Speed** average		

Name:_____
Age: _____
Grade:_____
Examiner:_____
Date of Evaluation: _____

Processing Speed: Ability to perform cognitive tasks fluently and automatically, especially when under pressure to maintain focused attention and concentration.

Perceptual Speed: Ability to search for and compare visual symbols rapidly when presented side by side or separated in a visual field.

Rate-of-test-taking: Ability to perform tests that are relatively easy or that require very simple decisions to be made rapidly.

Number Facility: Ability to manipulate and deal with numbers rapidly and accurately.

Sum/No. of Narrow Ability Averages

Cluster Average**
__ Broad (___)
__ Narrow (___)

Note. From *The intelligence test desk reference (ITDR): Gf-Gc Cross-Battery Assessment* (p. 422), by K. S. McGrew and D. P. Flanagan, 1998, Boston: Allyn & Bacon. Copyright 1998 by the publisher. Adapted with permission of Allyn & Bacon.

Description of Cognitive Ability Tests Within the CHC Framework

Battery	Age Range	Test[a]	BROAD (STRATUM II) ABILITY (code) / Narrow (Stratum I) Ability (code) / Test Description
			FLUID INTELLIGENCE (Gf) — Tests of Induction (I)
WAIS-III	16–89	**MATRIX REASONING**	The examinee is presented with a series of matrices in which one part of each matrix is missing, and is required to identify the missing part from a series of presented alternatives.
DAS	6–17	**MATRICES**	The examinee is required to complete a matrix of abstract designs by choosing the correct design from among four or six designs.
DAS	2–5	Picture Similarities	The examinee is required to match a target picture to one of four stimulus pictures.
KAIT	11–85+	**MYSTERY CODES**	The examinee is required to study the identifying codes associated with a set of pictorial stimuli and then figure out the code of a novel pictorial stimulus.
SB:IV	7–24	**MATRICES**	When presented with figural matrices in which one portion of each matrix is missing, the examinee is required to identify the missing elements from multiple-choice alternatives.
WJ-R/III	2–85+	**CONCEPT FORMATION**	The examinee is required to identify the rules for concepts when shown illustrations of instances of the concepts and noninstances of the concepts. This is a controlled-learning task that involves categorical reasoning based on principles of formal logic. The examinee is given feedback regarding the correctness of each response.
DTLA-4	6–17	**SYMBOLIC RELATIONS**	The examinee is required to select one of six options that best completes a matrix composed of geometric designs or line drawings.
CAS	5–17	Nonverbal Matrices	The examinee is required to select one of six options to complete a nonverbal progressive matrix.
CTONI	6–18	Geometric Sequences	The examinee is required to select a geometric shape from an array of shapes that best completes a sequentially ordered design. This test may also involve general sequential reasoning (RG).
K-BIT	4–90	Matrices	The examinee is required to complete either a 2 × 2 matrix or 3 × 3 matrix, or to complete a pattern of dots following a presentation of abstract visual stimuli.
KSNAP	11–85	Four-Letter Words	The examinee is required to identify secret words that are related to a series of clues. On one item, the examinee is required to rearrange jumbled sequences of four letters quickly into four-letter words.
Leiter-R	2–6	Classification	The examinee is required to categorize objects or geometric designs.
Leiter-R	5–18+	Design Analogies	The examinee is presented with 2 × 2 and 4 × 2 matrices and is required to complete these matrices using geometric shapes.
Leiter-R	2–18+	Repeated Patterns	The examinee is presented with patterns of pictorial or figural objects. These patterns are presented again and the examinee is required to supply the missing portion of the pattern by moving response cards into alignment with the easel.
Leiter-R	2–18+	Sequential Order	The examinee is presented with a progressive series of pictorial or figural objects and is required to select appropriate items that fit the progression.
MAT	5–17	Matrix Analogies	The examinee is required to solve four groups of matrices that include: Pattern Completion, Reasoning by Analogy, Serial Reasoning, and Spatial Visualization. This test may also involve general sequential reasoning (RG).
Raven's	5–18+	Raven's Progressive Matrices	The examinee is required to deduce relationships and solve problems involving a series of abstract figures and designs.
TONI-3	5–85	Test of Nonverbal Intelligence–3rd edition	The examinee is required to identify the rule that characterizes the relationship among a series of stimulus figures and select a correct response from an array of figures.
UNIT	5–17	**ANALOGIC REASONING**	The examinee is required to complete a matrix analogies task using common objects (e.g., hand/glove, foot/ [?]) and novel geometric figures.

(continued)

Battery	Age Range	Test[a]	BROAD (STRATUM II) ABILITY (code) Narrow (Stratum I) Ability (code) Test Description
			FLUID INTELLIGENCE (Gf) **Tests of General Sequential Reasoning (RG)**
KAIT	11–85+	**LOGICAL STEPS**	The examinee is required to attend to logical premises presented both visually and aurally, and then to respond to a question by making use of the logical premise.
WJ-R/III	4–85+	**ANALYSIS-SYNTHESIS**	The examinee is required to analyze the presented components of an incomplete logic puzzle and to identify the missing components. This is a controlled-learning task in which the examinee is given instructions on how to perform an increasingly complex procedure. The examinee is given feedback regarding the correctness of his or her response.
Leiter-R	2–10	Picture Context	The examinee is required to recognize an object that has been removed from a larger display using visual context clues.
Leiter-R	6–18+	Visual Coding	The examinee is required to code symbols associated with pictorial objects, geometric objects, and numbers.
UNIT	5–17	**CUBE DESIGN**	The examinee completes a three-dimensional block design task using between one and nine green-and-white blocks.
			FLUID INTELLIGENCE (Gf) **Tests of Quantitative Reasoning (RQ)**
DAS	6–17	**SEQUENTIAL & QUANTITATIVE REASONING**	The examinee is required to complete a series/sequence of abstract designs by identifying the missing designs or provide the missing number to match a pattern of numbers. This test may also involve induction (I).
SB:IV	12–24	**EQUATION BUILDING**	The examinee is required to take numerals and mathematical signs and resequence them in order to produce a correct solution (i.e., an equation).
SB:IV	7–24	Number Series	After reviewing a series of four or more numbers, the examinee is required to generate the next two numbers in the series in a manner consistent with the principle underlying the number series.
			CRYSTALLIZED INTELLIGENCE (G) **Tests of Language Development (LD)**
WECH	3–74	**COMPREHENSION**	The examinee is required to respond to a series of orally presented questions involving everyday problems or understanding of social rules and concepts. This test may also involve general information (K0).
WECH	3–74	**SIMILARITIES**	The examinee is required to determine how two objects or concepts are alike. This test may also involve lexical knowledge (VL).
DAS	6–17	**SIMILARITIES**	The examinee is required to say how three words are similar to one another.
DAS	2–5	Verbal Comprehension	The examinee is required to manipulate objects or identify objects in pictures in response to oral instructions given by the examiner. This test may also involve listening ability (LS).
SB:IV	12–24	**VERBAL RELATIONS**	When given four words, the examinee is required to state how three words of the four-word set are similar.
SB:IV	2–24	Comprehension	For items 1–6, the examinee is required to identify body parts on a card with a picture of a child. For items 7–42, the examinee is required to respond to questions about everyday problem situations ranging from survival behavior to civic duties. This test may also involve general information (K0).
SB:IV	2–14	Absurdities	The examinee is required to point to or describe the absurdity in a presented situation that is contrary to common sense.
DTLA-4	6–17	Word Opposites	The examinee is required to provide antonyms for a series of presented words.
DTLA-4	6–17	Story Construction	The examinee is required to construct stories following a presentation of a series of pictures.

Battery	Age Range	Test[a]	BROAD (STRATUM II) ABILITY (code) / Narrow (Stratum I) Ability (code) / Test Description
			CRYSTALLIZED INTELLIGENCE (Gc)
			Tests of Lexical Knowledge (VL)
WECH	3–74	VOCABULARY	The examinee is required to define a series of orally presented words. This test may also involve language development (LD).
DAS	6–17	WORD DEFINITIONS	The examinee is required to define words. This test may also involve language development (LD).
DAS	2–5	Naming Vocabulary	The examinee is required to name objects or pictures of objects. This test may also involve language development (LD).
SB:IV	2–24	VOCABULARY	The examinee is required to either point to pictures named by the examiner or (later) define words orally. This test may also involve language development (LD).
WJ-R	2–85	ORAL VOCABULARY	In Part A (Synonyms), the examinee is required to state a word similar in meaning to the word presented. In part B (Antonyms), the examinee must state a word that is opposite in meaning to the word presented. In the WJ III this test is combined with Picture Vocabulary (vocabulary test). This test may also involve language development (LD).
WJ-R	2–85	PICTURE VOCABULARY	The examinee is required to name familiar and unfamiliar pictured objects. In the WJ III this test is combined with Oral Vocabulary (Vocabulary test). This test may also involve general information (K0).
WJ III	2–85	VERBAL COMPREHENSION	In part A (Synonyms), the examinee is required to state a word similar in meaning to the word presented. In Part B (Antonyms), the examinee must state a word that is opposite in meaning to the word presented. In Part C (Picture Vocabulary) the examinee is required to name familiar and unfamiliar pictured objects. This test may also involve language development (LD) and general information.
NEPSY	3–4	Body Part Naming	The examinee is required to name specific body parts presented on a stimulus card. This test may also involve general information (K0).
EVT	2–85	Expressive Vocabulary Test	The examinee is required to name or provide a synonym for a series of presented pictures. This test may also involve language development (LD).
K-BIT	4–90	Expressive Vocabulary	The examinee is required to provide a name for each of 45 picture items. This test may also involve general information (K0) and language development (LD).
PPVT-3	2–85	Peabody Picture Vocabulary Test	The examinee is required to point to a picture that matches the word provided by the examiner. This test may also involve general information (K0) and language development (LD).
			CRYSTALLIZED INTELLIGENCE (Gc)
			Tests of Listening Ability (LS)
WJ-R	4–85	LISTENING COMPREHENSION	The examinee is required to listen to a short, tape-recorded passage and supply the single word missing at the end of the passage. This test may also involve language development (LD).
NEPSY	3–12	Comprehension of Instructions	The examinee is required to listen to and respond quickly to a series of increasingly complex verbal instructions (e.g., "point to the little, bright star"). Later, the examinee must point to items that are not as readily identifiable ("point to a shape that is not blue and is in between two triangles and under a circle"). This test may also involve language development (LD).
			CRYSTALLIZED INTELLIGENCE (Gc)
			Tests of General Information (K0)
WECH	3–74	INFORMATION	The examinee is required to answer orally presented questions regarding common events, objects, places, and people.
DTLA-4	6–17	Basic Information	The examinee is required to answer orally presented questions regarding common knowledge.
WJ III	2–85+	GENERAL INFORMATION	The examinee is required to answer orally presented questions regarding the common or typical characteristics of certain objects.
			CRYSTALLIZED INTELLIGENCE (Gc)
			Tests of Information about Culture (K2)
KAIT	11–85+	FAMOUS FACES	The examinee is required to name people of current or historical fame, based on their photographs and a verbal cue about each.

(continued)

Battery	Age Range	Test[a]	BROAD (STRATUM II) ABILITY (code) Narrow (Stratum I) Ability (code) Test Description
			VISUAL PROCESSING (*Gv*) Tests of Spatial Relations (SR)
WECH	3–74	**BLOCK DESIGN**	The examinee is required to reproduce a series of designs using blocks. This test may also involve visualization (Vz).
DAS	3–17	Pattern Construction	The examinee is required to use flat squares or blocks to construct a series of designs.
K-ABC	4–12	**TRIANGLES**	The examinee is required to reproduce a printed two-dimensional design using two-color triangles.
SB:IV	2–24	**PATTERN ANALYSIS**	For the first six items, the examinee is required to place puzzle pieces into a form board. In subsequent items the examinee reproduces patterns with blocks. This is a timed test.
Leiter-R	11–18+	Figure Rotation	The examinee is required to rotate a two- or three-dimensional object or geometric figure mentally. This test may also involve visualization (Vz).
UNIT	5–17	Cube Design	The examinee is required to complete a three-dimensional block design task using between one and nine green-and-white blocks. This test may also involve visualization (Vz).
			VISUAL PROCESSING (*Gv*) Tests of Visualization (Vz)
WPPSI-R	3–7	Geometric Designs	The examinee is required to view a stimulus design and to select the design that is exactly like the first from an array of four designs. Later, the examinee is required to draw geometric designs that are consistent with a printed model. This test may also involve finger dexterity (P2).
DAS	2–3	Block Building	The examinee is required to copy two- or three-dimensional designs with wooden blocks.
DAS	4–5	Matching Letter-like Forms	The examinee is required to find an identical match of a target letter-like shape.
WJ-R/III	4–85+	**SPATIAL RELATIONS**	The examinee is required to match shapes visually. The examinee must select, from a series of shapes, the component parts needed to make a given whole shape. This test may also involve spatial relations (SR).
Leiter-R	2–10	Matching	The examinee is presented with a series of visual stimuli and is required to select response cards to match these stimuli.
Leiter-R	2–18+	Form Completion	The examinee is required to recognize a whole object from a randomly displayed array of its parts. This test may also involve spatial relations (SR).
Leiter-R	11–18+	Paper Folding	The examinee is required to fold mentally an unfolded object displayed in two dimensions and to match it to a target.
NEPSY	3–12	Block Construction	The examinee is required to construct a series of three-dimensional designs using monochromatic blocks.
			VISUAL PROCESSING (*Gv*) Tests of Visual Memory (MV)
WMS-III	16–89	Visual Reproduction I	The examinee is required to view a design briefly and to draw it from memory.
CMS	5–16	Dot Locations	The examinee is required to place chips on an empty grid to replicate a previously presented dot pattern.
CMS	5–16	Dot Locations 2	The examinee is required to replicate the previously presented dot patterns shown in the immediate condition, after a 25- to 35- minute delay.
CMS	5–16	Picture Locations	The examinee is presented with pictures located on a grid and, when the stimulus card is removed from view, must place response chips on a blank grid to denote the locations of the previously presented pictures.
DAS	6–17	**RECALL OF DESIGNS**	The examinee is required to reproduce abstract line drawings from memory.
DAS	3–7	Recognition of Pictures	The examinee is required to view pictures of objects and identify those objects in a second picture that has a larger array of objects.
K-ABC	2–4	Face Recognition	The examinee is required to select from a group photograph the one or two faces that were shown briefly in a preceding photograph.

Battery	Age Range	Test[a]	BROAD (STRATUM II) ABILITY (code) / Narrow (Stratum I) Ability (code) / Test Description
KAIT	11–85+	MEMORY FOR BLOCK DESIGNS	The examinee is required to study a printed abstract design that is exposed briefly and then to copy the design from memory using six yellow-and-black wooden blocks and a tray.
SB:IV	2–24	Bead Memory	For the first 10 items, the examinee is required to recall which one of two beads was exposed. For items 11–42, the examinee is required to place beads on a stick in the same sequence as shown in a picture.
SB:IV	7–24	Memory for Objects	The examinee is required to identify objects in the correct order from a larger array of presented objects.
WJ-R/III	4–85+	Picture Recognition	The examinee is required to recognize a subset of previously presented pictures within a field of distracting pictures.
DTLA-4	6–17	Design Sequences	The examinee is required to replicate a series of pictured designs using a group of cubes.
DTLA-4	6–17	Design Reproduction	The examinee is required to draw a geometric figure from memory following a single presentation.
Leiter-R	4–10	Immediate Recognition	A stimulus array of pictured objects is shown for 5 sec. After its removal the examinee is required to discriminate between objects that are present and objects that are absent.
Leiter-R	2–18+	Forward Memory	After the examiner points to a series of pictures in a given sequence, the examinee is required to repeat the pointing sequence.
UNIT	5–17	OBJECT MEMORY	The examinee is shown a visual array of common objects (e.g., shoes, telephone, tree) for 5 sec, after which the examinee identifies the pictured objects from a larger array of pictured objects.
UNIT	5–17	SPATIAL MEMORY	The examinee is required to remember and recreate the placement of black and/or green chips on a 3 × 3 or 4 × 4 cell grid.
UNIT	5–17	SYMBOLIC MEMORY	The examinee is required to recall and recreate sequences of visually presented universal symbols (e.g., green boy, black woman).
NEPSY	3–12	Imitating Hand Positions	The examinee is required to imitate a series of hand positions as demonstrated by the examiner using both the preferred and nonpreferred hands within a specified time limit (e.g., 20 sec).
LAMB	20–60	Simple Figure	The examinee is required to view geometric designs for 15 sec and to reproduce them from memory and, later, with the design in view.
LAMB	20–60	Complex Figure	The examinee is required to view one complex design for 15 sec and reproduce it from memory and, later, with the design in view.
WRAML	5–17	Picture Memory	The examinee is required to view two scenes and identify which components have changed from the first to second scene.
WRAML	5–17	Design Memory	The examinee is required to draw four presented designs from memory following a 10-sec delay.
TOMAL	5–19	Facial Memory	The examinee is required to identify a particular series of faces among a set of distracter faces.
TOMAL	5–19	Abstract Visual Memory	The examinee is required to identify a particular stimulus among a set of six distracters.
TOMAL	5–19	Manual Imitation	The examinee is required to imitate a series of hand movements presented by the examiner.
TOMAL	5–19	DR: Visual Selective Remindin	The examinee is required to imitate a pointing sequence presented by the examiner 30 min earlier.
			VISUAL PROCESSING (Gv) / **Tests of Closure Speed (CS)**
WECH	3–74	OBJECT ASSEMBLY	The examinee is required to complete a series of puzzle sequences within a specified time limit. This test may also involve spatial relations (SR).
K-ABC	2–12	Gestalt Closure	The examinee is required to name an object or scene pictured in a partially completed ink blot drawing.
WJ-R	2–85+	Visual Closure	The examinee is required to identify a drawing or picture of a simple object that is represented by disconnected lines. The test requires the subject to combine the disconnected lines visually into a meaningful whole.
KSNAP	11–85	Gestalt Closure	The examinee is required to name an object or scene following the presentation of a partially completed inkblot drawing.
			VISUAL PROCESSING (Gv) / **Tests of Spatial Scanning (SS)**
WISC-III	6–16	Mazes	The examinee is required to complete a series of increasingly difficult mazes using a pencil.

(continued)

| | | | BROAD (STRATUM II) ABILITY (code) |
| | | | Narrow (Stratum I) Ability (code) |
Battery	Age Range	Test[a]	Test Description
WPPSI-R	3–7	Mazes	The examinee is required to complete a series of increasingly difficult mazes using a pencil.
UNIT	5–17	Mazes	The examinee completes a maze task by tracing a path through each maze from the center starting point to an exit.
NEPSY	5–12	Route Finding	The examinee is presented with a drawing of a target house in a small schematic map and is required to find a route to that house. Later, the examinee must find the target house again when it is presented within a larger map containing other houses and streets.
			VISUAL PROCESSING (Gv)
			Tests of Flexibility of Closure (CF)
CAS	5–17	FIGURE MEMORY	The examinee is required to identify a geometric figure within a more complex design. This test may also involve visual memory (MV).
Leiter-R	2–18+	Figure Ground	The examinee is required to identify imbedded figures or designs within a complex stimulus.
			VISUAL PROCESSING (Gv)
			Tests of Serial Perceptual Integration (PI)
K-ABC	2–4	Magic Window	The examinee is required to identify a picture that is exposed by being moved past a narrow slit or window (making the picture only partially visible throughout the presentation).
CAS	5–17	VERBAL SPATIAL RELATIONS	The examinee is required to choose one of six pictures in response to a verbal question about spatial relationships. This test may also involve Gc-related abilities, including language development and listening ability.
			SHORT-TERM MEMORY (Gsm)
			Tests of Memory Span (MS)
WAIS-III	16–89	DIGIT SPAN	The examinee is required to repeat a series of orally presented digits either verbatim or in reverse order. This test may also involve working memory (MW).
WISC-III	6–16	DIGIT SPAN	The examinee is required to repeat a series of orally presented digits either verbatim or in reverse order. This test may also involve working memory (MW).
CMS	5–16	Numbers	The examinee is required to repeat a series of orally presented number sequences either verbatim or in reverse order. This test may also involve working memory (MW).
CMS	5–16	Stories	The examinee is required to recall stories immediately following a single presentation. This test may also involve listening ability (LS).
WMS-III	16–89	Logical Memory I	The examinee is required to recall two brief stories immediately following a single presentation. This test may also involve listening ability (LS).
WMS-III	16–89	Digit Span	The examinee is required to repeat a series of digits both forward and backward. This test may also involve working memory (MW).
DAS	3–17	Recall of Digits	The examinee is required to repeat a series of orally presented digits.
K-ABC	2–12	NUMBER RECALL	The examinee is required to repeat verbatim orally presented number sequences.
K-ABC	4–12	WORD ORDER	The examinee is required to touch a series of pictures in the same sequence as named by the examiner.
SB-IV	7–24	MEMORY FOR DIGITS	The examinee is required to repeat digits exactly as they were stated by the examiner and, for some items, in reverse order. This test may also involve working memory (MW).
WJ-R/III	4–85+	MEMORY FOR WORDS	The examinee is required to repeat lists of unrelated words in the correct sequence after they are presented aurally by use of a tape player, or, in special cases, by an examiner.
CAS	5–17	WORD SERIES	The examinee is required to repeat a series of words in the same order as presented by the examiner.
CAS	5–17	SENTENCE REPETITION	The examinee is required to repeat sentences that are syntactically correct but essentially meaningless.
CAS	5–17	SENTENCE QUESTIONS	The examinee is required to answer questions about syntax-based but meaningless statements.
WPPSI-R	3–7	Sentences	The examinee is required to repeat verbatim a series of orally presented sentences.

Battery	Age Range	Test[a]	BROAD (STRATUM II) ABILITY (code) Narrow (Stratum I) Ability (code) Test Description
KSNAP	11–85	Number Recall	The examinee is required to repeat a series of number sequences verbatim.
LAMB	20–60	Digit Span	The examinee is required to repeat a series of number sequences verbatim or in reverse order.
LAMB	20–60	Supraspan Digit	The examinee is required to learn a number that is two digits longer than the longest number that was successfully recalled on the Digit Span subtest. Later, the examinee must recall the number during free-recall and retention-recall trials.
TOMAL	5–19	Digits Forward	The examinee is required to recall a series of number sequences.
TOMAL	5–19	Letters Forward	The examinee is required to recall a series of letter sequences.
WRAML	5–17	Number/Letter Memory	The examinee is required to repeat a combination of orally presented letters and numbers ranging from 2–10 units in length.
NEPSY	5–12	Rep of Nonsense Words	The examinee is required to repeat a series of tape-recorded nonsense words.
NEPSY	3–12	Sentence Repetition	The examinee must repeat a series of increasingly complex and lengthy sentences.
			SHORT-TERM MEMORY (Gsm) **Tests of Working Memory**
WAIS-III	16–89	LETTER-NUMBER SEQUENCING	The examinee is required to listen to orally presented letter-number sequences and to repeat the sequences back by arranging the numbers in ascending order, followed by the letters in alphabetical order.
WMS-III	16–89	Letter-Number Sequencing	The examinee is required to listen to orally presented letter-number sequences and to repeat the sequences back by arranging the numbers in ascending order, followed by the letters in alphabetical order.
WMS-III	16–89	Mental Control	The examinee is required to perform a series of simple tasks, which gradually increase in complexity, as quickly as possible (e.g., saying the months of the year forward and backward).
CMS	5–16	Sequences	The examinee is required to perform a series of simple tasks (e.g., saying the names of the months forward and backward as quickly as possible).
WJ-R/III	4–85	NUMBERS REVERSED	The examinee is required to repeat a series of number sequences presented aurally by use of a tape player.
WJ III	4–85+	AUDITORY WORKING MEMORY	The examinee is required to retain two types of orally presented information (numbers and words) and then repeat them in a specified order. The task requires the examinee to perform two different mental operations simultaneously (i.e., to retain and manipulate stimuli).
NEPSY	5–12	Knock and Tap	The examinee is required to watch the examiner produce different motor movements and must respond in a specified manner (e.g., if the examiner knocks, the examinee must tap).
			LONG-TERM RETRIEVAL (Glr) **Tests of Associative Memory (MA)**
WMS-III	16–89	Verbal Paired Associates I	The examinee is required to listen to eight novel word pairs, and, upon the presentation of the first word of each pair, the examinee must provide the second word of the pair.
WMS-III	16–89	Verbal Paired Associates II	The examinee is presented with the first word of each pair learned in Verbal Paired Associates I and must provide the corresponding word that completes the pair. Later, the examinee is read a list containing 24 word pairs and must identify each pair as a previously learned or newly presented pair.
CMS	5–16	Word Pairs	The examinee is read a list of word pairs and, following the presentation of the first word pair, the examinee must provide the second word of the pair. After 3 trials, the examinee is required to provide both words of the pairs from memory.
CMS	5–16	Word Pairs 2	Following a 25- to 35-min delay, the examinee is asked to recall previously learned word pairs. Later, the examinee is presented with word pairs and must identify the pairs as previously learned or newly presented pairs.

(continued)

Battery	Age Range	Test*	BROAD (STRATUM II) ABILITY (code) Narrow (Stratum I) Ability (code) Test Description
KAIT	11–85+	REBUS LEARNING	The examinee is required to learn the word or concept associated with a particular rebus (drawing) and then to read phrases and sentences composed of these rebuses.
KAIT	11–85+	REBUS DELAYED RECALL	The examinee is required to "read" phrases and sentences composed of rebuses he or she had learned about 45 min earlier during the rebus learning test.
WJ-R	2–85+	MEMORY FOR NAMES	The examinee is required to learn associations between unfamiliar auditory and visual stimuli (an auditory–visual association test).
WJ-R/III	2–85+	VISUAL AUDITORY LEARNING	The examinee is required to associate novel visual symbols (rebuses) with familiar words in oral language and to translate a series of symbols into verbal sentences (a visual-auditory association task). This test is a controlled-learning test in which the examinee's errors are corrected. This task simulates a learning-to-read test. This test may also involve meaningful memory (MM).
WJ-R	4–85+	DELAYED RECALL: MEMORY FOR NAMES	The examinee is required to recall (after 1–8 days) the space creatures presented in the Memory for Names test. The examinee is not told that subsequent testing will occur.
WJ-R/III	4–85+	Delayed Recall: Visual-Auditory Learning	The examinee is required to recall (after 1–8 days) the symbols (rebuses) presented in the Visual-Auditory Learning test. The examinee is not told that subsequent testing will occur. This test is a controlled-learning test in which the examinee's errors are corrected. This is a recall and relearning test in the WJ III.
Leiter-R	4–10	Delayed Recognition	After a 20-min delay, the examinee is required to recognize the objects associated in the Associated Pairs test.
Leiter-R	2–18+	Associated Pairs	Pairs of pictured objects are displayed for 5 to 10 sec. After their removal the examinee is required to make meaningful and nonmeaningful associations. This test may also involve meaningful memory (MM).
Leiter-R	6–18+	Delayed Pairs	After a 20-min delay the examinee is required to recognize the objects associated in the Associated Pairs test. This test may also involve meaningful memory (MM).
NEPSY	5–12	Memory for Names	The examinee is presented with a series of pictures depicting children and is given the name of each child. Following this presentation, the examinee is presented with the stimulus cards in random order and must provide the correct name. There is a delayed portion of this task. This test may also involve meaningful memory.
TOMAL	5–19	Paired Recall	The examinee is required to recall a previously presented word pair after the first word of the pair is presented by the examiner.
LAMB	20–60	Word Pairs	The examinee is required to recall the second word of 14 word pairs during a series of retention and recall trials. This test may also involve ideational fluency (FI).
WRAML	5–17	Sound Symbol	The examinee is required to recall sounds that were previously related to a series of abstract figures. A delayed recall trial is given.
		LONG-TERM RETRIEVAL (Glr) **Tests of Ideational Fluency (FI)**	
WJ III	4–85+	RETRIEVAL FLUENCY	The examinee is required to retrieve the names of objects fluently. The examinee is asked to state as many items as he or she can of three different types: "things to eat or drink," "names of people," and "animals." This test may also involve Associated Fluency (FA).
		LONG-TERM RETRIEVAL (Glr) **Tests of Figural Fluency (FF)**	
NEPSY	5–12	Design Fluency	The examinee is required to make as many unique designs as possible by connecting a series of dots.
		LONG-TERM RETRIEVAL (Glr) **Tests of Naming Facility (NA)**	
WJ III	4–85+	RAPID PICTURE NAMING	The examinee is required to identify and orally name pictures of common objects rapidly.

Battery	Age Range[a]	Test[a]	BROAD (STRATUM II) ABILITY (code) / Narrow (Stratum I) Ability (code) / Test Description
CAS	5–17	Expressive Attention	The examinee is required to identify the name of a color used to print a word when both are different (e.g., the word "red" is printed in green ink).
NEPSY	5–12	Speeded Naming	The examinee is required to name the color, size, and shape of a series of stimulus items rapidly.
			LONG-TERM RETRIEVAL (Gr) **Tests of Free Recall Memory (M6)**
WMS-III	16–89	Word Lists I	The examinee is required to recall as many words as possible from a list of 12 orally presented, unrelated words. Later, after a new word list is presented, the examinee must recall as many words from the first list as possible.
WMS-III	16–89	Word Lists II	The examinee is required to recall the original word list given in Word Lists I. Later, the examinee is read 24 words and must identify each word as belonging or not belonging to the original list. This test may also involve associative memory (MA).
CMS	5–16	Word Lists	The examinee is required to recall as many words as possible, in any order, from an orally presented list. Later, the examinee is presented with those words omitted in the first recall and asked to recall those words as well as the original words recalled from the first list.
CMS	5–16	Word Lists 2	After a 20- to 35-min delay, the examinee must recall as many words he or she can from Word List I. Later, the examinee is presented with a list of words and must identify the words as newly presented or previously presented words. This test may also involve associative memory (MA).
DAS	4–17	Recall of Objects	The examinee is required to view a picture card with 20 objects and recall the names of these objects after the card is removed.
NEPSY	7–12	List Learning	The examinee is required to listen to a list of orally presented words and to repeat as many words as he/she can remember, in any order. Later, the examinee is presented with a new list of words and must recall those words, in addition to the original list of words, in any order.
LAMB	20–60	Wordlist	The examinee is required to recall a 15-word list during a series of free-recall, cued-recall, and retention-recall trials. This test may also involve associative memory (MA).
TOMAL	5–19	Word Selective Reminding	The examinee is required to learn and recall a word list during a series of 8 trials.
TOMAL	5–19	DR: Word Selective Reminding	The examinee is required to recall the previously learned word list following a 30-min delay.
WRAML	5–17	Verbal Learning	The examinee is required to recall immediately an orally presented word list. Later, a delayed-recall trial is administered.
			LONG-TERM RETRIEVAL (Gr) **Tests of Meaningful Memory (MM)**
WMS-III	16–89	Logical Memory II	The examinee is asked to retell two previously presented stories from Logical Memory 1 and to respond to closed-ended (e.g., yes/no) questions about both sets of stories.
CMS	5–16	Stories 2	The examinee is asked to retell two previously presented stories from Stories in the absence of any stimulus cues. Later, the examinee is required to answer questions presented by the examiner for each story.
			AUDITORY PROCESSING (Ga) **Tests of Phonetic Coding–Analysis (PC-A)**
W-ADT	4–8	Wepman Auditory Discrimination	The examinee is required to recognize the fine differences between phonemes used in English speech by indicating, verbally or gesturally, whether the words in each pair are the same or different.
GFW-TAD	3–70+	G-F-W Test Auditory Discrimination	The examinee is required to discriminate speech sounds against two different backgrounds: quiet and noise. This test may also involve resistance to auditory distortion.
G-FTA	2–16+	G-F Test of Articulation	The examinee is required to produce spontaneous and imitative sounds and to produce correctly a previously misarticulated sound following a demonstration by the examiner.
WJ-R/III	2–85+	INCOMPLETE WORDS	After hearing a recorded word that has one or more phonemes missing, the examinee is required to identify the correct word.

(continued)

Battery	Age Range	Test[a]	BROAD (STRATUM II) ABILITY (code) — Narrow (Stratum I) Ability (code) — Test Description
TOPA	5–8	Test of Phonological Awareness	The examinee is required to isolate individual phonemes in spoken words.
TPAT	5–9	Segmentation	The examinee is required to divide sentences into words by clapping out the number of words in the sentences, and to divide words into syllables by clapping out the number of syllables in each word. Later, the examinee must segment words by phoneme or sound.
TPAT	5–9	Isolation	The examinee must identify the initial, medial, and final phonemes in a series of presented words.
TPAT	5–9	Deletion	The examinee is required to say a word, then, to repeat it leaving out a root word, syllable, or phoneme.
TPAT	5–9	Rhyming	The examinee is required to identify whether two presented words rhyme. Later, the examinee must produce a word that rhymes with a given stimulus word.
NEPSY	3–12	Phonological Processing	The examinee is required to identify words from word segments. Later, the examinee is required to construct a new word by either omitting a syllable or phoneme or by substituting a phoneme in one word for another. This test may also involve phonetic coding-synthesis (PC:S).
			AUDITORY PROCESSING (Ga) — Tests of Phonetic Coding-Synthesis (PC:S)
WJ-R/III	4–85+	SOUND BLENDING	The examinee is required to integrate and then say whole words after hearing parts (syllables and/or phonemes) of the words presented via an audio tape player.
TPAT	5–9	Substitution	The examinee must construct words by using blocks that represent sounds. Later, the examinee is required to transform a given word into a new word by changing one sound. This test may also involve phonetic coding-analysis.
TPAT	5–9	Blending	The examinee is required to blend together given sound units (e.g., syllables, phonemes) to construct words.
			AUDITORY PROCESSING (Ga) — Tests of Speech/General Sound Discrimination (US/U3)
WJ III	4–85+	AUDITORY ATTENTION	The examinee is required to discriminate similar-sounding words in the presence of increasing noise. This test requires selective attention and may also involve resistance to auditory stimulus distortion (UR).
WJ-R	4–85+	SOUND PATTERNS	The examinee is required to indicate whether pairs of complex sound patterns presented via an audio tape player are the same or different. The patterns may differ in pitch, rhythm, or content.
			PROCESSING SPEED (Gs) — Tests of Perceptual Speed (P)
WAIS-III	16–74	SYMBOL SEARCH	The examinee is required to scan a row of symbols and identify the matching symbols in the group. This test may also involve rate-of-test-taking (R9).
WISC-III	6–16	SYMBOL SEARCH	The examinee is required to scan a row of symbols and identify the matching symbols in the group. This test may also involve rate-of-test-taking (R9).
WJ-R/III	2–85+	VISUAL MATCHING	The examinee is required to locate and circle the two identical numbers in a row of six numbers. The task proceeds in difficulty from single-digit numbers to triple-digit numbers and has a 3-min time trial. For younger examinees, the task requires the examinee to identify two identical pictures of assorted shapes and colors by pointing. This test may also involve rate-of-test-taking.
WJ-R	4–85+	CROSS OUT	The examinee is required to scan and compare visual information quickly. The examinee must mark the 5 drawings in a row of 20 drawings that are identical to the first drawings in the row. The examinee is given a 3-min time limit to complete as many rows of items as possible. This test may also involve rate-of-test-taking.
CAS	5–17	PLANNED CONNECTIONS	The examinee is required to complete a pattern of letters and numbers. This test may also involve rate-of-test-taking (R9).
CAS	5–17	RECEPTIVE ATTENTION	The examinee is required to identify pairs of pictures or letters while resisting distractions. This test may also involve semantic processing speed (R4).

Battery	Age Range	Test[a]	BROAD (STRATUM II) ABILITY (code) Narrow (Stratum I) Ability (code) Test Description
Leiter-R	2–18+	Attention Sustained	The examinee is required to identify specific stimuli among an array of different stimuli. This test may also involve rate-of-test-taking (R9).
			PROCESSING SPEED (Gs) **Tests of Rate-of-test-taking (R9)**
WAIS-III	16–74	**DIGIT SYMBOL-CODING**	The examinee is required to draw symbols that are paired with a series of numbers quickly using a key.
WISC-III	6–16	**CODING**	The examinee is required to draw symbols that are paired with a series of letters (Coding A) or numbers (Coding B) quickly according to a key.
WPPSI-R	3–7	Animal Pegs	The examinee is required to place colored pegs into holes on a board quickly according to a key.
CAS	5–17	**PLANNED CODES**	The examinee is required to use a strategy to match symbols to letters as quickly as possible.
			PROCESSING SPEED (Gs) **Tests of Number Facility (N)**
DAS	6–17	Speed of Information Processing	The examinee is required to mark on each row the largest number or the circle with the most boxes as quickly as possible. This test may also involve rate-of-test-taking (R9).
CAS	5–17	**MATCHING NUMBERS**	The examinee is required to develop a plan to find two identical numbers on several rows. This test may also involve rate-of-test-taking (R9).
CAS	5–17	**NUMBER DETECTION**	The examinee is required to find specific numbers to match a sample while resisting response to distracting numbers. This test may also involve rate-of-test-taking (R9).
WJ III	4–85+	**DECISION SPEED**	The examinee is required to scan a row of pictures rapidly and to decide which of the two drawings are conceptually related. The decisions become slightly more abstract as the test progresses.

Note. CAS = Cognitive Assessment System; CMS = Children's Memory Scale; CTONI = Comprehensive Test of Nonverbal Intelligence; DAS = Differential Ability Scales; DTLA-4 = Detroit Tests of Learning Aptitude–Fourth Edition; K-ABC = Kaufman Assessment Battery for Children; KAIT = Kaufman Adolescent and Adult Intelligence Test; K-BIT = Kaufman Brief Intelligence Test; K-SNAP = Kaufman Short Neuropsychological Assessment Procedure; LAMB = Learning and Memory Battery; LEITER-R = Leiter International Performance Scale–Revised; SB:IV = Stanford-Binet Intelligence Scale–Fourth Edition; TOMAL = Test of Memory and Learning; TONI-3 = Test of Nonverbal Intelligence–Third Edition; TOPA = Test of Phonological Awareness; UNIT = Universal Nonverbal Intelligence Test; WAIS-III = Wechsler Adult Intelligence Scale–Third Edition; WISC-III = Wechsler Intelligence Scale for Children–Third Edition; WJ III = Woodcock-Johnson Psychoeducational Battery–Third Edition; WJ-R = Woodcock-Johnson Psychoeducational Battery–Revised; WMS-III = Wechsler Memory Scale–Third Edition; WPPSI-R = Wechsler Preschool nd Primary Scale of Intelligence; WRAML = Wide Range Assessment of Memory and Learning.

(continued)

Tests printed in bold, uppercase letters are strong measures; tests printed in bold, lowercase letters are moderate measures as defined empirically; tests printed in regular type lowercase letters are classified logically (see Flanagan, McGrew, & Ortiz, 2000; McGrew & Flanagan, 1998). In the case in which tests have two narrow ability classifications, the second classification is reported in parentheses following the test description. Tests of the major batteries that were classified either empirically or logically as mixed measures are not included in this table.

Sources: *Kaufman Adolescent and Adult Intelligence Test (KAIT)* by Alan Kaufman and Nadeen Kaufman. © 1993 American Guidance Service, Inc., 4201 Woodland Road, Circle Pines, MN 55014-1796. *Kaufman Assessment Battery for Children (K-ABC)* by Alan Kaufman and Nadeen Kaufman. © 1983 American Guidance Service, Inc., 4201 Woodland Road, Circle Pines, MN 55014-1796. Test definitions for the Leiter-R were reproduced by permission of Stoelting Co., Wood Dale, IL. Test definitions for the WMS-III, CMS, NEPSY, and DAS were adapted with permission for from The Psychological Corporation. Technical manual for the Wechsler Adult Intelligence Scale/Wechsler Memory Scale: Third Edition. Copyright © 1997 by The Psychological Corporation. Adapted and reproduced by permission. "Wechsler Memory Scale," "WMS," "Wechsler Adult Intelligence Scle," and "WAIS" are registered trademarks of The Psychological Corporation. Manual of the Children's Memory Scale. Copyright © 1997 by The Psychological Corporation. Adapted and reproduced by permission. All rights reserved. Manual of the NEPSY. Copyright © 1998 by The Psychological Corporation. Adapted and reproduced by permission. All rights reserved. "NEPSY" is a registered trademark of The Psychological Corporation. Administration and Scoring Manual for the Differential Ability Scales. Copyright © 1990 by The Psychological Corporation. Adapted and reproduced by permission. All rights reserved. "Differential Ability Scales" and "DAS" are registered trademark of The Psychological Corporation. Test definitions for the Phonological Awareness Test were adapted from Robertson, Carolyn and Wanda Salter. The Phonological Awareness Test. East Moline, IL: Lingui Systems, 1997. 1-800-PRO-IDEA. Test definitions for the SB:IV, UNIT, WJ-R, and Cas were adapted with permission from Riverside Publishing Company. Copyright © 1986 by Riverside Publishing Company. Reproduced from the Guide for administering and scoring *The Stanford-Binet Intelligence Scale, Fourth Edition*, by Robert L. Thorndike, Elizabeth P. Hagen, and Jerome M. Sattler, with permission of the publisher. Copyright © 1998 by The Riverside Publishing Company. Reproduced from the *Universal Nonverbal Intelligence Test Manual*, by Bruce A. Bracken and R. Steve McCallum, with permission of the publisher. Copyright © 1989 by The Riverside Publishing Company. Reproduced from the *WJ-R Tests of Cognitive Ability Standard and Supplemental Batteries: Examiners Manual* in the *Woodcock-Johnson Psychoeducational Battery–Revised*, by Richard W. Woodcock and M. Bonner Johnson, with permission of the publisher. Copyright © 1997 by The Riverside Publishing Company. Reproduced from the *Cognitive Assessment System Administration and Scoring Manual* in the *Cognitive Assessment System*, by J. P. Das and Jack A. Naglieri. Reproduced from the *Cognitive Assessment System Administration and Scoring Manual* in the *Cognitive Assessment System*, by J. P. Das and Jack A. Naglieri, with permission of the publisher. Test definitions for the DTLA-4 were adapted from the *Detroit Tests of Learning Aptitude, Fourth Edition (DTLA-4)*, 1998, Austin TX: Pro-Ed. Reproduced by permission.

Appendix C

Evaluation of Cognitive Ability Test Reliability

Reliability	2	3	4	5	6	7	8	9	10	11	12	13	14	15	16	17	18	19	20 24	25 29	30 34	35 39	40 44	45 49	50 54	55 59	60 64	65 69	70 74	75 79	80 84	85 +
DAS																																
Block Building																																
Verbal Comp.																																
Pict. Similarities																																
Naming Vocab.																																
Recall of Objects																																
Pattern Construct																																
Early Num. Con.																																
Copying																																
Match. Let-L F																																
Recall of Digits																																
Recog. ofPict.																																
Recall of Designs																																
Word Definitions																																
Matrices																																
Similarities																																
Seq./Quant. Res.																																
Speed of Inf.Proc.																																
K-ABC																																
Magic Window																																
Face Recognition																																
Hand Movements																																
Gestalt Closure																																
Number Recall																																
Triangles																																
Word Order																																
Matrix Analogies																																
Spatial Memory																																
Photo Series																																

(continued)

Reliability	2	3	4	5	6	7	8	9	10	11	12	13	14	15	16	17	18	19	20 24	25 29	30 34	35 39	40 44	45 49	50 54	55 59	60 64	65 69	70 74	75 79	80 84	85 +
KAIT																																
Definitions																																
Rebus Learning																																
Logical Steps																																
Auditory Comp																																
Mystery Codes																																
Double Meaning																																
Mem. Block. Des.																																
Famous Faces																																
Rebus Del'dRecall																																
Aud. Delayed Rec.																																
SB:IV																																
Vocabulary																																
Bead Memory																																
Quantitative																																
Mem. for Sent.																																
Pattern Analysis																																
Comprehension																																
Absurdities																																
Memory for Digits																																
Copying																																
Mem. for Objects																																
Matrices																																
Number Series																																
Paper Fold & Cut																																
Verbal Relations																																
Equation Building																																
WAIS-III																																
Picture Completion																																
Vocabulary																																
D-S Coding																																
Similarities																																
Block Design																																
Arithmetic																																
Matrix Reasoning																																

Reliability	2	3	4	5	6	7	8	9	10	11	12	13	14	15	16	17	18	19	20 24	25 29	30 34	35 39	40 44	45 49	50 54	55 59	60 64	65 69	70 74	75 79	80 84	85 +
Digit Span																																
Information																																
Pict. Arrangement																																
Comprehension																																
Symbol Search																																
L-N Sequencing																																
Object Assembly																																
WISC-III																																
Pict. Completion																																
Information																																
Coding																																
Similarities																																
Pict. Arrangement																																
Arithmetic																																
Block Design																																
Vocabulary																																
Object Assembly																																
Comprehension																																
Symbol Search																																
Digit Span																																
Mazes																																
WPPSI-R																																
Object Assembly																																
Information																																
Geometric Design																																
Comprehension																																
Block Design																																
Arithmetic																																
Mazes																																
Vocabulary																																
Pict. Completion																																
Similarities																																
Animal Pegs																																
Sentences																																

(continued)

Reliability	2	3	4	5	6	7	8	9	10	11	12	13	14	15	16	17	18	19	20 24	25 29	30 34	35 39	40 44	45 49	50 54	55 59	60 64	65 69	70 74	75 79	80 84	85 +
WJ-R																																
Mem. for Names																																
Mem. for Sent.																																
Visual Matching																																
Incomplete Words																																
Visual Closure																																
Pict. Vocabulary																																
Analysis-Synthesis																																
V-A Learning																																
Mem. for Words																																
Cross Out																																
Sound Blending																																
Pict. Recognition																																
Oral Vocabulary																																
Concept Formation																																
DR: Mem. for Names																																
DR: V-A Learning																																
Numbers Reversed																																
Sound Patterns																																
Spatial Relations																																
Listening Comp.																																
Verbal Analogies																																
WMS-III																																
Digit Span																																
Faces I																																
Faces II																																
Family Pict.I																																
Family Pict.II																																
Letter-Num. Seq.																																
Logical Mem. I																																
Logical Mem. II																																
Mental Control																																
Spatial Span																																
Verb Pair Assoc. I																																
Verb Pair Assoc. II																																
Visual Repro. I																																

Reliability	2	3	4	5	6	7	8	9	10	11	12	13	14	15	16	17	18	19	20 24	25 29	30 34	35 39	40 44	45 49	50 54	55 59	60 64	65 69	70 74	75 79	80 84	85 +
Visual Repro. II																																
Word Lists I																																
Word Lists II																																
CMS																																
Dot Locations																																
Dot Locations 2																																
Faces																																
Faces 2																																
Family Pictures																																
Family Pictures 2																																
Numbers																																
Picture Locations																																
Sequences																																
Stories																																
Stories 2																																
Word Lists																																
Word Lists 2																																
Word Pairs																																
Word Pairs 2																																

Low ☐ Medium ▨ High ■ No Information Available ☐

Appendix D

Percentile Rank and Standard Score Conversion Table

Percentile Rank and Standard Score Conversion Table

	Standard Score			
Percentile Rank	WJ-R/III CHC Cross-Battery (M = 100; SD = 15)	DAS, WASI (M = 50; SD = 10)	SB-IV (M = 50; SD = 8)	Wechsler (IQ and Memory Scales), K-ABC/KAIT, DTLA 4, CAS, Leiter-R, NEPSY, CMS, UNIT (M = 10; SD = 3)
99.99	160	90	82	
99.99	159	89		
99.99	158	89	81	
99.99	157	88		
99.99	156	87	80	
99.99	155	87		
99.99	154	86	79	
99.98	153	85		
99.98	153	85	78	
99.97	152	85		
99.96	151	84	77	
99.95	150	83		
99.94	149	83	76	
99.93	148	82		
99.93	147	81	75	
99.89	146	81		
99.87	145	80	74	19
99.84	144	79		
99.80	143	79	73	
99.75	142	78		
99.70	141	77	72	
99.64	140	77		18
99.57	139	76	71	
99	138	75		
99	138	75	70	
99	137	75		
99	136	74	69	
99	135	73		17
99	134	73	68	
99	133	72		
98	132	71	67	
98	131	71		
98	130	70	66	16
97	129	69		
97	128	69	65	
97	127	68		
96	126	67	64	
95	125	67		15
95	124	66	63	
94	123	65		
93	123	65	62	
92	122	65		
92	121	64	61	
91	120	63		14
89	119	63	60	
88	118	62		
87	117	61	59	
86	116	61		
84	115	60	58	13

354

	Standard Score			
Percentile Rank	WJ-R/III CHC Cross-Battery (M = 100; SD = 15)	DAS, WASI (M = 50; SD = 10)	SB-IV (M = 50; SD = 8)	Wechsler (IQ and Memory Scales), K-ABC/KAIT, DTLA 4, CAS, Leiter-R, NEPSY, CMS, UNIT (M = 10; SD = 3)
83	114	59		
81	113	59	57	
79	112	58		
77	111	57	56	
75	110	57		12
73	109	56	55	
71	108	55		
69	108	55	54	
67	107	55		
65	106	54	53	
65	105	53		11
62	104	53	52	
57	103	52		
55	102	51	51	
52	101	51		
50	100	50	50	10
48	99	49		
45	98	49	49	
43	97	48		
40	96	47	48	
38	95	47		9
35	94	46	47	
33	93	45		
31	93	45	46	
29	92	45		
27	91	44	45	
25	90	43		8
23	89	43	44	
21	88	42		
19	87	41	43	
17	86	41		
16	85	40	42	7
14	84	39		
13	83	39	41	
12	82	38		
11	81	37	40	
9	80	37		6
8	79	36	39	
8	78	35		
7	78	35	38	
6	77	35		
5	76	34	37	
5	75	33		5
4	74	33	36	
3	73	32		
3	72	31	35	
3	71	31		
2	70	30	34	4
2	69	29		
2	68	29	33	
1	67	28		

(continued)

	Standard Score			
Percentile Rank	WJ-R/III CHC Cross-Battery (M = 100; SD = 15)	DAS, WASI (M = 50; SD = 10)	SB-IV (M = 50; SD = 8)	Wechsler (IQ and Memory Scales), K-ABC/KAIT, DTLA 4, CAS, Leiter-R, NEPSY, CMS, UNIT (M = 10; SD = 3)
1	66	27	32	
1	65	27		3
1	64	26	31	
1	63	25		
1	63	25	30	
16	62	25		
.49	61	24	29	
.36	60	23		2
.30	59	23	28	
.25	58	22		
.20	57	21	27	
.16	56	21		
.16	55	20	26	1
.11	54	19		
.09	53	19	25	
.07	52	18		
.06	51	17	24	
.05	50	17		
.04	49	16	23	
.03	48	15		
.02	48	15	22	
.02	47	15		
.01	46	14	21	
.01	45	14		
.01	44	13	20	
.01	43	12		
.01	42	11	19	
.01	41	11		
.01	40	10	18	

Appendix E

CHC Cross-Battery Data, Normative, and Intracognitive Summary Sheets

Name:_____

Age:_____ Grade:_____

Examiner:_____ Date:_____

CHC Cross-Battery Summary Sheet
Part 1: Data Summary

Cluster	Test Battery	Subtest Name + (CHC ability code)	Standard Score	Standard Score Confidence Interval	Percentile Rank	Classification
Gf (Fluid Reasoning)		Gf Cluster Average =				
Gc (Crystallized Intelligence)		Gc Cluster Average =				
Gv (Visual Processing)		Gv Cluster Average =				
Gsm (Short-Term Memory)		Gsm Cluster Average =				
Glr (Long-Term Retrieval)		Glr Cluster Average =				
Ga (Auditory Processing)		Ga Cluster Average =				
Gs (Processing Speed)		Gs Cluster Average =				

Note. All standard scores are based on age norms. **Confidence Bands:** • Clusters = ±5 • Subtests = ±7

Name:_____

Age:_____ Grade: _____

Examiner:_____ Date: _____

CHC Cross-Battery Summary Sheet
Part 2: Normative Analysis Graph

Confidence Bands: • Clusters = ±5 • Subtests = ±7

−1 SEM ← 68 % → +1 SEM

Performance Classification	Very Low	Low	L. Avg.	Average	H. Avg.	Sup.	Very Superior
Percentile Ranks	≤2	3–8	9–24	25–75	76–97	92–97	98–99+

(CHC Code) 40 50 60 70 80 90 100 110 120 130 140 150 160

Broad/Narrow (___) Cluster

_____ (__)
_____ (__)
_____ (__)
_____ (__)
_____ (__)

Broad/Narrow (___) Cluster

_____ (__)
_____ (__)
_____ (__)
_____ (__)
_____ (__)
_____ (__)

Broad/Narrow (___) Cluster

_____ (__)
_____ (__)
_____ (__)
_____ (__)
_____ (__)
_____ (__)

Broad/Narrow (___) Cluster

_____ (__)
_____ (__)
_____ (__)
_____ (__)
_____ (__)
_____ (__)

Broad/Narrow (___) Cluster

_____ (__)
_____ (__)
_____ (__)
_____ (__)
_____ (__)
_____ (__)

Broad/Narrow (___) Cluster

_____ (__)
_____ (__)
_____ (__)
_____ (__)
_____ (__)
_____ (__)

Broad/Narrow (___) Cluster

_____ (__)
_____ (__)
_____ (__)
_____ (__)
_____ (__)
_____ (__)

40 50 60 70 80 90 100 110 120 130 140 150 160

NORMATIVE RANGE CLASSIFICATION	Normative Deficit	Normal Limits	Normative Strength
	<1 SD below mean	±1 SD from mean	>1 SD above mean

Name:_____

Age:_____ Grade:_____

Examiner:_____ Date:_____

CHC Cross-Battery Summary Sheet
Part 3: Intracognitive Analysis Graph

Performance Classification and Corresponding Percentile Rank Ranges

CHC FACTOR NAME	DIFF. SCORE (6)	REL. S, W, or NS (7)	Very Low ≤ 2		Low 3–8	L. Avg. 9–24	Average 25–75	H. Avg. 76–97	Sup. 92–97	Very Superior 98–99+		
			40	50	60	70	80	90	100	110	120	130	140	150	160

Gf   +/-___ ( )

Gc   +/-___ ( )

Gv   +/-___ ( )

Gsm +/-___ ( )

Ga   +/-___ ( )

Glr   +/-___ ( )

Gs   +/-___ ( )

40   50   60   70   80   90   100   110   120   130   140   150   160

NORMATIVE RANGE CLASSIFICATION	Normative Weakness <1 SD below mean	Normal Limits ±1 SD from mean	Normative Strength >1 SD above mean

Calculation and Interpretation of Scores:

	Cluster Averages (1)	Overall Average (5)	Difference Score (6)	Relative Interpretation Strength, Weakness, or NS (7)	Normative Interpretation Strength, Weakness, or NL (8)
Gf =	_____	− _____	= +/- _____	_____	_____
Gc =	_____	− _____	= +/- _____	_____	_____
Gv =	_____	− _____	= +/- _____	_____	_____
Gsm =	_____	− _____	= +/- _____	_____	_____
Ga =	_____	− _____	= +/- _____	_____	_____
Glr =	_____	− _____	= +/- _____	_____	_____
Gs =	_____	− _____	= +/- _____	_____	_____

Sum of Averages = _____ (2)

Number of Factors ÷ _____ (3)

Overall Average = _____ (4)

Relative Interpretation:
SS Diff. ≥ −15 = Relative Weakness
SS Diff. ≥ +15 = Relative Strength
SS Diff. ≤ ±14 = Not Significant (NS)

Normative Interpretation:
SS ≥ 116 = Normative Strength
SS ≤ 85 and ≥ 115 = Normal Limits (NL)
SS ≤ 84 = Normative Weakness

Appendix F

Definitions of Learning Disability

Source	Definition
National Joint Committee on Learning Disabilities (NJCLD)	*Learning disabilities* is a general term that refers to a heterogeneous group of disorders manifested by significant difficulties in the acquisition and use of listening, speaking, reading, writing, reasoning, or mathematical skills. These disorders are intrinsic to the individual and are presumed to be due to a central nervous system dysfunction, and may occur across the life span. Problems in self-regulatory behaviors, social perception, and social interaction may exist with the learning disabilities but do not, by themselves, constitute a learning disability. Although learning disabilities may occur concomitantly with other disabilities (e.g., sensory impairment, mental retardation, serious emotional disturbance), or with extrinsic influences (such as cultural differences, insufficient or inappropriate instruction), they are not the result of those conditions or influences.
Individuals with Disabilities Education Act (IDEA)	The term means a disorder in one or more of the basic psychological processes involved in understanding or in using language, spoken or written, that may manifest itself in an imperfect ability to listen, think, speak, read, write, or spell, or to do mathematical calculations, including such conditions as perceptual disabilities, brain injury, minimal brain dysfunction, dyslexia, and developmental aphasia. The term does not include learning problems that are primarily the result of visual, hearing, or motor disabilities, of mental retardation, of emotional disturbance, or of environmental, cultural, or economic disadvantage. A team may determine that a child has a specific learning disability if (a) the child's achievement is not commensurate with his or her age and ability levels in one or more of the seven areas listed below if provided with learning experiences appropriate for the child's age and ability levels; and (b) the team finds that a child has a severe discrepancy between achievement and intellectual ability in one or more of the following areas:

Source	Definition
	1. Oral expression.
	2. Listening comprehension.
	3. Written expression.
	4. Basic reading skill.
	5. Reading comprehension.
	6. Mathematics calculation.
	7. Mathematics reasoning.
	A team may not identify a child as having a specific learning disability if the severe discrepancy between ability and achievement is primarily the result of (a) A visual, hearing, or motor impairment; (b) Mental retardation; (c) Emotional disturbance; or (d) Environmental, cultural, or economic disadvantage.
Diagnostic and Statistical Manual of Mental Disorders– Fourth Edition (DSM-IV)	"Learning disorders are diagnosed when the individual's achievement on individually administered, standardized tests in reading, mathematics or written expression is substantially below that expected for age, schooling, and level of intelligence. The learning problems significantly interfere with academic achievement or activities of daily living that require reading, mathematical, or writing skills. A variety of statistical approaches can be used to establish that a discrepancy is significant. *Substantially below* is usually defined as a discrepancy of more than 2 standard deviations between achievement and IQ.
	A smaller discrepancy between achievement and IQ (i.e., between 1 and 2 standard deviations) is sometimes used, especially in cases where an individual's performance on an IQ test may have been compromised by an associated disorder in cognitive processing, a comorbid mental disorder or general medical condition, or the individual's ethnic or cultural background. If a sensory deficit is present, the learning difficulties must be in excess of those associated with the deficit."[1]

[1]American Psychiatric Association. (1994). *Diagnostic and statistical manual of mental disorders* (4th ed.). Washington, DC: Author.

Appendix G

Predicted Achievement Values and Critical Values for Statistical Significance (WJ-R BCA and WJ-R Achievement; WASI FSIQ-4 and WIAT)

WJ-R Predicted Achievement Values Based on WJ-R Cognitive Battery

SUBTEST STANDARD SCORES

BCA (Std)	Letter-Word Identification	Passage Comprehension	Calculation	Applied Problems	Dictation	Writing Samples	Science	Social studies	Humanities	Word Attack	Reading Vocabulary	Quantitative Concepts	Proofing	Writing Fluency	Punctuation and Capitalization	Spelling	Usage	Broad Reading	Broad Math	Broad Written Language	Broad Knowledge	Skills
46	65	64	69	64	66	69	62	63	62	68	63	63	66	68	67	67	68	61	64	64	58	60
47	66	64	70	64	67	70	63	64	62	68	64	63	67	68	68	68	68	61	64	65	59	60
48	66	65	70	65	67	70	64	65	63	69	65	64	67	69	68	68	69	62	65	66	59	61
49	67	66	71	66	68	71	64	65	63	69	65	65	68	69	69	69	69	63	66	66	60	62
50	68	67	72	67	69	72	65	66	65	70	66	65	69	71	70	70	70	64	67	67	61	63
51	68	67	72	67	69	72	66	67	65	71	67	66	69	71	70	70	71	64	67	68	62	63
52	69	68	73	68	70	73	66	67	66	71	68	67	70	72	71	71	71	65	68	68	63	64
53	69	69	73	69	70	73	67	68	67	72	69	68	70	72	72	72	72	66	69	69	63	65
54	70	69	74	69	71	74	68	69	67	72	69	68	71	73	72	73	72	66	69	70	64	66
55	71	70	74	70	72	75	69	70	68	73	69	69	72	73	73	73	73	67	70	70	65	66
56	71	71	75	71	72	75	69	71	69	74	70	70	72	74	73	74	74	68	71	71	66	67
57	72	71	75	71	73	75	70	71	69	74	71	70	73	74	74	74	74	69	71	72	66	68
58	73	72	76	72	74	76	71	71	70	75	71	71	74	75	74	75	75	69	72	72	67	69
59	73	73	77	73	74	77	71	72	70	75	72	72	74	76	75	76	75	70	73	73	68	69
60	74	73	77	73	75	77	72	73	72	76	73	72	75	76	76	76	76	71	73	74	69	70
61	75	74	78	74	75	78	73	73	72	77	73	73	75	77	76	77	77	72	74	74	70	71
62	75	75	78	75	76	78	74	74	73	77	74	74	76	78	77	78	78	72	75	75	70	72
63	76	75	79	75	77	79	74	75	74	78	75	74	77	78	77	78	78	73	75	76	71	72
64	77	76	79	76	77	80	75	76	74	78	76	75	77	78	78	79	79	74	76	77	72	73
65	77	77	80	77	77	80	76	76	75	79	76	76	78	79	79	79	80	74	77	77	73	74
66	78	78	81	77	78	81	76	77	76	80	77	77	79	80	79	80	80	75	77	78	73	75
67	79	78	81	78	79	81	77	78	77	80	78	77	79	80	80	80	81	76	78	78	74	75
68	79	79	82	79	80	82	78	78	77	81	78	78	80	81	80	81	81	77	79	79	75	76

SUBTEST STANDARD SCORES

BCA (Std)	Letter-Word Identification	Passage Comprehension	Calculation	Applied Problems	Dictation	Writing Samples	Science	Social studies	Humanities	Word Attack	Reading Vocabulary	Quantitative Concepts	Proofing	Writing Fluency	Punctuation and Capitalization	Spelling	Usage	Broad Reading	Broad Math	Broad Written Language	Broad Knowledge	Skills
70	81	80	83	80	81	83	79	80	79	82	80	79	81	82	82	82	82	78	80	80	77	78
71	81	81	83	81	82	83	80	80	79	83	80	80	82	83	82	82	83	79	81	81	77	78
72	82	81	84	81	82	84	80	81	80	83	81	81	82	83	83	83	83	80	81	82	78	79
73	82	82	85	82	83	85	81	82	81	84	82	81	83	84	84	84	84	80	82	82	79	80
74	83	83	85	83	84	85	82	82	82	84	82	82	84	84	84	84	84	81	83	83	80	81
75	84	83	86	83	84	86	83	83	82	85	83	83	84	85	85	85	85	82	83	84	81	81
76	85	84	86	84	85	86	83	84	83	86	84	83	85	86	85	86	86	82	84	84	81	82
77	85	85	87	85	86	87	84	84	84	86	85	84	86	87	86	86	87	83	85	85	82	83
78	86	85	87	85	86	87	85	85	84	87	85	85	86	87	87	87	87	84	85	85	83	84
79	86	86	88	86	87	88	85	86	85	87	86	86	87	87	87	87	87	85	86	86	84	84
80	87	87	89	87	87	89	86	86	86	88	86	86	87	88	88	88	88	85	87	87	84	85
81	88	87	89	87	88	89	87	87	87	89	87	87	88	89	88	88	89	86	87	87	85	86
82	88	88	90	88	89	90	87	88	87	89	88	88	89	89	89	89	89	87	88	88	86	87
83	89	89	90	89	89	90	88	88	88	90	88	88	89	90	90	90	90	88	89	89	87	87
84	90	89	90	89	90	90	89	89	89	90	89	89	90	90	90	90	90	88	89	89	88	88
85	90	90	91	90	90	91	90	90	90	91	90	90	91	90	91	91	91	89	90	90	88	89
86	91	91	92	91	91	92	91	91	91	92	90	90	91	91	91	91	92	90	91	91	89	90
87	92	91	93	91	92	93	92	92	92	93	92	92	92	92	93	92	93	91	91	92	90	90
88	92	92	93	92	92	93	92	93	92	93	93	92	93	93	93	93	93	91	92	93	90	91
89	93	93	94	93	94	94	93	93	93	94	93	93	94	94	94	94	94	92	93	93	91	92
90	94	93	94	93	94	94	94	93	94	95	94	94	94	95	95	95	95	93	94	94	92	93
91	94	94	95	94	94	95	94	94	94	95	94	94	94	95	95	95	95	93	94	94	93	93
92	95	95	95	95	95	95	94	95	94	95	95	94	95	95	95	95	95	94	95	95	94	94
93	95	95	96	95	96	96	95	95	95	96	95	95	96	96	96	96	96	95	95	95	95	95

(continued)

WJ-R Predicted-achievement Values Based on WJ-R Cognitive Battery (*continued*)

SUBTEST STANDARD SCORES

BCA (Std)	Letter-Word Identification	Passage Comprehension	Calculation	Applied Problems	Dictation	Writing Samples	Science	Social studies	Humanities	Word Attack	Reading Vocabulary	Quantitative Concepts	Proofing	Writing Fluency	Punctuation and Capitalization	Spelling	Usage	Broad Reading	Broad Math	Broad Written Language	Broad Knowledge	Skills
94	96	96	97	96	96	97	96	96	96	96	96	96	96	96	96	96	96	96	96	96	95	96
95	97	97	97	97	97	97	97	97	96	97	97	97	97	97	97	97	97	96	97	97	96	96
96	97	97	98	97	97	98	97	97	97	98	97	97	97	98	98	98	98	97	97	97	97	96
97	98	98	98	98	98	98	98	98	98	98	98	98	99	98	98	98	98	98	98	98	98	97
98	99	99	99	99	99	99	99	99	98	99	99	99	99	99	99	98	98	99	99	99	98	98
99	99	99	99	99	99	99	99	99	99	99	99	99	99	99	99	99	99	99	99	99	99	99
100	100	100	100	100	100	100	100	100	100	100	100	100	100	100	100	100	100	100	100	100	100	100
101	101	101	101	101	101	101	101	101	101	101	101	101	101	101	101	101	101	101	101	101	101	101
102	101	102	102	102	102	101	102	102	101	102	101	101	102	102	102	102	102	102	102	102	102	102
103	102	103	102	103	103	102	103	103	102	102	102	102	103	102	103	102	103	103	103	103	102	102
104	103	103	103	103	103	103	104	104	104	103	103	103	103	103	104	103	104	104	103	103	104	103
105	104	104	103	104	104	103	105	105	104	104	105	104	104	104	104	104	104	105	105	104	104	104
106	105	105	104	105	105	104	106	105	105	105	105	105	105	105	105	104	105	106	105	105	105	105
107	105	105	104	105	105	104	106	106	106	105	106	106	106	105	105	105	106	107	105	105	106	105
108	106	106	105	106	106	105	107	107	107	106	107	106	106	106	106	105	107	107	106	106	107	106
109	107	107	106	107	107	106	108	108	108	107	108	107	107	107	107	106	108	108	107	107	108	107
110	107	107	106	107	107	106	108	109	109	108	108	108	107	107	107	107	108	109	107	107	109	108
111	108	108	107	108	108	107	109	109	109	108	109	108	108	108	108	107	109	109	108	108	109	108
112	108	109	107	109	108	107	110	110	110	109	110	109	108	108	109	108	110	110	109	109	110	109
113	109	109	108	110	109	108	111	110	111	110	110	110	109	108	109	109	110	110	109	109	110	110
114	110	110	109	110	109	109	111	110	111	110	111	110	109	108	109	109	110	110	109	109	111	110
115	110	111	109	111	110	109	112	112	111	110	112	110	110	109	110	109	111	112	110	110	112	111
116	111	111	109	111	111	110	112	112	112	111	112	111	111	110	110	110	111	112	111	111	112	112
117	111	111	110	111	111	110	112	112	112	110	112	112	111	110	110	110	111	112	111	111	113	113

SUBTEST STANDARD SCORES

BCA (Std)	Letter-Word Identification	Passage Comprehension	Calculation	Applied Problems	Dictation	Writing Samples	Science	Social studies	Humanities	Word Attack	Reading Vocabulary	Quantitative Concepts	Proofing	Writing Fluency	Punctuation and Capitalization	Spelling	Usage	Broad Reading	Broad Math	Broad Written Language	Broad Knowledge	Skills
118	112	112	110	112	111	110	113	112	113	111	112	112	111	111	111	111	111	113	112	112	114	114
119	112	113	111	113	112	111	113	113	113	111	113	113	112	111	112	112	111	114	113	113	115	114
120	113	113	111	113	113	111	114	114	114	112	114	114	113	112	112	112	112	115	113	113	116	115
121	114	114	112	114	113	112	115	114	115	113	114	114	113	113	113	113	113	115	114	114	116	116
122	114	115	113	115	114	113	115	115	116	113	115	115	114	113	113	113	113	116	115	115	117	117
123	115	115	113	115	114	113	116	116	116	114	116	116	114	114	114	114	114	117	115	115	118	117
124	116	116	114	116	115	114	117	116	117	114	116	117	115	114	115	115	114	118	116	116	119	118
125	116	117	114	117	116	114	118	117	118	115	117	117	116	115	115	115	115	118	117	116	120	119
126	117	117	115	117	116	115	118	118	118	116	118	118	116	116	116	116	116	119	117	117	120	120
127	118	118	115	118	117	115	119	118	119	116	118	118	117	117	117	117	117	120	118	118	121	120
128	118	119	116	119	118	116	120	119	120	117	119	119	118	118	118	118	118	120	119	118	122	121
129	119	119	117	119	118	117	120	120	121	117	120	120	118	118	118	118	117	121	119	119	123	122
130	120	120	117	120	119	117	121	120	121	118	120	121	119	119	119	119	118	122	120	120	123	123
131	120	121	118	121	120	118	122	121	122	119	121	121	120	119	119	120	119	123	121	120	124	123
132	121	122	118	121	120	119	122	122	123	119	122	122	120	120	120	120	119	123	121	121	125	124
133	121	123	119	122	121	120	124	122	123	120	122	123	121	120	120	121	120	124	122	122	126	125
134	122	123	119	123	122	120	124	123	124	120	123	123	122	121	121	121	120	125	123	123	127	126
135	123	123	120	123	122	121	125	124	125	121	124	124	122	122	121	121	121	126	123	123	127	126
136	123	124	121	124	123	122	126	124	126	122	124	125	123	122	122	122	122	126	124	124	128	127
137	124	125	121	125	123	122	127	125	126	122	125	126	123	123	123	123	122	127	125	124	129	128
138	125	125	122	125	124	123	127	126	127	123	126	126	124	123	123	124	123	128	125	125	130	129
139	125	126	122	126	125	123	127	127	128	123	127	127	125	124	124	124	123	128	126	126	130	129
140	126	127	123	127	125	125	128	127	128	124	127	128	125	125	124	124	124	129	127	126	131	130
141	127	127	123	127	126	126	129	128	129	125	128	128	126	125	125	125	125	130	127	127	132	131

(continued)

WJ-R Predicted-achievement Values Based on WJ-R Cognitive Battery (*continued*)

SUBTEST STANDARD SCORES

BCA (Std)	Letter-Word Identification	Passage Comprehension	Calculation	Applied Problems	Dictation	Writing Samples	Science	Social studies	Humanities	Word Attack	Reading Vocabulary	Quantitative Concepts	Proofing	Writing Fluency	Punctuation and Capitalization	Spelling	Usage	Broad Reading	Broad Math	Broad Written Language	Broad Knowledge	Skills
142	127	128	124	128	126	124	129	129	130	125	129	129	126	125	126	126	125	131	128	128	133	132
143	128	129	125	129	127	125	130	129	131	126	129	130	127	126	126	126	126	131	129	128	134	132
144	129	129	125	129	128	125	131	130	131	126	130	130	128	126	127	127	126	132	129	129	134	133
145	129	130	126	130	128	126	132	131	132	127	131	131	128	127	127	127	127	133	130	130	135	134
146	130	131	126	131	129	126	132	131	133	128	131	132	129	128	128	128	128	134	131	130	136	135
147	131	131	127	131	130	127	133	132	133	128	132	132	130	128	129	129	128	134	131	131	137	135
148	131	132	127	132	130	127	134	133	134	129	133	133	130	129	129	129	129	135	132	132	137	136
149	132	133	128	133	131	128	134	133	135	129	133	134	131	129	130	130	129	136	133	132	138	137
150	133	134	129	134	132	129	135	134	136	130	134	135	132	130	131	131	130	137	134	133	139	138
151	133	134	129	134	132	129	136	135	136	131	135	135	132	131	131	131	131	137	134	134	140	138
152	134	135	130	135	133	130	136	135	137	131	135	136	133	131	132	132	131	138	135	134	141	139
153	134	136	130	136	133	130	137	136	138	132	136	137	133	132	132	132	132	139	136	135	141	140
154	135	136	131	136	134	131	138	137	138	132	137	137	134	132	133	133	132	139	136	136	142	141
155	136	137	131	137	135	131	139	137	139	133	137	138	135	133	134	134	133	140	137	136	143	141

Note. Ability and achievement scores for the WJ-R were measured in z-score units where $z = (SS - 100)/15$. Then a predicted achievement z score was obtained through the regression equation $z_p = r_{xy}z_{ab}$, where z_p is the predicted achievement score, r_{xy} is the correlation between ability and achievement, and z_{ab} is the z score of the ability measure. In order to calculate the predicted-achievement standard score, z_p is converted to that metric using the equation $SS_p = 15_z + 100$, where SS_p is the predicted-achievement standard score.

Differences Required for Significance Between WJ-R Predicted and Actual Achievement Subtest Scores (achievement predicted from the BCA [Std])

	p	mean	6	7	8	9	10	11	12	13	14	15	16	17	18	19	20-29	30-39
Letter-Word Identification	0.05	11.57	16.08	13.23	11.92	11.49	13.17	13.10	9.89	9.44	12.84	10.24	9.43	10.38	9.88	11.94	11.03	11.05
	0.01	18.18	23.39	19.66	18.21	17.94	20.05	19.94	16.53	16.11	20.04	16.18	15.59	16.61	16.32	18.62	17.96	17.71
Passage Comprehension	0.05	8.97	16.08	12.41	8.48	7.93	7.94	7.24	9.16	7.26	10.01	6.70	6.34	8.10	8.03	9.53	9.02	9.21
	0.01	15.28	23.66	18.85	14.41	13.99	14.22	13.32	16.18	14.17	16.84	11.84	12.15	14.14	14.06	15.56	15.49	15.58
Calculation	0.05	13.17	16.08	13.44	12.12	12.26	14.73	12.86	11.08	13.52	12.27	11.48	11.29	13.27	14.66	12.56	16.76	12.41
	0.01	20.33	23.94	20.66	19.21	19.57	22.27	19.97	18.27	21.10	19.33	17.70	18.08	20.32	21.95	19.13	24.60	19.20
Applied Problems	0.05	10.15	9.11	7.87	8.95	8.96	7.91	8.83	8.95	10.95	10.64	11.75	11.39	10.23	11.68	10.44	12.65	12.08
	0.01	16.59	15.97	13.52	15.05	15.16	14.27	15.14	15.59	17.89	17.42	17.96	17.86	16.43	18.25	16.33	19.58	18.98
Dictation	0.05	10.53	13.85	9.92	9.85	11.09	11.04	9.69	12.48	9.09	10.39	8.99	7.30	10.01	9.29	12.25	11.19	11.97
	0.01	17.22	21.28	16.11	16.15	17.80	17.76	16.22	20.03	16.10	17.03	14.89	13.36	16.33	16.14	19.28	18.20	18.76
Writing Samples	0.05	12.64	18.70	16.57	16.56	17.91	13.15	10.74	7.84	11.93	9.89	7.06	8.60	12.64	11.61	13.55	13.18	12.27
	0.01	19.77	26.50	24.02	24.13	25.78	20.81	17.98	14.98	19.55	16.85	12.43	15.19	19.97	18.13	20.71	20.29	18.96
Science	0.05	7.12	6.04	3.91	5.04	7.23	5.56	5.99	7.05	6.81	7.72	7.58	7.34	7.17	6.66	9.39	10.51	9.98
	0.01	13.16	12.34	9.31	10.64	13.28	11.53	11.70	13.27	13.57	13.97	13.17	13.29	12.72	12.50	15.40	17.20	16.68
Social Studies	0.05	8.29	5.02	5.00	6.38	5.95	8.06	6.04	8.86	9.56	10.11	8.54	9.35	8.84	8.93	10.42	10.45	11.13
	0.01	14.57	11.47	11.11	12.26	11.97	14.41	11.99	15.51	16.51	16.77	14.08	15.43	14.74	15.21	16.60	17.06	17.98
Humanities	0.05	7.29	8.35	8.17	5.95	7.67	8.10	7.66	6.06	6.42	6.58	5.34	6.23	6.38	5.21	9.62	8.55	10.36
	0.01	13.30	14.98	14.35	11.47	13.79	14.42	13.68	12.11	12.79	12.47	10.56	12.01	11.71	10.96	15.89	14.74	16.90
Word Attack	0.05	11.83	15.80	12.86	14.15	13.03	12.42	11.91	13.41	12.94	14.19	10.15	8.96	8.06	11.92	11.03	9.20	9.32
	0.01	18.79	23.22	19.60	21.22	20.20	19.41	19.02	20.85	20.56	22.01	16.46	15.74	14.25	18.69	17.74	15.89	15.85
Reading Vocabulary	0.05	10.74	16.15	13.01	9.37	8.82	10.99	10.08	8.01	10.27	8.88	9.60	6.87	8.89	9.42	14.53	14.72	12.31
	0.01	17.07	23.46	19.52	15.04	14.66	17.58	16.18	13.82	17.13	14.97	15.35	12.50	14.68	15.39	21.34	22.23	19.24

(continued)

Differences Required for Significance Between WJ-R Predicted and Actual Achievement Subtest Scores (achievement predicted from the BCA [Std]) (*continued*)

	p	mean	6	7	8	9	10	11	12	13	14	15	16	17	18	19	20-29	30-39
Quantitative Concepts	0.05	7.15	8.33	6.29	7.31	7.19	6.03	7.08	7.47	6.50	7.16	6.19	6.39	4.56	7.86	8.08	10.99	7.01
	0.01	13.28	14.67	12.12	13.18	13.28	12.16	13.22	13.93	13.38	13.74	12.06	12.13	10.00	13.84	13.67	17.73	13.35
Proofing	0.05	10.98	14.32	11.06	10.21	10.18	11.83	11.38	12.13	11.73	10.63	9.45	8.81	10.04	9.87	11.56	11.31	11.14
	0.01	17.69	21.96	17.69	16.71	16.83	18.67	17.93	19.44	18.98	17.31	15.19	15.11	16.23	16.81	18.25	18.16	17.75
Writing Fluency	0.05	6.03	13.31	7.66	4.95	4.67	1.77	1.14	6.57	3.98	7.98	2.89	10.30	7.49	4.41	10.38	5.09	3.97
	0.01	12.75	21.05	14.56	11.69	11.54	8.03	7.41	13.67	11.29	15.32	8.88	17.77	13.76	10.46	16.78	11.53	10.24
Punctuation & Capitalization	0.05	9.29	12.70	11.48	9.92	9.38	8.84	8.04	10.76	9.29	9.57	5.91	7.94	9.08	7.01	10.09	9.54	9.12
	0.01	16.09	20.24	18.11	16.80	16.38	15.75	14.58	18.28	16.45	16.42	11.48	14.63	15.56	13.84	16.75	16.46	15.73
Spelling	0.05	11.01	11.73	8.99	10.12	9.81	10.99	11.56	12.44	10.61	10.52	10.89	9.31	10.13	11.64	13.53	12.35	11.48
	0.01	17.84	19.07	15.36	16.61	16.39	17.80	18.16	19.94	17.86	17.25	17.21	15.72	16.61	18.80	20.92	19.53	18.24
Usage	0.05	9.29	9.99	11.51	8.24	9.10	7.51	10.69	10.50	10.39	9.11	8.87	6.03	7.95	8.04	10.11	10.20	10.39
	0.01	16.10	17.26	18.29	14.61	16.10	14.34	17.87	17.86	17.70	15.93	14.85	12.24	14.06	14.94	17.03	17.31	17.28
Broad Reading	0.05	8.86	3.95	10.60	10.50	11.03	9.99	9.98	8.77	11.67	7.93	7.41	9.28	8.51	10.71	10.64	10.71	0.00
	0.01	14.26	7.55	16.37	16.49	17.25	15.87	16.31	15.03	18.28	12.85	12.73	14.90	14.12	16.60	16.93	16.84	0.00
Broad Mathematics	0.05	12.17	14.10	10.40	10.93	10.82	12.05	10.96	10.71	12.55	11.44	12.05	11.98	12.30	13.59	12.14	15.80	12.85
	0.01	18.63	21.31	16.32	17.11	17.13	18.71	17.22	17.23	19.44	17.92	17.99	18.31	18.63	20.24	18.16	23.04	19.39
Broad Written Language	0.05	11.21	17.61	15.02	13.10	14.44	13.17	12.30	10.00	9.60	8.00	6.79	7.42	10.40	9.92	10.29	10.20	11.09
	0.01	17.76	25.14	21.89	19.62	21.41	20.11	19.12	16.89	16.56	14.33	12.01	13.53	16.97	16.04	16.61	16.53	17.43
Broad Knowledge	0.05	8.50	8.56	7.44	7.25	7.40	8.17	7.38	8.46	9.44	8.99	7.66	8.17	7.67	7.21	10.28	10.43	11.47
	0.01	13.97	14.49	12.74	12.32	12.69	13.73	12.55	14.10	15.64	14.69	12.44	13.43	12.57	12.32	15.84	16.29	17.62
Skills	0.05	10.29	14.22	10.64	9.60	10.29	10.85	10.90	10.25	9.61	10.23	8.84	7.72	9.21	9.50	10.62	11.32	10.89
	0.01	16.05	21.00	16.18	14.97	16.04	16.86	16.79	16.35	15.66	16.20	13.78	12.81	14.53	15.13	16.24	17.45	16.80

Note. Critical values are based on the following formula: 1.96 SD [sqrt $(1 - r^2_{xy})$] $- 2.24$ SE$_{resid}$. This allows for multiple comparisons (up to four) operating within a 95% confidence level.

WIAT Subtest and Composite Predicted-Achievement Values Based on WASI FSIQ-4

FSIQ-4	SUBTEST STANDARD SCORES								COMPOSITE STANDARD SCORES			
	Basic Reading	Math Reasoning	Spelling	Reading Comprehension	Numerical Operations	Listening Comprehension	Oral Expression	Written Expression	Reading	Math	Language	Writing
46	66	65	68	62	70	69	75	65	61	65	65	61
47	67	66	69	62	70	70	75	66	62	66	66	62
48	67	67	69	63	71	70	76	67	63	67	67	63
49	68	67	70	64	71	71	76	67	63	67	67	63
50	69	68	71	65	72	72	77	68	64	68	68	64
51	69	69	71	65	73	72	77	69	65	69	69	65
52	70	69	72	66	73	73	77	69	65	69	69	65
53	70	70	72	67	74	73	78	70	66	70	70	66
54	71	71	73	67	74	74	78	71	67	71	71	67
55	72	71	73	68	75	74	79	71	68	71	71	68
56	72	72	74	69	75	75	79	72	68	72	72	68
57	73	72	75	69	76	75	80	72	69	72	72	69
58	74	73	75	70	76	76	80	73	70	73	73	70
59	74	74	76	71	77	77	81	74	70	74	74	70
60	75	74	76	72	78	77	81	74	71	74	74	71
61	75	75	77	72	78	78	82	75	72	75	75	72
62	76	76	78	73	79	78	82	76	73	76	76	73
63	77	76	78	74	79	79	83	76	73	76	76	73
64	77	77	79	74	80	79	83	77	74	77	77	74
65	78	78	79	75	80	80	84	78	75	78	78	75
66	79	78	80	76	81	81	84	78	76	78	78	76
67	79	79	81	77	82	81	84	79	76	79	79	76
68	80	80	81	77	82	82	85	80	77	80	80	77

(continued)

WIAT Subtest and Composite Predicted-Achievement Values Based on WASI FSIQ-4 (*continued*)

FSIQ-4	SUBTEST STANDARD SCORES								COMPOSITE STANDARD SCORES			
	Basic Reading	Math Reasoning	Spelling	Reading Comprehension	Numerical Operations	Listening Comprehension	Oral Expression	Written Expression	Reading	Math	Language	Writing
69	80	80	82	78	83	82	85	80	78	80	80	78
70	81	81	82	79	83	83	86	81	78	81	81	78
71	82	81	83	79	84	83	86	81	79	81	81	79
72	82	82	83	80	84	84	87	82	80	82	82	80
73	83	83	84	81	85	85	87	83	81	83	83	81
74	84	83	85	82	85	85	88	83	81	83	83	81
75	84	84	85	82	86	86	88	84	82	84	84	82
76	85	85	86	83	87	86	89	85	83	85	85	83
77	86	85	86	84	87	87	89	85	83	85	85	83
78	86	86	87	84	88	87	90	86	84	86	86	84
79	87	87	88	85	88	88	90	87	85	87	87	85
80	87	87	88	86	89	89	91	87	86	87	87	86
81	88	88	89	87	89	89	91	88	86	88	88	86
82	89	88	89	87	90	90	92	88	87	88	88	87
83	89	89	90	88	90	90	92	89	88	89	89	88
84	90	90	91	89	91	91	92	90	88	90	90	88
85	91	90	91	89	92	91	93	90	89	90	90	89
86	91	91	92	90	92	92	93	91	90	91	91	90
87	92	92	92	91	93	93	94	92	91	92	92	91
88	92	92	93	91	93	93	94	92	91	92	92	91
89	93	93	94	92	94	94	95	93	92	93	93	92
90	94	94	94	93	94	94	95	94	93	94	94	93
91	94	94	95	94	95	95	96	94	94	94	94	94
92	95	95	95	94	96	95	96	95	94	95	95	94

	SUBTEST STANDARD SCORES								COMPOSITE STANDARD SCORES			
FSIQ-4	Basic Reading	Math Reasoning	Spelling	Reading Comprehension	Numerical Operations	Listening Comprehension	Oral Expression	Written Expression	Reading	Math	Language	Writing
93	96	96	96	95	96	96	97	96	95	95	96	95
94	96	96	96	96	97	97	97	96	96	96	96	96
95	97	97	97	96	97	97	98	97	96	97	97	96
96	97	97	98	97	98	98	98	97	97	97	97	97
97	98	98	98	98	98	98	99	98	98	98	98	98
98	99	99	99	99	99	99	99	99	99	99	99	99
99	99	99	99	99	99	99	100	99	99	99	99	99
100	100	100	100	100	100	100	100	100	100	100	100	100
101	101	101	101	101	101	101	100	101	101	101	101	101
102	101	101	101	101	101	101	101	101	101	101	101	101
103	102	102	102	102	102	102	101	102	102	102	102	102
104	103	103	102	103	102	102	102	103	103	103	103	103
105	103	103	103	104	103	103	102	103	104	103	103	104
106	104	104	104	104	103	103	103	104	104	104	104	104
107	104	104	104	105	104	104	103	104	105	104	104	105
108	105	105	105	106	104	105	104	105	106	105	105	106
109	106	106	105	106	105	105	104	106	106	106	106	106
110	106	106	106	107	106	106	105	106	107	106	106	107
111	107	107	106	108	106	106	105	107	108	107	107	108
112	108	108	107	109	107	107	106	108	109	108	108	109
113	108	108	108	109	107	107	106	108	109	108	108	109
114	109	109	108	110	108	108	107	109	110	109	109	110
115	109	110	109	111	108	109	107	110	111	110	110	111
116	110	110	109	111	109	109	108	110	112	110	110	112

(continued)

WIAT Subtest and Composite Predicted-Achievement Values Based on WASI FSIQ-4 (continued)

FSIQ-4	SUBTEST STANDARD SCORES								COMPOSITE STANDARD SCORES			
	Basic Reading	Math Reasoning	Spelling	Reading Comprehension	Numerical Operations	Listening Comprehension	Oral Expression	Written Expression	Reading	Math	Language	Writing
117	111	111	110	112	110	110	108	111	112	111	111	112
118	111	112	111	113	110	110	108	112	113	112	112	113
119	112	112	111	113	111	111	109	112	114	112	112	114
120	113	113	112	114	111	111	109	113	114	113	113	114
121	113	113	112	115	112	112	110	113	115	113	113	115
122	114	114	113	116	112	113	110	114	116	114	114	116
123	114	115	114	116	113	113	111	115	117	115	115	117
124	115	115	114	117	113	114	111	115	117	115	115	117
125	116	116	115	118	114	114	112	116	118	116	116	118
126	116	117	115	118	115	115	112	117	119	117	117	119
127	117	117	116	119	115	115	113	117	119	117	117	119
128	118	118	117	120	116	116	113	118	120	118	118	120
129	118	119	117	121	116	117	114	119	121	119	119	121
130	119	119	118	121	117	117	114	119	122	119	119	122
131	120	120	118	122	117	118	115	120	122	120	120	122
132	120	120	119	123	118	118	115	120	123	120	120	123
133	121	121	119	123	118	119	116	121	124	121	121	124
134	121	122	120	124	119	119	116	122	124	122	122	124
135	122	122	121	125	120	120	116	122	125	122	122	125
136	123	123	121	126	120	121	117	123	126	123	123	126
137	123	124	122	126	121	121	117	124	127	124	124	127
138	124	124	122	127	121	122	118	124	127	124	124	127
139	125	125	123	128	122	122	118	125	128	125	125	128
140	125	126	124	128	122	123	119	126	129	126	126	129

| | SUBTEST STANDARD SCORES | | | | | | | | COMPOSITE STANDARD SCORES | | | |
FSIQ-4	Basic Reading	Math Reasoning	Spelling	Reading Comprehension	Numerical Operations	Listening Comprehension	Oral Expression	Written Expression	Reading	Math	Language	Writing
141	126	126	124	129	123	123	119	126	130	126	126	130
142	126	127	125	130	124	124	120	127	130	127	127	130
143	127	128	125	131	124	125	120	128	131	128	128	131
144	128	128	126	131	125	125	121	128	132	128	128	132
145	128	129	127	132	125	126	121	129	132	129	129	132
146	129	129	127	133	126	126	122	129	133	129	129	133
147	130	130	128	133	126	127	122	130	134	130	130	134
148	130	131	128	134	127	127	123	131	135	131	131	135
149	131	131	129	135	127	128	123	131	135	131	131	135
150	132	132	130	136	128	129	124	132	136	132	132	136
151	132	133	130	136	129	129	124	133	137	133	133	137
152	133	133	131	137	129	130	124	133	137	133	133	137
153	133	134	131	138	130	130	125	134	138	134	134	138
154	134	135	132	138	130	131	125	135	139	135	135	139
155	135	135	132	139	131	131	126	135	140	135	135	140

Note. Ability and achievement scores for the WJ-R were measured in z-score units where $z = (SS - 100)/15$. Then a predicted achievement z score was obtained through the regression equation $z_p = r_{xy} z_{ab}$, where z_p is the predicted achievement score, r_{xy} is the correlation between ability and achievement, and z_{ab} is the z score of the ability measure. In order to calculate the predicted-achievement standard score, z_p is converted to that metric using the equation $SS_p = 15_z + 100$, where SS_p is the predicted-achievement standard score.

Differences Required for Significance between Predicted and Actual WIAT Achievement Subtest and Composite Scores (achievement predicted from WASI FSIQ-4)

WIAT Subtests	p	Mean	age 6	age 7	age 8	age 9	age 10	age 11	age 12	age 13	age 14	age 15	age 16	ages 17 to 19
Basic Reading	0.05	12.30	13.95	13.95	13.34	13.58	13.34	12.99	12.65	11.90	11.59	10.45	10.72	11.39
	0.01	19.09	20.82	20.82	20.18	20.43	20.18	19.81	19.46	18.68	18.36	17.17	17.46	18.16
Math Reasoning	0.05	10.29	8.72	10.93	10.00	11.13	11.94	11.13	11.33	11.13	11.33	10.18	10.45	10.65
	0.01	19.09	20.82	20.82	20.18	20.43	20.18	19.81	19.46	18.68	18.36	17.17	17.46	18.16
Spelling	0.05	12.02	12.73	13.25	13.25	14.00	13.80	13.44	13.09	11.44	11.15	10.13	10.84	10.99
	0.01	19.09	20.82	20.82	20.18	20.43	20.18	19.81	19.46	18.68	18.36	17.17	17.46	18.16
Reading Comp.	0.05	8.09	10.34	10.34	9.30	9.55	9.30	9.06	8.82	7.26	7.05	5.67	5.12	5.30
	0.01	19.09	20.82	20.82	20.18	20.43	20.18	19.81	19.46	18.68	18.36	17.17	17.46	18.16
Numerical Ops.	0.05	10.44	9.49	10.68	10.27	12.60	13.43	12.13	11.37	10.40	11.37	10.00	9.49	9.24
	0.01	19.09	20.82	20.82	20.18	20.43	20.18	19.81	19.46	18.68	18.36	17.17	17.46	18.16
Listening Comp.	0.05	9.72	9.66	10.88	10.05	10.59	11.75	10.59	8.77	9.02	8.77	9.02	8.53	9.40
	0.01	19.09	20.82	20.82	20.18	20.43	20.18	19.81	19.46	18.68	18.36	17.17	17.46	18.16
Oral Expression	0.05	15.21	14.75	15.27	15.27	15.39	15.81	15.94	15.51	15.39	15.51	15.39	14.26	15.39
	0.01	19.09	20.82	20.82	20.18	20.43	20.18	19.81	19.46	18.68	18.36	17.17	17.46	18.16
Written Exp.	0.05	7.24	---	---	5.44	5.91	6.81	6.25	6.75	8.48	8.24	8.08	8.32	8.08
	0.01	19.09	20.82	20.82	20.18	20.43	20.18	19.81	19.46	18.68	18.36	17.17	17.46	18.16

WIAT Composites	p	Mean	age 6	age 7	age 8	age 9	age 10	age 11	age 12	age 13	age 14	age 15	age 16	ages 17 to 19
Reading	0.05	10.92	12.46	12.46	11.78	12.12	11.78	11.47	11.80	10.28	10.02	9.22	8.48	9.22
	0.01	19.09	20.82	20.82	20.18	20.43	20.18	19.81	19.46	18.68	18.36	17.17	17.46	18.16
Mathematics	0.05	12.08	10.93	12.48	11.94	13.30	13.67	13.30	12.95	12.16	12.95	11.63	11.94	11.63
	0.01	19.09	20.82	20.82	20.18	20.43	20.18	19.81	19.46	18.68	18.36	17.17	17.46	18.16
Language	0.05	11.26	11.42	11.94	11.42	12.16	12.48	12.16	10.84	10.65	10.84	10.18	10.00	11.13
	0.01	19.09	20.82	20.82	20.18	20.43	20.18	19.81	19.46	18.68	18.36	17.17	17.46	18.16
Writing	0.05	8.86	---	---	8.02	9.22	9.47	8.73	8.98	9.22	8.98	8.73	8.48	8.73
	0.01	19.09	20.82	20.82	20.18	20.43	20.18	19.81	19.46	18.68	18.36	17.17	17.46	18.16
Total	0.05	12.30	13.95	13.95	13.34	13.58	13.34	12.99	12.65	11.90	11.59	10.45	10.72	11.39
	0.01	19.09	20.82	20.82	20.18	20.43	20.18	19.81	19.46	18.68	18.36	17.17	17.46	18.16

Annotated Bibliography

Valdés, G., & Figueroa, R. A. (1994). *Bilingualism and testing: A special case of bias.* Norwood, NJ: Ablex Publishing Corporation.

This volume is perhaps the definitive treatise on the issue of bias in the assessment of culturally and linguistically diverse children. The authors provide an extensively detailed discussion regarding both the historical and contemporary literature with respect to bias as well as an outstanding presentation on the relevant issues in assessment, including a chronology of the judicial decisions governing the practice. Research findings are reviewed and examined in critical detail, often revealing insights not found in other sources. The volume is not intended, however, to be a guide to assessment as much as it is meant to offer an extended discussion of the important and far-ranging aspects of bilingual assessment. For individuals interested in fully appreciating the issues in assessing culturally and linguistically diverse individuals, there is no better source.

Cummins, J. C. (1984). *Bilingual and special education: Issues in assessment and pedagogy.* Austin, TX: Pro-Ed.

This volume has become a somewhat classic text in the area of bilingual assessment, especially with respect to the issue of language proficiency. Cummins provides discussion of his dichotomous language-proficiency concepts, which include Basic Interpersonal Communicative Skills (BICS) and Cognitive Academic Language Proficiency (CALP). These are extremely important concepts related to the fair and equitable assessment of bilingual individuals. A unique feature of this volume is the presentation of research that begins to provide a basis for the cultural and linguistic classifications that extend the CHC Cross-Battery approach. Cummins also integrates assessment issues as they relate to special education and to implications for remedial instruction. Overall, it is an extremely informative and ground-breaking work that deserves the attention it has received over the years.

Carroll, J. B. (1993). *Human cognitive abilities: A survey of factor-analytic studies.* Cambridge, UK: Cambridge University Press.

This work represents perhaps the most important recent contribution to the understanding of human cognitive abilities. Carroll's ambitious endeavor covers the results of more than seventy years and more than 460 data sets from factor-analytic investigations on cognitive abilities, including abilities related specifically to language, thinking, memory, visual and auditory perception, creativity, and more. From this data, Carroll concludes that 9–10 broad cognitive abilities are consistently identified, and about 70 narrow abilities are subsumed under the broad factors. Of the theoretical models of intelligence extant at the time, Carroll suggested that the results provide convincing support for the

Cattell-Horn modern Gf-Gc *theoretical framework. Carroll extends his results further to provide a basis for developing his own, three-stratum theory of intelligence, which serves primarily as a way to demonstrate the importance of all cognitive abilities in the understanding of human intellectual functioning. Carroll also addresses the relevance and meaning of his findings with respect to other, still-controversial issues related to human intelligence, in particular the existence of a "g" (general ability) factor. This volume is fast becoming a classic in the field and is a must-read for anyone interested in understanding modern intelligence theory.*

McGrew, K. S., & Flanagan, D. P. (1998). *The intelligence test desk reference (ITDR):* Gf-Gc *Cross-Battery assessment.* Boston: Allyn & Bacon.

This book provides comprehensive information about the most important psychometric, theoretical, and qualitative characteristics of the major intelligence batteries, including WISC-III, WAIS-III, WPPSI-R, KAIT, K-ABC, SB:IV, DAS, and WJ-R. In addition, test characteristics are summarized for more than 20 special-purpose cognitive ability tests that are used to assess the cognitive capabilities of diverse populations and to supplement intelligence tests (e.g., Leiter-R, UNIT, CAS, C-TONI, WRAML, etc.). This information, contained in an easy-to-read, visual-graphic format, is a foundational source that is invaluable to practitioners, particularly those who employ cross-battery techniques. In addition, this book was the first to introduce formally cross-battery assessment to practitioners. Therefore, it offers an in-depth discussion and presentation of the theory and research underlying cross-battery assessment.

Flanagan, D. P., McGrew, K. S., & Ortiz, S. O. (2000). *The Wechsler Intelligence Scales and* Gf-Gc *theory: A contemporary approach to interpretation.* Boston: Allyn & Bacon.

This book presents cross-battery assessment and interpretation principles and procedures as a means to modernize the use of the Wechsler Intelligence Scales. In this book, the Wechsler Scales are described in terms of their contributions to research and practice and are placed firmly in the current, theory-based trend of intelligence-test interpretation. The Wechsler Scales are described according to the extent to which they operationalize prominent abilities specified in contemporary theory on the structure of intelligence. This book shows how contemporary theory can be linked to the applied measurement of cognitive abilities using the Wechsler Scales. More specifically, it imposes a strong substantive framework to the interpretation of the Wechsler Scales via Flanagan and McGrew's cross-battery approach. The end result is the derivation of more valid inferences from Wechsler test scores. The Wechsler-Based Cross-Battery *approach to assessment described in this book provides practitioners with the knowledge and skills necessary to ground cognitive ability assessment and interpretation with the Wechsler Scales in strong theory and research, and to conduct assessments in a more psychometrically and theoretically defensible manner.*

Index

Acknowledgments

We are deeply grateful for the contributions of Kevin S. McGrew, co-founder of the CHC Cross-Battery approach. His research and writings directly influenced this current work and will continue to enrich and inform the research foundation upon which our cross-battery approach was built. We are also grateful to Jennifer Mascolo for her unwavering dedication and commitment to this project. Her substantial efforts greatly enhanced the quality of this book.

Our deep appreciation is also extended to Alan and Nadeen Kaufman for their support of this project and for providing us with the opportunity to teach our methods of cognitive ability assessment to the readership of the *Essentials* series. The contributions of Tracey Belmont and the rest of the staff at Wiley are gratefully acknowledged as well. Their expertise and pleasant and cooperative working style made this book an enjoyable and productive endeavor.

And finally, we would like to thank some of the many people who have contributed in a variety of other ways for their generous assistance in bringing this book into full bloom. We thank (in no particular order) John Willis, Ron Dumont, Robert Misak, Gale Wyman, and Larry Pristo for their work on automating the CHC Cross-Battery scoring process; J. Ryan Burke for his original ideas and work on the CHC Culture-Language Matrix; Craig Carter, Anna Lee Speer, and the entire school psychology staff of the Washington Elementary School District for their commitment to and feedback on the CHC Cross-Battery approach; and Dave Mirich for reviewing portions of the manuscript.

About the Authors

Dawn P. Flanagan, PhD (Ohio State University, Columbus), Associate Professor of School Psychology at St. John's University in New York, is a nationally recognized author, editor, researcher, and recipient of APA's Lightner-Witmer Award. Her research and publications focus on the structure of in-telligence, psychoeducational assessment, and theory-based methods of cognitive assessment.

Samuel O. Ortiz, PhD (University of Southern California), Associate Professor of School Psychology at St. John's University in New York, is a nationally recognized consultant and trainer throughout the United States who combines practical and research-based experience as well as specialized education and training in working with Hispanics and other cultural groups. His research and publications focus on nondiscriminatory assessment methods and equitable practices and procedures in psychoeducational evaluation.